AF895569

Juvenile Justice in African and Western Criminal Justice Systems

Simeon Peter Sungi
https://orcid.org/0000-0003-4172-6222
United States International University-Africa, Kenya

Henry K. Murigi
https://orcid.org/0000-0001-6734-050X
Pan-African Christian University, Kenya

IGI Global
Scientific Publishing
Publishing Tomorrow's Research Today

Vice President of Editorial	Melissa Wagner
Director of Acquisitions	Mikaela Felty
Director of Book Development	Jocelynn Hessler
Production Manager	Mike Brehm
Cover Design	Jose Rosado

Published in the United States of America by
IGI Global Scientific Publishing
701 East Chocolate Avenue
Hershey, PA, 17033, USA
Tel: 717-533-8845 | Fax: 717-533-7115
Website: https://www.igi-global.com E-mail: cust@igi-global.com

Library of Congress Cataloging-in-Publication Data

No LCCN (CIP Data Pending)
ISBN13: 978-1-6684-9343-4
Isbn13Softcover: 978-1-6684-9347-2
EISBN13: 978-1-6684-9344-1
British Cataloguing in Publication Data
A Cataloguing in Publication record for this book is available from the British Library.

Table of Contents

Detailed Table of Contents

in Western countries. With better policies, training, and community support, they can be improved and used more widely in African legal systems.

The study titled "Public & Police Response to Juvenile Offenders in India" examines the social and institutional responses to juvenile delinquency, focusing on the influence of media, public perception, and police practices. Juvenile delinquency in India is a complex issue, influenced by socio economic factors, media portrayals, and societal attitudes towards crime and punishment. Public fear, often driven by sensationalized media coverage, demands punitive measures rather than rehabilitative approaches, hindering reintegration efforts for juvenile offenders. The research emphasizes the need for police sensitization programs and the development of specialized juvenile units to align policing practices with the rehabilitative goals of the justice system. Through a blend of criminological theories, including Merton's Strain Theory and Social Learning Theory, the study underscores how public attitudes and institutional responses can either perpetuate or reduce juvenile recidivism.

Youth crime is a problem throughout the world and the most common methods of dealing with it often rely on retribution and imprisonment as the ultimate goals. This approach of "warehousing" youths through the institution of prison has been argued to undermine sustainable youth development and crime prevention. This paper and its findings are adapted by the author from his earlier field survey on: "Opinions of victims of crime and criminal justice professionals" conducted in Nigeria (Omale, 2009), and suggests initiatives to tackle this problem. A total number of 151 respondents comprising 74 victims of crime and 77 professionals of the criminal justice system took part in this study. This paper is evidence-based research; with a review of relevant literature to support its argument. The paper highlights some theoretical explanations (with a focus on sociological positivism and social constructionism) to explain the complex interaction of the variables which might be implicitly and explicitly implicated in youth offending behaviour in Nigeria and globally.

This chapter presents findings from a study exploring the extent to which formal interactions with social control agents may propel youth toward delinquent self-perceptions. Using the West Indian island of Barbados as a case study, this research examined the juvenile justice system and juveniles perception of their experiences with the law. This research investigated how youths' exposure to arrest and incarceration affected the likelihood that the juveniles would label themselves negatively, assessed the importance of perceived negative labeling on delinquency, and examined the impact of detention on youths' perceptions of their future possibilities. Findings show that being publicly branded as a deviant does not equate to the acceptance of a deviant label. This research shows that labeling was less likely to be internalized based on the juvenile's social environment; personal, family, and peer history with the law; view of the offenses; personal characteristics and strength; and the practices of social control agents that may acts as a buffer to accepting a deviant label.

This chapter presents a comparative analysis of juvenile justice systems in Kenya and Tanzania, with a focus on the implications of diversion programs on child development. Although both countries emphasize rehabilitation over punitive measures, significant gaps in aligning with international standards remain. Through an analysis of secondary data from legislative documents, policy reports, and case studies, the chapter highlights Kenya's structured interventions and their implementation challenges, as well as Tanzania's community-based approach, which lacks detailed guidelines. The study concludes with recommendations for developing training programs, addressing resource limitations, and enhancing research to foster evidence-based improvements in both systems.

This paper examines the practical challenges of safeguarding children's rights within Kenya's criminal justice system, focusing on gaps in legal representation, professional training, privacy protections, and support systems for vulnerable groups such as child parents, victims, and youth offenders. Drawing on lessons from jurisdictions like South Africa, Canada, the United Kingdom, and the United States, the paper offers actionable recommendations to strengthen Kenya's child justice framework. These include ensuring continuous legal assistance, enhancing accessibility of information, implementing individualized assessments, and safeguarding children's privacy in criminal proceedings. The study advocates for a child-centered, rights-based approach to justice that prioritizes rehabilitation and reintegration over punitive measures, aiming to align Kenya's practices with international standards and best practices.

According to the Consortium of street children, there are about 60,000 street children in the country. While on the streets, these children are exposed to a hard life with drug abuse. This scenario puts them in a conflict situation with law enforcement. Drug abuse is criminalized in Kenya through the Narcotic Drugs and Psychotropic Substances Act (1994) and other legal frameworks. The study's objectives were to establish the legislative framework to curb drugs among street children and explore the challenges these laws face. The study adopted a Case Study design in which Nairobi, Kenya's capital, was the case study. Sampling was stratified among the 17 sub-counties in the city, and each had an equal representation of 4, making a total of 68 respondents. The target population consisted of social workers, law enforcers (particularly in the children's department), and administrators such as chiefs and Sub County commissioners. Data was collected using KIIS (Key Informant Interviews), document analysis, and desktop review.

Children in Somalia confront several challenges, including being exposed to many types of criminality and violence. Due to decades of violence and instability, Somalia's legal system has been disrupted, leaving a dearth of institutions and legal protections to protect children. The protection of children in Somalia has been demanded by the UN, especially in light of the country's current 15-year-old criminal responsibility age. Also, Somalia's courts and jails are not set up to meet the needs of young victims or offenders. Street children and child soldiers are particularly vulnerable to abuse and exploitation, with many facing re-victimization by the government. In general, Somalia's children are in terrible condition, and immediate action is required to guarantee that their rights are upheld and that they may lead secure lives. The building of a strong legislative framework in Somalia that can adequately meet children's needs and stop further harm to this vulnerable group requires the cooperation of the international community.

Egyptian society is heavily rooted in ancient traditions and religious practices. Islam is the cornerstone of Egypt's social, intellectual, and political cohesion, offering the logical force that bonds communities into a broad nation. Since independence, the Egyptians have modeled the criminal justice system on the existing religious and colonial ideological influences. Despite being one of Africa's largest countries, only a few scholars have examined the Egyptian juvenile justice system. The chapter will explore various aspects of the juvenile justice system in Egypt, its history, organization, and contemporary issues in juvenile justice. The chapter highlights the age of majority and criminal responsibility, trends and statistics of youth crimes, and custodial and non-custodial treatment of young offenders. Through the comparison with western juvenile justice systems, the chapter intends to offer policy implications for the existing problems that youth face and suggest future research areas on youth crime and the juvenile justice system.

This chapter explores the reframing of juvenile justice through a human rights lens, using Kenya and the United States as comparative case studies. Both nations

Preface

In recent decades, juvenile justice has moved from the periphery of criminal justice scholarship to a central position in global debates about rights, development, and social protection. Across Africa and the wider Global South, countries are grappling with the realities of rapid urbanization, economic disparities, emerging security threats, and evolving social norms that profoundly influence the lives of children and young people. This book emerges from the recognition that understanding juvenile justice in such diverse contexts requires multidisciplinary, comparative, and empirically grounded perspectives.

This edited volume brings together scholars, practitioners, policymakers, and researchers who examine the complexities of children's encounters with criminal justice systems across Africa, complemented by comparative insights from the Caribbean and the United States. The chapters explore themes ranging from diversion, rights protection, youth crime prevention, and labeling theory to street children, prosecutorial perspectives, and the lived experiences of children in conflict-affected settings. While each chapter stands as an independent contribution, together they form a comprehensive mosaic of the challenges, innovations, and ongoing transformations shaping juvenile justice today.

The book is structured to guide readers from conceptual foundations to regional analyses, and finally toward reform-oriented reflections. It is meant not only for scholars of criminology and law but also for practitioners, students, social workers, community activists, and policymakers committed to advancing the rights and well-being of children.

Our goal is that this book serves as both a resource and a catalyst: a resource for understanding and teaching juvenile justice in African contexts, and a catalyst for reform, collaboration, and deeper scholarly inquiry. As editors, we hope the volume will stimulate critical debates, inspire further research, and contribute to the broader efforts toward building justice systems that are humane, rights-based, and responsive to the needs of all children.

CHAPTER OVERVIEW

Chapter 1: Juvenile Justice and Human Rights: A Comparative Study

In this opening chapter, the authors present a far-reaching comparative analysis of juvenile justice systems across African and Western contexts, grounding their evaluation in international human rights instruments such as the CRC and ACRWC. They illuminate the enduring impact of punitive colonial legacies in many African systems—manifested in overcrowded facilities, inadequate rehabilitative structures, and resource constraints—while simultaneously acknowledging Western models' rhetorical commitment to restorative justice alongside persistent issues like racial disproportionality. Through case studies from South Africa, Kenya, the United States, and Europe, the chapter offers a nuanced portrait of diverse reform trajectories: South Africa's promising yet under-resourced Child Justice Act, Kenya's struggle with overcrowding despite legislative reform, the U.S. efforts to reduce detention amid equity challenges, and Europe's comparatively successful rehabilitation-focused systems. The authors conclude by emphasizing the need for reforms that center human rights, community-based alternatives, and systemic equity to strengthen juvenile justice worldwide.

Chapter 2: Juvenile Diversion Programs

This chapter examines the critical role of diversion programs in interrupting pathways to further offending and addressing structural drivers of juvenile crime such as poverty, educational barriers, and family instability. The authors synthesize evidence on informal and formal diversion, community justice initiatives, and restorative service models, noting consistent reductions in recidivism and improvements in youth outcomes across varied contexts. While diversion has demonstrated significant success in many Western jurisdictions, the chapter underscores the persistent obstacles to implementation in African justice systems, including resource limitations, inconsistent application, and stigmatizing community attitudes. The authors advocate for stronger policy frameworks, sustained training, and deeper community engagement to ensure that diversion becomes an equitable and widely accessible tool for youth development.

Chapter 3: Public and Police Response to Juvenile Offenders

Focusing on India, this chapter interrogates the complex social and institutional dynamics shaping public and police responses to juvenile offending. The authors trace how socio-economic pressures, sensationalized media narratives, and culturally embedded punitive attitudes heighten public fear and foster demands for harsher measures that impede rehabilitative goals. Employing criminological theories—most notably Merton's Strain Theory and Social Learning Theory—the analysis reveals how institutional practices and public perceptions can either reinforce or mitigate youth recidivism. The chapter highlights the pressing need for police sensitization programs and specialized juvenile units designed to align frontline practices with the rehabilitative ethos envisioned in India's juvenile justice legislation.

Chapter 4: How Might We Prevent Youth Crime?: Lessons from Research in Nigeria

Drawing on empirical findings from a field survey of victims and criminal justice professionals in Nigeria, this chapter challenges punitive, incarceration-centered approaches that have long dominated responses to youth crime. The authors argue that such "warehousing" of young people not only undermines rehabilitation but also perpetuates cycles of marginalization. Through theoretical lenses grounded in sociological positivism and social constructionism, the chapter unpacks the complex interplay of structural and social variables contributing to youth offending. It ultimately presents a range of evidence-based strategies and community-driven interventions aimed at fostering sustainable youth development and strengthening crime-prevention efforts in Nigeria and comparable settings.

Chapter 5: Force Feeding in Africa: Juvenile Justice in Africa and Western Criminal Justice Systems

This chapter offers a striking examination of *leblouh*—the Mauritanian practice of force-feeding young girls to prepare them for early marriage—and juxtaposes it with Western cultural pressures surrounding thinness and beauty. The authors delve into the cultural, behavioral, and health-related implications of leblouh, highlighting the physical and psychological risks borne by girls subjected to the practice, as well as its intersection with underage marriage and gendered expectations. The chapter further analyzes government actions, advocacy efforts by non-governmental organizations, and the broader implications for children's rights and juvenile justice in Mauritania. Through this cross-cultural comparison, the chapter brings important attention to how societal norms around body image and gender can constitute profound child-protection challenges.

Chapter 6: Comparing Street Children in Sub-Saharan African Countries (Ghana and Nigeria) and the West

In this chapter, the authors address the persistent and alarming phenomenon of street children in Ghana and Nigeria, situating the issue within broader socio-economic conditions across Sub-Saharan Africa. Drawing on UNICEF data and country-level analyses, the chapter explores the factors that push children onto urban streets, the daily survival challenges they face, and the governmental and community responses aimed at addressing their needs. It offers a comparative assessment of Ghanaian and Nigerian programs—highlighting their achievements, shortcomings, and the structural limits they encounter—while contrasting these approaches with Western models that often provide more extensive social support and child-protection mechanisms. The chapter illuminates both the urgency of the crisis and the opportunities for reform.

Chapter 7: Exploring the Labeling Theory of Deviance in Barbados

This chapter provides an in-depth exploration of labeling theory within the context of Barbados, focusing on how youth interpret and respond to being formally labeled as "deviant." Drawing from empirical research on juvenile experiences with arrest, detention, and institutional contact, the authors reveal that public branding does not necessarily result in internalized deviant identities. Instead, acceptance or rejection of such labels is mediated by social environments, personal resilience, family and peer histories with the law, and the nature of interactions with social control agents. The findings underscore the importance of humane and developmentally sensitive policing and adjudication practices that avoid reinforcing stigmatizing identities among youth.

Chapter 8: Comparative Analysis of Diversion Programs for Children in Kenya and Tanzania

This comparative chapter analyzes the structure, implementation, and developmental implications of diversion programs in Kenya and Tanzania. While both nations articulate commitments to rehabilitation and international child-rights standards, the authors expose significant disparities in program design, clarity of guidelines, and resource allocation. Kenya's comparatively structured interventions face challenges in execution, whereas Tanzania's community-driven model suffers from a lack of standardized procedures. The chapter concludes by recommending investments in workforce training, systematic data collection, and evidence-based program development to ensure that diversion fulfills its intended rehabilitative potential in both countries.

Chapter 9: Challenges in Safeguarding Children's Rights in Kenya's Criminal Justice System: A Prosecutor's View

In this practitioner-informed chapter, the authors present an incisive critique of the obstacles that impede the protection of children's rights within Kenya's criminal justice system. Key concerns include inadequate legal representation, insufficient professional training, limited information access, and the vulnerability of special populations such as child parents and young victims. Drawing on comparative insights from South Africa, Canada, the United Kingdom, and the United States, the chapter outlines actionable reforms—including individualized assessments, privacy protections, and continuous legal assistance—that would align Kenya's juvenile justice framework more closely with international norms. Emphasizing rehabilitation and reintegration, the authors advocate for a child-centered, rights-based model of justice.

Chapter 10: The Legal Dilemma in Implementing Drug-Abuse Laws Among Street Children in Nairobi

This chapter investigates the intersection of drug-abuse laws and the lived realities of Nairobi's estimated 60,000 street children, highlighting the legal and practical challenges that arise when criminalization frameworks confront entrenched social vulnerabilities. Through a case study design involving social workers, law enforcement officials, and local administrators, the authors analyze key legislation—including the Narcotic Drugs and Psychotropic Substances Act of 1994—and identify gaps that hinder effective responses to drug use among street-connected youth. The chapter illustrates how enforcement practices often exacerbate children's marginalization and calls for a more holistic, welfare-oriented approach informed by field-level insights.

Chapter 11: Children of Somalia

This chapter offers a sobering account of the precarious circumstances facing children in Somalia, where decades of conflict, institutional collapse, and systemic instability have left youth—especially street children and child soldiers—highly vulnerable to exploitation, abuse, and re-victimization. The authors highlight the urgent need for legal reforms, noting the inadequacies of existing protections, including the high age of criminal responsibility and the lack of child-responsive court and correctional facilities. Emphasizing calls from the international community, particularly the United Nations, the chapter argues for collaborative, multi-sectoral efforts to build a robust child-protection framework capable of meeting the needs of Somalia's most at-risk youth.

Chapter 12: The Juvenile Justice System in the Arab Republic of Egypt

In this chapter, the authors trace the historical, cultural, and religious influences that continue to shape Egypt's juvenile justice system, noting the centrality of Islam and colonial-era legacies in the country's legal development. Despite the significance of Egypt within Africa and the Middle East, scholarly attention to its juvenile justice framework remains limited. This chapter seeks to address that gap by examining the age of criminal responsibility, youth-crime trends, custodial and non-custodial responses, and contemporary challenges. Through comparison with Western juvenile justice systems, the authors offer a series of policy recommendations and identify future research directions essential to addressing the evolving needs of Egyptian youth.

Chapter 13: Reframing Juvenile Justice Through a Human Rights Lens: Kenya and the United States

The final chapter provides a comparative human-rights-based evaluation of juvenile justice systems in Kenya and the United States. Highlighting Kenya's formal commitment to international conventions and its emphasis on rehabilitation and diversion, the authors contrast these structures with the U.S. system's decentralization, punitive tendencies, and persistent racial disparities. Through this juxtaposition, the chapter critically assesses both nations' alignment with global human rights norms, identifying significant implementation challenges such as Kenya's resource constraints and the U.S.'s equity crises. The authors conclude by calling for reforms that foreground dignity, fairness, and holistic rehabilitation as core principles of juvenile justice across all societies.

Acknowledgement

This book is the product of the collective efforts, insights, and dedication of many people and institutions.

We extend our deepest gratitude to all contributing authors. Their scholarship, fieldwork, and commitment to advancing the rights of children are the cornerstone of this volume. Each chapter reflects countless hours of research, analysis, and revision, and we are immensely grateful for their willingness to share their expertise and collaborate across borders and disciplines.

We also acknowledge the invaluable support of our peer reviewers, whose constructive feedback strengthened the intellectual clarity and coherence of the chapters. Their careful reading and thoughtful critiques enriched the quality of the final work.

Our appreciation goes to the universities, research centers, and organizations that facilitated data collection, provided institutional backing, and supported the authors' scholarly endeavors. Special thanks to practitioners—prosecutors, police officers, social workers, community leaders, and child protection officers—who provided the real-world insights that animate many chapters in the volume.

We are grateful to our families, colleagues, and mentors, whose encouragement sustained this project through its various stages. Their patience, understanding, and belief in the importance of this work made it possible to bring the volume to completion.

Finally, we acknowledge the countless children—those on the streets of Nairobi, the families negotiating life in conflict-affected Somalia, the youth navigating the justice systems of Ghana, Nigeria, Kenya, Tanzania, Egypt, and beyond—whose resilience and lived experiences inspire our pursuit of justice, protection, and dignity for every child. This book is dedicated to them.

Henry Murigi, Editor

Nairobi, Kenya

Introduction

The study of juvenile justice across the African continent continues to evolve as societies confront new social, economic, and security challenges that shape the lives of children and young people. This edited volume responds to these shifts with a rich collection of scholarship that examines the lived realities of justice-involved youth, the institutional strengths and weaknesses of justice systems, and the innovative pathways that countries are forging to protect and rehabilitate children. Spanning East, West, North, and parts of the Caribbean, the chapters collectively illuminate how juvenile justice is simultaneously locally and globally embedded in cultural contexts yet shaped by international human rights norms.

The opening chapters establish the conceptual and normative foundation for the book. The discussion on juvenile justice and human rights offers a crucial framework that anchors the volume in principles of dignity, participation, and protection. This is followed by a comprehensive examination of diversion programs and an insightful chapter on police and public responses to juvenile offending, both of which underscore the need for approaches that are preventive rather than punitive. The section closes with evidence-based research from Nigeria, which highlights how youth crime prevention strategies must be grounded in community realities and responsive to structural drivers of vulnerability.

From these foundational concepts, the book advances into a set of comparative and regional analyses that broaden the reader's understanding of the interconnected forces shaping juvenile justice systems. The chapter on force feeding and disciplinary practices juxtaposes African experiences with Western approaches, drawing attention to ethical tensions and differing philosophies of youth correction. The examination of street children in Ghana, Nigeria, and Western nations highlights the universal yet context-specific challenges faced by children living on the margins. A compelling contribution on labeling theory in Barbados brings a Caribbean perspective into the discourse, demonstrating how identity, stigma, and youth agency intersect in complex ways across diverse societies.

The heart of the volume lies in its detailed East African case studies. The comparative analysis of diversion programs in Kenya and Tanzania reveals how legal frameworks, resource capacities, and community systems influence the success of restorative approaches. The prosecutorial viewpoint on safeguarding children's rights in Kenya provides an insider account of the legal and institutional hurdles that persist despite progressive legislative reforms. Equally important is the chapter examining drug abuse and street children in Nairobi, which exposes the legal dilemmas and social contradictions that arise when punitive frameworks are applied to children who are themselves victims of structural neglect. The section concludes with a sobering yet necessary discussion on the plight of children in Somalia, reminding us of the compounded vulnerabilities faced by youth in conflict-affected settings.

Beyond East Africa, the volume expands to North Africa with an examination of Egypt's juvenile justice system. This contribution enriches the comparative scope of the book by revealing how historical legacies, legal traditions, and contemporary reforms shape the treatment of children in conflict with the law in a region often underrepresented in juvenile justice scholarship.

The final chapter synthesizes these diverse insights by reframing juvenile justice through a human rights lens using case studies from Kenya and the United States. This concluding contribution challenges readers to rethink traditional justice models and consider how rights-based approaches can transform systems, empower children, and strengthen accountability. By bridging African and Western experiences, it offers a compelling vision for future reforms that prioritize rehabilitation, dignity, and social reintegration.

Across the chapters, several themes emerge with clarity and urgency. First, juvenile justice systems cannot be divorced from the broader social structures that shape children's lives, poverty, insecurity, family instability, and limited access to social services often precede contact with the law. Second, the criminalization of childhood is a pervasive phenomenon, particularly for children in street situations, conflict zones, or impoverished communities. Third, the success of reform requires more than legislative alignment with international standards; it demands well-resourced institutions, trained personnel, community engagement, and sustained political will.

Collectively, these chapters paint a vivid and often challenging portrait of juvenile justice today. Yet they also offer hope by documenting innovative practices, emerging reforms, and the resilience of children who navigate difficult circumstances. Readers will find in this volume not only a rigorous academic contribution but also an urgent call to transform juvenile justice systems into spaces of protection, opportunity, and fairness.

I commend the editors and contributors for assembling an insightful, timely, and truly global collection. May this work inspire new research, inform policy debates, and strengthen the collective effort to ensure justice for every child, regardless of circumstance, geography, or identity.

Simeon P. Sungi, Editor

Nairobi, Kenya

Chapter 1
Juvenile Justice and Human Rights:
A Comparative Study

M. K. Nikitha
https://orcid.org/0009-0001-7323-6511
PES University, India

S. Likitha
https://orcid.org/0009-0002-2970-6042
PES University, India

ABSTRACT

This chapter compares juvenile justice systems in African and Western contexts, focusing on their alignment with international frameworks like the CRC and ACRWC. African systems often reflect punitive colonial legacies, leading to overcrowded facilities and inadequate rehabilitation, while Western systems emphasize restorative justice but face challenges like racial disparities. Case studies from South Africa, Kenya, the U.S., and Europe highlight diverse issues. South Africa's Child Justice Act promotes diversion but lacks resources, and Kenya faces overcrowding despite legal reforms. The U.S. reduces detention through initiatives like JDAI but struggles with equity, while European nations achieve success with rehabilitation-based models. The chapter advocates reforms prioritizing human rights, community-based alternatives, and systemic equity to create effective, rights-based juvenile justice systems.

DOI: 10.4018/978-1-6684-9343-4.ch001

INTRODUCTION

The Importance of Juvenile Justice

Juvenile justice represents a critical domain within the broader criminal justice system, focused on addressing the unique needs and challenges faced by young offenders. Unlike adult offenders, juveniles are in a critical developmental stage, where their cognitive, emotional, and social capacities are still evolving. This distinction underlines the imperative to approach juvenile justice not merely as a mechanism for punishment but as an opportunity for rehabilitation and reintegration into society.

The importance of juvenile justice is multifaceted. Firstly, it acknowledges that children and adolescents are not yet fully matured, meaning that their actions often stem from a combination of immaturity, environmental influences, and social pressures. Understanding this is crucial for crafting responses that are appropriate and constructive rather than punitive. The juvenile justice system, therefore, plays a vital role in shaping future behaviors and providing young people with the tools necessary for responsible citizenship.

Secondly, juvenile justice systems aim to protect the community while ensuring that young offenders are treated with dignity and respect. The emphasis on rehabilitation, rather than retribution, aligns with developmental theories that argue that juveniles are capable of change when provided with appropriate interventions. Research has shown that rehabilitative approaches, which focus on education, counselling, and community support, yield better long-term outcomes than punitive measures, ultimately reducing recidivism rates among young offenders (Lipsey, 2009).

Finally, the juvenile justice system serves as a reflection of societal values and norms regarding childhood and youth. A society's treatment of its young people can be seen as a measure of its commitment to justice, equity, and human rights. Therefore, developing an effective juvenile justice system is not only a legal obligation but also a moral imperative.

Overview of International Human Rights Standards

The international landscape of juvenile justice is shaped by a robust framework of human rights standards, which assert the rights of children and establish guidelines for their treatment within the legal system. The United Nations Convention on the Rights of the Child (CRC), adopted in 1989, is the cornerstone of this framework, providing comprehensive guidelines that emphasize the protection of children's rights, including those who come into conflict with the law. Key provisions of the CRC, particularly Article 37, prohibit torture and inhumane treatment of children and mandate that detention be used only as a last resort and for the shortest appropriate time.

In addition to the CRC, the African Charter on the Rights and Welfare of the Child (ACRWC), adopted in 1990, addresses the specific needs and challenges faced by children in the African context. It emphasizes the right to a fair trial, the importance of rehabilitation, and the need for children to be treated in a manner consistent with their dignity and worth. These international instruments collectively underscore the imperative that juvenile justice systems operate within a framework of human rights, ensuring that the fundamental rights of young offenders are respected and upheld.

Despite the existence of these international standards, their implementation varies significantly across different regions. Western countries have made notable strides in aligning their juvenile justice systems with CRC and ACRWC principles, often driven by advancements in developmental psychology and social science research. In contrast, many African nations continue to grapple with colonial legacies and punitive frameworks that prioritize punishment over rehabilitation. This divergence highlights the need for a comparative analysis to better understand how these frameworks function in practice.

Comparative Approach: African and Western Systems

The comparative approach adopted in this chapter seeks to explore the divergent trajectories of juvenile justice systems in Africa and the West. It aims to analyse how historical, cultural, and socio-economic factors have influenced the development of these systems, particularly regarding their adherence to international human rights standards.

In African countries, the historical context of colonialism has left an indelible mark on juvenile justice systems, many of which continue to operate under punitive legal frameworks inherited from colonial rule. These systems often fail to adequately address the needs of young offenders, leading to high rates of incarceration and limited access to rehabilitative services. Conversely, Western nations have, over time, reformed their juvenile justice systems to incorporate principles of restorative justice and rehabilitation, reflecting a broader understanding of the developmental differences between juveniles and adults. By comparing these two contexts, this chapter will uncover both the successes and challenges faced by juvenile justice systems worldwide. This comparative analysis will not only highlight best practices but will also identify key areas where reforms are necessary to enhance the protection of juvenile offenders' rights.

HISTORICAL DEVELOPMENT OF JUVENILE JUSTICE

Colonial Legacy in African Juvenile Justice

Historical Background: Colonialism and the Justice System

The colonial era significantly shaped the legal systems of African countries, introducing legal frameworks that prioritized control over rehabilitation. European powers established laws designed to suppress dissent and maintain order among colonized populations. These laws often treated indigenous people, including children, as criminals deserving harsh punishment. The imposition of these legal systems disregarded local customs and practices, leading to the criminalization of behaviors that were previously accepted within the context of indigenous cultures.

In many colonies, including British East Africa and French West Africa, the legal system was characterized by punitive measures aimed at enforcing compliance with colonial authority. Juvenile offenders were frequently subjected to the same legal processes as adults, with little consideration for their age or developmental stage. For instance, under the British colonial legal system in Kenya, children as young as 12 could be charged with serious offenses and face the possibility of imprisonment alongside adults, reflecting a broader trend across the continent (Mugambi, 2013).

This punitive framework was rooted in a broader ideology of colonialism, which viewed indigenous populations as inherently criminal or uncivilized. The justice systems imposed by colonial powers aimed not only to control crime but also to instil a sense of order and morality according to European standards. This often meant harsh punishments for relatively minor offenses, with little focus on rehabilitation or the individual circumstances of young offenders.

Impact of Colonial Legal Frameworks on Post-Colonial Juvenile Justice

After gaining independence, many African countries inherited these colonial legal frameworks, which continued to influence their juvenile justice systems. Although new laws were introduced in an attempt to modernize and localize the justice system, many of these retained the punitive characteristics of colonial laws. As a result, juvenile justice systems in countries such as Kenya, Nigeria, and Uganda often mirrored the punitive approaches of their colonial pasts, with little emphasis on rehabilitation or alternative sentencing.

For instance, in Kenya, the Children Act of 2001 was intended to align the juvenile justice system with international standards, including the CRC. However, the practical implementation of the Act has been hampered by a lack of resources and infrastructure, leading to significant gaps in its effectiveness. Juvenile offenders in Kenya frequently find themselves in overcrowded remand homes, where they are held for extended periods without trial, often alongside adult offenders (Odongo, 2012). This situation not only contravenes international human rights standards but also exacerbates the psychological and social issues faced by young people in conflict with the law.

Similarly, in Nigeria, the legal system continues to operate under the colonial-era Children and Young Persons Act, which emphasizes punitive measures over rehabilitation. Despite the introduction of the Child Rights Act in 2003, which aimed to improve the treatment of children in conflict with the law, many states have failed to fully implement its provisions, leaving children vulnerable to harsh treatment and inadequate legal protections (Amnesty International, 2016).

The colonial legacy has thus created a cycle of punitive responses to juvenile offending in many African countries, undermining efforts to reform juvenile justice systems in line with international human rights standards. The challenge for post-colonial African nations is to break free from these historical constraints and establish juvenile justice systems that prioritize rehabilitation and support for young offenders.

Western Reforms in Juvenile Justice

The Rise of Separate Juvenile Courts in Western Countries

The development of separate juvenile courts in Western countries marked a significant shift in the treatment of young offenders. The United States was a pioneer in this movement, establishing the first juvenile court in Cook County, Illinois, in 1899. This court was founded on the belief that children should be treated differently from adults, acknowledging their developmental differences and potential for reform. The establishment of juvenile courts aimed to provide a more compassionate and rehabilitative approach to juvenile offending, focusing on guidance and support rather than punishment.

The early 20th century saw the spread of juvenile courts across the United States and into other Western countries. These courts operated under the principle of parens patriae, which granted the state the authority to act as a guardian for children, particularly those who were neglected or in conflict with the law. The juvenile court system sought to address the underlying causes of delinquency, providing educational and social services to support rehabilitation.

In the United Kingdom, the establishment of the Children Act 1908 marked a similar transition toward recognizing the distinct needs of juvenile offenders. This legislation established separate procedures for dealing with young offenders and introduced the concept of "youth courts" that focused on rehabilitation rather than punitive measures. The Act aimed to protect children from the harsh realities of the adult justice system, recognizing that young people required special consideration in legal proceedings.

Influence of Social Science and Developmental Psychology

The evolution of juvenile justice in Western countries was significantly influenced by advancements in social science and developmental psychology. Researchers began to highlight the differences between juvenile and adult offenders, particularly in terms of cognitive development, emotional maturity, and susceptibility to social influences. Studies by psychologists such as G. Stanley Hall in the early 20th century emphasized the importance of understanding adolescence as a distinct developmental phase that requires tailored interventions.

By the mid-20th century, the field of developmental psychology had firmly established itself, influencing public policy and legal practices surrounding juvenile justice. The recognition that adolescents possess a unique capacity for change led to reforms aimed at promoting rehabilitation and education rather than incarceration. Social science research demonstrated that punitive approaches often led to negative outcomes, including increased recidivism rates among young offenders.

The incorporation of these insights into juvenile justice practices prompted significant changes in legislation and policy. For instance, the establishment of diversion programs and community-based interventions became more widespread in the United States, focusing on providing juveniles with the support they need to address underlying issues contributing to their offending behaviour.

Key Moments in Juvenile Justice Reform (US, UK, Germany, etc.)

Several landmark reforms have significantly shaped the trajectory of juvenile justice in Western countries:

United States: The Juvenile Justice and Delinquency Prevention Act (JJDPA) of 1974 represented a pivotal moment in U.S. juvenile justice reform. This legislation aimed to deinstitutionalize status offenders and promote alternatives to detention. The Act established guidelines for the treatment of juveniles and emphasized the need for community-based programs that address the root causes of delinquency.

United Kingdom: The Youth Justice and Criminal Evidence Act 1999 introduced significant reforms to the juvenile justice system, focusing on preventing offending behavior through early intervention and community-based alternatives. This legislation established Youth Offending Teams (YOTs) to coordinate services for young offenders, emphasizing rehabilitation and support rather than punitive measures.

Germany: The Jugendgerichtsgesetz (Juvenile Court Act) enacted in 1953 established a legal framework for addressing juvenile delinquency that prioritizes education and rehabilitation. This law promotes educational measures over punitive sentences and has been influential in shaping a juvenile justice system that emphasizes restorative justice principles.

International Trends: Globally, the adoption of the United Nations Convention on the Rights of the Child (CRC) in 1989 further reinforced the importance of treating juvenile offenders with dignity and respect. The CRC established standards for juvenile justice that many Western countries have adopted into their legal frameworks, promoting rehabilitation and limiting the use of detention.

These key moments illustrate the significant shifts that have taken place in juvenile justice reform across Western countries, with an increasing focus on rehabilitation, community involvement, and adherence to international human rights standards. However, while progress has been made, challenges remain in ensuring that all juveniles receive fair treatment and adequate support within the justice system.

THEORETICAL FRAMEWORKS

Restorative Justice and Its Application

Restorative justice is an innovative approach to addressing crime that emphasizes the importance of repairing harm rather than imposing punishment. It is grounded in the belief that crime is fundamentally a violation of people and relationships, and as such, it calls for the offender to take responsibility for their actions and make amends. This approach contrasts sharply with traditional punitive systems, which often prioritize retribution over rehabilitation. The principles of restorative justice revolve around several key tenets, including the need to repair the harm caused by criminal behaviour, involve all stakeholders in the process, empower victims, reintegrate offenders, and actively engage the community in resolving conflicts.

At the heart of restorative justice is the focus on repairing the damage inflicted on victims and the community. This includes addressing not only the physical harm but also the emotional and psychological impacts of the crime. Offenders are encouraged to engage directly with victims and understand the consequences of their actions. This process promotes accountability and fosters empathy, which can lead to genuine remorse and the desire to make amends. In many instances, restorative justice practices facilitate open dialogue among victims, offenders, and community members, allowing them to collaboratively explore the root causes of the offense and develop a plan for restitution and healing.

Examples of restorative justice applications can be found in both African and Western contexts, highlighting the versatility of this approach in addressing juvenile delinquency. In South Africa, the Child Justice Act of 2008 has established restorative justice as a key component of the juvenile justice system. This landmark legislation emphasizes the importance of diversion programs that aim to keep young offenders out of formal court processes. Instead, the law encourages participation in restorative justice conferences, where victims and offenders come together with community representatives to discuss the offense and collaboratively determine how to make amends. This model has shown promise in reducing recidivism rates and fostering community cohesion, as it actively involves all stakeholders in the healing process.

In New Zealand, restorative justice practices have been successfully integrated into the juvenile justice system, particularly through the Youth Court. Here, family group conferences bring together young offenders, their families, victims, and community representatives to discuss the impact of the offending behaviour and develop a comprehensive plan for reparation and support. This process empowers victims by giving them a voice and allowing them to express their feelings and needs directly to the offender. Research indicates that this model effectively promotes accountability and significantly reduces recidivism rates among young offenders, as the rehabilitative focus fosters a sense of responsibility and connection to the community.

In the United States, restorative justice has gained traction in various jurisdictions, particularly through victim-offender mediation programs. For example, Minneapolis has implemented a restorative justice initiative within its juvenile court system that allows young offenders to engage directly with victims. This interaction fosters a sense of accountability and encourages offenders to make meaningful amends for their actions. Studies have shown that such restorative practices can lead to lower recidivism rates and increased victim satisfaction compared to traditional punitive measures, emphasizing the effectiveness of community-based approaches in the rehabilitation of juvenile offenders.

The role of community involvement in juvenile rehabilitation is critical within the restorative justice framework. Community engagement serves as a support network for young offenders, facilitating their reintegration into society after they have made amends. In many cultures, particularly in African contexts, traditional justice systems have long relied on community-based approaches to conflict resolution, which can be seamlessly integrated into modern juvenile justice practices. By involving community members in the rehabilitation process, restorative justice fosters a sense of collective responsibility for the well-being of young offenders and helps to restore broken relationships.

Moreover, community involvement can enhance the effectiveness of rehabilitative programs by ensuring that young offenders receive the support they need from their families, peers, and local organizations. This holistic approach not only aids in the emotional and psychological healing of the offender but also promotes community healing and cohesion. The collaborative nature of restorative justice encourages communities to address the social issues that contribute to juvenile delinquency, such as poverty, lack of education, and exposure to violence, thereby reducing the likelihood of reoffending.

Rehabilitation Theory

Rehabilitation theory serves as another crucial framework within the context of juvenile justice, focusing on the potential for young offenders to reform and reintegrate into society. This theory posits that juvenile delinquents can be rehabilitated through targeted interventions that address their unique needs and circumstances. Central to rehabilitation theory is the understanding that juvenile offenders, unlike adult criminals, are still in a formative stage of development and possess the capacity for change. This perspective is supported by extensive research in developmental psychology, which emphasizes that adolescents are particularly susceptible to positive influences and can learn from their mistakes when provided with the appropriate support and resources.

In the realm of juvenile justice, rehabilitation involves a range of interventions designed to address the underlying factors contributing to delinquent behaviour. These may include educational programs, vocational training, mental health counselling, and family support services. By focusing on these areas, rehabilitation theory seeks to equip young offenders with the skills and knowledge necessary to make better life choices and avoid future criminal behaviour. This approach contrasts sharply with punitive models that often fail to consider the developmental needs of juveniles, leading to increased recidivism rates.

Psychological perspectives play a significant role in understanding the capacity for reform among juveniles. Research has shown that adolescents possess a high degree of neuroplasticity, meaning their brains are still developing and can adapt to new experiences and learning opportunities. This inherent capacity for growth and change is particularly relevant in the context of rehabilitation, as it suggests that juveniles can be effectively redirected away from criminal behaviour when provided with appropriate interventions. Furthermore, studies indicate that juveniles are more likely to respond positively to rehabilitative efforts, particularly when these efforts involve family engagement and community support (Lipsey, 2009).

Comparative applications of rehabilitation across different legal systems reveal both successes and challenges in implementing this framework effectively. In the United States, rehabilitation has become a cornerstone of juvenile justice reform, particularly in the context of community-based programs designed to prevent recidivism. Programs such as Functional Family Therapy (FFT) and Multisystem Therapy (MST) have been shown to significantly reduce reoffending rates among juveniles by addressing the familial and social dynamics that contribute to delinquent behaviour (Mendel, 2011). These interventions emphasize the importance of family involvement in the rehabilitation process and have been widely adopted in various jurisdictions.

In contrast, many African nations face substantial barriers to implementing effective rehabilitation programs for juvenile offenders. While there is recognition of the need for reform, systemic challenges such as lack of funding, inadequate infrastructure, and insufficiently trained personnel hinder the development of comprehensive rehabilitation services. For example, in Kenya, the Children Act 2001 aims to align the juvenile justice system with international standards, yet many young offenders remain incarcerated in overcrowded facilities without access to educational or rehabilitative programs (Odongo, 2012).

Despite these challenges, there are promising developments in some African countries. In South Africa, the Child Justice Act emphasizes rehabilitation and restorative justice, allowing for community-based interventions that prioritize the needs of young offenders. The focus on rehabilitation has led to the implementation of diversion programs that keep juveniles out of the formal justice system and provide them with opportunities for growth and development. However, the effectiveness of these programs is often limited by resource constraints and the need for further training of personnel involved in the juvenile justice system.

Overall, both restorative justice and rehabilitation theory offer valuable insights into the treatment of juvenile offenders. By prioritizing the needs of young people and emphasizing rehabilitation over punishment, these frameworks provide a foundation for developing effective juvenile justice systems that promote the rights and dignity of children. As societies continue to grapple with the complexities of juvenile crime, adopting these approaches can lead to better outcomes for both young offenders and the communities they inhabit.

LEGAL FRAMEWORKS AND HUMAN RIGHTS STANDARDS

International Human Rights Standards for Juveniles

International human rights law has established comprehensive frameworks that specifically address the rights of children, particularly those who come into conflict with the law. Two of the most significant instruments in this regard are the United Nations Convention on the Rights of the Child (CRC) and the African Charter on the Rights and Welfare of the Child (ACRWC). Both of these treaties seek to ensure that the rights of juvenile offenders are respected and protected, yet they operate within different regional contexts and frameworks.

The United Nations Convention on the Rights of the Child, adopted in 1989, is a landmark treaty that outlines the civil, political, economic, social, and cultural rights of children. It recognizes that children are entitled to special protection and assistance due to their vulnerability and developmental needs. The CRC establishes that children in conflict with the law must be treated with dignity and respect, with a focus on their rehabilitation rather than punishment. Central to the CRC is the principle of the best interests of the child, which serves as a guiding standard for all actions concerning children. Article 40 specifically addresses the rights of children accused of violating the law, emphasizing their right to be treated in a manner consistent with the promotion of their sense of dignity and worth. It calls for the establishment of laws, procedures, and institutions designed to promote the rehabilitation of juvenile offenders and their reintegration into society.

The African Charter on the Rights and Welfare of the Child, adopted in 1990, builds upon the principles set forth in the CRC while addressing the unique challenges faced by children in the African context. The ACRWC recognizes that African children are often subjected to specific vulnerabilities, including poverty, armed conflict, and cultural practices that may violate their rights. The Charter emphasizes the need for states to create laws and policies that promote the welfare and rights of children, including those in conflict with the law. Importantly, the ACRWC calls for children to be treated with dignity and for their rights to be protected in the justice system. It echoes the CRC in advocating for the use of detention only as a last resort and for the shortest possible time, while promoting the importance of rehabilitation and the need to consider the child's age and circumstances in legal proceedings.

Both the CRC and ACRWC are critical in shaping the legal frameworks for juvenile justice in their respective regions, yet their effectiveness depends heavily on how they are implemented at the national level. In many cases, while countries may have ratified these treaties, the actual application of their principles in domestic law and practice remains inconsistent. This inconsistency can lead to significant gaps in protections for juvenile offenders, particularly in countries where the justice system is under-resourced or influenced by cultural norms that prioritize punitive measures over rehabilitation.

Comparative Legal Analysis

A comparative legal analysis reveals both the successes and challenges faced by juvenile justice systems in African and Western nations. By examining the legal frameworks and practices in countries such as Kenya, South Africa, Nigeria, the United States, the United Kingdom, and Germany, we can identify key divergences and similarities in how juvenile offenders are treated and what protections are afforded to them.

In Kenya, the Children Act of 2001 was introduced to align the country's juvenile justice system with the principles established by the CRC. The Act seeks to promote the rights of children and provide mechanisms for their protection and rehabilitation. It established the Children's Courts and introduced provisions for diversion and alternative sentencing, aiming to prevent children from being subjected to the adult justice system. However, despite these progressive laws, the implementation of the Children Act has faced numerous challenges. Overcrowding in juvenile detention facilities, inadequate legal representation, and a lack of resources have hindered the effectiveness of the Act, often leaving many children in pre-trial detention for extended periods without access to necessary rehabilitative services (Odongo, 2012).

In South Africa, the Child Justice Act of 2008 represents a significant advancement in juvenile justice reform. This legislation emphasizes restorative justice and the use of diversion programs to keep young offenders out of formal court proceedings. The Act aims to address the specific needs of juvenile offenders by focusing on rehabilitation and reintegration into society. Despite these positive developments, challenges remain in ensuring that all children, particularly those in rural areas, have access to the benefits provided by the Act. Resource constraints and a lack of trained personnel continue to limit the effectiveness of rehabilitation programs, highlighting the on-going need for reform and support within the system (Gallinetti, 2009).

In Nigeria, the legal framework governing juvenile justice has been slower to adapt to international human rights standards. The Children and Young Persons Act, inherited from colonial rule, continues to dominate the legal landscape. While the Child Rights Act was passed in 2003 to improve protections for children, many states have yet to implement its provisions fully. As a result, juvenile offenders in Nigeria often face harsh treatment, including lengthy pre-trial detention and inadequate access to legal representation. The lack of enforcement of child rights legislation undermines the potential for reform and highlights the significant disparities between the laws on paper and their application in practice (Amnesty International, 2016).

Turning to Western nations, we see a different trajectory in juvenile justice reform, shaped by a greater emphasis on rehabilitation and adherence to international human rights standards. In the United States, the Juvenile Justice and Delinquency Prevention Act (JJDPA) of 1974 was a pivotal piece of legislation aimed at improving the treatment of juvenile offenders. The Act mandated the deinstitutionalization of status offenders and emphasized the importance of community-based alternatives to detention. Despite these advancements, significant racial disparities persist within the U.S. juvenile justice system, with African American and Latino youth disproportionately represented in detention facilities. Furthermore, recent years have seen a backlash against rehabilitative approaches, leading to a renewed focus on punitive measures in some jurisdictions, raising concerns about the future of juvenile justice reform in the U.S. (Feld, 1999).

In the United Kingdom, the Youth Justice and Criminal Evidence Act of 1999 marked a significant reform in the approach to juvenile offenders. This legislation introduced a framework focused on prevention and rehabilitation, promoting early intervention and the establishment of Youth Offending Teams (YOTs) to coordinate services for young offenders. The UK has made substantial progress in aligning its juvenile justice practices with the principles outlined in the CRC, yet challenges remain, particularly regarding the over-representation of minority youth in the justice system and the continued use of custodial sentences for non-violent offenses (Cavadino & Dignan, 2007).

In Germany, the juvenile justice system is characterized by a strong emphasis on rehabilitation and education. The Juvenile Court Act, enacted in 1953, establishes a legal framework that prioritizes the rehabilitation of young offenders and promotes restorative justice principles. Germany's approach to juvenile justice has been influenced by its commitment to human rights and social welfare, resulting in lower recidivism rates and more effective reintegration of young offenders into society. However, challenges such as varying regional practices and disparities in resources persist, highlighting the need for on-going efforts to maintain and improve the system (Weijers, 2004).

In summary, a comparative analysis of juvenile justice systems in African and Western nations reveals both significant advancements and persistent challenges. While many African countries are striving to align their legal frameworks with international human rights standards, they continue to face systemic issues that undermine their effectiveness. Conversely, Western nations have made considerable progress in implementing rehabilitative approaches, but they too grapple with issues such as racial disparities and the overuse of detention. Understanding these complexities is essential for informing future reforms and ensuring that the rights of juvenile offenders are protected globally.

DETENTION PRACTICES AND ALTERNATIVES

Juvenile Detention in Africa

Juvenile detention practices in Africa present a complex and often troubling landscape marked by overcrowding and inadequate conditions. In countries like Nigeria, juvenile detention facilities are characterized by extreme overcrowding, poor sanitation, and insufficient access to education and healthcare. For example, many juvenile facilities in Nigeria operate well beyond their intended capacity, leading to conditions that violate basic human rights standards. Reports indicate that juveniles are frequently detained with adult offenders, exposing them to violence and abuse, further compounding the detrimental effects of incarceration. Overcrowding not only makes it difficult for staff to provide adequate supervision and support but also undermines any rehabilitative efforts. In this environment, young offenders often experience heightened levels of stress, anxiety, and trauma, which can exacerbate their behavioural issues and hinder their ability to reintegrate into society after release.

Kenya faces similar challenges within its juvenile detention system. Despite the existence of the Children Act 2001, which was intended to improve conditions and provide for the rehabilitation of juvenile offenders, many children continue to be held in overcrowded remand homes and police cells. These facilities often lack basic amenities and adequate educational programs, resulting in a neglect of the physical and psychological needs of juveniles. Studies have shown that the lack of access to education and mental health services negatively impacts the development and well-being of these young people, leading to long-term psychological consequences, including depression and post-traumatic stress disorder (PTSD). The prolonged exposure to such harsh conditions in detention facilities can create a cycle of reoffending, as juveniles exit the system without the necessary support to make positive changes in their lives.

The impact of these inadequate detention conditions on the psychological well-being of juveniles cannot be overstated. In environments where children are subjected to violence, neglect, and abuse, the likelihood of developing mental health issues increases significantly. Research indicates that exposure to such adverse conditions can lead to emotional disturbances, behavioral problems, and a lack of trust in authority figures. Furthermore, the stigma associated with being incarcerated can hinder a juvenile's ability to reintegrate into their community, perpetuating a cycle of marginalization and recidivism. Addressing the issues of overcrowding and poor conditions in juvenile detention facilities is critical to improving the outcomes for young offenders and ensuring that their rights are respected.

Juvenile Detention in Western Nations

In contrast to the challenges faced in African nations, juvenile detention practices in Western countries often reveal a different set of issues, particularly concerning racial disparities. In the United States, significant racial and ethnic disparities exist within the juvenile justice system, with African American and Latino youth being disproportionately represented in detention facilities. Numerous studies have demonstrated that these youth are more likely to be arrested, detained, and incarcerated than their white counterparts, even for similar offenses. This overrepresentation can be attributed to systemic biases in policing practices, judicial decisions, and socioeconomic factors that disadvantage minority communities.

For example, African American youth are often subjected to harsher treatment at every stage of the juvenile justice process, from arrest to sentencing. This trend raises critical questions about the equity of the juvenile justice system and highlights the need for reforms that address these disparities. Programs aimed at reducing racial bias and promoting equitable treatment of all juveniles are essential to ensuring that the system operates fairly and justly.

Meanwhile, European nations have developed alternative approaches to juvenile detention that prioritize rehabilitation and community-based interventions. In Germany, for instance, the juvenile justice system emphasizes educational measures and probation over detention. The Juvenile Court Act encourages judges to consider alternative sentences that focus on the offender's rehabilitation and reintegration into society. Similarly, in the Netherlands, the youth justice system has implemented comprehensive diversion programs that keep young offenders out of detention. These programs often involve counselling, family support, and community service, reflecting a broader commitment to restorative justice principles.

The emphasis on rehabilitation in European juvenile justice systems has resulted in lower recidivism rates compared to more punitive systems, demonstrating the effectiveness of community-based alternatives. This contrasts sharply with practices observed in the U.S. and some African countries, where detention is often used as a first response rather than a last resort.

Alternatives to Detention

As the limitations of detention become increasingly apparent, many jurisdictions are exploring alternatives that prioritize rehabilitation over incarceration. One promising avenue is the implementation of restorative justice programs, which focus on repairing the harm caused by criminal behaviour through dialogue and community involvement. Restorative justice emphasizes the active participation of victims, offenders, and community members in addressing the impact of the offense, fostering a sense of accountability and encouraging offenders to make amends. In South Africa, for example, restorative justice practices have been integrated into the juvenile justice system through programs that allow young offenders to engage directly with their victims and develop restitution plans.

In addition to restorative justice, community service and educational programs serve as effective alternatives to detention. These initiatives allow young offenders to contribute positively to their communities while receiving the support and guidance necessary for rehabilitation. Community service programs have been implemented in various jurisdictions, providing juveniles with opportunities to engage in meaningful work that fosters a sense of responsibility and belonging. Similarly, educational programs that focus on skill development and vocational training can help juveniles acquire the tools they need to reintegrate successfully into society. In the United States, programs like Functional Family Therapy (FFT) and Multisystem Therapy (MST) have shown success in reducing recidivism by addressing the familial and social dynamics that contribute to delinquent behaviour (Mendel, 2011).

Comparative effectiveness of these alternatives demonstrates the importance of community involvement and support in the rehabilitation process. Research indicates that community-based alternatives to detention, such as those found in many European countries, not only result in lower recidivism rates but also enhance the overall well-being of young offenders. In contrast, traditional detention practices often fail to address the underlying issues that lead to delinquency and can exacerbate the challenges faced by juveniles upon re-entry into society.

Overall, the exploration of detention practices and alternatives in both African and Western contexts reveals the need for systemic reforms that prioritize rehabilitation over punishment. By addressing the root causes of juvenile offending and implementing effective community-based alternatives, juvenile justice systems can promote the rights and dignity of young offenders while ensuring the safety and well-being of society as a whole.

CASE STUDIES

South Africa's Child Justice Act

The Child Justice Act of 2008 represents a landmark achievement in South Africa's efforts to reform its juvenile justice system by integrating restorative justice principles and emphasizing alternatives to incarceration. The Act aims to address the needs of young offenders by creating a legal framework that prioritizes rehabilitation and reintegration into society rather than punitive measures. One of the key provisions of the Child Justice Act is the establishment of specialized Child Justice Courts, which are designed to handle cases involving children accused of crimes with sensitivity and expertise. These courts emphasize the importance of diversion from the formal justice system, allowing young offenders to participate in restorative justice processes such as victim-offender mediation and community service, which can lead to more constructive outcomes (Gallinetti, 2009).

In practice, the implementation of the Child Justice Act has shown significant success in reducing the number of juveniles held in detention. For instance, the Act promotes the use of diversion programs, which aim to divert young offenders away from the formal justice system, thus preventing them from entering detention facilities. Research has indicated that these programs not only help in reducing recidivism rates but also foster a sense of accountability and restitution among young offenders (Makoae, 2015). While the Act has been a step in the right direction, challenges remain, particularly in ensuring that all children, especially those from marginalized communities, have access to the benefits of these programs. Continued investment in training for judicial personnel and community-based organizations is crucial to sustaining and expanding these positive outcomes.

The impact of the Child Justice Act on the broader social context cannot be overstated. By prioritizing rehabilitation and community involvement, the Act has fostered a more nuanced understanding of juvenile offending in South Africa. The legislation recognizes the socio-economic factors that contribute to delinquent behaviour, such as poverty, lack of education, and exposure to violence, and seeks to address these underlying issues through support and intervention programs. For example, community-based initiatives that provide counselling, educational support, and vocational training have emerged as essential components of the juvenile justice system, further emphasizing the need for a holistic approach to addressing youth crime (Skelton & Tshehla, 2008). However, the sustainability of these programs relies on adequate funding and resources, which remain a concern in a country still grappling with socio-economic inequalities.

US Juvenile Justice Reform

In the United States, juvenile justice reform has focused on reducing the reliance on detention and addressing the significant racial disparities that exist within the system. One of the most notable initiatives in this regard is the Juvenile Detention Alternatives Initiative (JDAI), launched by the Annie E. Casey Foundation in 1992. JDAI seeks to promote alternatives to detention and improve the overall juvenile justice system by emphasizing the importance of community-based interventions. The initiative is rooted in the recognition that many juveniles can be effectively supervised and rehabilitated without the need for incarceration, which often exacerbates the challenges they face (Annie E. Casey Foundation, 2013).

The JDAI framework encourages jurisdictions to implement data-driven decision-making processes that assess the risk and needs of juvenile offenders. By employing standardized risk assessment tools, jurisdictions can identify youth who do not pose a threat to public safety and can be safely diverted from detention. This approach has led to a significant reduction in the number of youths held in detention facilities across participating jurisdictions. For example, in several cities where JDAI has been implemented, reductions in juvenile detention populations have ranged from 30% to 70% (Peters & Hennessey, 2018).

Moreover, JDAI has highlighted the systemic racial disparities present in the juvenile justice system. African American and Latino youth are disproportionately represented in detention facilities, often facing harsher treatment than their white peers for similar offenses. The initiative has prompted a revaluation of policies and practices that contribute to these disparities, advocating for culturally competent practices and community engagement strategies that address the unique needs of minority youth (Feld, 1999). Through community-based alternatives, such as restorative justice programs and intensive supervision, JDAI aims to not only reduce racial disparities but also provide more equitable treatment for all juveniles.

However, despite the successes achieved through JDAI and other reform efforts, significant challenges remain within the U.S. juvenile justice system. The on-going debate around the appropriate age for criminal responsibility, the increasing criminalization of status offenses and the punitive policies that disproportionately affect marginalized communities continue to complicate efforts to achieve comprehensive reform (Mendel, 2011). Addressing these systemic issues is essential to ensuring that the juvenile justice system serves the best interests of all youth and aligns with the principles of rehabilitation and restorative justice.

Kenya's Struggles with Overcrowded Juvenile Prisons

In Kenya, the challenges facing the juvenile justice system are pronounced, particularly in relation to overcrowded juvenile prisons and inadequate access to rehabilitation services. Despite the existence of progressive legislation, such as the Children Act of 2001, which aims to promote the rights and welfare of children in conflict with the law, the realities of the juvenile detention system often fall short of these ideals. Many juvenile facilities in Kenya operate well beyond their intended capacity, leading to severe overcrowding. Juvenile offenders are frequently detained in adult facilities due to a lack of separate, adequately resourced juvenile institutions, exposing them to risks of abuse and violence (Odongo, 2012).

The impact of overcrowding on the psychological well-being of juveniles is significant. Research has indicated that young people held in overcrowded detention facilities experience heightened levels of stress, anxiety, and depression, which can exacerbate existing behavioural issues. The lack of access to educational programs and mental health services further compounds these challenges, leaving many juveniles without the support they need to address the underlying issues contributing to their delinquency (Wanjiru, 2015). The failure to provide appropriate rehabilitative services not only hinders the potential for positive change among young offenders but also perpetuates a cycle of recidivism that can have long-term consequences for both individuals and society.

Moreover, the struggle to implement child-cantered reforms in Kenya's juvenile justice system is often compounded by systemic issues such as limited funding, inadequate infrastructure, and a shortage of trained personnel. Although the Children Act articulates a vision for a more rehabilitative and supportive approach to juvenile justice, the gap between policy and practice remains wide. Many children are subjected to prolonged pre-trial detention, often without legal representation, which violates their rights and undermines the objectives of rehabilitation outlined in the Act. As a result, efforts to reform the juvenile justice system in Kenya face substantial barriers, necessitating a concerted commitment from the government and civil society to ensure that children in conflict with the law receive the protection and support they deserve (Skelton & Tshehla, 2008).

In conclusion, the case studies of South Africa, the United States, and Kenya illustrate the complexities and challenges inherent in juvenile justice systems across different contexts. While South Africa has made significant strides through the implementation of the Child Justice Act, the on-going issues of access and resource allocation remain critical for the success of rehabilitation efforts. The United States has demonstrated the potential for reform through initiatives like JDAI, yet racial disparities persist, highlighting the need for continued vigilance and advocacy. In Kenya, the struggle against overcrowded juvenile facilities and inadequate resources underscores the urgent need for comprehensive reforms that prioritize the rights and rehabilitation of young offenders. These case studies underscore the importance of learning from both successes and challenges in order to inform future policy and practice in juvenile justice globally.

POLICY RECOMMENDATIONS AND CONCLUSION

Comprehensive Reforms Needed in African Juvenile Justice Systems

The challenges facing juvenile justice systems in Africa are multifaceted and deeply rooted in historical, social, and economic contexts. To create a more effective and equitable juvenile justice framework, comprehensive reforms are essential. First and foremost, African nations must prioritize the alignment of their legal frameworks with international human rights standards, particularly the United Nations Convention on the Rights of the Child (CRC) and the African Charter on the Rights and Welfare of the Child (ACRWC). This requires a thorough review of existing legislation to identify and amend punitive provisions that do not account for the developmental needs of juveniles.

Moreover, investment in infrastructure and resources is crucial for improving detention facilities and rehabilitation programs. Many juvenile detention centres in Africa are overcrowded and lack basic amenities, which not only violate the rights of young offenders but also hinder effective rehabilitation. Governments should allocate funds to renovate and expand juvenile facilities, ensuring they provide safe and supportive environments that prioritize education, counselling, and vocational training. Additionally, the training of staff in juvenile facilities should be prioritized to ensure that they are equipped to provide the necessary support and rehabilitation to young offenders. By enhancing the capacity of detention facilities and improving the qualifications of personnel, African nations can create environments that promote rehabilitation and reduce recidivism.

Another critical component of reform is the implementation of community-based alternatives to detention. Diversion programs that focus on restorative justice and rehabilitation can effectively keep juveniles out of the formal justice system while addressing the underlying issues contributing to their delinquent behaviour. African countries should invest in community engagement initiatives that provide counselling, mentorship, and educational support to at-risk youth. By fostering a collaborative approach that involves families, schools, and community organizations, these programs can address the root causes of juvenile delinquency and create pathways for positive development.

Finally, it is imperative that African nations strengthen their legal aid services to ensure that all young offenders have access to legal representation. Many juveniles face lengthy pre-trial detention without the support of a lawyer, which violates their rights and undermines the fairness of the judicial process. Establishing accessible legal aid programs and training legal professionals in child rights issues will help ensure that juveniles receive the protections they deserve within the justice system.

Steps Western Nations Must Take to Address Racial Disparities and Improve Outcomes

In Western nations, addressing racial disparities in juvenile justice requires a multifaceted approach that acknowledges the systemic biases present in the justice system. First, policymakers must conduct comprehensive assessments of the factors contributing to these disparities, including discriminatory policing practices and inequitable access to resources. Data collection is essential for identifying trends and patterns related to race and ethnicity within the juvenile justice system. By collecting disaggregated data, states can better understand the extent of racial disparities and develop targeted interventions to address them.

Moreover, training and education programs for law enforcement and judicial personnel are crucial in promoting cultural competence and sensitivity. By providing training that addresses implicit biases and promotes equitable treatment of all juveniles, Western nations can begin to dismantle the systemic issues that contribute to disparities in the juvenile justice system. This includes revising training programs for police officers, judges, and social workers to ensure that they understand the unique challenges faced by minority youth and are equipped to provide appropriate interventions.

Additionally, Western nations should expand access to community-based alternatives to detention, particularly for minority youth. Programs that prioritize restorative justice, counselling, and education can effectively divert young offenders from the formal justice system, addressing the root causes of delinquency while promoting rehabilitation. By investing in community resources, such as mentorship programs, after-school activities, and family support services, policymakers can help create a more supportive environment for at-risk youth, reducing the likelihood of reoffending.

Finally, on-going evaluation and accountability measures are essential to ensure that reforms are effective and that progress is being made toward reducing racial disparities. Establishing independent oversight bodies to monitor the implementation of reforms and assess their impact on juvenile justice outcomes will help ensure that commitments to equity and fairness are upheld. By fostering transparency and accountability, Western nations can build public trust in the juvenile justice system and demonstrate their commitment to creating a more just and equitable society.

Role of International Organizations in Supporting Reform Efforts

International organizations, including the United Nations, UNICEF, and the African Union, play a vital role in supporting juvenile justice reform efforts around the world. These organizations can provide technical assistance, funding, and expertise to help countries implement effective reforms that align with international human rights standards. For African nations, international organizations can facilitate capacity-building initiatives aimed at strengthening legal frameworks, improving detention conditions, and enhancing the skills of personnel working within the juvenile justice system.

Furthermore, international organizations can promote the sharing of best practices and knowledge among countries facing similar challenges. By creating platforms for collaboration and dialogue, these organizations can help facilitate partnerships between governments, civil society, and community-based organizations that work to support juvenile offenders. This collaborative approach not only enhances the effectiveness of reform efforts but also ensures that solutions are culturally relevant and context-specific.

In addition to providing technical assistance, international organizations can advocate for the prioritization of juvenile justice reform on national and regional agendas. By raising awareness of the importance of protecting the rights of young offenders, these organizations can help mobilize political will and resources necessary for comprehensive reform. Engaging with stakeholders at all levels, from government officials to local communities, can help create a sense of ownership and commitment to the reform process.

Finally, on-going monitoring and evaluation of juvenile justice systems by international organizations can help ensure accountability and transparency in reform efforts. By conducting assessments and providing feedback, these organizations can support countries in identifying areas for improvement and measuring the impact of reforms on juvenile justice outcomes. This commitment to evaluation not only enhances the effectiveness of reform initiatives but also reinforces the importance of aligning juvenile justice practices with international human rights standards.

In conclusion, achieving effective juvenile justice systems requires a collaborative effort that encompasses comprehensive reforms in African nations, targeted actions to address racial disparities in Western nations, and active support from international organizations. By prioritizing rehabilitation over punishment, fostering community involvement, and ensuring that the rights of young offenders are respected, we can create a more equitable and effective juvenile justice system that meets the needs of all youth and promotes their successful reintegration into society.

Comparative Study of Juvenile Justice Systems

United States

The U.S. juvenile justice system operates at the state level, with significant variation in policies. Despite its progressive roots, recent decades have seen a shift toward punitive measures, particularly for serious offenses. Human rights concerns include racial disparities in sentencing and the use of solitary confinement, which contravenes UNCRC principles. The case of Kalief Browder, a minor detained for three years without trial in New York's Rikers Island, exemplifies systemic failures and human rights violations (Gonnerman, 2015).

India

India's Juvenile Justice (Care and Protection of Children) Act, 2015, aligns with international standards by emphasizing rehabilitation and defining juveniles as individuals under 18 years. However, challenges persist, including inadequate age determination mechanisms and societal stigma toward juvenile offenders. Cases such as the aftermath of the 2012 Delhi gang rape highlighted contentious debates on the age threshold for serious crimes, leading to amendments allowing adult trial for heinous offenses committed by 16-18-year-olds (Jha, 2015).

Scandinavian Countries

Countries like Norway and Sweden adopt a rehabilitative approach, ensuring that juveniles receive community-based support instead of incarceration. The Norwegian justice system, for example, limits detention to severe cases and integrates education and psychological counselling into its framework. These practices have resulted in low recidivism rates and are often held as global benchmarks for child-friendly justice (Smith, 2018).

South Africa

Post-apartheid reforms in South Africa emphasize restorative justice, with a focus on reconciliation and rehabilitation. The Child Justice Act, 2008, established specialized child justice courts and prioritized diversion programs over formal sentencing (Skelton & Tshehla, 2008). These measures underscore the integration of human rights principles into national legislation.

Key Human Rights Violations in Juvenile Justice Systems

Children in juvenile justice systems often face severe rights violations, such as prolonged pre-trial detention, lack of access to education, and exposure to inhumane conditions. In the U.S., for instance, racial minorities disproportionately face harsher penalties and longer detention periods, highlighting systemic discrimination (Poe-Yamagata & Jones, 2000). Globally, the denial of legal counsel and inadequate mental health support remain critical issues, as evidenced in detention facilities in conflict-affected regions (Human Rights Watch, 2022).

REFERENCES

African Union. (1990). *African Charter on the Rights and Welfare of the Child (ACRWC)*. African Union. Retrieved from https://au.int/en/treaties/african-charter-rights-and-welfare-child

Amnesty International. (2016). *Nigeria: Trapped in the Cycle of Violence: Nigeria's Justice System and the Detention of Children*. Amnesty International. Retrieved from https://www.amnesty.org/en/documents/afr44/4961/2016/en/

Annie E. Casey Foundation. (2013). *Juvenile Detention Alternatives Initiative: Lessons from the States*. Annie E. Casey Foundation. Retrieved from https://www.aecf.org/resources/juvenile-detention-alternatives-initiative/

Cavadino, M., & Dignan, J. (2007). *The Penal System: An Introduction* (4th ed.). Sage Publications.

Feld, B. C. (1999). *Bad Kids: Race and the Transformation of the Juvenile Court*. Oxford University Press.

Gallinetti, J. (2009). *Getting to Know the Child Justice Act*. Child Justice Alliance. Retrieved from https://www.childjustice.org.za/

Gonnerman, J. (2015). Kalief Browder, 1993–2015. *The New Yorker, 7*.

Lipsey, M. W. (2009). The Primary Factors that Characterize Effective Interventions with Juvenile Offenders: A Meta-Analytic Overview. *Victims & Offenders*, *4*(2), 124–147.

Makoae, M. G. (2015). *Experiences of caregivers implementing HIV and AIDS services within community-based organizations (CBOS) in rural Maseru: Lesotho* (Doctoral dissertation, University of the Free State).

Mendel, R. A. (2011). *No Place for Kids: The Case for Reducing Juvenile Incarceration*. Annie E. Casey Foundation. Retrieved from https://www.aecf.org/resources/no-place-for-kids/

Mugambi, M. K. (2013). *Effects of e-government strategy on service delivery in the government ministries in Kenya* (Doctoral dissertation, University of Nairobi).

Odongo, G. (2012). Juvenile Justice in Kenya: A Human Rights Perspective. *African Human Rights Law Journal*, *12*(2), 274–293.

Poe-Yamagata, E., & Jones, M. (2000). And justice for some: Building blocks for youth. *Retrieved July, 12*, 2009.

Skelton, A., & Tshehla, B. (2008). Child Justice in South Africa. *Institute for Security Studies Monographs*, *2008*(150), 72.

Smith, M. (2018). For the Love of 'Bad, Foreign Habits': Anglo-Saxon and Scandinavian Cultural Development and Identity Differentiation from 750 to 950 CE.

UNICEF. (2017). *A Familiar Face: Violence in the Lives of Children and Adolescents*. United Nations. Retrieved from https://data.unicef.org/resources/a-familiar-face/

United Nations. (1989). *Convention on the Rights of the Child (CRC)*. United Nations. Retrieved from https://www.ohchr.org/en/instruments-mechanisms/instruments/convention-rights-child

Wanjiru, F. W. (2015). *The effect of dividend pay out ratio on the financial performance of companies listed on the Nairobi Securities Exchange* (Doctoral dissertation, University of Nairobi).

Weijers, I. (2004). The Moral Dialogue: Juvenile Justice, Criminal Law, and Restorative Justice. *Journal of Social Philosophy*, *35*(3), 466–480.

Chapter 2
Juvenile Diversion Programs

Poorvi Ravikumar
https://orcid.org/0009-0003-8585-8785
PES Univeristy, India

S. Likitha
https://orcid.org/0009-0002-2970-6042
PES University, India

ABSTRACT

Juvenile Diversion Programs play a vital role in the legal system. They aim to stop young people from committing more crimes and tackle root causes like poverty, poor education, and unstable homes. These programs focus on stopping crime before it happens, helping kids change, and making things right. They come in different forms, such as informal and formal diversion, community-based justice, and volunteer work. Studies show these programs help reduce repeat offenses, avoid lasting criminal records, and support personal growth. However, putting these programs in place, especially in African justice systems, faces issues like limited funds, uneven use, and social judgment. Despite these problems, youth programs have shown good results in Western countries. With better policies, training, and community support, they can be improved and used more widely in African legal systems.

INTRODUCTION

Worldwide, the juvenile justice systems are based on the consideration of children and adolescents being different from adults in cognitive, moral, and emotional development and decision-making processes and their ability to learn and change.

DOI: 10.4018/978-1-6684-9343-4.ch002

This underlying assumption has led to the proliferation of special-purpose and restorative justice systems that seek to reform, rather than just to punish, young law violators. Among the key elements of the juvenile justice system, especially in the African and Western criminal systems, is the juvenile diversion program. The attempts of this type of program are to help young people not to be caught in formal court proceedings and the usual strict measures, but through alternative interventions that are more restorative and reintegrative.

The very conception at the core of juvenile diversion is that the referral of young people to traditional justice institutions probably does more harm than good. A juvenile offense would lead to the imposition of educational, work-related, and social barriers that worsen the situation by the stigma of youth thereby making them recidivate (Howell, 2009). Instead of criminalizing the youth and sending them to court, diversion programs intend to provide alternatives that help them develop a proper sense of self while taking care of the issues related to family instability and lack of education and employment and economic status.

In African and Western criminal justice systems, diversion programs for juveniles can have various shapes because they are influenced by different local laws, cultural norms, financial resources, and historical context. For example, in several African nations, the traditional justice methods often act as a major force in the conception and implementation of juvenile diversion programs (Skelton, 2015). This sort of rehabilitation is based on restorative justice and usually requires the involvement of the community, reconciliation, and restitution; besides, the youngsters are given the responsibility to reconcile the harm they caused by their misconduct. Alternatively, diversion programs for young offenders in the Western criminal justice systems are often more institutionalized and focused on therapeutic interventions. Counselling is often used to help in working through any underlying issues along with drug abuse treatment and educational help (Cipriani, 2009). In various cases, these programs administer behavioural and psychological tests to identify what particular needs the adolescents are facing and then customize the therapies accordingly.

Despite the fact that the main objectives of rehabilitation programs for juveniles in Africa and the Western world are quite similar—avoiding re-offending, fostering rehabilitation, and making them rejoin-local areas—Differences in the use of these goals are clearly visible. In Africa, informal justice and community-based approaches are typically used, being that the region's socio-cultural nature and historical dependence on collective decision-making are apparent (Muncie, 2008). Conversely, Western countries are more likely to use formal state institutions, where individualized treatment plans that incorporate psychological and legal expertise are developed (Haines & Case, 2015).

The global community, through legal structures like the United Nations Convention on the Rights of the Child (UNCRC), pushes for diversion programs as a key part of youth justice. Article 40 of the UNCRC stresses the need to handle young offenders in ways that help them rejoin society instead of just punishing them. Even with this worldwide agreement different areas put these programs into action in various ways. Big hurdles still exist to make sure these programs work well, treat everyone, and reach all young convicts.

For instance, in Africa, there are very limited resources, the infrastructure is weak, and there are extremely high levels of poverty, which makes it very difficult to fully enforce juvenile diversion programs. The other concern is that, although they are more readily available and culturally acceptable, the traditional justice systems do not have the same due process protections and checks and balances as the formal court systems. However, in Western nations, while resources and laws are readily available, juvenile diversion programs are not always distributed fairly, and access is often determined by race, class, and location (Haines Case, 2015). Another thing is that western society's focus on individual treatment fails to take into account the larger social and structural aspects of juvenile delinquency, such as poverty, educational inequity, and systemic discrimination.

The objective of this chapter is to delve into these involved issues by comparing two or more diversion programs for young offenders in Africa and the West. This allows for an analysis of the level of resemblance and divergence of various programs and their results with the intention of offering solutions to improving juvenile justice systems for the benefit of both the young offenders and the communities they belong to.

Juvenile Diversion Program

Diversion can be understood from many angles but above all implies opportunities extending beyond formal judicial processes. It saves resources and also allows a better social integration for children in conflict with the law. The process of disposing or unambiguously resolving judicial affairs is termed as pre-trial diversion. A variety of other broader definitions can be incorporated including the eluding more complex and negative surroundings of the formal judicial proceedings in some cases reducing the burden upon the court or the child within judicial jurisdiction. All these help the child follow the rules better without a reward or punishment system being instituted. The particular aim of this particular operational principal rests primarily in prevention of the initiation of judicial proceedings against or suspension of judicial proceedings against children in need of protection, support and guidance so as to improve their growth and development and acceptance within the community. (Crime & Unicef, 2007) Central to the concept of diversion is the acknowledgment that youth crime is often a product of environmental factors such as poverty, lack of education, and social instability. Therefore, the aim is to address these underlying issues rather than impose penalties that may stigmatize or further alienate young offenders (Feld, 1993).

Core Principles of Juvenile Diversion Programs

Prevention: Diversion programs essentially focus on preventing a youth from further involvement in crime. These diversion programs attempt to break the cycle of reoffending by diverting the youth away from the formal justice system. Some preventive techniques within these diversion programs include workshops on education, vocational training, and life skills courses that are tailored to address the needs and circumstances specific to the youth.

Rehabilitation: The methodology of diversion programs is based on rehabilitation instead of punishment. Counselling, therapy, and education towards guiding youngsters to understand why they did that, and how could they not do that in the future are some typical rehabilitative methods under such programs. Rehabilitative approaches have been found to lower the recidivism levels as well, because the youngsters are being equipped with the development of emotional and psychological skills needed for such a fight (Wilson & Hoge, 2012)

Restorative Justice: One of the lead principles is on restorative justice, where through this, the harm occasioned and the relationships involved between the offender, the victim, and even the community will be restored. The approach includes mediation-or perhaps the meeting of the offenders with their victims to acknowledge what they have done and try to provide restitution and perhaps reconcile (Zehr, 2002). Restoration of justice is a model that can be classified as humane and effective when tackling juvenile offenses with a focus on making an offender accountable while also being empathetic.

Purpose of Diversion Programs

It is said that diversion programs reduce the chances of another offense by a juvenile. It has been found that youths diverted out of the criminal justice system during processing are less likely to offend than those who have undergone the traditional court process. This will help the youth revert to rehabilitation and skill building, which will eventually equip them with better means of life patterns, thus reducing the likelihood of criminal actions through their later years.

The core objective of juvenile diversion is to prevent the long-term consequences of a criminal record. In most jurisdictions, a criminal record, technically obtained and subsequently served, has far-reaching collateral consequences, including restricting educational and employment opportunities, thereby creating a vicious cycle of poverty and crime. In this sense, diversion programs aim to keep youth out of the formal justice system, ensuring that they do not have long-term futures disrupted and contributing to good citizenship

The juvenile diversion programs make possible interventions that can trigger personal growth and development. Interventions might be mentorship programs, counselling sessions, anger management classes, and community service projects among many others. For instance, youth can take educational projects ensuring completion of education or vocational training in different professions to enhance prospects for a stable future. Such programmes increase the likelihood of desistance, although they encourage also the overall development of the young offender himself or herself (Umbreit & Armour, 2010).

Types of Juvenile Diversion Programs

Informal Diversion: This method of dealing with cases involves resolving cases outside the court system, without any formal charges against them. Law enforcement officers or social workers may refer juveniles to community service activities and counselling or other rehabilitative measures. It is used for first-time or low-level offenses, in order to correct behaviour without resulting in legal repercussions (Lundman, 1994).

Formal Diversion: It occurs when a juvenile is sent to the programme on the understanding of an agreement that could carry suspended prosecution. Under good performance, the charges may be dropped, or in extreme cases, the case may be dismissed. Various programs in form formal diversion include drug treatment programs, educational courses, and probation-based supervision with therapeutic support.

Restorative Justice Models Restorative justice is focused on providing restoration, that is, harm repair and relationship restoration, rather than retribution. Mediation and Victim-Offender Reconciliation where offenders and victims meet together in a controlled setting to discuss the impact of the crime and agree on a form of restitution. These meetings provide education to offenders and victims, often leading to the signing of agreements that benefit each party and the community as well (Van Ness & Strong, 2014). Family Group Conferencing approach, the offender, their family, the victim, and community members all come to form a plan to confront the offense and have the youth make things right. That creates opportunities to ensure that families and communities can be an active participant in juvenile rehabilitative efforts.

Community Service Programs: In this program, youngsters are engaged in activities which would help their community and improve them, such as clearing from public areas or taking part in a local charity program. Community service holds the juvenile communities accountable as it develops a sense of responsibility and belonging to the environment (Shelden, 1999).

Counselling and Therapy: This can be one to one or group or even family therapy sessions aimed at behavioural, emotional, or psychological issues that might be causing delinquency (Henggeler et al., 2009). Skills Building Programs: Many diversionary programs focus on equipping the youths with vocational and life skill training education. This will build relevant competency amongst them to lead to employment, livelihood, and self-sufficiency but in a responsible and contributive manner in society, and greatly reduce recidivism (Miller et al., 2016).

JUVENILE DIVERSION PROGRAMS IN AFRICAN CRIMINAL JUSTICE SYSTEMS

African juvenile justice has developed extensively and transformed due to indigenous practices, colonial and other legacies, and also due to modern reform efforts. A lot of African societies handled youth offenses through community-led action and restorative justice practices focused on reconciliation and reparation rather than punishment (Skelton & Batley, 2006). Traditional justice systems incorporated family and members of society in the resolution of conflicts; re-integration was usually given priority for young offenders back into society.

Colonization, however, brought Western-type punitive justice systems that often conflicted with traditional methods. Colonial powers established formal judicial systems that emphasized punishment and incarceration, often siding with this approach at the expense of others, like those of indigenous people, that focus more on restorative and community-driven approaches (Olowu, 2008). This duality is reflective of many post-colonial African countries where formal juvenile justice systems coexist with customary methods.

Many of the recent efforts across the continent toward the harmonization of traditional practices with more contemporary juvenile justice models have favoured rehabilitation and diversion rather than the punitive approach. This shift is an offshoot of global human rights norms, such as the United Nations Convention on the Rights of the Child (CRC), ratified by most African countries. These are the reforms about building a juvenile justice system accepted both culturally and internationally (Muntingh, 2011).

A few diversion programs have been incorporated into the reform of juvenile justice in South Africa. The Child Justice Act passed in 2008 has established a statutory basis for diverting young offenders away from the traditional court system to community-based programs. A few of the diversion programs that have been launched are family group conferencing, victim-offender mediation, and life skills training workshops. These programs are diversionary in as much as they will depend on personal accountability and responsibility within the community for rehabilitation of the offender.

In Kenya, among others, diversion programs are found to integrate with customary justice structures such as community elders' councils. The centrepiece is juvenile cases with offenders, victims, and other members in the community taking part in dialogue and reconciling efforts, as noted by Cheserek in 2013. In Kenya, the Children Act of 2001 gives legal provisions for diversion, furthering the engagement of children in performing community service, counselling, or training or education away from the jail cell. Nigeria: Nigeria juvenile justice combines traditional approaches with formal diversion programs. Most of the programs employ local community and religious leaders to conduct restorative justice sessions between the offender and victim to work towards restitution and reconciliation. Besides, NGOs collaborated with the government in skill building and vocational training interventions aimed at improving recidivism among the youths.

Many African communities employ councils made up of either older members or respected leaders to help resolve disputes where the combatants are minors. The councils encourage the aggressor and the victim to engage with each other in consensus-seeking resolution methods. This approach is designed to reconvene harmony and prevent the adverse implications associated with criminal record documentation. Juveniles are sometimes ordered to perform community service or reparative work. As a form of reparation, this makes sure that juveniles face the consequence of their actions, while also making them stronger in their attachment to the communities around them and fostering a sense of responsibility and belonging.

Community involvement is another characteristic feature of most juvenile diversion programs in many African countries. Most programs use local leaders, religious bodies, and NGOs to complement their rehabilitative efforts at the community level. Other aspects of culture such as stories, mentorship, and traditional rites are also reinforced in diversion efforts to make these programs appealing to the youth and the larger community. In Tanzania, for instance, the diversion programs include traditional ceremonies that reintegrate the juveniles into the community through reclaiming their status and identity as responsible members of society.

Challenges and Limitation

Despite the many promising characteristics of these programs in Africa, several challenges and constraints are placed upon their effectiveness. This varies according to the country in question, but generally includes the lack of resources, inconsistencies in applying programmes between an urban and a rural context, and societal opinions on juvenile offending.

One of the big challenges African juvenile diversion programs faces is a lack of financial and infrastructural resources. In some countries, budgets are meagrely set aside for juvenile justice programs, leaving them with poor facilities and service delivery (Gallinetti, 2009). Diversion programs may be absent or lacking in rural settings altogether; thereby denying youth living within those regions an alternative to incarceration. A greater barrier to the successful functioning of diversion programs is the unavailability of adequately trained professionals. Policemen, social workers, and other personnel working on these initiatives rarely receive training in child psychology, restorative practices, and cultural sensitivity. Such lack of training does not help implement diversion programs effectively and may yield inconsistent results.

Urban locations usually have more developed infrastructure and capabilities, making it more possible to offer a greater range of diversion services. In contrast, rural locations usually lack the needed infrastructure support; and hence, well-planned and effective diversion services cannot be as easily set up. Differential application in urban versus rural locations results in imbalanced service accessibility wherein rural youth are more often exposed to traditional court processes and possibly incarceration (Muntingh, 2011). Efforts are in place to redress this imbalance as several countries have committed their resources to mobile judicial systems and community engagement projects that offer diversion for rural dwellers. However, the effectiveness of these interventions requires enormous funding and operational support, which remains a challenge for different contexts.

Social perceptions and stigma surrounding juvenile delinquency. Public attitudes toward young offenders also limit the success of diversion programs. For instance, in many African societies, the issue of delinquency is characterized by stigma, which inhibits the willingness to embrace non-punitive approaches. Such stigma may discourage the willingness of victims and the community to take part in restorative justice practices, besides affecting how officials are willing to divert the youth from traditional judicial procedures. The general public perception influences the policy-making process and diversion program approval. The change in mindset and need for such benefits calls for community education and awareness programs, which are very vital for changing attitudes. Programs that show success stories and show long-term benefits of diversion have helped alleviate stigmatization of such programs and gained public support for them

JUVENILE DIVERSION PROGRAMS IN WESTERN CRIMINAL JUSTICE SYSTEMS

In the western nations including the United States, the United Kingdom and Canada, the juvenile justice systems have transformed in many aspects over the last one century or so. Such systems were traditionally retributive, focusing on imprisonment and deterrent. Young offenders were for example, sentenced like any other adult without considering their age and chances of reformation and rehabilitation (Sickmund & Puzzanchera, 2014). Since the second half of the 20th century, the situation dramatically changed in the Western countries with respect to dealing with juvenile offenders or delinquents. This includes not only punishment of the offenders on account of the offense they committed but also supporting the rehabilitation of the offenders back into the society (Lipsey et al., 2010). That shift created emergence and further enhancement of such measures as juvenile diversion that were designed to offer young offenders the opportunities which do not require court and incarceration.

In Western countries, diversion programs are intended to lessen the negative effects that people experience by engaging with the formal justice system. These approaches seek to curtail the factors underlying the tendency towards delinquency like mental and emotional health, abusing drugs, or being in marginal conditions and strive to rehabilitate and reintegrate young delinquent individuals into the communities (Howell et al., 2013). In doing so these accounts apply responsivity by making juveniles accept responsibility, acquire skills and alter behaviours which enable them live productive and law-abiding lives.

In United Sates, Juvenile Mental Health Courts (JMHCs) are special courts that help young people with mental health problems who get in trouble with the law. JMHCs aim to keep kids out of detention centres and give them personalized treatment plans to tackle their mental health issues while encouraging good behaviour changes (Herz, 2017). These courts work together with judges, social workers mental health experts, and families. Young people in JMHCs must go to counselling, take their medications, and use community services as part of their plan to stay out of trouble. Studies show that JMHCs cut down on repeat offenses and boost mental health for those who take part, because they focus on treatment instead of punishment (Herz & Ryan, 2010).

In UK, teen courts sometimes called youth or peer courts, are programs that divert young lawbreakers from the usual justice system. In these courts other young people, not judges or lawyers, decide the cases. These programs try to teach and help offenders while making sure they take responsibility for their actions. They also get young people involved in their community. The UK has started several of these teen court programs. Research by Snow and Sanger in 2011 shows these courts have helped lower repeat offenses and helped young offenders grow as people. During a standard peer court meeting, a young offender faces a panel of fellow teens who choose suitable consequences. These may include serving the community, writing apology notes, or attending therapy. The aim is to provide a helpful, community-centred method that allows young wrongdoers to grasp how their actions affect others. At the same time, it helps them avoid the shame linked to official criminal records. Peer courts also focus on practices to make things right. They make sure to include the opinions of victims and community members when making decisions (Hine, 2020).

Restorative justice programs play a key role in Canada's approach to juvenile diversion. These programs aim to fix the damage an offense causes through mediation, talks between victims and offenders, and community participation. They bring together the victim, the offender, and community members to find a solution that helps healing and holds people responsible (Choi et al., 2011). In Canada restorative justice programs often include indigenous practices when dealing with First Nations youth. By incorporating traditional cultural practices into these programs, they recognize the need to address the long-standing and widespread unfairness faced by indigenous communities. Studies show that these programs have an impact on lowering repeat offenses and boosting victim satisfaction. They offer a more meaningful solution compared to typical punishment-based approaches (Marshall 2018).

Effectiveness and Outcomes

Studies show that youth diversion programs in Western nations help cut down repeat offenses and boost rehabilitation when they're custom-fit to what each kid needs. Many research studies show that diversion programs cut down repeat offenses among young people more than regular court processes do. Let's look at an example: Lipsey and his team's 2010 study found that when kids in the US took part in community-based diversion programs, they were 30% less likely to break the law again. We see the same kind of results in the UK and Canada. In these countries, programs like restorative justice and peer courts give young lawbreakers chances to turn their lives around and grow as people. The success of these programs stems from their aim to tackle root causes like mental health issues, drug problems, and family situations. These programs help young people by offering specific help and support. This allows teens to learn how to cope, get better at interacting with others, and stay out of trouble with the law in the future (Wilson & Hoge, 2013).

Diversion programs in Western countries have proved quite helpful in meeting the needs of at-risk young people such as those struggling with mental health, drug abuse, or past trauma. Take Juvenile Mental Health Courts as an example. These programs blend legal action with therapy, which leads to fewer repeat offenses and improved mental health results (Herz, 2017). But some people say that even though these programs work well, they might not fix big problems like unfairness based on race or money. Young people from minority groups African American and indigenous kids still end up in the youth justice system more often than others. They might also find it harder to get into programs that keep them out of trouble (Wilson & Hoge, 2013). To make things fairer, we need to change policies in a big way and put more money into programs that understand different cultures and are easy for everyone to use.

COMPARATIVE ANALYSIS OF EFFECTIVENESS AND OUTCOMES OF DIVERSION PROGRAM IN AFRICAN AND WESTERN COUNTRIES

Juvenile diversion programs aim to steer young offenders away from the formal justice system. These programs focus on rehabilitating offenders holding them accountable, and preventing future criminal behaviour. They offer alternatives like counselling educational support, community service, and restorative justice approaches. These programs have an impact on reducing repeat offenses tackling the root causes of delinquency, and helping juveniles rejoin society (Wilson & Hoge, 2013). Studies show that diversion programs can meet their goals when they're well-planned and put into action. But how well these programs work depends on things like what kind of program it is, who it's for, what resources they have, and the bigger picture of society and laws (Petrosino et al. 2010).

A key aim of youth diversion programs is to lower repeat offenses. This shows how well they can help offenders and stop them from getting into trouble with the law again. Research from different countries and program types reveals that diversion programs lead to fewer repeat offenses than traditional punishment methods. Studies that look at many juvenile diversion programs show strong proof of how they cut down on repeat offenses. Take, for example, a big study by Petrosino and his team in 2010. They looked at more than 30 different studies and found that young people who took part in diversion programs were much less likely to break the law again compared to those who went through regular juvenile courts. Their study showed that, on average, these programs led to about 25% fewer repeat offenses among the youth who participated. This shows how well these programs work.

A separate meta-analysis conducted by Wilson and Hoge (2013) reached comparable conclusions suggesting that programs incorporating therapeutic components—like cognitive-behavioural therapy (CBT) or family counselling—tend to have a strong impact on reducing recidivism. Programs that aim to change behaviour instead of just punishing or deterring offenders, prove most successful in decreasing repeat offenses.

Comparative Studies: Formal Processing vs. Diversion Programs

Research shows that putting kids through the formal juvenile justice system often makes them more likely to break the law again. This happens because it can label them as troublemakers and close doors for their future. On the flip side, programs that steer kids away from the system and offer support services help tackle the root causes of bad behaviour. These include family problems, drug use, and mental health issues (Lipsey et al. 2010). A U.S. study found some interesting results. Kids who took part in community-based programs to keep them out of court were 40% less likely to break the law again. This is compared to those who went through formal court proceedings and ended up behind bars (Howell et al. 2013). Another way to measure how well diversion programs work is to look at how they help young offenders change for the better. These programs aim to give kids the tools and support they need to stay on the right path. Many of them offer classes, job training, life lessons, and counselling. This has an impact on how teens handle tough situations, get along with others, and learn skills to find work.

Programs with job training and education have a big impact on helping young offenders turn their lives around. These programs keep kids busy and give them skills to get jobs, which makes them less likely to commit crimes later. A long-term study in the UK looked at young people who went through programs that offered job training. Over five years, these kids were more likely to have jobs and less likely to reoffend compared to those who didn't get this help (Snow & Sanger, 2011). Educational support, like tutoring and mentorship, plays a key role in helping people get back on track. Programs that aim to boost grades and get young people interested in school again have worked well. These programs have cut down on dropouts and helped kids behave better. A study in Canada showed that young lawbreakers who joined programs to get back into school were more likely to finish their education and stay out of trouble later on (Marshall 2018).

Programs that deal with mental health and drug abuse problems work well for young offenders who have underlying mental or behavioural issues. Take Juvenile Mental Health Courts (JMHCs) in the US, for example. They offer a complete plan that mixes legal oversight with personalized treatment, including therapy and managing medications. Research shows that young people who finish these programs end up with better mental health and are much less likely to commit crimes again (Herz & Ryan 2010). Substance abuse treatment programs for young offenders aim to rehabilitate rather than punish. These programs offer counselling, family therapy, and help to manage addiction. In Australia, diversion programs that include substance abuse treatment have cut down repeat offenses among those who take part. These programs tackle addiction as a main reason for bad behaviour (Allard et al. 2015).

Restorative justice methods have a significant impact on many diversion programs. They aim to fix damage, encourage responsibility, and help offenders, victims, and the community make peace. Studies show that restorative justice programs are good at lowering repeat offenses and making victims feel better. These programs give offenders a chance to see how their actions affect others and take responsibility in a helpful setting (Sherman et al., 2015).

Victim-offender mediation (VOM) programs play a key role in restorative justice for juvenile diversion. These programs bring together offenders and victims to talk about the offense how it affected people, and what needs to happen next. Studies of VOM programs in the US and Canada show that both victims and offenders are very happy with them. Many offenders say they now understand their actions better and want to make changes (Umbreit & Armour, 2010). Research in Canada showed that young offenders who took part in VOM programs had a 28% lower chance of committing another crime within two years than those who went through regular court processes. The study also stressed how important it is to include community members in the mediation. This helped create support networks for the offender and made it easier for them to rejoin society (Choi et al. 2011).

Family group conferencing (FGC) has an impact on restorative justice in several Western countries, including New Zealand, Australia, and the UK. FGC brings together the offender, their family, the victim, and community members to create a plan to make amends and rehabilitate. Research shows that FGC programs help cut down on repeat offenses and boost family bonds giving young offenders the backing they need for good results in the long run (Daly, 2016).

Diversion programs prove their worth not just through short-term results like lower repeat offenses, but also by how they help young people rejoin society and thrive in the long run. Good programs teach teens essential life skills, help them find jobs, and form healthy relationships. This makes them less likely to get in trouble with the law again. Finding work and having a stable place to live show that diverted teens are on the right track. Programs that offer job training, career advice, and help with housing give young offenders a much better shot at success. In the US, Youth Build teaches young offenders building skills and provides education. This leads to fewer unemployed participants and less chance they'll break the law again (Howell et al. 2013).

ETHICAL DILEMMAS IN IMPLEMENTING YOUTH DIVERSION PROGRAMS

Youth diversion programs offer alternatives to formal justice processes, aiming to help young offenders grow and reintegrate. While these programs seek positive outcomes, they also bring up ethical issues. These include worries about fairness, bias, responsibility, and protecting young people's rights. We must address these ethical questions to ensure diversion programs work with honesty, fairness, and respect for all participants' dignity and rights.

Equity and Fairness in Program Access

A key ethical issue in running youth diversion programs is making sure everyone can access them equally. Studies show not all young people have the same chances to join these programs. Things like race, wealth, and where they live can affect whether a young person is offered diversion instead of going to court.

Research in the US and other Western countries shows that minority youth, especially Black, Latino, and indigenous young people, are less likely to be in diversion programs, even though they're more likely to be in the justice system overall (Wilson & Hoge, 2013). These differences suggest unfair treatment and raise ethical concerns about discrimination. For example, Rovner (2016) found that Black youth were much less likely to be diverted than white youth, even for similar offenses. To fix these unfair gaps, diversion programs need rules that focus on including everyone and actively try to reduce bias. This might mean training police and justice workers to spot and stop unfair practices, and creating specific programs for minority and disadvantaged communities (Holman & Ziedenberg, 2006).

Where young people live also affects their access to diversion programs, especially in rural areas and poor urban neighbourhoods where resources are limited. Youth in these areas might not have the same diversion options as those in richer or better-resourced communities. This raises ethical questions about fairness and applying justice consistently. For a diversion program to be ethically sound, it must be available to all young people, no matter where they live or how much money their family has (Mears et al., 2014).

Informed Consent and Autonomy

Another ethical issue is making sure young people and their families understand their rights and what it means to join a diversion program. Young people, especially those from disadvantaged backgrounds, might not fully grasp the legal results of their choices or what options they have. This means they might agree to join diversion programs without really understanding their rights or what the program requires.

To ensure ethical practices, diversion programs must provide clear, easy-to-understand information about their goals, expectations, and possible outcomes to young people and their families. This includes explaining the difference between joining a diversion program and going through formal court proceedings and outlining the rights and duties that come with each option (Hartjen, 2008). For instance, when young people are offered a chance to join a restorative justice program, they should get a detailed explanation of what it involves. This might include victim-offender mediation sessions, community service requirements, and potential behaviour or education interventions. Also, young people should have access to legal advice or a guardian to help them make informed choices, ensuring their rights and independence are respected throughout the process (Umbreit & Armour, 2010).

Balancing Public Safety and Rehabilitation

One of the toughest ethical challenges in youth diversion programs is balancing the need for public safety with the goal of rehabilitation. These programs aim to give young people chances to improve while keeping them out of formal justice systems, which can have long-lasting negative effects. However, ethical questions come up when deciding which young people qualify for diversion, especially in cases involving serious or violent offenses. Risk assessment tools are often used to determine if a young person is suitable for diversion. These tools look at factors like past behaviour, family environment, and mental health. While they're designed to protect public safety by identifying young people who might be more likely to reoffend, they also raise ethical concerns about potential biases and how accurate their predictions are. There's a risk that these tools might unfairly label minority youth as "high risk," continuing unfair treatment in the justice system (Schwalbe, 2008). To ethically balance safety and rehabilitation, diversion programs should have clear, open criteria for who can join. They should also make sure risk assessment tools work fairly for all groups of people. Additionally, ethical practices must include regular reviews and updates to these tools to reduce bias and improve their accuracy in predicting outcomes (Vincent et al., 2012).

Ethical challenges also come up in making sure young people in diversion programs take responsibility for their actions while getting the support they need to improve. Programs must find a balance between imposing consequences and providing opportunities for growth. For example, restorative justice programs require offenders to take responsibility and make amends, but they must also ensure that the consequences are fair and aimed at helping the young person develop (Sherman et al., 2015).

Privacy and Confidentiality

Another ethical consideration in youth diversion programs involves protecting participants' privacy and confidentiality. Young offenders often have complex personal histories that may include trauma, abuse, or mental health issues. Programs must handle this sensitive information carefully to protect the privacy and dignity of young people. Diversion programs need strong privacy rules to protect participants' personal info. This means keeping records safe and only sharing them with authorized staff. Programs should tell young people and their families how their info will be used and get their okay before sharing it with outside groups like service providers or community organizations (International Association for Juvenile and Family Judges, 2018).

While privacy is key, programs also need to be open about how they work and what they achieve. Ethical issues come up when balancing these two needs, especially when programs are checked for effectiveness or when stakeholders want to see participant data. To handle these issues, diversion programs can make data anonymous for research and evaluation, keeping individual privacy safe while still being accountable and open (Mears et al., 2014).

Cultural Sensitivity and Inclusivity

Making sure juvenile diversion programs are culturally aware and inclusive is vital for ethical implementation. Programs that don't consider cultural differences or the specific needs of minority communities might accidentally reinforce existing unfairness or push participants away. Diversion programs must be designed with cultural awareness, offering services that reflect participants' diverse backgrounds. For example, programs working with indigenous youth should include culturally relevant practices and involve community elders or leaders in the rehabilitation process. Studies in Canada have shown that indigenous youth in culturally tailored diversion programs, like healing circles, do better than those in standard programs (Marshall, 2018). To ethically implement such interventions, programs must actively work with the communities they serve, getting input from cultural leaders and making sure staff are trained in cultural awareness and competence.

BARRIERS AND CHALLENGES TO IMPLEMENTING EFFECTIVE JUVENILE DIVERSION PROGRAMS

Juvenile diversion programs offer alternatives to traditional justice system paths. They aim to cut repeat offenses, help rehabilitation, and stop young offenders from being labelled. These programs could help, but many things get in the way of putting them to work well in different areas and justice systems.

Legal and Policy Limitations

A major roadblock in setting up good juvenile diversion programs is the lack of consistency and the broken-up nature of legal and policy frameworks. Different policies in different areas, along with not enough laws, can restrict how far and how well diversion efforts can go. Many countries those with federal or decentralized systems, show different juvenile justice policies at the national, state, or local levels. In the United States, for instance, diversion policies can differ a lot between states. This creates gaps in how the system treats juveniles based on where they live (Torbet et al. 2000). In the same way, in African countries like Nigeria, policies might not be the same in cities and rural areas. This leads to uneven use and results (Okorie 2020). These differences bring up ethical and practical issues. Juveniles in some places might have better access to diversion options and support services than others. To tackle these obstacles, we need uniform and standard rules to make sure young offenders in all areas have equal and steady chances to avoid court. Setting up national plans with clear rules that still allow some local changes could help fix these differences.

One more problem is that juvenile justice systems don't work well with other social services, like school's mental health centres, and child welfare agencies. Programs that try to keep kids out of court often need different groups to team up to give young people the full support they need. But when the legal system doesn't push for or make these team-ups happen, these programs don't work as well as they could (Schwartz, 2009). For example, if these programs aren't linked to mental health services, kids with underlying mental health issues might not get the help they need, which makes it more likely they'll break the law again. To get better results, lawmakers should focus on changing laws to bring juvenile justice and other social services closer together. Making agreements between agencies and creating teams with people from different fields can lead to a more complete approach to helping young people turn their lives around.

Resource Constraints

Resource shortages pose a significant challenge in both developing and developed nations impacting the accessibility and effectiveness of diversion programs. Limited funds, a shortage of skilled staff, and inadequate facilities hamper efforts to set up and maintain successful diversion initiatives. Setting up good youth diversion programs costs a lot. You need money to build stuff, train people, and create programs. But many countries don't have enough cash for this. Poor and middle-income countries struggle. They have to spend their money on other things to help their people (Chitsamatanga & Rembe, 2019). Even rich countries can have problems. When the economy goes bad or leaders change their minds, they might cut money for these programs. To fix this, governments and other groups need to look for different ways to get money. They could team up with businesses or ask for help from other countries. Also, they could try to make programs that don't cost as much. These could use what's already in the community and get people to volunteer. This might help them do more with less money.

Juvenile diversion programs' success relies on skilled and dedicated professionals like social workers, psychologists, police officers, and educators. But many places struggle to find enough trained staff in areas with few resources or where juvenile justice isn't a top concern. For example, many African countries don't have enough experts to carry out restorative justice programs or to provide counselling and mentoring (Muntingh, 2011). This shortage of qualified personnel poses a big problem for these programs. To tackle this issue, we need to create training programs that give staff the skills and knowledge they need. This includes lessons on cultural awareness dealing with trauma, and using methods that fix problems instead of just punishing. Governments should also offer perks, like school money and chances to move up in their careers, to get more people to work in juvenile justice.

Cultural and Societal Attitudes

How our culture and society view young offenders and justice has a big impact on how we use and accept programs that keep kids out of court. People often look down on young offenders and don't like approaches that aren't about punishment. This affects public policy and how willing communities are to get involved with these programs. In many places, society labels young people who get caught up in the legal system. This labelling makes it hard for them to fit back in and turn their lives around. The negative view often includes diversion programs too. Some folks in the community and some decision-makers think these programs are too easy on crime or don't punish enough (Bazemore & Umbreit, 1995). Because of these views, those in charge might not want to send young offenders to diversion programs. This cuts down on who can use these programs and how much good they can do. Fighting stigma needs public awareness programs that show how diversion programs help people and focus on getting better instead of being punished. Getting important community leaders, lawmakers, and news outlets involved can change how people see these programs and build support for diversion efforts.

In Western and African settings, people often resist non-punitive methods because of deep-rooted cultural ideas about discipline, punishment, and justice. Some Western nations see punitive measures like jail time as crucial to keep the public safe, which leads them to prefer "tough on crime" policies (Mears et al., 2014). In the same way certain African communities have traditional justice systems that focus on payback and group responsibility. These clash with modern diversion programs that aim to rehabilitate (Skelton & Tshehla 2008). To tackle these issues, diversion programs need changes to match local cultural beliefs while pushing for restorative justice ideas. Using fitting practices, like community work and talks, and getting respected local leaders involved can help connect old and new ways of handling youth justice.

Challenges in Sustaining Community-Based Programs

Keeping programs running is another big roadblock to successful youth diversion programs those that depend on community help and local resources. While community-based programs are often easier to access and more relevant, they also struggle to maintain long-term funding, support, and involvement. Many diversion programs rely on volunteers to mentor, counsel, and supervise. This approach can engage local communities, but it also creates problems when volunteers lose interest or when programs find it hard to attract and keep volunteers. For instance, research in Western and African settings has shown how tough it is to keep volunteer-led programs going over time when the economy or society changes (Sherman et al. 2015). To make community-based programs last longer, we need to come up with ways to keep volunteers around. We could offer rewards or give them chances to train and grow. Also, teaming up with local groups, businesses, and non-profits can build a stronger support system for these efforts.

Juvenile diversion programs need good monitoring and evaluation to last and get better. But many programs don't have enough money or know-how to set up strong evaluation systems. Without good data gathering and analysis, it's hard to measure how well programs work, spot areas to improve, and keep getting funds.

JUVENILE DIVERSION PROGRAMS: RECOMMENDATIONS FOR IMPROVEMENT

Juvenile diversion programs hold significant promise in reducing recidivism rates, promoting rehabilitation, and preventing the stigmatization of young offenders. These programs aim to redirect youth away from the traditional justice system and into supportive environments that foster personal growth and accountability. However, the effectiveness of these programs is often hindered by various legal, resource, and societal barriers that can impede their success. This section outlines several recommendations to improve juvenile diversion programs, focusing on essential areas such as policy and legislative reforms, capacity building, and community engagement. By addressing these critical areas, stakeholders can enhance the implementation and outcomes of diversion initiatives, ensuring they are accessible, culturally sensitive, and sustainable for all involved.

Policy and Legislative Reforms

Reforming policies and legislation are crucial to establishing a supportive framework for juvenile diversion programs. Consistent, comprehensive, and integrated policies are necessary to ensure that programs operate effectively and that juveniles receive equitable treatment regardless of their location. This means that all young people, no matter where they live, should have access to the same quality of diversion programs. To overcome inconsistencies in how juvenile diversion programs are implemented across different jurisdictions, it is essential to advocate for unified national policies. These policies should establish clear guidelines and minimum standards for diversion programs, ensuring that juveniles in different regions receive similar opportunities for rehabilitation. For example, countries with federal systems, such as the United States, can develop national frameworks that provide consistency while allowing for local adaptability (Schwartz, 2009). This approach can help ensure that all young offenders, regardless of their geographic location, have access to the same resources and support. Moreover, African nations can also benefit from harmonizing policies across urban and rural areas to reduce disparities and improve access to services (Okorie, 2020). By creating a more uniform policy landscape, we can ensure that all young people have the same chances for rehabilitation and support, regardless of where they live.

Implementing national juvenile justice frameworks that incorporate diversion as a key component can create a standardized approach that is adaptable to local contexts. Collaboration among government agencies, non-profits, and international organizations is critical for developing and enacting these comprehensive policies. This collaboration can help ensure that the policies are not only effective but also relevant to the communities they serve. Effective juvenile diversion programs require adequate funding and institutional support to thrive. Governments should allocate sufficient resources to ensure that diversion programs are well-funded and adequately staffed. This means that there should be enough financial backing to hire qualified personnel, provide necessary training, and maintain facilities that support the programs. Advocacy efforts should also focus on integrating diversion programs into broader juvenile justice policies, making them an integral part of the legal framework rather than optional or peripheral initiatives (Chitsamatanga & Rembe, 2019). This integration can help elevate the importance of diversion programs within the justice system and ensure that they receive the attention and resources they deserve.

To secure funding, governments and organizations can explore partnerships with international donors, non-governmental organizations (NGOs), and private sector entities. Public-private partnerships can provide additional resources and expertise to strengthen programs, while international aid can support capacity-building efforts in low- and middle-income countries. By leveraging these partnerships, diversion programs can gain the financial and technical support needed to operate effectively and reach more young people.

Capacity Building and Training

Investing in the training and development of professionals involved in juvenile diversion programs is essential to their success. Capacity-building initiatives should focus on equipping staff with the skills and knowledge necessary to provide effective, culturally sensitive services. This training is vital to ensure that staff can address the unique needs of the youth they serve and create an environment that fosters trust and understanding. Professionals involved in juvenile diversion, including social workers, counsellors, law enforcement officers, and educators, need specialized training to address the complex needs of young offenders. Training programs should emphasize restorative justice practices, trauma-informed care, and skills for managing behavioural issues. In African countries, where there are often shortages of trained professionals, targeted training programs can help build the capacity of those working in juvenile justice (Muntingh, 2011). Governments and NGOs should collaborate to develop professional development opportunities, such as workshops, certification programs, and exchange programs with other countries, to enhance the skills of juvenile justice practitioners. Investing in these programs not only improves the quality of services provided but also increases the overall effectiveness of diversion initiatives.

Training programs should also focus on cultural sensitivity, particularly in diverse societies where cultural beliefs and practices influence perceptions of justice. Involving local community leaders and culturally knowledgeable individuals in the design and implementation of training can ensure that diversion programs align with cultural values and practices (Skelton & Tshehla, 2008). Restorative practices, which emphasize reconciliation and rehabilitation, are effective in many contexts but require skilled facilitation. Training juvenile justice personnel in restorative techniques, such as mediation, family conferencing, and victim-offender reconciliation, can enhance the effectiveness of these approaches and promote healing within communities.

Community Engagement and Support

Community engagement is vital for the success and sustainability of juvenile diversion programs. Engaging communities not only builds support for non-punitive approaches but also leverages local resources and knowledge to enhance program implementation. Developing and supporting community-based programs is an effective strategy for making diversion programs more accessible and relevant to local populations. Governments and NGOs should partner with community organizations, religious groups, and local leaders to implement and manage programs that meet the specific needs of their communities. This approach ensures that diversion initiatives are culturally appropriate and have the support needed to succeed. To build and sustain these partnerships, stakeholders should engage in regular dialogue with community members, providing opportunities for them to participate in program development and decision-making. Involving communities in this way not only strengthens their commitment to the program but also increases its effectiveness and sustainability (Sherman et al., 2015).

Public perception plays a significant role in the acceptance and success of juvenile diversion programs. Stigmatization of juvenile offenders and skepticism toward non-punitive approaches can undermine efforts to implement these programs effectively. Governments and organizations should prioritize awareness-raising campaigns that educate the public about the benefits of diversion programs and the importance of rehabilitation and reintegration (Bazemore & Umbreit, 1995). Engaging local media, community leaders, and influential figures in advocacy efforts can significantly help shift public opinion and reduce the stigma associated with juvenile delinquency. By actively involving these stakeholders, we can create a more supportive environment for young offenders. Highlighting success stories and positive outcomes of diversion programs can also demonstrate their effectiveness, building trust and support within communities. When people see real-life examples of how these programs have positively impacted youth, it can change their perceptions and encourage broader acceptance.

Enhancing Monitoring and Evaluation Mechanisms

Monitoring and evaluation (M&E) are critical for understanding the impact of juvenile diversion programs and identifying areas for improvement. Effective M&E mechanisms allow stakeholders to collect data, measure outcomes, and refine programs to achieve better results. This process is essential for ensuring that programs remain relevant and effective in meeting the needs of the youth they serve.

Governments and organizations should establish standardized M&E frameworks that are adaptable to different contexts and regions. These frameworks should include indicators for measuring recidivism rates, behavioural changes, and the overall well-being of participants. By collecting consistent and reliable data, stakeholders can assess program effectiveness, identify best practices, and make informed decisions about future program development. This data-driven approach ensures that programs are continually improved based on evidence rather than assumptions. Providing training for staff on data collection and analysis is essential to ensure that M&E processes are implemented effectively. Staff members need to understand how to gather and interpret data accurately. Additionally, collaborating with academic institutions and research organizations can enhance the rigor and reliability of evaluation efforts. These partnerships can provide valuable insights and methodologies that strengthen the evaluation process.

Data collected through M&E processes should be used to inform decision-making and drive continuous improvement. Regular analysis of program outcomes can highlight successful strategies, identify areas for improvement, and guide the allocation of resources. Governments and organizations should develop feedback loops that allow program staff to use data insights to adjust and refine their approaches in real-time. This adaptability is crucial for responding to the changing needs of participants and the community. Sharing evaluation findings with stakeholders, including policymakers, community members, and international donors, can also demonstrate program impact and build support for scaling up successful initiatives. Transparency in sharing results fosters trust and encourages further investment in diversion programs.

CONCLUSION

Juvenile Diversion Programs play a key role in seeking justice for juveniles. They offer an option besides formal court proceedings and give young offenders chances to rehabilitate, restore, and grow. These programs have core principles that include prevention, rehabilitation, and restorative justice. They aim to tackle the root causes of youth crime and help juveniles rejoin society. Different types of diversion programs exist. These include informal and formal diversion restorative justice models, and community service programs. All these contribute to the main goal: to reduce repeat offenses and encourage positive growth among young offenders.

The rollout of youth diversion programs in African justice systems runs into several roadblocks and constraints such as not enough resources uneven use, and social stigma. To tackle these issues, we need to make policy changes that work, build up skills, and get the community involved. To make youth diversion programs better and use them more in African justice systems, we should set up national rules and guidelines, provide enough money and resources, put money into training and growing professionals, and work with local communities. The track record of youth diversion programs in Western countries shows how these efforts can make a difference in young offenders' lives and boost community health. African justice systems can learn from what works well in the West to build and upgrade their own youth diversion plans. Also, by teaming up across borders key players can swap know-how, tools, and skills to roll out better diversion programs worldwide and get better results.

To wrap up, programs that divert juveniles from the criminal justice system show great potential to tackle youth crime and help young offenders get back on track and rejoin society. By improving policies, building up resources, and getting the community involved, these programs can grow and take root in both Western and African legal systems. In the end, this has an impact on making neighbourhoods safer and more supportive for everyone.

REFERENCES

Allard, T., Chrzanowski, A., & Stewart, A. (2015). The Effectiveness of Juvenile Diversion Programs in Australia. *Australian and New Zealand Journal of Criminology, 48*(4), 543–559.

Bazemore, G., & Umbreit, M. (1995). Balanced and Restorative Justice for Juveniles: A Framework for Juvenile Justice in the 21st Century. *Juvenile & Family Court Journal, 46*(1), 1–26.

Chitsamatanga, B. B., & Rembe, N. (2019). Exploring the Challenges of Juvenile Diversion Programmes in Africa: A Case Study of Zimbabwe. *African Journal of Criminology and Justice Studies, 12*(1), 71–85.

Choi, J. J., Green, D. L., & Gilbert, M. J. (2011). Victim-Offender Mediation: A Meta-Analysis of Program Effectiveness. *Justice Quarterly, 28*(4), 745–772.

Cipriani, D. (2009). *Children's Rights and the Minimum Age of Criminal Responsibility: A Global Perspective*. Ashgate Publishing.

Crime, U. N. O. O. D. A., & Unicef. (2007). *Manual for the Measurement of Juvenile Justice Indicators*. United Nations Publications.

Feld, B. C. (1993). *Justice for Children: The Right to Counsel and the Juvenile Courts*. Harvard University Press.

Gallinetti, J. (2009). *The Impact of the Child Justice Act on Juvenile Offenders in South Africa*. University of Cape Town.

Haines, K., & Case, S. (2015). *Positive Youth Justice: Children First, Offenders Second*. Policy Press.

Henggeler, S. W., Schoenwald, S. K., & Borduin, C. M. (2009). *Multisystemic therapy for antisocial behavior in children and adolescents, 2nd ed.* https://psycnet.apa.org/record/2009-06165-000

Herz, D. C. (2017). Juvenile Mental Health Diversion: A Collaborative Court Approach. *Children and Youth Services Review, 83*, 91–100.

Herz, D. C., & Ryan, J. P. (2010). Exploring the Effectiveness of Juvenile Mental Health Courts. *Youth Violence and Juvenile Justice, 8*(2), 136–152.

Hine, J. (2020). The Role of Peer Courts in the UK Juvenile Justice System. *Journal of Youth Studies, 13*(5), 587–604.

Holman, B., & Ziedenberg, J. (2006). *The Dangers of Detention: The Impact of Incarcerating Youth in Detention and Other Secure Facilities*. Justice Policy Institute.

Howell, J. (2009). *Preventing and reducing Juvenile Delinquency: A Comprehensive framework*. https://doi.org/DOI: 10.4135/9781452274980

Howell, J. C., Lipsey, M. W., & Wilson, D. B. (2013). A Handbook of Evidence-Based Juvenile Diversion Programs. *Crime and Delinquency*, *62*(5), 823–841.

Lipsey, M. W., Howell, J. C., Kelly, M. R., Chapman, G., & Carver, D. (2010). Improving the Effectiveness of Juvenile Justice Programs: A New Perspective on Evidence-Based Practice. *Juvenile Justice Research and Policy*, *11*(1), 27–45.

Lundman, R. J. (1994). Demeanor or crime? The Midwest city police-citizen encounters study. *Criminology*, *32*(4), 631–656.

Marshall, A. (2018). Restorative Justice for Indigenous Youth in Canada: Addressing Historical Injustices. *Canadian Journal of Criminology and Criminal Justice*, *60*(3), 289–306.

Mears, D. P., Shollenberger, T. L., & Willison, J. B. (2014). Juvenile Diversion Programs: A Meta-Analysis of Program Effects. *Youth Violence and Juvenile Justice*, *12*(4), 325–348.

Miller, D.. (2016). Vocational Skills Programs for At-Risk Youth: An Evaluation. *Journal of Youth Development*, *11*(2), 45–61.

Muncie, J. (2008). *Youth and Crime* (3rd ed.). SAGE.

Muntingh, L. (2011). *Diversion Programmes for Juvenile Offenders in Africa: Challenges and Opportunities*. University of the Western Cape.

Okorie, M. A. (2020). *Juvenile Justice Systems in Nigeria: Challenges and Opportunities. Nigerian Journal of Legal Studies, Hartjen, C. A. (2008). Youth, crime, and justice: A global inquiry*. Rutgers University Press.

Olowu, D. (2008). The Impact of Colonization on African Juvenile Justice Systems. *African Legal Review*, *42*(1), 103–117.

Rovner, J. (2016). *Racial Disparities in Youth Incarceration Persist*. The Sentencing Project.

Schwalbe, C. S. (2008). A Meta-Analysis of Juvenile Risk Assessment Instruments: Predictive Validity by Gender. *Criminal Justice and Behavior*, *35*(11), 1367–1381.

Schwartz, S. H. (2009). Basic human values. *sociologie, 42*, 249-288.

Shelden, R. G. (1999). *Delinquency and Juvenile Justice in American Society*. Waveland Press.

Sherman, L. W., Strang, H., & Woods, D. J. (2015). Recidivism Outcomes for Restorative Justice Diversion Programs. *Journal of Youth Studies*, *18*(6), 725–742.

Sickmund, M., & Puzzanchera, C. (2014). *Juvenile Offenders and Victims: 2014 National Report*. U.S. Department of Justice.

Skelton, A. (2015). Juvenile Justice in Africa: Reflections on Restorative Justice and Children's Rights. *International Journal of Children's Rights*, *23*(2), 335–351.

Skelton, A., & Batley, M. (2006). *Restorative Justice in South Africa: From Traditional Practice to Formal Adoption*. South African Legal Reform Institute.

Skelton, A., & Tshehla, B. (2008). *Child Justice in South Africa*. Google Books. https://books.google.co.in/books/about/Child_Justice_in_South_Africa.html?id=WWYxAQAAIAAJ&redir_esc=y

Torbet, P., Griffin, P., Hurst, H., & MacKenzie, L. (2000). *Juveniles facing criminal sanctions: Three states that changed the rules*. US Department of Justice, Office of Justice Programs, Office of Juvenile Justice and Delinquency Prevention.

Umbreit, M. S., & Armour, M. P. (2010). *Restorative Justice Dialogue: An Essential Guide for Research and Practice*. Springer Publishing Company.

Van Ness, D. W., & Strong, K. (2014). *Restoring Justice: An Introduction to Restorative Justice* (5th ed.). ResearchGate., https://www.researchgate.net/publication/287587203_Restoring_Justice_An_Introduction_to_Restorative_Justice_Fifth_Edition

Vincent, G. M., Guy, L. S., & Grisso, T. (2012). *Risk Assessment in Juvenile Justice: A Guidebook for Implementation*. Models for Change Initiative.

Wilson, H. A., & Hoge, R. D. (2012). The effect of youth diversion programs on recidivism. *Criminal Justice and Behavior*, *40*(5), 497–518. DOI: 10.1177/0093854812451089

Zehr, H. (2002). *The Little Book of Restorative Justice*. Good Books.

Chapter 3
Public and Police Response to Juvenile Offenders

P. R. Muhsina
https://orcid.org/0009-0008-7531-4836
PES University, India

S. Likitha
https://orcid.org/0009-0002-2970-6042
PES University, India

ABSTRACT

The study titled "Public & Police Response to Juvenile Offenders in India" examines the social and institutional responses to juvenile delinquency, focusing on the influence of media, public perception, and police practices. Juvenile delinquency in India is a complex issue, influenced by socio economic factors, media portrayals, and societal attitudes towards crime and punishment. Public fear, often driven by sensationalized media coverage, demands punitive measures rather than rehabilitative approaches, hindering reintegration efforts for juvenile offenders. The research emphasizes the need for police sensitization programs and the development of specialized juvenile units to align policing practices with the rehabilitative goals of the justice system. Through a blend of criminological theories, including Merton's Strain Theory and Social Learning Theory, the study underscores how public attitudes and institutional responses can either perpetuate or reduce juvenile recidivism.

DOI: 10.4018/978-1-6684-9343-4.ch003

INTRODUCTION

Juvenile delinquency poses significant challenges to societies, affecting not only young offenders but also the communities in which they live. In India, this issue is deeply intertwined with the country's cultural, social, and legal fabric. The juvenile justice system, primarily governed by the Juvenile Justice (Care and Protection of Children) Act, 2015, aims to rehabilitate rather than punish juvenile offenders, recognizing their unique vulnerabilities and potential for reform. However, despite legislative efforts to address juvenile delinquency, the complex interplay between public perceptions and police practices often hinders these young offenders' reintegration into society.

Public attitudes toward juvenile offenders in India are shaped by several factors, including media portrayals, community safety concerns, and societal beliefs about crime and punishment. The media often sensationalizes juvenile crimes, which can fuel public fear and drive demands for stricter punishment. This heightened fear frequently overshadows efforts at rehabilitation, perpetuating a punitive mindset that may lead to the stigmatization and alienation of juveniles. Research indicates that negative public perceptions can impede the success of rehabilitative measures, trapping young offenders in a cycle of reoffending and social isolation (Mears et al., 2007).

The media plays a significant role in shaping public perception, often sensationalizing juvenile crimes and portraying young offenders as threats to public safety. This contributes to a fear-driven narrative that calls for harsher punishments rather than focusing on the underlying causes of juvenile delinquency, such as socioeconomic factors, peer pressure, and familial instability. When the public is influenced by such narratives, the push for stricter laws and punitive measures grows, limiting the space for rehabilitative programs that could potentially redirect juveniles away from a life of crime (Zai & Zani, 2020). In India, societal beliefs around crime and punishment are further influenced by cultural values that emphasize collective safety and honour. Juvenile offenders are often viewed through the lens of morality, with their actions seen as reflecting poorly on their families and communities (Garg, 2021). Such beliefs can hinder efforts to reintegrate juveniles back into society, as the stigma of their criminal past may remain long after their legal punishments have been served. This stigmatization can lead to difficulties in finding employment, education, and social acceptance, ultimately contributing to a cycle of recidivism.

The police are often the first point of contact for juveniles who come into conflict with the law. Their approach to handling juvenile offenders can significantly impact the trajectory of a young person's life. In India, police practices are shaped by training, departmental policies, and the expectations of the communities they serve. While the Juvenile Justice (Care and Protection of Children) Act, 2015 emphasizes the importance of treating juveniles differently from adult offenders, there is often a gap between policy and practice. Studies have shown that police officers who adopt a supportive and rehabilitative approach towards juvenile offenders are more likely to contribute to positive outcomes, such as reduced recidivism and better reintegration into society (Young et al., 2017). However, many police officers in India may lack the training or resources needed to adopt such an approach. Instead, juveniles may be treated punitively, with little consideration given to their developmental stage or the root causes of their criminal behaviour.

The pressure to maintain public order and respond to community fears can lead police officers to prioritize punitive measures over rehabilitation. This is particularly true in cases involving serious crimes, where the public and media often demand swift and harsh justice (Garg, 2021). The tension between upholding the law and addressing the underlying social issues that contribute to juvenile delinquency makes the role of police in the juvenile justice system a delicate balancing act. Efforts to improve police handling of juvenile offenders have focused on training and sensitization programs that aim to align police practices with the principles of juvenile justice. Such programs seek to educate police officers about the developmental differences between juveniles and adults, the importance of rehabilitation, and the legal protections afforded to young offenders under the Juvenile Justice Act. Sensitization training can help officers understand the psychological, social, and economic factors that may lead a juvenile to commit a crime, encouraging a more compassionate and rehabilitative approach.

In some regions of India, police forces have implemented specialized juvenile units that are trained to handle cases involving minors. These units often work closely with social workers, psychologists, and community organizations to ensure that juveniles receive the support they need to avoid reoffending. However, the effectiveness of such initiatives varies widely across the country, with resource constraints and a lack of uniform implementation hindering progress in many areas (Garg, 2021). Reintegration is a key goal of the juvenile justice system, but it is often one of the most challenging aspects of dealing with juvenile offenders. The stigma attached to being labelled a criminal, even as a minor, can be difficult to overcome. This stigma is exacerbated by public attitudes that view juvenile offenders as inherently dangerous or morally corrupt (Zai & Zani, 2020). Reintegration efforts, such as vocational training programs, counselling, and community service, are critical in helping juveniles rebuild their lives, but they are often underfunded or poorly executed.

The lack of a supportive social environment can make it difficult for juvenile offenders to successfully reintegrate into society. Many juveniles come from disadvantaged backgrounds, and without adequate support systems in place, they may struggle to find employment, complete their education, or form positive relationships. This can lead to a sense of hopelessness, which in turn increases the likelihood of reoffending (Garg, 2021). The issue of juvenile delinquency in India is a complex problem that requires a multifaceted response from both the public and law enforcement. While the Juvenile Justice (Care and Protection of Children) Act, 2015 provides a strong legal framework for addressing juvenile crime, the success of this system depends on the effective implementation of rehabilitative measures and the support of society as a whole. Public attitudes toward juvenile offenders must shift away from punishment and toward rehabilitation if these young individuals are to have any chance of reintegrating into society (Zai & Zani, 2020). Police practices also play a critical role in determining the outcomes for juvenile offenders. Sensitization programs and specialized training can help bridge the gap between the legal framework and the day-to-day realities of law enforcement. However, without sustained efforts to change public perceptions and provide adequate resources for rehabilitation, the cycle of juvenile delinquency is likely to continue (Panag et al., 2024).

THEORETICAL FRAMEWORK

Criminological theories provide insights into why juveniles engage in criminal acts and how society responds to them. Merton's Strain Theory, for instance, posits that individuals may resort to delinquency when societal goals are unattainable through legitimate means. In India, factors such as poverty and limited access to education can foster feelings of frustration among youth, driving them towards delinquent behaviour. A. Mishra (2019), Social Learning Theory also plays a role in explaining how juveniles learn criminal behaviours through associations with family or peer groups, an especially relevant concept in a country where community and family structures exert strong influences.

Merton's Strain Theory: This theory suggests that when individuals cannot achieve societal goals through legitimate means, they may turn to delinquency as an alternative. In India, widespread issues like poverty, unemployment, and inadequate access to quality education create significant barriers for youth (Nickerson, 2023). These barriers can lead to frustration and a sense of hopelessness, prompting some to engage in criminal behaviour as a means to achieve success or recognition that feels otherwise unattainable. Merton's Strain Theory is important in understanding the link between societal structures and juvenile delinquency, particularly within the context of public and police responses in India. Merton posited that societal pressure to achieve culturally approved goals, such as financial success or social status, creates strain when the legitimate means to achieve these goals such as education, employment, or access to resources are limited or unavailable. In India, systemic issues like poverty, unemployment, and inadequate access to quality education exacerbate this strain, especially among disadvantaged youth (Kaur, 2023). This frustration often leads to the adoption of deviant behaviours, including criminal activities, as an alternative to achieving these societal goals

The public perception of juvenile offenders in India is often shaped by the socio-economic challenges faced by the offenders. Juvenile delinquency is frequently associated with poverty, marginalization, and lack of educational opportunities. Many in the public view juvenile offenders as victims of their circumstances rather than inherently criminal individuals. The understanding that these juveniles are responding to systemic failures rather than personal failings has led to calls for rehabilitative approaches rather than punitive measures (Nickerson, 2023). But this perspective is not universally shared. In cases of serious offenses, public opinion may shift towards favouring harsher punishment, as seen in cases involving heinous crimes committed by juveniles. This often creates tension between public sentiment and legal frameworks, which emphasize rehabilitation.India's juvenile justice system, governed by the Juvenile Justice (Care and Protection of Children) Act, 2015, aims to balance public safety with the need for rehabilitation. The law reflects a growing acknowledgment of the strain that societal inequities place on juveniles. Reforms in the juvenile justice system have increasingly focused on providing education, vocational training, and counselling as alternatives to incarceration, addressing the root causes of delinquency rather than merely punishing the behaviour (Kaur, 2023).

The police, as primary enforcers of the law, play a crucial role in shaping the juvenile justice process. Historically, law enforcement agencies in India have been more focused on punitive measures rather than rehabilitative approaches when dealing with juvenile offenders. However, recent years have seen a shift toward a more balanced approach, partially influenced by public sentiment and legal mandates. Police officers are required to handle juvenile offenders differently from adult offenders, often with the aim of diverting them from formal criminal proceedings. Special juvenile police units (SJPU) have been established to handle cases involving minors, reflecting the understanding that juveniles should not be exposed to the harsh realities of adult criminal justice systems. This aligns with Merton's Strain Theory, which suggests that structural inequities lead juveniles to delinquency. The police are tasked not only with enforcing the law but also with working within a framework that addresses the socio-economic pressures these juveniles face.But still these challenges remain. Resource constraints, lack of training, and societal pressures sometimes result in police officers adopting a more punitive stance, especially in cases where public outcry for justice is strong. In such instances, juveniles may be treated with suspicion and subjected to the same harsh treatments as adult criminals. This reflects a disconnect between the ideal of rehabilitation and the reality of law enforcement practices in certain regions of India (The Editors of Encyclopaedia Britannica, 2024).

Merton's Strain Theory provides a useful lens for understanding juvenile delinquency in India, especially in the context of public and police responses. The public is increasingly advocating for rehabilitative approaches that acknowledge the socio-economic factors contributing to delinquency. Meanwhile, the police are gradually adopting more sensitive practices when handling juvenile offenders, although challenges remain. By addressing the structural inequities that create strain for these youth, society can better prevent delinquency and promote rehabilitation, rather than perpetuate a cycle of crime and punishment.

Social Learning Theory: This theory posits that individuals learn behaviours through their interactions with others, particularly through family and peer influences. In India, where community ties and familial structures are often strong, juveniles may adopt criminal behaviours by associating with peers or family members involved in delinquency (Jensen, 2015). This theory highlights the importance of the social environment in shaping behaviour, suggesting that delinquency can spread within close-knit groups where criminal behaviour is normalized or glamorized.

In India, public perception of juvenile offenders can often reflect frustration and fear due to rising crime rates, particularly when juveniles are involved in serious offenses. Social Learning Theory posits that many juveniles may not inherently possess criminal tendencies but learn these behaviours from their environment. This understanding can help shift the public's view from seeing juvenile delinquents as purely criminal to acknowledging the social factors influencing their behaviour. Unfortunately, the stigma around juvenile delinquency can lead to social exclusion and lack of rehabilitation opportunities, which in turn reinforces criminal behaviour rather than addressing the root causes of their deviant actions. Educating the public on how social influences contribute to delinquency may promote a more empathetic and supportive approach, advocating for community-based interventions rather than punitive responses (Sharma & Gupta, 2023).

Indian law enforcement agencies are tasked with responding to juvenile crime under the framework of the Juvenile Justice (Care and Protection of Children) Act, 2015. However, the police response often mirrors the broader public sentiment, focusing on immediate containment rather than addressing the social dynamics contributing to delinquency. Social Learning Theory provides a framework for police to consider the family and peer influences that shape juvenile behaviour. Instead of merely punishing the juvenile, police can work in collaboration with community organizations, schools, and families to mitigate the social influences driving the juvenile towards crime (Jensen, 2015).

The Social Learning Theory (SLT), developed by Albert Bandura, focuses on how the environment, role models, and reinforcement influence behaviour. According to SLT, young people often learn delinquent behaviours by watching and copying others, especially their peers and family members. Both public and police responses to young offenders can either contribute to or reduce juvenile delinquency, depending on how they interact with these environmental factors.

The theory highlights the importance of understanding the environment in shaping juvenile delinquency. In India, where community and family structures are closely connected, it's important for public and police responses to young offenders to shift from punishment to rehabilitation. Addressing the peer and family influences that drive delinquency through education, community involvement, and police reform can lead to long-term solutions for juvenile crime. By focusing on changing the social environment that supports criminal behaviour, the police and the public can help young people reintegrate into society as productive and law-abiding citizens.

In India, family and community structures play a significant role in shaping a juvenile's environment, making them critical to preventing delinquency. According to SLT, when juveniles observe criminal behaviour in their social environments and see it rewarded or unpunished, they are likely to imitate it (StudyCorgi, 2023). Public responses should therefore focus on community-based interventions that promote positive role models and environments. By encouraging educational and social programs that provide constructive alternatives, communities can help juveniles learn pro-social behaviours. Awareness campaigns and parental education are key tools to modify family dynamics, ensuring that children are not exposed to criminal behaviour from family members or peers.

Further, the public's perception of juvenile offenders must shift from stigmatization to understanding and rehabilitation. If the community treats juvenile offenders as irredeemable criminals, it reinforces negative self-perceptions that juveniles may already have. This can exacerbate delinquent behaviours, in line with SLT's notion of internalizing observed patterns. Community-based approaches that focus on rehabilitation, mentoring, and skill-building can create an environment where juveniles can model positive behaviours and reintegrate successfully into society (Theories of Delinquency, 2018).

Police play a crucial role in shaping the social environment of juveniles through their interactions. Traditional punitive approaches to juvenile crime, such as harsh interrogations or detainment, often reinforce the very behaviours police aim to curb. When juveniles experience aggressive treatment by law enforcement, they may internalize these negative interactions, resulting in a reinforcement of criminal identities (StudyCorgi, 2023).

To align with SLT, police responses should shift from punitive to rehabilitative. Officers must be trained to recognize the environmental factors that contribute to juvenile delinquency, such as negative peer influence and family dysfunction. Collaborative efforts between law enforcement, social workers, and mental health professionals can create interventions that address these root causes. For instance, police mentoring programs, where officers serve as positive role models, can help juveniles model pro-social behaviour (Awati & Fitzgibbons, 2024). Along with this, problem-solving policing where officers focus on identifying and addressing the underlying social and environmental causes of crime aligns with SLT's emphasis on modifying behaviour through environmental change Through such strategies, police can contribute to an environment that deters crime and encourages juveniles to adopt law-abiding behaviours.

These frameworks collectively illustrate how systemic social issues and interpersonal relationships contribute to juvenile delinquency in India, underscoring the need for a holistic approach in addressing these challenges within the juvenile justice system.

PUBLIC PERCEPTION OF JUVENILE OFFENDERS IN INDIA

Public perception plays a pivotal role in shaping juvenile justice policies in India. Juvenile offenders, particularly those involved in heinous crimes, are often viewed with fear and mistrust, which significantly impacts law enforcement practices and the legal system. The broader Indian society tends to favour punitive measures over rehabilitation, reflecting a deep-seated belief that juveniles involved in serious crimes should face strict punishment rather than second chances.

The 2012 Delhi gang rape case serves as a prime example of how public sentiment can drive changes in the juvenile justice system. In this case, one of the accused was a juvenile, which led to widespread public outrage and demands for stricter laws. The case ignited a national debate over whether juveniles committing heinous crimes should be treated differently than adult offenders. (Shah, 2024)

A notable example of how public perception can shape juvenile justice policies in India is the 1992 Ajmer rape case. In this case, a minor was involved in the abduction and sexual assault of a schoolgirl, which created a public outcry demanding that the juvenile be punished severely. At the time, the juvenile justice system in India followed a rehabilitative model, with the aim of reintegrating young offenders into society (Dadwal, 2018). However, due to widespread public anger and the demand for justice for the victim, this case brought the juvenile justice system under scrutiny. People began questioning the effectiveness of rehabilitation for juveniles involved in heinous crimes, pushing the government to consider more punitive measures (Dadwal, 2018). This intense public outcry led to amendments in the Juvenile Justice (Care and Protection of Children) Act in 2015, allowing juveniles aged 16-18 to be tried as adults for serious crimes such as rape and murder (A. Mishra, 2019).

Before the amendment, the juvenile justice system in India emphasized rehabilitation and reformation, following the principle that children and adolescents are not fully tauter and can be reformed with the right interventions. Yer, public pressure significantly influenced this shift towards more punitive measures. A. Mishra (2019), the amendment reflects the public's demand for retribution rather than rehabilitation in cases involving heinous crimes. While some viewed this legal change as a necessary step toward justice, others raised concerns that it undermined the juvenile justice system's rehabilitative focus.

Media coverage, especially in high-profile cases, often fuels public calls for harsher punishments against juvenile offenders. The sensationalized portrayal of juvenile crime in the media tends to focus on the offense and its impact on society, rather than the underlying socio-economic or psychological factors that drive delinquency (Orr, 2020). This biased representation can create a skewed image of juvenile offenders as hardened criminals, leading to a societal push for retribution over rehabilitation.

As a result, the public's demand for tougher laws places immense pressure on law enforcement agencies to adopt more punitive practices. Officers may feel compelled to treat juvenile offenders more harshly, even in cases where rehabilitative measures could be more appropriate, this can be detrimental to the goal of reintegrating juveniles into society, as it reinforces negative behaviours rather than addressing the root causes of delinquency (Dadwal, 2018).

Despite legal reforms that aim to balance punishment with rehabilitation, societal support for rehabilitative measures remains limited. Public sentiment tends to favour punitive responses, especially when the crimes committed by juveniles are severe or widely publicized. The perception that rehabilitation is "soft" on crime creates a barrier to implementing more compassionate approaches. This societal attitude undermines the efforts of juvenile justice reformers, who advocate for a system focused on education, counselling, and skill-building to prevent recidivism (Kaur, A.,2023). And also, families and communities often struggle with accepting rehabilitated juveniles back into society, which can result in further marginalization. Without public support, the chances of successful reintegration diminish, leaving juveniles more vulnerable to re-offending.

Public perception of juvenile offenders in India, driven by fear, mistrust, and media sensationalism, has significantly influenced both law enforcement and legal frameworks. The public's demand for punitive measures has led to legislative changes that allow juveniles to be tried as adults for serious crimes (Mears et al., 2007). However, these shifts towards retribution over rehabilitation pose challenges to the juvenile justice system's core principles. To address juvenile delinquency effectively, India must cultivate public support for rehabilitative measures, fostering an environment where young offenders can reform and reintegrate into society. Only then can the juvenile justice system achieve its goal of reducing recidivism and protecting the rights of young offenders.

ROLE OF POLICE IN THE JUVENILE JUSTICE SYSTEM

The role of police in the juvenile justice system is crucial, especially in a country like India, where law enforcement officers are often the first point of contact for juveniles in conflict with the law. Their interaction with young offenders sets the tone for subsequent legal proceedings and rehabilitation efforts. However, the police response in India has often been punitive, driven by traditional societal attitudes and a lack of adequate training in handling juvenile offenders.

In India's juvenile justice system, police officers play a dual role acting as law enforcers and as gatekeepers of justice for juvenile offenders. The Juvenile Justice (Care and Protection of Children) Act, 2015, mandates that Special Juvenile Police Units (SJPUs) be established across the country to ensure that juvenile cases are handled with sensitivity and care. Each SJPU is supposed to include trained Child Welfare Officers (CWOs) who understand the developmental needs of juveniles and can approach cases from a rehabilitative perspective. However, the implementation of these provisions is inconsistent across states, leading to significant disparities in how juvenile offenders are treated (Mittal & Law, 2024). In 2013, another gang rape case in Shakti Mills, Mumbai, involved a juvenile offender. This case reignited the debate about juvenile justice in India, especially since the offense was committed after the Nirbhaya case. The public once again voiced strong opposition to the leniency extended to juvenile offenders, pressing for stricter penalties.

The police's role in this case was vital in apprehending the offenders swiftly, including the juvenile. The case showcased the importance of proper coordination between the police and the juvenile justice system, ensuring that while the offenders were brought to justice, the juvenile received treatment according to the law. Police response in such cases tends to focus on both punitive and rehabilitative measures. While they are required to follow due process under the Juvenile Justice Act, ensuring that juveniles are treated differently from adult criminals, public pressure often pushes the police towards harsher treatments, which can conflict with the legal standards set for juvenile offenders (Vidya, 2021).

Juvenile involvement in extremist activities presents a unique challenge to law enforcement, especially in conflict areas like Jammu and Kashmir. The recruitment of minors by terrorist organizations complicates the legal and ethical responses required from the police. In one case, a 16-year-old was recruited by a terrorist organization and apprehended during an anti-terror operation. This situation highlighted the divide in public opinion—while some view these juveniles as victims of radicalization, others consider them serious threats to national security (Press Trust of India, 2022). The police response in these cases must balance the protection of national security with the rehabilitation of juveniles. According to the Juvenile Justice (Care and Protection of Children) Act, juveniles involved in crimes, including serious offenses like terrorism, must be treated differently from adults. This legal framework mandates collaboration between law enforcement, social workers, and psychologists to help in the de-radicalization and rehabilitation of young offenders, focusing on reintegration into society (Khan, 2021).

In 2020, a case of a juvenile stabbing his classmate to death in Delhi once again brought public attention to the issue of juvenile delinquency. The police were able to apprehend the juvenile quickly, but the case revealed a gap in police sensitization to juvenile offenders. The juvenile's background was one of neglect and abuse, which were contributing factors to his violent behaviour. The police, in this case, were criticized for initially treating the juvenile as an adult criminal, before following proper protocol under the Juvenile Justice Act (H. Mishra, 2024). The case highlighted the need for ongoing police training and education on handling juvenile offenders, ensuring that the legal rights of these juveniles are respected even in serious cases

Despite legal mandates, many police officers continue to approach juvenile delinquency from a punitive standpoint. Research has shown that this is due to deeply ingrained societal biases, where juvenile offenders are often seen as "criminals" rather than vulnerable children in need of support and rehabilitation. A report by A. Mishra (2019) found that many police officers are not fully aware of their roles under the Juvenile Justice Act, leading to inappropriate handling of juvenile cases. In many instances, juveniles are detained in police stations or treated as adult offenders, which can have lasting psychological impacts and hinder their rehabilitation.

Efforts have been made to improve police training and sensitize law enforcement officers to the unique needs of juvenile offenders. The training programs include familiarization with international standards, such as the United Nations Convention on the Rights of the Child (UNCRC), which India is a signatory to. These programs emphasize the importance of adopting a child-centric approach in dealing with juvenile cases (Santosh Kumar Yadav, 2021). However, challenges remain, particularly in rural and semi-urban areas, where traditional policing methods often take precedence over the child welfare principles outlined in the Juvenile Justice Act

In many cases, police officers lack specialized training, and the institutional support for SJPUs is weak, leading to a situation where juveniles are not provided the care and protection they are entitled to under the law. Furthermore, societal attitudes towards juvenile offenders often influence police behaviour, reinforcing the view that punitive measures are the most effective response to delinquency. For the police to play a constructive role in the juvenile justice system, there is an urgent need for comprehensive reforms. These reforms should include regular and mandatory training for all police officers in handling juvenile cases, as well as sensitization to the socio-economic and psychological factors that lead to juvenile delinquency. Police training should also focus on understanding the rights of children, as outlined in the Convention on the Rights of the Child (UNCRC,1989) and the need for a rehabilitative, rather than punitive, approach to juvenile justice.

PUBLIC VS POLICE RESPONSE: A COMPARATIVE PERSPECTIVE

A comparative analysis of international models reveals that many Western countries have adopted restorative justice principles in their juvenile justice systems. These models emphasize reconciliation and community-based solutions rather than punishment.

Restorative Justice and Juvenile Justice in India: Restorative justice is an alternative approach to traditional punitive justice, emphasizing reconciliation, accountability, and the healing of relationships between offenders, victims, and the community (Vashishth et al., 2024). It aims to address the harm caused by crime while reintegrating offenders back into society as law-abiding citizens. In many Western countries, restorative justice is a cornerstone of juvenile justice systems, focusing on rehabilitation rather than punishment. Implementing such principles in India can provide a transformative pathway for the country's juvenile justice system.

The Indian juvenile justice system, as guided by the Juvenile Justice (Care and Protection of Children) Act, 2015, already incorporates several principles aligned with restorative justice, such as prioritizing rehabilitation over retribution (Vashishth et al., 2024). However, full integration of restorative justice models has been limited. Restorative justice seeks to repair the harm caused by delinquency, involving victims, offenders, and the community in a process of healing and accountability. In India, adopting restorative justice could shift the focus from punitive measures, such as detention, to community-based solutions where juvenile offenders are encouraged to take responsibility for their actions and make amends to their victims (Marwah, 2020).

Restorative justice encourages offenders to recognize the impact of their crimes and work toward restitution, whether through apologies, compensation, or community service. This process can be particularly effective in the Indian context, where family and community play central roles in an individual's life. By involving the family and community in the process, the juvenile offender can receive the emotional and moral support needed for rehabilitation.

One key benefit of restorative justice is that it can prevent juveniles from reoffending. Traditional punitive measures, such as incarceration, often expose juveniles to hardened criminals, leading to further criminal behaviour. In contrast, restorative justice creates a supportive environment that fosters personal growth, accountability, and a sense of belonging, this approach can be particularly effective in addressing the socio-economic factors that often contribute to juvenile delinquency in India, such as poverty, lack of education, and peer pressure (Marwah, 2020).

Restorative justice also benefits the victims. In India, victims of juvenile crimes often feel neglected by the justice system. Restorative practices give victims a voice, allowing them to express how the crime has affected them and participate in the resolution process, this can promote healing for both the victim and the offender and reduce feelings of fear and anger and implementing restorative justice in India presents challenges (Marwah, 2020). For one, there is a lack of awareness and understanding of the concept among law enforcement, the judiciary, and the general public. Kaur (2023) says, police officers and judicial officials often adhere to more punitive, traditional forms of justice, which can delay the adoption of restorative approaches and there is also a need for trained mediators and facilitators who can guide restorative justice processes. Restorative justice may be perceived as being too lenient, especially in cases involving serious offenses. Educating the public and stakeholders about the long-term benefits of this approach is crucial to its success.

Incorporating restorative justice principles into India's juvenile justice system can foster healing, accountability, and reintegration. By focusing on reconciliation between offenders and victims, restorative justice can create an alternative to punitive measures that often fail to address the root causes of juvenile crime. As India continues to reform its juvenile justice system, adopting restorative justice practices will not only benefit juvenile offenders but also contribute to a more humane and effective justice system overall.

According to ("The Juvenile Justice System in India and Children Who Commit Serious Offences – Reflections on the Way Forward," 2013) The Juvenile Justice Act (JJ Act) advocates a child-friendly approach by emphasizing the need for correctional homes and social reintegration rather than incarceration. The law focuses on creating environments where young offenders can reform, learning skills that would enable them to lead productive lives in the future. Juvenile Justice Boards (JJBs) were established under the Act to determine appropriate rehabilitative measures based on individual cases, stressing that the primary aim is to "reform, not punish." According to the Act, institutionalization of juveniles is considered a last resort, and whenever possible, non-institutional care in the form of foster care or sponsorship is preferred. In this sense, India's legal framework aligns with the global trend of restorative justice, emphasizing rehabilitation over retribution

Despite the progressive and reformative intent of the law, public sentiment often gravitates towards retributive justice, particularly when juvenile offenders are involved in serious crimes such as rape or murder. In high-profile cases, the public outcry frequently calls for harsher punishment, mirroring societal pressures to deliver quick justice. This dichotomy between the law's rehabilitative focus and the public's call for retribution poses challenges for the effective implementation of the JJ Act ("India's Juvenile Justice Dilemma: Balancing Punishment and Potential," 2024). While the law mandates that police officers dealing with juveniles receive specialized training, the implementation of this requirement is inconsistent across different states in India. Without adequate training and resources, the police often lack the knowledge or tools necessary to handle juvenile cases appropriately, resorting instead to conventional crime control methods that focus on punishment rather than reform

The role of the police is pivotal in the execution of the juvenile justice system. However, in practice, police responses to juvenile delinquency often lean towards punitive measures, influenced by public pressure and the nature of the crime. In cases of violent offenses, the police sometimes treat juveniles similarly to adult criminals, prioritizing arrest and detention over rehabilitation. This practice undermines the reformative principles of the JJ Act and reinforces a cycle of marginalization and reoffending among juveniles

Public Sentiment Towards Juvenile Offenders: Public outrage following high-profile cases involving juveniles often leads to calls for stricter penalties. For example, after the 2012 Delhi gang rape case, in which one of the perpetrators was a minor, there was widespread public demand for harsher punishments for juveniles involved in serious crimes. This case highlighted the public's dissatisfaction with the Juvenile Justice (Care and Protection of Children) Act of 2000, which, at the time, set a maximum sentence of three years for minors convicted of serious crimes. As a result of public pressure, the law was amended in 2015, allowing juveniles aged 16 and older to be tried as adults for heinous offenses such as rape and murder. In India, the public sentiment towards juvenile offenders, particularly in cases involving severe crimes, tends to lean heavily toward retribution. Many people advocate for harsher penalties for juveniles, viewing such offenders as deserving of the same punishments as adults (Scott et al., 2006). This creates tension between societal attitudes and the country's progressive legal framework, which emphasizes rehabilitation over punishment.

While public sentiment generally favours punitive measures, these attitudes often stem from a desire for justice and deterrence rather than a deeper understanding of juvenile behaviour (Scott et al., 2006). Social Learning Theory suggests that juveniles are products of their environment, and their criminal behaviour is often influenced by factors such as family dysfunction, peer pressure, and socio-economic conditions. Despite this, public opinion continues to favour retributive justice, particularly when the crime is viewed as morally repugnant or particularly violent (Scott et al., 2006).

Police officers in India, who are tasked with enforcing the law and maintaining public order, often find themselves caught between the country's rehabilitative legal framework and public demands for retribution (Malimath et al., 2003). The Juvenile Justice (Care and Protection of Children) Act, 2015, places a strong emphasis on rehabilitation and reintegration of juvenile offenders into society. It mandates a child-friendly approach, focusing on counselling, education, and rehabilitation, rather than punishment. However, police officers often face immense pressure from the public and media to take punitive action against juvenile offenders, particularly in high-profile cases.

This pressure can lead to instances where law enforcement authorities adopt more punitive measures than those outlined in the legal framework. Police officers, at times, may be inclined to treat juveniles as adults, especially in cases involving heinous crimes, to appease public sentiment. This is especially true when the crimes evoke strong emotions, such as rape, murder, or terrorism. However, such an approach contradicts the principles of juvenile justice, which are rooted in the belief that children, even those who commit serious crimes, are capable of reform and should be given the opportunity to rehabilitate.

BRIDGING THE GAP BETWEEN PUBLIC SENTIMENT AND LEGAL FRAMEWORK

To resolve the tension between public sentiment and the legal framework, efforts must be made to educate the public about the factors contributing to juvenile delinquency and the importance of rehabilitation. Public awareness campaigns can play a crucial role in shifting the focus from retribution to rehabilitation by explaining that punitive measures may not necessarily lead to long-term solutions to juvenile crime. Additionally, law enforcement agencies must adhere to the principles of juvenile justice and ensure that their actions align with the legal framework, rather than public demands for retribution.

The conflict between public sentiment favouring harsher penalties for juvenile offenders and the legal framework emphasizing rehabilitation is a significant challenge in India. While the public often pushes for punitive measures, it is essential to prioritize rehabilitation, as it offers a more sustainable solution for reducing juvenile crime. Police and policymakers must work together to educate the public and ensure that juvenile offenders are treated in accordance with the law, focusing on reform rather than retribution (Malimath et al., 2003).

In India, the tension between public sentiment and the legal framework surrounding juvenile delinquency presents a significant challenge. The Juvenile Justice (Care and Protection of Children) Act, 2015 emphasizes the rehabilitation and reintegration of juvenile offenders, there is often a disconnect between this legal framework and public sentiment, which tends to favour harsher penalties, especially in cases involving serious crimes (Malimath et al., 2003). The public, often driven by emotions and a desire for justice, can demand punitive actions that conflict with the rehabilitative goals of the juvenile justice system. The primary challenge lies in reconciling these two perspectives and ensuring that juvenile offenders are treated in a manner that aligns with both legal standards and long-term societal benefits.

As mentioned by Malimath et al. (2003), Juvenile delinquency refers to illegal or antisocial behaviours committed by individuals under the age of 18. In India, the causes of juvenile delinquency are often rooted in socio-economic factors such as poverty, lack of education, unemployment, and family dysfunction. Adolescents from disadvantaged backgrounds are more likely to engage in criminal activities due to the absence of positive role models, peer pressure, or a lack of access to opportunities for personal development.For example, in slum areas and impoverished communities, children and adolescents are often exposed to environments where criminal behaviour is normalized. Gangs and organized crime syndicates may recruit young people, taking advantage of their vulnerable socio-economic position. The children are often manipulated into committing crimes such as theft, drug trafficking, or even violent offenses. These juveniles are typically unaware of the long-term consequences of their actions, and punitive measures, while satisfying public demand for justice, often fail to address the root causes of their behaviour (Goyal, 2022).

This sentiment is further fuelled by media coverage that often portrays juvenile offenders as hardened criminals, ignoring the complexities of their socio-economic backgrounds and developmental immaturity. The perception that the juvenile justice system is too lenient can create pressure on policymakers and law enforcement to adopt a more punitive stance, even though this may conflict with the principles of juvenile justice (Goyal, 2022).

The Juvenile Justice Act, 2015, reflects India's commitment to international standards of child rights and justice, focusing on rehabilitation and reintegration of juvenile offenders into society (A. Mishra, 2019). The Act recognizes that juveniles, due to their age and developmental stage, are more amenable to reform than adults. It advocates for interventions that address the underlying causes of delinquency, such as providing education, vocational training, and psychological counselling. However, the 2015 amendments to the Act introduced provisions allowing juveniles aged 16 to 18 to be tried as adults in cases of heinous crimes. This amendment was a response to public pressure following the Nirbhaya case and reflects a shift towards a more punitive approach for serious offenses. While the amendment addresses public demands for justice, it also raises concerns about the long-term impact of trying juveniles as adults. Research suggests that juveniles who are processed through the adult criminal justice system are more likely to reoffend than those who go through the juvenile system, which focuses on rehabilitation

Police play a crucial role in shaping the public's perception of juvenile offenders. In India, law enforcement agencies are often seen as the first point of contact for juveniles entering the justice system. Their interactions with juveniles can significantly influence the outcomes of cases. Traditionally, the Indian police force has been criticized for taking a more punitive approach when dealing with juvenile offenders. For example, juvenile offenders are often subjected to the same detention facilities as adult criminals, which can expose them to hardened criminals and reinforce criminal behaviour. Such practices, though not always legal, reflect a broader tendency in law enforcement to prioritize punishment over rehabilitation.

Reforming police practices is essential to aligning the actions of law enforcement with the principles of juvenile justice. Police officers need to be trained to handle juvenile offenders with empathy and understanding, recognizing the developmental and psychological differences between juveniles and adults. Community policing initiatives, where officers work closely with local communities to prevent juvenile delinquency through early intervention, can be effective in reducing juvenile crime rates.

To resolve the tension between public sentiment and the legal framework, efforts must be made to educate the public about the factors contributing to juvenile delinquency and the importance of rehabilitation. Public awareness campaigns can play a crucial role in shifting the focus from retribution to rehabilitation by explaining that punitive measures may not necessarily lead to long-term solutions to juvenile crime (A. Mishra, 2019).For example, community outreach programs that involve discussions with parents, teachers, and local leaders about the causes of juvenile delinquency, such as peer pressure, family dysfunction, and socio-economic challenges, can help change public perceptions. These campaigns can highlight the benefits of rehabilitation, such as reducing recidivism rates and providing juveniles with the opportunity to become productive members of society.

One successful example is the Balsena initiative in Gujarat, which empowers children and adolescents by providing them with education, life skills, and vocational training. This program has been instrumental in preventing children from vulnerable communities from falling into delinquency. By focusing on early intervention and addressing the root causes of delinquency, the program has successfully reintegrated numerous juveniles into mainstream society.

Law enforcement agencies have a critical role in ensuring that their actions align with the principles outlined in the Juvenile Justice Act (Dadwal, 2018). This requires training police officers to handle juvenile cases with a focus on rehabilitation rather than punishment. For instance, the Delhi Police have initiated programs to train officers on juvenile justice, emphasizing alternative responses to juvenile offenses that prioritize counselling and community service over detention

Policymakers play a critical role in bridging the gap between public sentiment and the legal framework. By enacting laws that reflect a balanced approach to juvenile justice, they can ensure that the focus remains on rehabilitation rather than retribution. Additionally, policymakers must work closely with law enforcement agencies to ensure that juvenile justice laws are implemented effectively and that police officers are trained to handle juvenile cases in accordance with the law. Collaboration between policymakers, law enforcement, and civil society organizations is essential for creating a juvenile justice system that prioritizes the well-being and rehabilitation of offenders (Dadwal, 2018). This can include developing more diversion programs that offer alternatives to formal judicial proceedings, such as community service, counselling, and education programs that aim to prevent reoffending.

The conflict between public sentiment favoring harsher penalties for juvenile offenders and the legal framework emphasizing rehabilitation is a significant challenge in India. While the public often pushes for punitive measures, it is essential to prioritize rehabilitation, as it offers a more sustainable solution for reducing juvenile crime. Police and policymakers must work together to educate the public and ensure that juvenile offenders are treated in accordance with the law, focusing on reform rather than retribution. By addressing the root causes of juvenile delinquency and implementing rehabilitative measures, India can create a more just and effective juvenile justice system that benefits both individuals and society as a whole.In contrast, while India's legal framework advocates for rehabilitation, the public and police often lean towards retributive measures, particularly in cases of violent crime. This disparity highlights the tension between India's progressive legal intentions and the practical challenges of implementing these policies in a society that largely favours punitive justice (Goyal, 2022).

CHALLENGES IN IMPLEMENTING A REHABILITATIVE APPROACH

One of the significant challenges in promoting a rehabilitative approach to juvenile justice in India is the socio-economic background of many offenders. Juveniles from lower socio-economic groups, particularly those from marginalized communities, are disproportionately represented in the criminal justice system. Poverty, lack of access to education, and unstable family environments contribute to their vulnerability to crime. However, the biases held by law enforcement officials often exacerbate their plight, leading to mistreatment during arrest and detention. This, in turn, creates additional barriers to their rehabilitation and reintegration into society.

In India, juveniles from disadvantaged backgrounds are often subject to harsher treatment by law enforcement agencies (Goyal, 2022). Police officers may hold prejudices against individuals from lower socio-economic classes, minority groups, and certain castes, which influence how they interact with these juveniles. For example, juveniles from slum areas or underprivileged sections of society may be stereotyped as habitual offenders, increasing the likelihood of abuse and mistreatment during arrest. This bias not only violates the basic human rights of these juveniles but also leads to unlawful detention, poor legal representation, and, in some cases, custodial violence.

Juvenile offenders from impoverished backgrounds face systemic discrimination that hinders their access to justice. They may not have the financial means to hire competent legal representation, and as a result, they are often unable to advocate for themselves within the judicial system. Additionally, their families may lack the knowledge or resources to navigate the complex legal process, further disadvantaging these young offenders. This mistreatment undermines the potential for rehabilitation, which is the key principle behind juvenile justice laws in India. The Juvenile Justice (Care and Protection of Children) Act, 2015, emphasizes rehabilitation over punishment, with a focus on reintegrating juveniles into society through counselling, education, and skill-building programs. However, when juveniles are mistreated by police and other authorities, their chances of successful rehabilitation diminish significantly (Tatia & Patel, 2011). The experience of violence and discrimination during their arrest or detention can have a traumatic effect on young offenders, exacerbating feelings of alienation and distrust towards law enforcement and society as a whole.

Juveniles from disadvantaged backgrounds often lack access to rehabilitative programs, such as education or vocational training, due to their socio-economic status. These programs are essential for preparing young offenders to reintegrate into society and avoid re-offending. The failure to provide these resources perpetuates a cycle of poverty and crime, as these juveniles are more likely to remain marginalized and resort to criminal activities as a means of survival. To address these issues, India needs to implement reforms that ensure equal treatment for juveniles from all socio-economic backgrounds. Training police officers on the importance of unbiased treatment and human rights can help reduce the mistreatment of marginalized juveniles during arrest and detention. Furthermore, improving access to legal aid and ensuring that juveniles are treated with dignity and respect throughout the judicial process will promote a more rehabilitative approach.

Investment in community-based programs that provide education, skill-building, and psychological support for at-risk juveniles can help mitigate the socio-economic factors that drive delinquency. By addressing the root causes of juvenile crime, such as poverty and lack of opportunity, these programs can help reduce the overrepresentation of disadvantaged juveniles in the criminal justice system. The socio-economic background of juveniles plays a critical role in their treatment within the Indian justice system. Disadvantaged juveniles are often subject to mistreatment, which hinders their chances of rehabilitation and reintegration into society (Tatia & Patel, 2011). To promote a fair and rehabilitative juvenile justice system, India must address the socio-economic disparities that lead to bias and mistreatment. By focusing on equal treatment, access to justice, and comprehensive rehabilitative programs, India can improve outcomes for juvenile offenders from all backgrounds.

Public discourse plays a pivotal role in shaping societal attitudes and, subsequently, the juvenile justice system in India. It is through collective conversations spanning media, schools, public forums, and government discussions that society forms its perspectives on juvenile crime, rehabilitation, and retribution. In India, where societal norms are deeply ingrained and often punitive, fostering public discourse that emphasizes rehabilitation over retribution is essential for changing public perception and improving outcomes for juvenile offenders.

The media holds considerable influence over public discourse and can either reinforce punitive attitudes or advocate for rehabilitative approaches. Unfortunately, the portrayal of juvenile offenders in Indian media often leans towards sensationalism, focusing on punishment rather than reform. This shapes public opinion, fostering a view that juvenile offenders are dangerous and deserve harsh penalties. However, when media platforms shift their narrative to focus on the rehabilitative aspects of juvenile justice, they can play a significant role in shaping public discourse toward empathy and understanding.

Public forums, including debates, panel discussions, and seminars, offer platforms for experts, legal professionals, activists, and citizens to engage in constructive dialogue about juvenile justice. These discussions often bring forward diverse perspectives, addressing the root causes of juvenile delinquency, such as poverty, peer pressure, and dysfunctional family environments. In these forums, experts can stress the importance of a rehabilitative rather than punitive approach, grounded in psychological and sociological insights into adolescent development.

Civil society organizations in India, such as child rights groups, play a crucial role in facilitating these discussions. They organize public awareness campaigns, rallies, and workshops to inform the public and policymakers about the importance of rehabilitation in juvenile justice. Government discussions and legislative debates are the final and most formal component of public discourse in shaping juvenile justice. In India, policies surrounding juvenile justice, such as the Juvenile Justice (Care and Protection of Children) Act, 2015, are products of these conversations. Public pressure, generated through media and civil society, often plays a significant role in influencing policy. Lawmakers, when informed by rehabilitative-focused discourse, are more likely to push for laws that prioritize the reform and reintegration of juveniles into society over punitive measures (A. Mishra, 2019).

Incorporating rehabilitation into public policy discussions ensures that laws reflect a more humane and constructive approach to juvenile justice. This has already begun to take place in India, as recent amendments to the Juvenile Justice Act aim to balance the need for accountability with the importance of rehabilitation. Public discourse is a powerful tool for reshaping societal attitudes toward juvenile justice in India. By fostering conversations across various platforms that emphasize rehabilitation over retribution, India can move toward a more compassionate, effective, and reformative juvenile justice system, and media, educational institutions, public forums, and government discussions must work together to shift the narrative from punishment to rehabilitation, ensuring that juvenile offenders have the opportunity to reform and reintegrate into society (A. Mishra, 2019).

There is a shortage of proper rehabilitation infrastructure, such as counselling services and vocational training centers. Many of the institutions designed to help juveniles are underfunded and overwhelmed, making it difficult for them to effectively address the needs of young offenders. This further limit the ability to rehabilitate juveniles and prevent recidivism. These challenges reflect systemic issues within the Indian juvenile justice system, calling for reforms to create a more supportive and fairer environment for rehabilitation. The lack of adequate rehabilitation infrastructure, such as counselling and vocational training centers, further hampers the success of the Juvenile Justice Act's rehabilitative goals. The few existing institutions are often underfunded and lack the capacity to address the large number of juvenile offenders entering the system each year (Kaur, 2023).

Police Training and Sensitization are shortcomings, various states in India have introduced training programs aimed at sensitizing police officers to the specific needs of juveniles. These programs focus on educating officers about the Juvenile Justice Act and international child rights conventions. In India, the Juvenile Justice Act (JJ Act) and international conventions such as the United Nations Convention on the Rights of the Child emphasize the need for special treatment of juveniles in conflict with the law. To align police practices with these standards, various states have implemented training programs aimed at sensitizing officers to the specific needs of juveniles. (Tatia & Patel, 2011). These training programs are designed to equip police personnel with knowledge about child rights, the JJ Act, and appropriate procedures for dealing with juvenile offenders. The training typically includes modules on rehabilitation, reintegration, and the significance of treating children in conflict with the law with dignity and care. Additionally, the programs stress the importance of creating a child-friendly atmosphere during interactions with juveniles.

CONCLUSION

In conclusion, the study of juvenile delinquency in the context of public and police responses in India provides valuable insights into the complex interplay of societal structures, individual behaviour, and the criminal justice system. Merton's Strain Theory offers a compelling framework for understanding the relationship between societal pressures, structural inequities, and the adoption of deviant behaviours by juveniles. The theory highlights the impact of limited access to legitimate means of achieving culturally approved goals, particularly in the face of systemic issues such as poverty, unemployment, and inadequate education.

The public perception of juvenile offenders in India is deeply influenced by the socio-economic challenges faced by these individuals. There is a growing recognition that juveniles involved in delinquent behaviour often emerge from disadvantaged backgrounds characterized by poverty, marginalization, and lack of educational opportunities. This understanding has led to calls for rehabilitative approaches that address the root causes of delinquency, rather than punitive measures that fail to address the underlying structural inequities. Yet it is important to acknowledge that public sentiment regarding juvenile offenders is not uniform. In cases of serious offenses, there is a tendency for public opinion to shift towards favouring harsher punishment, reflecting a tension between the desire for rehabilitation and the demand for justice. This divergence in public sentiment presents a challenge for the juvenile justice system in India, which seeks to balance public safety with the need for rehabilitation.

The Juvenile Justice (Care and Protection of Children) Act, 2015 reflects a growing acknowledgment of the strain that societal inequities place on juveniles and aims to provide a balanced approach that prioritizes education, vocational training, and counselling as alternatives to incarceration. The law represents a significant step towards addressing the root causes of delinquency and promoting rehabilitation, signalling a shift towards a more nuanced understanding of juvenile offenders within the legal framework.

But still the challenges persist yet as resource constraints, lack of training, and societal pressures can lead to instances where police officers adopt a more punitive stance, especially in response to strong public outcry for justice. This reflects a disconnect between the ideal of rehabilitation and the reality of law enforcement practices in certain regions of India. Addressing these challenges requires ongoing efforts to provide adequate resources and training for law enforcement personnel, while also promoting a greater understanding of the structural inequities that contribute to juvenile delinquency.

In addition to Merton's Strain Theory, the Social Learning Theory offers valuable insights into the influence of family and peer interactions on juvenile delinquency. The theory underscores the importance of the social environment in shaping behaviour, particularly in close-knit communities where criminal behaviour may be normalized or glamorized. Understanding the role of family and peer influences is essential for developing effective interventions that address the social dynamics contributing to delinquent behaviour.

Moving forward, it is crucial to continue advocating for rehabilitative approaches that address the root causes of juvenile delinquency in India. This requires a multifaceted approach that encompasses educational, social, and economic interventions aimed at reducing structural inequities and providing meaningful opportunities for vulnerable youth. Law enforcement agencies should continue to prioritize training and resources that support a balanced approach to handling juvenile offenders, while also promoting greater awareness of the societal factors that contribute to delinquency.

Addressing juvenile delinquency in India requires a comprehensive understanding of the societal, economic, and cultural factors that shape the behaviours of young individuals. By addressing these complex issues, society can work towards preventing delinquency, promoting rehabilitation, and breaking the cycle of crime and punishment. Through thoughtful policy interventions and a commitment to addressing systemic inequities, India can create a more just and equitable future for its youth.

The public and police responses to juvenile delinquency in India are shaped by a combination of societal attitudes, legal frameworks, and institutional limitations. While the Juvenile Justice Act, 2015, emphasizes rehabilitation, both public opinion and law enforcement practices often reflect a preference for retributive justice. This creates a dissonance between the law's intent and its execution. For India to move towards a more rehabilitative approach to juvenile justice, greater efforts must be made to educate both the public and law enforcement about the benefits of rehabilitation over punishment (A. Mishra, 2019). This includes expanding police training programs, increasing funding for juvenile rehabilitation centers, and fostering public discourse that emphasizes the need for reform over retribution. Ultimately, a shift in societal attitudes and law enforcement practices is essential for achieving the goals of the Juvenile Justice Act and ensuring that juvenile offenders are given the opportunity to reintegrate into society successfully.

REFERENCE

Awati, R., & Fitzgibbons, L. (2024). *What is social learning theory?* WhatIs. https://www.techtarget.com/whatis/definition/social-learning-theory

Dadwal, L. (2018). Juvenility: From criminality to responsibility. *International Journal of Reviews and Research in Social Sciences*, *6*(4), 381–395. DOI: 10.5958/2454-2687.2018.00031.x

Garg, R. (2021). *Juvenile delinquency : a social problem* - iPleaders. https://blog.ipleaders.in/juvenile-delinquency-social-problem

Goyal, A. (2022). Juvenile Justice system in india. *ResearchGate*. https://www.researchgate.net/publication/360540963_Juvenile_Justice_system_in_india

India's juvenile Justice dilemma: balancing punishment and potential. (2024). *Bharat Law AI*. https://www.bharatlaw.ai/post/balancing-justice-and-rehabilitation-transforming-juvenile-offenders-in-india-for-a-safer-society

Jensen, G. F. (2015). Delinquency, Sociology of. In *Elsevier eBooks* (pp. 68–74). https://doi.org/DOI: 10.1016/b978-0-08-097086-8.45021-x

Kaur, A. (2023). *Juvenile delinquency in India*. iPleaders. https://blog.ipleaders.in/juvenile-delinquency-related-legislations-india/

Malimath, V. S. Government of India, Ministry of Home Affairs, Varadachary, S., Gupta, A., Menon, N. R. M., Rao, D. V. S., Gupta, D., Basavarya, C. M., Girither, K., Menon, B., Reddy, S. M., Raja, V., & Uthaiah, M. K. (2003). Report. In *Committee on Reforms of Criminal Justice System*. Government of India, Ministry of Home Affairs. https://www.mha.gov.in/sites/default/files/criminal_justice_system_2.pdf

Marwah, A. (2020). RESTORATIVE JUSTICE AND REFORMATION OF OFFENDERS. In *ILI. Law Review*, *2020*(Winter Issue), 157–159. https://ili.ac.in/pdf/amar.pdf

Mears, D. P., Hay, C., Gertz, M. G., & Mancini, C. (2007). Public opinion and the foundation of the juvenile court. *Criminology*, *45*(1), 223–257. DOI: 10.1111/j.1745-9125.2007.00077.x

Mishra, A. (2019). Juvenile Justice and the role of Police: Indian Scenario - Academike. *Academike*.https://www.lawctopus.com/academike/juvenile-justice-role-police-indian-scenario/

Mishra, H. (2024). Delhi teen stabbed to death for refusing to throw party over new phone. *India Today*. https://www.indiatoday.in/cities/delhi/story/delhi-boy-stabbed-dies-party-new-phone-purchase-shakarpur-2605626-2024-09-24

Mittal, Y., & Law, L. (2024). Supreme Court: Juvenile accused cannot be tried as adult without preliminary assessment by JJB. *Live Law*. https://www.livelaw.in/supreme-court/jj-act-juvenile-accused-cant-be-tried-as-adult-in-absence-of-preliminary-assessment-report-by-jjb-supreme-court-253459

Nickerson, C. (2023). *Merton's Strain Theory of Deviance and Anomie in Sociology*. Simply Psychology. https://www.simplypsychology.org/mertons-strain-theory-deviance.html

Orr, J. (2020). Public Perceptions of Police Interactions with Juveniles. Undergraduate Review, 15, 256-275. https://vc.bridgew.edu/undergrad_rev/vol15/iss1/22

Panag, S., Ganguli, T., & Chopra, L. (2024). The Practitioner's Guide to Global Investigations. *Global Investigation Review*. https://globalinvestigationsreview.com/guide/the-practitioners-guide-global-investigations/2024/article/india

Pti. (2017). Ryan school murder case: Class 11 student confessed he killed Pradyuman Thakur, says CBI. https://www.livemint.com/Politics/acQQwygFhJcUqOdo2VkrbM/Ryan-School-murder-Accused-Class-XI-student-admits-killing.html

Scott, E. S., Reppucci, N. D., Antonishak, J., & DeGennaro, J. T. (2006). Public attitudes about the culpability and punishment of young offenders. *Behavioral Sciences & the Law*, *24*(6), 815–832. DOI: 10.1002/bsl.727

Shah, C. (2024). India's juvenile Justice dilemma: balancing punishment and potential. *Bharat Law AI*. https://www.bharatlaw.ai/post/balancing-justice-and-rehabilitation-transforming-juvenile-offenders-in-india-for-a-safer-society

Sharma, K., & Gupta, K. (2023). An analysis of social learning theory to the changing nature of juvenile crimes and legal responses to…ResearchGate. https://www.researchgate.net/publication/378976490_AN_ANALYSIS_OF_SOCIAL_LEARNING_THEORY_TO_THE_CHANGING_NATURE_OF_JUVENILE_CRIMES_AND_LEGAL_RESPONSES_TO_NAVIGATE_THE_CHANGE

StudyCorgi. (2023). *How Social Learning Theories Impact Juvenile Delinquency and Crime*. https://studycorgi.com/how-social-learning-theories-impact-juvenile-delinquency-and-crime/

Tatia, P., & Patel, D. N. (2011). Training of child welfare officers on special juvenile police unit on the juvenile justice. In Report Regarding Compliance of Direction of Hon'ble Supreme Court of India in Sampurna Behrua V Union of India. https://jhalsa.org/pdfs/JJB_Report.pdf

The Editors of Encyclopaedia Britannica. (2024). *Strain theory | Social Control, Anomie & Deviance*. Encyclopedia Britannica. https://www.britannica.com/topic/strain-theory-sociology

The juvenile justice system in India and children who commit serious offences – reflections on the way forward. (2013). *Observatorio Internacional De Justicia Juvenil*. https://www.oijj.org/sites/default/files/documentos/the_juvenile_justice_system_in_india_and_children_who_commit_serious_offences.pdf

Theories of delinquency. (2018). https://sandratrappen.com/2018/12/30/theories-of-delinquency/

Vashishth, A., Dudeja, S., & Teena, N. (2024). System of Restorative Justice and Juvenile Justice in India: A Brief Comparative Study with Latin American System. *Mexican Law Review*, •••, 131–143. DOI: 10.22201/iij.24485306e.2024.2.18895

Vidya. (2021). Shakti Mills gang rape case: Bombay HC asks Maha govt to "shun unscientific two-finger test" *India Today*. https://www.indiatoday.in/india/story/shakti-mills-gang-rape-case-bombay-high-court-two-finger-test-maharashtra-1881118-2021-11-26

Young, S., Greer, B., & Church, R. (2017). Juvenile delinquency, welfare, justice and therapeutic interventions: A global perspective. *BJPsych Bulletin*, *41*(1), 21–29. DOI: 10.1192/pb.bp.115.052274

Zai, A. F., & Zani, G. (2020). Juvenile Delinquency: A global challenge in modern society. *ResearchGate*, *10*, 2020. DOI: 10.61841/V24I10/400370

Chapter 4
How Might We Prevent Youth Crime?
Lessons From Research in Nigeria

Don John Omale
https://orcid.org/0000-0001-6787-0674
University of Derby, UK

ABSTRACT

Youth crime is a problem throughout the world and the most common methods of dealing with it often rely on retribution and imprisonment as the ultimate goals. This approach of "warehousing" youths through the institution of prison has been argued to undermine sustainable youth development and crime prevention. This paper and its findings are adapted by the author from his earlier field survey on: "Opinions of victims of crime and criminal justice professionals" conducted in Nigeria (Omale, 2009), and suggests initiatives to tackle this problem. A total number of 151 respondents comprising 74 victims of crime and 77 professionals of the criminal justice system took part in this study. This paper is evidence-based research; with a review of relevant literature to support its argument. The paper highlights some theoretical explanations (with a focus on sociological positivism and social constructionism) to explain the complex interaction of the variables which might be implicitly and explicitly implicated in youth offending behaviour in Nigeria and globally.

INTRODUCTION

There have been growing international demands for research information on the causes and strategic preventive measures of youth crime and violence around the world. And the question that is often asked is: why do some youths get involved

DOI: 10.4018/978-1-6684-9343-4.ch004

in offending behaviour? And how might we prevent youth crime? To answer these questions, researchers and criminologists have investigated a variety of factors to develop relevant theories of offending and recommend effective interventions (Palmer, 2003). So, understanding the factors that increase the risk of youths being the victims or perpetrators of youth crime is essential for developing effective policies and programmes to preventing it. Hence, the problems associated with youth offending are issues which should interest all of us. But whether they interest us or not, as Justice Oputa (1975) put it: 'they deeply and sometimes sadly involve and concern us rather intimately'. So, a complete or total disinterested attitude towards youth crime and violence is therefore not easy to achieve. But the more serious the youth crime problem is, the more important it is that society should look at it coolly and rationally. If youth crime is becoming a real threat, (as we have seen in Boko Haram insurgencies; Niger Delta Militancy, etc in Nigeria) then, the primary step is to try to understand the phenomena of increase, and the causes of such offending behaviour. Because in the word of Socrates '*Fundamentum Omnius Cultus animae*' (i.e., the soul of all improvement is the improvement of the soul). Put differently, this could mean that, to treat youth offending, we first, need to know something about it, diagnose it, isolate the push, and pull factors, and then prescribe appropriate remedy. Because just as a headache, though unpleasant, is no more than a symptom of an underlying disease, so could the problem of youth crime in Nigeria and around the world, be the outward indication that something is fundamentally going wrong in the society (see Justice Oputa, 1975, Omale 2005, 2006, 2009, 2012). Therefore, understanding the psycho-social and econometric factors that predisposes, and increase the risk of young people being the victims or perpetrators of youth crime and violence is essential for developing effective policies and programmes to preventing it.

So, what should be the response to this endemic and epidemic situation which affects so many youths in so many countries of the world? Is retributive justice and imprisonment the best response? Are tougher laws and policing such as 'operation fire for fire'; 'operation sweep', 'operation flush' as was (and is) the case in Nigeria (Omale, 2005. p.3) or building more prisons and longer sentencing the answer? Are youth offenders to be treated in the same way as adults? In treating young offenders, should our attention be focused on the youths themselves or on the socio-econometric and systemic factors that put these vulnerable groups at risk? (Shaw, 2005. p.2). Perhaps, there is no cap fit all solution because the complexities of youth crime and violence in terms of its causes, and the wide variety of forms it takes in different countries and regions, means that 'no simple or single approach is sufficient to provide lasting and sustainable solutions' (Shaw 2005. p.2). However, are there any lessons to learn from research? This paper present findings from a field survey in Nigeria and suggests initiatives to tackle the problem.

METHODOLOGY

The methodological approach is a mixed method (survey and interview). The primary research instruments used in data collection for this paper are the Victims Questionnaire/Interview Schedule (VQIS) and the Professionals Questionnaire/ Interview Schedule (PQIS). Both instruments contained structured, semi-structured and open-ended questions used for an in-depth interview and a self completed questionnaire where necessary. Respondents were victims of crime and professionals in the criminal justice system in Nigeria. Respondents were selected using the snowballing sampling technique. This sampling technique was used because respondents were hard-to reach category of persons. Fifteen victims of crime consented and participated in a face-face interview. As the victims preferred their interviews not to be recorded, notes were taken directly on the questionnaire sheets throughout the interview. The remaining sixty-nine victims were surveyed through a self completed questionnaire which were completed in their own time and collected by the researcher. For the criminal justice professionals, the PQIS was used as a self completed questionnaire. They were requested to advice government on the way forward for youth crime control and prevention in Nigeria.

LITERATURE/THEORETICAL REVIEW

In recent times, the problems of youth crime and violence and the danger it poses to law and order and to security of life and property have become a global concern. In the UK and USA for instance, the increase in gun and knife crimes, and youth gangs in schools and cities have been of great concern to both the people and government. Similarly, the new dimensions of youth crime and violence in Nigeria which have metamorphosed from street crime, campus cultism to hostage taking, violent extremism and suicide bombing have been of great concern and threat to Nigeria's security and democracy. The causes of these youth offending behaviours, like all other criminal behaviours, are multifaceted. However, the circumstances which place young people at risk of violence, either as victims or offenders, are very similar across countries, and they are also points for intervention (Shaw 2005). For instance, Reiner (2007) argues that the rise in youth crime, and the increasing appeal of law-and-order campaigns against youth crime and violence are due to the same cause: 'the dominance of the neo-liberal political economy', and 'the revolution of the rich', and its associated negative economic, ethical and sociopolitical consequences. Hence, the United Nations Guidelines for the Prevention of Crime adopted in 2002 agreed with international stakeholders that the best, most effective, and perhaps sustainable response to youth crime is to develop 'a balanced and strategic prevention approach' (UNODC, 2005). In the same vein, Shaw (2005) argues that this approach includes strengthening local communities, changing attitudes and (perhaps cognitive behavioural re-orientation to criminal offending), providing alternatives to young people growing up, and reducing availability of what I might call "criminal opportunities" (such as cheap and availability of small arms, and psychotropic substances), as well as working with those young persons (who are already involved with the criminal justice system) to help them return to a safer community and live a healthier childhood life.

Although, the causes of youth crime appear to be very similar across cultures and nations, there is however, a need to adopt and adapt strategies and interventions to a wide variety of contexts found in different countries and regions. Hence, projects and programmes that are developed and judged effective in certain country may not be appropriate in another if transposed without regard to tackling the socio-econometric factors of the country concerned. Because according to Lewin Kurt's (1943) equation, B=f (P+ E). That is, every behaviour (including youth offending behaviour) is a factor of the offenders' personality plus the environment they find themselves. This is why it could be argued that the most appropriate intervention model for youth offending behaviour is perhaps for policies and programmes to invest in preventative approaches, and supports for young people and their families, rather than to exclude and "warehouse" them through the institution of prison. Shaw (2005) agreed with this point of view when she argues that there is 'clear evidence of the problems inherent in the social exclusion of young people from mainstream society, including those from ethnic and cultural minorities'. Hence, she advocates for the importance of recognizing the rights of children including their rights to quality education, and gainful employment, and the inclusion of young persons in planning and delivery of programmes that concern their welfare. Thus Shaw (2005) argues that promoting the participation of youth at risk is increasingly being recognized as an important way to respond to their social exclusion and to development of effective intervention strategies and programmes. Similarly, the UN-HABITAT (2004) noted that young people are a major source of knowledge of their own needs and on what can be done, and as such are well placed to work with their peers and can (if given the opportunity) act as powerful researchers, trainers, advocates, and designers of effective programmes and projects. To this end, Jack Straw (2007) argues that government's attention on youth crime prevention should be focused on where talents are under-developed; aspirations unfulfilled; and youth potential wasted.

Hence, a reasonable government should be able to identify factors that have potential to aggravate youth offending behaviour. At the individual level, these include biological, psychological, and behavioural characteristics. Some children exhibit challenging behaviour in early childhood that gradually escalates to more severe forms of anti-social behaviour before and during adolescence. Dahlberg and

Potter (2001) theorised this pattern of child development as a life-course persistent development pathway. The life-course persistent developmental pathway helps to explain the continuity over time in challenging violent youth behaviour. The crux of the theory is that there are certain individuals who persist in having a greater underlying tendency than others towards violent behaviour. That is, those who are relatively more aggressive at a given age also tend to be relatively more aggressive later in life, even though their absolute levels of violence may vary. These factors could be related to pre-natal and post-natal reasons, including child weaning and parenting skills. For instance, in a study entitled 'some child-rearing antecedents and criminal behaviour' McCord (1979) found that parental conflict in early childhood and poor attachment between parents and children has positive correlation to youth violent behaviour. Similarly, studies conducted in the UK-England, Scotland, and Wales (Wadsworth, 1978), the USA (Farrington, 1998) and New Zealand (Henry et al, 1996) found that children who grow up in single-parent households, and experienced parental separation between birth and the age of ten are at greater risk for youth crime and violence. In the same vein, Kury et al (2002), in a study of why youths in Germany get involved in drug use offending found that the growing rate of divorce and the number of single parents (usually mothers) was inversely implicated in the rise of youth involvement in drug use offending. It could be argued that because these groups of children are more likely to be delinquent, they often tend to seek out delinquent peers hence, Elliot and Menard (1996) conclude that 'delinquency caused peer bonding and, at the same time, bonding with delinquent peers caused delinquency'. Whereas peer influences during adolescence are generally considered positive and important in shaping interpersonal relationships 'delinquent peer-bonding' however, have negative consequences. Hence, there are popular sayings that birds of the same feather flock together or show me your friend and I will tell who you are.

In another development, Farrington (1998) found that many children in a family with a low level of family cohesion in the absence of other social support can affect children's social and emotional functioning and behaviour. This finding might be true to some extent in the case of youth crime and violence behaviour in Nigeria. In Nigeria, having a large family is often encouraged in some cultures for several reasons. For instance, some parents from low socioeconomic backgrounds fear that their inability to afford quality healthcare services for their children might make some siblings not survive the danger of malaria and other childhood diseases, so some parents give birth to as many 'backups' as possible so that as some die of childhood diseases those that are able to survive this 'war' would remain.

This pitiable attitude of some poor families in Nigeria echoes the argument of Reiner (2007) that the massive rise in crime (including youth crime and violence) in recent times, and the increasing appeal of law-and-order campaigns and philosophies are due to the same cause: 'the effect of the revolution of the rich', which produces negative economic, ethical, and sociopolitical consequences. These include harm associated with the formation of 'monopolies, growing inequality, egoism, poor health services, irresponsibility, private affluence (including corruption) and public squalor'. This argument was supported by Bedoya et al (1991) who found that the increase in youth gangs in Colombia was largely due to the growing social acceptance of 'easy money' and of whatever means are necessary to obtain it, as well as corruption in the police, judiciary, military, and local administration. Reiner (2007) thus argues that this spread of a culture whereby winning by any means is preferable to losing by the rules has huge consequences for crime at all levels of society. He further argues that, with the politics of law and order leaving out many forms of crimes committed by corporations, the states, (and the powerful), the criminal justice system ends up processing, almost exclusively, a narrow range of (offenders and), offences committed by the poor and the disadvantaged (such as unemployed youths, and youths from poor and ethnic minorities for instance). Hence, Sanjuan (1998) argues that a sense that justice depend on socioeconomic status was an important factor in the emergence of a culture of crime and violence among the marginalized youths in Caracas, Venezuela. Perhaps, the increase in youth crime and violence by disadvantaged youths could be viewed as a social tactics to challenge a failing social system especially in a 'paradox of plenty' because perhaps, they wonder and cannot understand why ‘they should stand in a plenty of water and still wash their hands with spittle’ (Omale, 2005, 2009, 2012).

Similarly, Shaxon (2007) noted that in some oil rich African countries, as income from oil rose at the international market, the more the countries slip places down the United Nations Human Development ranking in terms of youth development, social welfare, and per capita income. This money Shaxon (2007) argues is not earned by innovation and hard work but instead appears to come out of the ground as a gift from God to the privileged few. So, instead of this 'paradox of plenty to national (and youth development), they have tended to lower most measures of living standards for most of the population and leave a minority extremely wealthy and very well connected politically. Hence, the illegal wealth controlled by these groups of privileged few could enables old grievances to be fought out, as well as generating new ones.

FINDINGS FROM RESEARCH

This study presents findings from a total number of 151 respondents comprising 74 victims and 77 professionals that took part in this study.

Table 1. Frequency table of respondents

Type of Respondents		Frequency	Percent	Valid Percent	Cumulative Percent
Valid	Victim	74	49.0	49.0	49.0
	Professional	77	51.0	51.0	100.0
	Total	151	100.0	100.0	

When victims of crime and the criminal justice professionals were asked to recommend to government on possible ways to control and reduce youth crime and violence in Nigeria, the study found that 85.1% of victims of crime, and 66.2% of the criminal justice professionals affirm that transforming the social system would be a better way of controlling youth crime and violence, while 14.9% of victims of crime, and 33.8% of the criminal justice professional suggests rehabilitative punishment. This finding resonates with that of Kury et al (2002) who found that 70.8% of their respondents had a level of anomia due to expected worsening conditions of the people; 33.7% of the respondents felt that it is no longer reasonable to believe in the future or bring children into this world, and 79.1% believe that politicians are uninterested in the people.

The concept of social transformation in the view of researcher includes positive, and effective socialization of young persons (good parenting and parental controls, religious and citizenship education in school curriculum), giving youth a voice in the social scheme that affects their wellbeing, providing employment and training opportunities for those who want to work, or earn qualification and skills, and leaders and 'significant others' to live exemplary life worthy of emulation. Where these factors are in place, then young persons who clearly could not be control in the society should be placed in rehabilitative programmes in prisons under the care of professionals. The chart below shows the analysis of the respondents' opinion.

Figure 2. Crime control advice for government by respondents

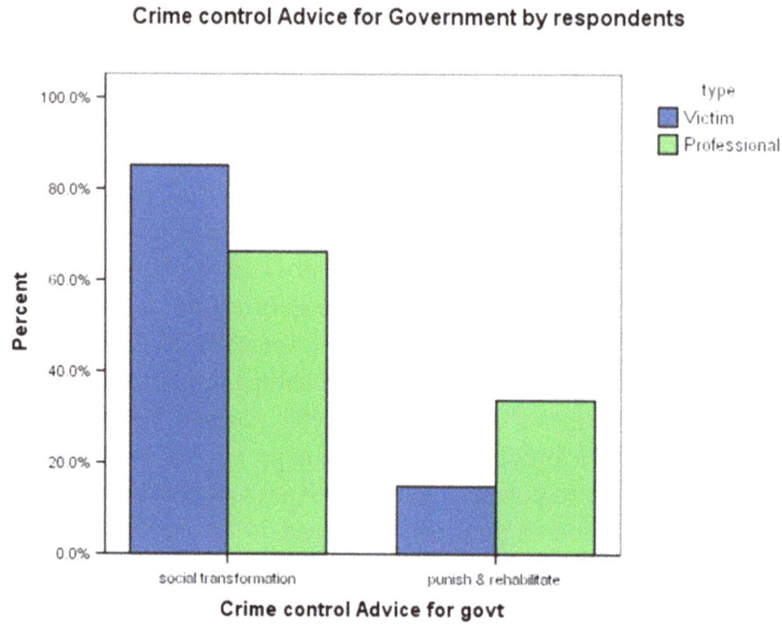

Result by Professions of the criminal justice Respondents

A further breakdown of the finding by criminal justice professions shows that 68.2% of police officers, 50.0% of judges, 75.0% of magistrates, 73.1% of prison officers, and 57.1% of public prosecutors and private practitioners respectively believe that transforming the social system would go along way at preventing and controlling youth crime and violence in Nigeria. And 31.8% of police officers, 50.0% of judges, 25.0% of magistrates, 26.9% of prison officers, 42.9% of public prosecutors and private practitioners respectively suggest rehabilitative punishments. The chart below shows the breakdown of analysis.

Figure 3. Crime control advice for government by profession of respondents

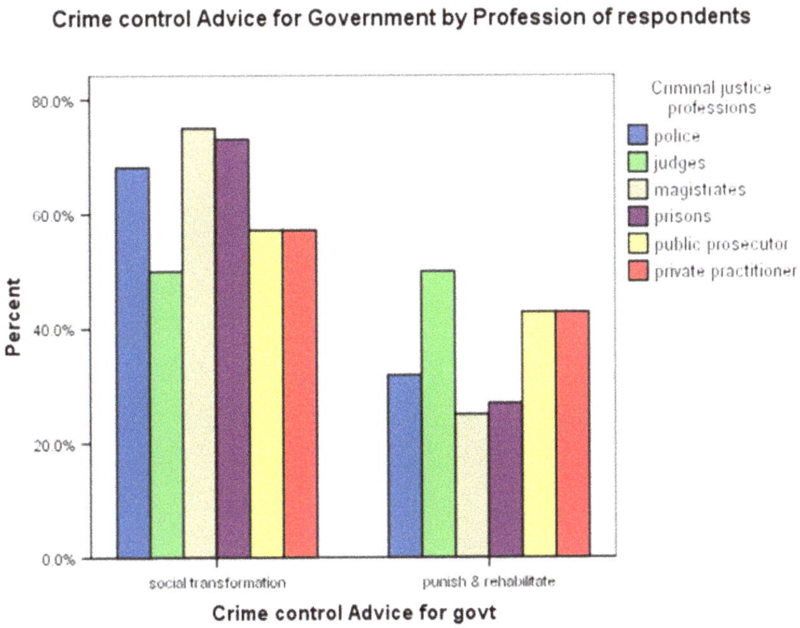

Result by Taxonomy of Victim Respondents

In another development, this study attempt to find out the opinion of different kind of victims that participated in the research regarding the way forward for crime prevention, and control in Nigeria. The study found that 87.5% of personal crime victims, 92.3% of sex crime victims, 80.0% of property/economic crime victims, and 86.7% of miscellaneous crime victims recommended the "social transformation" model; while 12.5% of personal crime, 7.7% of sex crime, 20.0% of property/economic crime, and 13.3% of miscellaneous crime victims recommended the "rehabilitative punishment" model.

It is important for the reading audience to note that there was no rule of thumb in the classification of crime in this study. However, in this study, personal crimes comprise robbery, common assault, death from auto crash, poisoning, ethno-religious violence, and campus cult violence as reported by primary and secondary victims. Sex crimes include rape/sexual assault, wife battery/domestic violence, and human trafficking victims. Economic/property crime here include fraud (419), debt, land dispute, theft and burglary victims; while miscellaneous offences include: slander, character assassination, police brutality, fight, and unlawful arrest victims.

See the chart below for the cross-tabulation of victim's classification/ victims' taxonomy.

Figure 4. Crime control advice for govt by taxonomy of victims

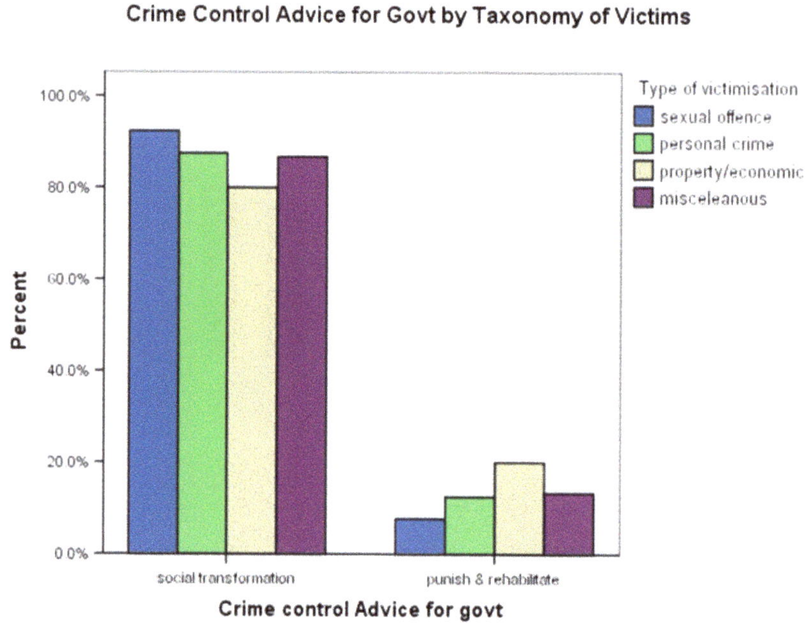

DISCUSSION

The findings of this study have shown that youth crime, like any other social ills is a complex phenomenon. However, the proliferation of this social problem bothers far more on social factors rather than individualistic as the respondents of this study have unanimously demonstrated across, professions, and taxonomy of victimization.

Looking at the social transformation argument in this study, it could be argued that when youths begin to have a sense of feelings of hopelessness in the society they belong, they tend to indulge in risky behaviour. For instance, in my international working experience as a correctional officer with some young offenders, a young person once said, 'what have I got to lose anyway? I have got no life to live'. This sense of hopelessness resonates in the finding of Kury et al (2002) where 33.7% of the respondents felt that it is no longer reasonable to believe in the future or bring children into this world, and 79.1% believe that politicians are uninterested in the people. In a state of hopelessness, the affected youths are potential time bomb to society because the one who is down fears no falls. Thus, social factors such as extreme poverty, social deprivation, and exclusion, arising from disproportionate opportunities, segregation or discrimination of neighborhoods, bullying arising from hate crime, and child abuse amongst others need to be checked in our society to prevent youths falling into this form of hopelessness. Extreme social conditions, therefore, could lead to a sense of social insecurity among some youths.

Youths therefore should be encouraged or given opportunities to speak out the ills they suffered or continues to suffer without fear of being castigated. This opportunity for youth ventilation or catharsis brings healings not only to the affected voice but to the society at large. Because, according to the US Surgeon-General Report (2001) experiences of youth shootings in the US for instance, have shown that most of these youths are troubled youths yearning to be heard. When they are denied the opportunities, or repressed, they would never say a word to us. They will be nursing their wounds in silence, and be quiet as a tortoise, but as deadly as the tiger. Suddenly, they would commit suicide bombings or mass murder, and leave many questions unanswered, but leave their unknown names in the front page of newspapers and news headlines.

It is in view of this argument that Males (1994) argues that most often, the media demonized the youth too often undermining that youth themselves could have been victims of state or adult crime. For instance, most often the negative adult violence on youth (such as pedophilia, child abuse) are under reported and ignored because perhaps, media coverage on youth crimes is a guaranteed crowd pleaser; while reporting adult violence against youth is not popular because most news consumers are adults. But one important truth with this intentional obscurity is that if youth are not protected from their adult abusers, and society or state crime, then the public will one day have to be protected from the youth (see Males, 1994).

What the above argument point at is that there should be respect for 'rule of law' by all and sundries (young, old, rich, or poor). Because the situation whereby in some jurisdictions the rule of law as a legal principle is only effective when an ordinary criminal is to be punished, but not when the 'rich and powerful' commit crime de-legitimate the concept of the 'rule of law'. And once the legitimacy of the law to punish is discredited by youths, the implication is 'anomie', and 'vengeance' against the state. For instance, in some western jurisdictions, where often laws to deal with youth crimes are lopsided: one law for the majority, and another for the minority, de-legitimates the law especially among those groups who considers themselves to be disproportionately treated.

Hence it is imperative for all jurisdictions to note the difference of ruling by law and the rule of law. Differentiating between the 'rule of law' and 'ruling by law' Kayode Oladele at a press interview with Laolu Akande (2007) explained that 'the rule of law' is a regulator of government and institutional power and no one is above the law (white, black, rich, poor, young or old) but in 'rule by law', the law becomes a manipulative instrument by social institutions and government, and the government; and its agencies interpret the law as it suit them, and they are above the law even when they commit *ultra vires* against the vulnerable groups. This unfortunate attitude in some jurisdictions around the world need remedy if youth violence is to be curtail, and youths are to be made to respect the law.

In view of this argument therefore, there are needs to reform the electoral process, and strengthen the anti-corruption crusade in Africa and Nigeria for instance. Because, when youths see 'significant others' (such as senators, ministers, and politicians) looting public funds with impunity (as often the case in Nigeria for instance), illegality would therefore be seen as legality by youth watchers. So, the efforts of the Anti-Corruption Commission, and the Economic and Financial Crimes Commission (EFCC) are welcome developments in Nigeria provided they are not selective but holistic in their modus operandi.

This reform advocacy is imperative because, when the electoral process becomes a do or dies affair, the need to use youths as political thugs arise. And, when there is demand for youth gangs, there must be a supply. So no matter how much the society criminalizes the youth gangs, in so far as thuggery is a means to meal tickets (sponsored by unscrupulous politicians) and, also serves as a ticket to political power and connections (should their sponsors win or rig elections) so far that illegitimate route to success become a well threaded route for youths in the absence of unavailable legitimate route (such as employment opportunities). Hence, Adams Oshiomole (2008) argues that the moments there are employment opportunities for the teaming jobless youths in our society, the sooner the thugs and armed robbers among them 'will know that it is better to work in the daytime and rest at night'.

Whereas the failure of the state institutions contributes to the proliferation of youth crime and violence, Smith (2007) argues that it is also important to address the growing lack of personal responsibility on parents who often blame society, or somebody else for the anti social behaviour of their children rather than looking closer home for their own actions or inactions. Most often these days some of the teens grow up in single parenthood. Whereas single parenting itself might not be the problem, it is however clear that very often most single parents want to be successful in their career at the same time a parent, and some lack parenting skill. In most cases, they often become uninvolved in the social, emotional, and psychological developments of their children. Only very few children with high morality would remain 'clean' in such circumstances. How do we fix it?

Hine (2007) was of the view that parents should spend quality times with their children because in contemporary times, rather than parents spending quality contact hours with their children they prefer to buy all sort of toys and computer games. The proliferation of violent computer games in modern times Hine (2007) argues seems not to help matters as they contribute to youths' involvement in gun violence. Though some parents would argue that because of the rate of street violence, they want to engage their children in computer games at home to keep them off the streets but there are problems with this line of argument.

CONCLUSION

The findings of this study and the discussion above have demonstrated the need to rejuvenate or restore some or all of our societal and family values if we are to overcome the proliferation of youth crime and violence in contemporary times. The problem of youth crime and violence as this study has demonstrated stem from the failure of the state, its institutions, and the family as agents of socializations. These social issues must be thoroughly dealt with if youth offending is to be prevented because; youths surrounded by those who actively commit crimes may feel the need to 'fit in with the crowd'. To keep their friends, youths may be peer pressured into committing a crime. This can be hard to resist due to the fear of being bullied or lonely at school. Hence, the failures of the microcosm have great impact on the macrocosm.

In another development, our unemployed and frustrated youths would continue to remain vulnerable to recruitment by leaders of youth gangs, and as thugs by unscrupulous politicians until we are able to provide employments and other better opportunities. These youths would also continue to be involved in local and political conflicts because contenders to these highly sought-after local and political positions would guarantee them access to financial resources, political and power connections should they get there by hooks or crooks. This situation would continue in Nigeria for instance, until we are able to ensure political and economic accountability and transparency through good governance, and reform of political and electoral process. This paper therefore concludes in line with Wood and Kemshall (2010, p.56) that the key solution to youth crime prevention should 'focus on risk management that is based on robust research evidence about the most effective ways of reducing risky behaviours in the community'.

REFERENCES

Akande, L. (2007). Nigerians in the Diaspora list Tasks for Bankole. *Guardian Newspaper*, *7*(December), 3.

Bedoya, M., & Martinez, J. (1991). *From football supporter to gang member*. El Propio Bolsillo.

Dahlberg, L. L., & Potter, L. B. (2001). Youth violence: Developmental pathways and prevention challenges. *American Journal of Preventive Medicine*, *20*(1), 3–14.

Elliot, D. S., & Menard, S. (1996). Delinquent friends and delinquent behaviour: temporal and developmental patterns. In Hawkins, J. D. (Ed.), *Delinquency and crime: current theories* (pp. 28–67). Cambridge University Press.

Farrington, D. P. (1998). Predictors, Causes, and Correlates of Male Youth Violence. In Tonry, M., & Moore, M. H. (Eds.), *Youth Violence* (pp. 421–475). University of Chicago Press.

Henry, B. (1996). 'Temperamental and Familial predictors of violent and nonviolent criminal convictions: Age 3 to age 18'. *Developmental Psychology*, *32*, 614–623.

Hine, J. (2007). Youth-A Waste of space? *CCJ Newsletter*, (17), 4.

Kury, H., Obergfell-Fuchs, J., & Ferdinand, T. (2002). The Background of Illegal Drug Abuse: a German View. In Brochu, S., Da Agra, C., & Cousineau, M. (Eds.), *Drugs and Crime Deviant Pathways* (pp. 197–218). Ashgate Publishing.

Lewin, K. (1943). 'Defining the "Field at a Given Time". *Psychological Review*, *50*, 292–310.

Males, M (1994) 'Bashing Youth: Media Myths about Teenagers', *Fair News bulletin,* March.

McCord, J. (1979). Some child rearing antecedents of criminal behaviour in adult men. *Journal of Personality and Social Psychology*, *37*, 1477–1486.

Omale, D. J. O. (2005). *Understanding restorative justice: A Handbook for criminal justice stakeholders*. Trinity Biz.

Omale, D. J. O. (2006). Justice in History: An Examination of the African Restorative Traditions and the Emerging Restorative Justice Paradigm. *African Journal of Criminology and Criminal Justice*, *2*(2), 30–60. http://www.umes.edu/WorkArea/showcontent.aspx?id=7012

Omale, D. J. O. (2009) Restorative justice as an alternative dispute resolution model: opinions of victims of crime and criminal justice professionals in Nigeria, PhD Thesis submitted to De Montfort University, Leicester. Available at: https://dora.dmu.ac.uk/items/879404ae-0e77-454c-b56d-4768cdee1d10

Omale, D. J. O. (2012). *Restorative Justice and Victimology: Euro-Africa Perspectives*. Wolf Legal Publishing.

Oputa, C. A. (1975). Crime and the Nigerian Society. In Elias, T. O., Nwagbara, S. N., & Akpamgbo, C. O. (Eds.), *African Indigenous Laws*. Government Printer.

Oshiomole, A. (2008). Osunbor Needs Time to pack out of Government House. *Thisday Newspaper*, (March), 1.

Reiner, R. (2007). *Law and Order: An Honest Citizen's Guide to Crime and Control*. Polity Press.

Sanjuan, A. M. (1998). Youth and Violence in Caracas: the paradoxes of a loss of citizenship. In Pinheiro, P. S. (Ed.), *Sao Paul without fear: a diagnosis of urban violence* (pp. 155–171). Garamond.

Shaw, M (2005) *Youth and Gun Violence: The Outstanding Case for Prevention*, International Centre for the Prevention of Crime (ICPC)

Shaxon, N. (2007). *Poisoned Wells: The Dirty politics of African Oils*. Macmillian.

Smith, A. (2007) 'Parental time a key factor in gang violence', *Leicester Mercury*, 29 August, p.15

Straw, J. (2007) 'What Next for Our Democracy', *Leicester Mercury*, 11 December, p.5

Surgeon-General Report, U. S. (2001). *Youth Violence: A Report of the Surgeon-General*. US Department of Health and Human Services.

UN-HABITAT. (2004) Strategy Paper on Urban Youth in Africa: A focus on the most vulnerable groups, Policy Dialogue Series No.2, Nairobi, Kenya: UN-HABITAT Safer Cities Project.

UNODC. (2005) *Strategies and Best Practices in Crime Prevention, in relation to Urban Areas and Youth at Risk,* Background Paper, in Workshop No.3 at the 11th UN Congress on Crime Prevention and Criminal Justice, Bangkok, Thailand: 18-25 April. Also available as File: A/CONF.203/11 at www.unodc.org

Wadsworth, M. E. J. (1978). 'Delinquency Prediction and its uses: The experience of a 21-year follow-up study. *International Journal of Mental Health*, 7, 43–62.

Wood, J., & Kemshall, H. (2010) 'Effective multi-agency public protection: learning from research', in K.Harisson (ed) *Managing high risk and sex offenders in the community: Risk management, treatment and social responsibility*, Collompton: Willan, pp 39-60

Chapter 5
Force Feeding in Africa: Juvenile Justice in Africa and Western Criminal Justice Systems Abstract

Danielle Elizabeth Wetuski
Prairie View A&M University, USA

ABSTRACT

Around the world, beauty standards are associated with women's attractiveness to men. In America, it is a cultural standard for women to be super thin to enhance their beauty. However, in Mauritania, young girls are force-fed to become voluptuous young women in preparation for the prospects of marriage (Thompson, 2014). Leblouh is noteworthy of several threats to children who are forced to commit to this tradition. For example, not only is the child eating until she is sick, but the child must also prep for an underage marriage by becoming obese (Melograno, 2022). Thus, the chapter will cover the behaviors, traditions, and risks of Leblouh in Mauritania and compare these concepts to the American idea of body image and eating habits. In addition, the chapter will identify the Mauritanian's government involvement and prevention in Leblouh practices, as well as the non-governmental groups that have actively combatted Leblouh and how this practice effects the juvenile justice system.

INTRODUCTION

Leblouh in Mauritania

Around the world, beauty standards are associated with women's attractiveness to men. In America, the cultural standard is for women to be exceedingly thin to

DOI: 10.4018/978-1-6684-9343-4.ch005

enhance their beauty. However, in Mauritania, adults force-feed their girls to become voluptuous young women, ready to prime the girl for marriage (Thompson, 2014). *Leblouh,* also known as gavage, is a French word meaning "force feeding" (Ouldzeidoune et al., 2013). Gavage was initially meant to fatten geese for livestock. Although the fattening process of livestock is meant as a preparation for human consumption, the practice of *Leblouh* on girls and women is enforced to mold them for early marriage. Therefore, girls and women are treated more like property for marriage than a person. This form of treatment is a women's rights issue that the Mauritania government is actively trying to prevent due to the underlining health issues *Leblouh* enforces.

The practice of force-feeding girls in Mauritania is known as *Leblouh* and is a cultural practice in Mauritania dating back to the nomadic era, where obesity signified wealth. This practice is a norm for Arab families in the region (Ouldzeidoune et al., 2013) to feed their daughters up to 1,600 calories daily to gain considerable amount of weight to catch a man's attention for marriage (Thompson, 2014). Therefore, *Leblouh* has a significant reference to the two main goals of the Mauritanian Arab culture for women: to produce children and to be a comfortable body for husbands (Ouldzeidoune et al., 2013). Harworth (2021) states that the perfect body, according to the men in Mauritania, would be women who have achieved bellies that overlap past their thighs, and the girl's neck should have multiple layers of fat. While Thompson (2014) describes the golden body image as stretch marks scarred down the girl's arms.

Leblouh could begin as early as six years old (Ouldzeidoune et al., 2013). It is customary for families to start force-feeding their daughters early to help provide an image of early body maturity and development (Ouldzeidoune et al., 2013). If the girl provides the illusion that she is more mature for her age through her body form, then she is perceived as ready for marriage. Although it is illegal to marry a girl under the age of eighteen years of age, many law enforcement undermines this law (Melograno, 2022).

Leblouh as Child Abuse

The *leblouh* practice tends to host two known forms of abuse to children—these two forms of abuse are physical and psychological abuse (*Physical Abuse*, 2023). Physical abuse is defined as a person who purposefully inflicts harm on another (Dag, 2021). In other words, physical abuse is when an elder maliciously harms a child after a child expresses an undesirable behavior. Psychological abuse, also known as emotional abuse, is characterized as abuse that targets another person's mental state (Sarwer, 2018). Specifically, psychological abuse can cause a person to experience anxiety or depression due to their experiences (*Emotional Abuse*, 2022).

Correspondlingly, Mauritanian girls experience physical and psychological abuse in three ways. First, the girls are forced to eat a severe amount of food, even if their bodies reject it, or they will be physically punished by their mothers and elders (Esposito, 2021; Haworth, 2021). Some girls are even subjected to the same medication intended for livestock's fat growth for later manufacturing and consumption (Haworth, 2021). Second, the girls experience psychological abuse due to the expectations placed upon them if they do not meet the obese beauty standards that Mauritania requires (Esposito, 2021). For example, it is common for girls and young women to have feelings of depression due to *Leblouh* (Ouldzeidoune et al., 2013). Last, girls are expected to gain weight to become eligible for early marriage (Knox, 2021). Prior research states that forced weight gain, excessive consumption of calories and child marriage are associated with psychological health risks (Sarwer, 2018). Reports have been collected of girls as young as fifteen years old becoming married because they have been successful in appearing older due to their obese state (Knox, 2021; Ouldzeidoune et al., 2013).

Leblouh and Physical Abuse

According to the Harvard International Review, the extremity of *Leblouh* equates to a form of child abuse (Esposito, 2021). Not only are the girls forced to eat a behemoth amount of food and consume up to five gallons of milk a day, they are also subjected to physical and mental abuse when resisting the *Leblouh* practice (Esposito, 2021). If a girl refuses to eat or drink her calories, a *zayar* technique is utilized on the girls. *Zayar* is when an elder woman squeezes the girl's toes between two sticks to cause great pain for not consuming her daily calories (Esposito, 2021). In addition to *zayar,* girls can also be punished by being pinched in their inner thighs, pulled by the ear, having their fingers bent backward, or forced to eat or drink their vomit if their stomach rejects the amount of food, she intakes. According to Ouldzeidoune et al. (2013), 61% of girls forced to practice *Leblouh* reported that they experienced forms of physical abuse when force-fed. One-third of girls encouraged to participate in *Leblouh* stated that their fingers were broken as punishment (Ouldzeidoune et al., 2013).

In 2021, a journalist for Marie Claire, Abigail Haworth, interviewed Mauritanian women to seek a better understanding of the *Leblouh* practice and traditions. Thus, Haworth met a girl named Tijanniya from Atar in Mauritania and she agreed to be interviewed for the Marie Claire journal. Tijanniya expressed that she was enrolled in what seemed like a summer camp when she was fourteen-year-old (Haworth, 2021). However, the camp was more in line with a structured organization to augment

Mauritanian girl's weight. Tijanniya recalls being forced to eat meals with several courses containing heavy amounts of goat milk, oily couscous, and millet (Haworth, 2021). Tijanniya states that if she or her peers were to refuse the food, then the elder women would physically beat them (Haworth, 2021). If the girls were to become sick from the amount of food and vomit, then she would be forced to consume her vomit to ensure she does not miss out on the calories (Haworth, 2021; Smith, 2009)

Like Tijanniya, many Mauritania girls are not only force-fed but are expected to attend camps in the summer to help the girls gain weight (Haworth, 2021). These organizations are called "fat farms" (Haworth, 2021; Smith, 2009). In addition to "fat farms," there are seasonal eating practices during the holidays and summers because goat's milk and millet are more accessible at that time (Smith, 2009). During these holidays, it is also common to send girls to the "fat farms" with the guise that the girl is not attending a weight specialty campsite (Smith, 2009). While at the "fat farm" it is understood that if the girl does not finish her meal or refuses to eat, then one of the elder women will cause severe physical pain to the girl by squeezing her toe between two wooden rods (Smith, 2009).

Leblouh and Health Issues

Leblouh's practice introduces several health issues and mental disorders. World Health Organization (WHO, 2023) states that three million adults worldwide die from obesity. According to the Centers for Disease Control and Prevention (CDC) (2023), obesity could cause one to have high blood pressure, high LDL cholesterol, low HDL cholesterol or high levels of triglycerides, type 2 diabetes, coronary heart disease, strokes, gallbladder disease, osteoarthritis, sleep apnea, breathing problems, several forms or types of cancer, low quality of life, and body pain with difficulty in physical functioning. Individuals with a body mass index (BMI) over 25 or higher are defined as overweight, and a BMI of 30 or higher is defined as obesity (CDC, 2023). BMI is a health care practice to meaure the height of a person and compare it to the weight they have to understand if the person is obtaining a healthy height to weight ratio (CDC, 2023).

In addition, The American College of Obstetricians and Gynecologists (ACOG) (2023) states that if one is obese while pregnant, then she is at greater risk for gestational hypertension, high blood pressure, preeclampsia, and obstructive sleep apnea. Gestational hypertension is when a pregnant girl experiences high blood pressure (ACOG, 2023). High blood pressure is also linked to preeclampsia, a medical condition that pregnant girls face during their second trimester or after the baby is born (ACOG, 2023). Preeclampsia also affects the kidneys, increases the risk of strokes, and heightens the risk for the placenta and fetus to have pre-birthing complications (ACOG, 2023). Obstructive sleep apnea is a sleep condition that causes the pregnant person to stop breathing. Sleep apnea is known to cause fatigue and increases the risk of high blood pressure, preeclampsia, heart problems, and lung complications in the pregnant individual (ACOG, 2023).

Last, a girl or woman who is obese and becomes pregnant is inclined to have issues with the pregnancy. The American College of Obstetricians and Gynecologists (2023) states that obesity can affect a pregnancy through congenital disabilities, complicate ultrasound exams, increase the risk for macrosomia, and cause the fetus to have a preterm birth or a stillbirth. Birth defects can be characterized as a baby born with a heart defect or may need neural tube defects, which are developmental issues for the brain, spinal cord, or the covering of the brain and spinal cord (ACOG, 2023). Ultrasound complications can occur due to the pregnant person having too much body fat, which will cause the technician to be unable to properly assess the growing fetus (ACOG, 2023). Macrosomia is a condition that causes the baby to be larger than average. A large baby can increase the risk of injury to the mother while giving birth (ACOG, 2023). Preterm birth is also an increased risk for girls and women who are obese because the pregnant person is more likely to have complications that may cause medical professionals to deliver the baby before the initial due date (ACOG, 2023). A preterm baby is at greater risk for long-term health problems when compared to a full-term baby (ACOG, 2023). Last, stillbirth increases alomg with the obesity of the girl or women (ACOG, 2023). Therefore, it is important to be in good health to become and maintain a pregnancy (ACOG, 2023).

Leblouh and Psychological Issues

In addition to physical health, mental health is at risk for those experiencing obesity. For example, Sarwer et al. (2018) state that obesity is significantly associated with psychosocial burdens such as mood, self-esteem, quality of life, and obstructed body image. Specific disorders linked to obesity are depression, eating disorders, anxiety, and substance abuse (CDC, 2023; Sarwer, 2018). In addition to psychological disorders, a person who is obese also has an increased risk of sexual abuse, physical abuse, and emotional neglect (Sarwer, 2018). For instance, prior studies have stated that individuals who seek medical professionals' help with obesity report that between 16% and 32% have experienced a form of sexual abuse (Grilo, 2005; Gustafson et al., 2006). Also, about 50% of individuals who are obese state they have experienced emotional neglect during their adolescents (Grilo, 2005; Gustafson et al., 2006). These forms of emotional neglect can range from verbal abuse to emotional neglect due to family divorce, family separation, substance abuse, or a parent or guardian becoming incarcerated (Sarwer, 2018). In sum, obesity tends to have multiple adverse effects on the human body and brain. Thus, individuals who experience it are more likely to have increased physical, medical, and psychological disorders (Grilo, 2005).

Furthermore, girls are subjected to psychological abuse from adults within Mauritania once they begin practicing *Leblouh* (Ouldzeidoune et al., 2013). For instance, girls are told that beauty lies within obesity, that thinness symbolizes poverty and a repulsive body figure (Knox, 2021). Young girls are then encouraged to believe that being obese is a form of unprecedented wealth and charm (Esposito, 2021). Mothers who pressure their daughters to partake in *Leblouh* state that it is out of love and guidance that their child eats enough to become married quickly (Esposito, 2021). In general, Mauritania women believe that obesity is not only about beauty but about power. If one is obese enough to be beautiful, then she will go on to marry and have a more powerful status as an obese wife. In addition, daughters are told by their mothers and elders that they are meant to be overweight to fulfill their two purposes in life- to be large and soft enough for their husbands to lie on comfortably and to have children (Esposito, 2021). If a girl does not meet beauty standards, she may feel depression, anxiety, and anxiousness (Ouldzeidoune et al., 2013).

Last, Children are already vulnerable to mental health issues and psychological challenges due to the pressures and circumstances that adolescence brings (Dag, 2021). Nevertheless, children forced into marriage early on are even more likely to experience anxiety, depression, suicidal ideations and suicidal attempts (Dag, 2021). Previous research has found that girls prepped for childhood marriages are experiencing anxiety and depression due to the burden of committing to a grown man, having children, and maintaining a marriage (Dag, 2021). In addition to the marriage, the girls tend to feel that their bodies have never been their own (Dag, 2021). For example, girls were forced to be obese, married for a man's pleasure, and expected to give birth to multiple children if possible (Dag, 2021). These occurrences affect the girl's psychological development and self-image by stripping her of her autonomy and self-choices.

MAURITANIA, *LEBLOUH* AND JUVENILE JUSTICE

Although the girls tend to experience feelings of depression and anxiety, they are still held to their promise to eat as much as they can to obtain a husband. In Mauritania, it is illegal to be wed under eighteen years old (Knox, 2021). However, girls are found to be promised and legally bound to a man by the time she is fifteen years old. About 37% of Mauritanian girls are married before the age of eighteen (Ouldzeidoune et al., 2013). In an interview provided by *The Sun,* a young woman named Annie stated that she began her descent into *Leblouh* at the age of four, was married by the age of twelve, received her first period at thirteen, and became pregnant in that same year with her first child (Knox, 2021). Annie describes her childhood as coming from a low-income family and being locked in a room alone until she finished her food (Knox, 2021). At one point, Annie informs Knox that she used to empty her food outside a window so she did not have to endure another bite, but then she was reported by another Mauritanisn, resulting in her mother physically abusing her and watching her while Annie ate her future meals. Annie also describes the most challenging part about *Leblouh* is not throwing up the food once she is full, stating that it was often that she would get sick when she over ate (Knox, 2021). Once Annie was promised to a man, she stated she was scared to marry because she did not know him (Knox, 2021). Annie stated that she has been traumatized by her childhood, her practice in *Leblouh*, the physical abuse she received from her mother and elders to continue eating, the pain of being full, the early marriage, and the fear of becoming a wife and mother (Knox, 2021). At the time of the interview, Annie was twenty-nine years old with seven children and one more on the way (Knox, 2021).

Mauritania has a history of ignoring the cries of women like Annie. *Leblouh* is a continued a practice detrimental to the Mauritanian women population because it places Mauritanian men's outdated wants and expectations of how a girl should look and perform as a woman above women;s overall health. Although the Mauritanian justice system has made some small leaps in helping the practice of *Leblouh* and child marriage, these practices are still at large today. For example, in 2001, Mauritanian law makers made it illegal for girls to participate in marriages to older men (Melograno, 2022). However, a loophole in the law allows parents to betroth their girls to older men so long that the girl agrees to the marriage (Melograno, 2022). Nevertheless, if the girl does not answer the engagement request, than this silence is seen as consent to marry (Melograno, 2022). Therefore, the justice system has not been as successful as intended.

MAURITANIA GOVERNMENT RESPONSE TO *LEBLOUH*

The Mauritania government has turned a blind eye to the presents of the *Leblouh* practice. However, in the late 20th century, media influences began to surface in Mauritania, leading the girl's and women's ability to observe female bodies from other parts of the world (Thompson, 2014). Women and children began to adapt other cultural norms into their daily lives. For example, girls were particularly interested in Sari, worn in Indian culture. The girls of Mauritania began to use fabric from their markets and develop their sense of the Sari fashion (Thompson, 2014). In addition, women began miming dances seen through the media, and women and children became more active in sports (Thompson, 2014). At the turn of the 21st century, the Mauritanian government began to recognize the health risks that accompany obesity and the trauma that develops when being force-fed from a young age to be married in the girl's youth (Leiter, 2020). Therefore, the government took a more active role in prevention.

First, Mauritania's government understood that *Leblouh's* customs and practices were outdated, creating several health risks for their women (Thompson, 2014). As a result, in 2003, a Mauritanian women's ministry started a campaign that supported a slimmer figure for both women and girls. In addition, media in the Mauritania household displayed commercials that depicted obese women being carried in wheel barrels by their husbands, becoming sick from their health, and being depicted as unattractive (Thompson, 2014). In time girls began to view obesity as a body form that was not beautiful and thinness as the most attractive body type one could have (Thompson, 2014).

Second, in 2008, ABC News interviewed the director of a campaign to combat *Leblouh,* approved by the Mauritania government, Yenserha Mint Mohamed Mahmoud (Hasan, 2008). Mahmoud has confirmed that he has broadcasted the dangers and difficulties of being overweight to Mauritanians (Hasan, 2008). Mahmoud states that there have been mixed results on the government's involvement, however, due to the areas the broadcast can reach (Hasan, 2008). Cities can listen to and view the broadcast on radios and televisions, yet, those in rural areas do not have the privilege of these networks. In addition to the broadcast, Mahmoud holds seminars about health, dieting, and educating women on what foods are good nourishment and which promote fat within their bodies (Hasan, 2008; Leiter, 2020).

Third, as of 2011, women-only gyms have been developed and manufactured in several areas of Mauritania to help women lose weight (Leiter, 2020). The most popular gym in Nouakchott has three hundred members (Leiter, 2020). Women joining the gym are not only finding motivation within themselves to exercise but are also being encouraged by doctors, health professionals, and societal change associated with beauty (Leiter, 2020). Recently, Western ideas of beauty, thinness, and muscular tones are becoming recognized as attractive and desirable body features in Mauritania (Leiter, 2020).

Last, two women-led non-government organization (NGOs) have taken it upon themselves to fight the practice of *Leblouh* by advocating for force-fed girls and women (Leiter, 2020). One of the groups is known as Espoire (Leiter, 2020). Some of the members of Espoire were forced to practice *Lebouh* when they were growing up. Therefore, Espoire aims to give women more opportunities to become educated by providing books, classes on health, and credits to women (Leiter, 2020). In addition, Espoire encourages women to become employed by offering them chances to gain work while providing health care and education for their children so that they do not have to attend "fat camps" (Leiter, 2020). In addition, the Sahel Women

Empowerment and Demographic Dividend (SWEDD) aim to educate young girls, help keep them in school and stigmatize child marriage to help prevent these forms of abuse (Melograno, 2022).

MAURITANIA AND AMERICA COMPARISON

Body image is just as important in America as it is in Mauritania because both countries associate body image with status (Smith, 2009; Mayeux et al., 2020). As Mauritania associates obesity with high social status, America associates thinness with high social status (Mayeux et al., 2020). Specifically, a thin girl will be viewed as a more popular person among her peers, which tends to boost her self-confidence (Elkind, 1967). Peer opinions, parental views of their children and American media have significant leverage when shaping youth's understadning of body image (Thompson et al., 1999). In addition to shaping the standard to body ideas, peers, parents, and media tend to place unnecessary pressure on young girls to meet the standard being thin (Thompson, 2014). Prior research has noted that girls who feel they do not meet these set standards are more likely to experience anxiety and depression (Thompson et al., 1999).

Contrary to Mauritania, American culture does not promote obesity (Smith, 2020). Ongoing research has and continues to develop new ways to prevent and control obesity (Smith, 2020). Due to this cultural dynamic, families try not to overfeed or force-feed their children into an overweight status. In addition, the American government provides schedule a time for children to have exercise and outdoor play in the child's school day, have physical exams to assess the child's health, has annual doctor appointments to check the child's growth and provides early education on helath foods to children.

Although the American body ideals are the opposite of the Mauritania nation, both countries have similar causes of increased mental and physical health risks (Aparicio et al., 2016; Smith, 2020). For example, children who live in America tend to feel pressure to be thin, physically fit, and popular among their peers, which is also a known risk factor for anxiety, depression, and suicidal ideations and suicide attempts (Smith, 2020). Girls who live in Mauritania are pressured to be obese by physical and psychological abuse form their parents, gaurdians, and elders (Cassidy, 1991).

LESSONS LEARNED

Leblouh is a form of force-feeding common in Mauritania, and it continues the tradition of child abuse by physically and mentally harming Mauritian girls. The inequality and challenges the Mauritanian girls and women face are not thoroughly addressed by the government. For instance, the government has not made strong strides in banning *Leblouh* traditions and practices, as well as extinguishing the wrongful expectation that girls should be prepared to marry young and produce children as soon as possible. Although the NGO's efforts are admirable and a great place to start, the Mauritania government must take a more active role in preventing *Leblouh* and child marriages. As previously stated, Mauritania emphasized the importance for their girls and women to fulfill their duties of being a plump and solf resting point for their husbands and giving birth to as many children as possible. However, both formalities are slowly killing their population thrpugh physical and mental health problems. Due to the Leblouh standards, Mauritanian girls and women are becoming so unhealthy that they are not able to live, let alone bare children. In conclusion, greater actions are needed to prevent the abuse and trauma that girls and women face in the depths of the traditional practice of *Leblouh.*

REFERENCES

ACOG. (2023). Obesity And Pregnancy. *The American College Of Obstetricians And Gynecologists*. Https://Www.Acog.Org/Womens-Health/Faqs/Obesity-And-Pregnancy

Aparicio, E., Canals, J., Arija, V., De Henauw, S., & Michels, N. (2016). The Role Of Emotion Regulation In Childhood Obesity: Implications For Prevention And Treatment. *Nutrition Research Reviews*, *29*(1), 17–29. PMID: 27045966

Cassidy, C. (1991). The Good Body: When Big Is Better. *Medical Anthropology*, *13*(3), 181–213. PMID: 1961102

CDC. (2023). Health Effects Of Overwright And Obseity. *Centers For Disease Control And Prevention* Https://Www.Cdc.Gov/Healthyweight/Effects/Index.Html

Dag, H. Y. A.; Altikrdesler, Ö. K. & Törün, S. H. (2021). A Child Abuse: Marriage At Childhood Age. *Turkish Archives Of Pediatrics*(6). Https://Doi.Org/Doi: DOI: 10.5152/Turkarchpediatr.2021.21093

Emotional Abuse. (2022). Psychology Today. Https://Www.Psychologytoday.Com/Us/Basics/Emotional-Abuse

Esposito, A. (2021). Force-Feeding And Drug Abuse: The Steep Price Of Beauty In Mauritania. *Harvard International Review*. Https://Doi.Org/Https://Hir.Harvard.Edu/Force-Feeding-And-Drug-Abuse-The-Steep-Price-Of-Beauty-In-Mauritania/

Grilo, C. M., Masheb, R. M., Brody, M., Toth, C., Burke-Matindale, C. H., & Rothschild, B. S. (2005). Childhood Maltreatment In Extremely Obese Male And Female Bariatric Surgery Candidates. *Obesity Research*, *13*(1), 123–130. PMID: 15761171

Gustafson, T. B., Gibbons, L. M., & Sarwer, D. B. (2006). History Of Sexual Abuse Among Bariatric Surgery Candidates. *Surgery for Obesity and Related Diseases*, *2*(3), 369–374. PMID: 16925354

Hasan, L. (2008). Mauritania Tries To Reverse Obesity Tradition: Women In This West African Country Are Still Force-Fed To Stay Fat. *ABC News*. Https://Abcnews.Go.Com/GMA/Story?Id=4322187&Page=1

Haworth, A. (2021). Forced To Be Fat. Https://Doi.Org/Http://Www .Marieclaire.Com/World-Reports/News/Forcefeeding- In-Mauritania.

Knox, M. (2021). FAT SHAME: 'I Was Force-Fed Five Times A Day To Fatten Me Up For Marriage Aged 12 – If I Refused Or Threw Up I'd Be Beaten'. *The Sun*. Https://Www.Thesun.Co.Uk/News/13727356/Force-Fed-5-Times-Day-Beaten

Leiter, S. (2020). *Force-Feeding In West Africa: 5 Facts About Leblouh In Mauritania*. Https://Borgenproject.Org/Leblouh-In-Mauritania/

Melograno, V. (2022). Childhood Interruped: Child Marraige In Mauritania. *The Borgen Project*. Https://Borgenproject.Org/Child-Marriage-In-Mauritania/

Ouldzeidoune, N. K. J., Bertrand, J., & Rice, J. (2013). A Description Of Female Genital Mutilation And Force-Feeding Practices In Mauritania: Implications For The Protection Of Child Rights And Health. *PLoS One*, *8*(4). Https://Doi.Org/Doi: 10.1371/Journal.Pone.0060594 PMID: 23593257

Physical Abuse. (2023). American Psychological Association. Https://Dictionary .Apa.Org/Physical-Abuse

Sarwer, D. B. P., H. M. (2018). The Psychological Burden Of Obesity. *Endocrinology and Metabolism Clinics of North America*, *45*(3), 677–688. PMID: 27519139

Smith, A. (2009). Girls Being Force-Fed For Marriage As Fattening Farms Revived. *The Observer*.

Smith, J. D. F., E. & Kobayahi, M. A. (2020). Prevention And Management Of Childhood Obesity And Its Psychological And Health Comorbidities. *Annual Review of Clinical Psychology*, •••, 351–380. PMID: 32097572

Thompson, C. (2014). Body Image In Mauritania: Bigger Is Better. *Utah Historical Review*, 1-7.

WHO. (2023). Obesity. *World Health Organization*. Https://Www.Who.Int/Health -Topics/Obesity#Tab=Tab_1

Chapter 6
Comparing Street Children in Sub-Saharan African Countries (Ghana and Nigeria) and the West

Kaviya Shankar
Prairie View A&M University, USA

ABSTRACT

Street children are a common and alarming issue in most developing countries, particularly Sub-Saharan Africa. According to UNICEF (2021), there are around 30 million street children on the continent due to the deterioration of incomes and livelihoods, the impact of rising family poverty, malnutrition, and restricted access to essential health services. These conditions force children to depend on scrounging for food and money on the streets, sleeping in vacant buildings, abandoned basements, and sometimes open air. Western African countries like Ghana and Nigeria are not exceptions in dealing with street children. Both countries are relatively developed and have a significantly large population of street children. This study emphasizes the general aspects of street children in Ghana and Nigeria, including the background, contemporary issues, governmental reactions, and approaches. The chapter will also examine the strengths and limitations of Ghana and Nigeria's methods of dealing with street children, a comparison with Western perspectives.

INTRODUCTION

Protecting children is society's fundamental moral and ethical obligation. Vulnerable children stand a much better chance of growing up in a society that allows

DOI: 10.4018/978-1-6684-9343-4.ch006

them to thrive. Access to social protection is a universal human right, especially for children (ILO & UNICEF, 2023). Social protection empowers marginalized children and is a critical cornerstone to reaching their basic needs in many countries and its deficiency leads to the abandonment of children on the streets. The phenomenon of street children is not restricted to one society; there are cultural differences (Aptekar, 1994). One of the earliest studies about street children was by Henry Mayhew noted in 1851, "The number of street children increases with each passing year" (Briggs et al., 1966). Mayhew coined *street children* because it logically followed his other descriptors of individuals, including *street-sellers*. UNESCO repurposed the term *street children* to refer to war-vagrant children after World War II. Later in 1980, UNICEF created three street children's classifications concentrating on developing countries. The first *Children for the street* are street-working kids who live with their families; c*hildren on the street* who get little family assistance are the second type, and finally, *Street children* without familial support are the third type (Williams, 1993).

The association of street children positions their status as both victims and perpetrators of crime (Nhapi & Agere, 2019). Furthermore, street children's lack of formal representation excludes them from policy development. Since multiple definitions of *street children* exist in various contexts, they may prove that they are not a homogenous group, and that the specific context determines whether youngsters should be included in the criteria. In contemporary times, four rigid classifications of street children have been identified: *children of the street, children on the street, children who are part of a street family, and children in institutional care* (Owoaje et al., 2009). However, the United Nations defined the term' street children' to include "any boy or girl… for whom the street in the widest sense of the word… has become his or her habitual abode and/or source of livelihood, and who is inadequately protected, supervised, or directed by responsible adults" (UNICEF, 2012). Street children face significant hazards as they lack access to a secure family environment, essential services such as economic problems, healthcare, education, and safeguards against exploitation.

Street children are one of the clear indicators of poverty and marginalization in the urban environment of a country's growth. Still, their rights are frequently disregarded (Van Blerk, 2015). According to the UN (2022), the estimation of street children worldwide has increased to 150 million, however, the COVID-19 pandemic has increased the population by 100 million more children experiencing multidimensional poverty. Further, the global economic recession does not mitigate for many countries, especially in the Sub-Saharan regions of Africa. Sub-Saharan Africa consists of 48 countries south of the Sahara Desert. The youth in the Sub-Saharan region face complex issues because of rapid societal change. Ghana and Nigeria have the same colonial pasts and are the most populous English-speaking countries in West Africa. They are also the main contributors to the Economic Community of West African States (ECOWAS), which aims to facilitate the unrestricted movement of goods and people in the region. Additionally, Ghana is classified as a lower middle-income economy, the second largest in West Africa after Nigeria (Bosiakoh & Obeng, 2021).

According to the World Bank (2023), the economic growth of these countries is slowed; Nigeria -3.6% in 2022 from 4.1% in 2021 and Ghana- 3.2% in 2022, down from 5.4% in 2021. Also, the Ukraine war disrupted the fiscal consolidation efforts of several countries in the region that had commenced following the COVID-19 pandemic. As a result, the government has increasingly turned to measures such as subsidies, temporary tariffs, levy waivers, and providing income support to the most vulnerable segments of the population. Several studies found that street children are constantly exposed to substance abuse, diseases, violence, and hunger, resulting in various mental health challenges, including low self-esteem, unhappiness, and a negative outlook on life (McAlpine et al., 2010; Myburgh et al., 2015; Boakye-Boaten, 2008; Ayenew et al., 2020). The present chapter focuses on the issue of street children in Ghana and Nigeria, both of which are emerging nations that are not immune to this predicament. Although child survival rates have exhibited an upward trend in Sub-Saharan Africa, leading to more adolescents, these demographics encounter distinctive obstacles. They are more likely to live in poverty, have limited access to education, experience higher population growth, face higher risks of maternal mortality and HIV prevalence than their peers in other parts of the world (Blum, 2007).

Consequently, studies regarding street children to comprehend and address the obstacles encountered by one of the most marginalized segments of the population are an important aspect. This chapter discusses Ghana and Nigeria, from Sub-Saharan Africa, since they have a similar situation with street children. This chapter will explore the background, contemporary issues, governmental reactions, and approaches to reducing street children in both countries compared to the Western perspective. The rationale for this chapter is that Ghana and Nigeria have a high population of street children and are in similar economic situations; nonetheless, neither country has specific laws and policies related to the issue. The child welfare systems in Ghana and Nigeria have similarities and differences. Both countries have policies and programs to protect children's rights and well-being. However, significant differences exist in implementing these policies and programs due to variations in the countries' socioeconomic and political contexts.

STREET CHILDREN OF GHANA

Ghana is a multiethnic country in Western Africa. The country is politically divided into 16 administrative regions, with Accra as the capital city. Ghanaians speak about 50 indigenous languages, including Akan, Ewe, Ga, Dagaare, and Dagbani; however, English is the official language. According to the World Bank (2021), the population of Ghana is over 32.83 million. Conversely, Ghana has a young population of about 6.9 million adolescents or about 22% of the total population. Most children (35%) live or work on the streets of major cities in Ghana. The most populated cities with street children are Greater Accra, Kumasi, and Sekondi-Takoradi – the golden triangle cities (Dankyi & Huang, 2021). The golden triangle cities also attract migrants searching for jobs since the discovery of oil and gas (Dankyi, 2022). There is also a growing number of second-generation street children.

Street children in Ghana have become a complex problem attributed to several causal factors. These factors include income inequality between rural and urban areas, urbanization, and the disintegration of the extended family (Beauchemin, 1999). The essential services like toilets, showers, water, and food become expensive. The children who live on the street also work on the Street (Awumbila & Ardayfio-Schandorf, 2008). The country's development pace suggests a rapid transformation in the probable future. While research has paid significant attention to the focal issue, policy efforts and actions appear to have reached a standstill. The Ghanaian government was the first nation to ratify the UN Convention on the Rights of a Child in 1990 and passed the Children Act in 1998, which was later amended in 2016. The laws mention the rights of all children, including street children, and the protection of children from abuse, exploitation, and neglect. The law also establishes a legal structure for reintegrating and rehabilitating street children into society (Fred et al., 2022).

The Ministry of Gender, Children, and Social Protection is responsible for implementing programs and activities affecting children in Ghana. Through advocacy, research, and other development initiatives, its mission is to enhance children's welfare and full integration into the development process. This is consistent with Article 28 of the 1992 Constitution and the Children's Act, which require the government to protect children's rights. These legal documents demonstrate Ghana's dedication to promoting Ghanaian children's physical, mental, and social health. The department strives to uphold these provisions of Ghana's laws.

In addition, the Ghanaian administration has endorsed international declarations comprising the Universal Declaration of Human Rights (1948), Education for All (EFA) (1990), Salamanca Declaration (1994), and Dakar Framework for Action (2000). The labor laws in Ghana protect from child labor, according to the ILO Convention on the Worst Forms of Child Labor in 2000 and the African Charter on the Rights and Welfare of the Child of the African Union (Boateng & Dako-Gyeke, 2022). The government, Ministry of Gender, Children and Social Protection (2015) has around 44 social intervention programs for children and families on the streets. One such program was the Child and Family Welfare Policy in 2015. The policy incorporated multiple facets, such as the Children's Act, which delineated the entitlements of minors and the obligations of both guardians and the state. Several initiatives, such as the Free Compulsory Universal Basic Education Act, have been implemented to facilitate access to high-quality education. Additionally, the Livelihood Empowerment Against Poverty program has been designed to mitigate poverty among households that are vulnerable and have children.

Apart from the government, non-governmental organizations (NGOs) and faith and religious-based organizations collaborate with the government and work with street children. Though the policies and implications are available, the nation lacks financial commitments, policy and practice gaps, and a more inclusive approach that tackles the problem of street children (Dankyi, 2022). Recently the Department of Social Welfare, UNICEF, Catholic Relief Services, and the Consortium conducted a one-day workshop to commemorate the 2023 International Day for Street Children. The Safety for All Children festival raised awareness of street-connected individuals' challenges nationwide. Stakeholders might also endorse the 5-year Street Connected People Strategy Plan. The Deputy Minister for Women, Children, and Social Protection, Hon. Francisca Oteng Mensah, lamented the plight of street-connected children and urged well-meaning Ghanaians to collaborate with the government to combat street. She counseled parents, guardians, and caregivers to build a loving household to keep kids from running away. The 5-year Street Connected People Strategy Plan was developed with stakeholder involvement (MoGCSP, 2023). The effectiveness of these programs is still a matter of debate. The problem of street children in Ghana has become inextricably between policies and results of reducing street children.

STREET CHILDREN IN NIGERIA

Nigeria is a multicultural country with over 250 ethnic groups and over 500 languages spoken (World Atlas, 2021). Nigeria is also located in West Africa, with a population of over 206 million people, making it the most populous country in Africa and the seventh most populous country globally (World Bank, 2021). Among this population, 52 percent are individuals aged 0-17 years. The country gained independence from the British in 1960 and has since struggled with political instability, corruption, and economic challenges. Nigeria is known for its oil reserves, which account for a significant portion of its economy (BBC, 2019).

According to the Organization of the Petroleum Exporting Countries (OPEC), Nigeria has the largest oil reserves in Africa and is the continent's largest oil producer (OPEC, 2021). However, the over-reliance on oil exports has made Nigeria vulnerable to fluctuations in global oil prices, contributing to the country's economic disputes. Despite these positive developments, Nigeria still faces many challenges, including poverty, unemployment, and insecurity. The country has struggled with conflicts and violence, particularly in the northern part, where the Boko Haram insurgency has caused significant harm to civilians and displaced millions of people. (Council on Foreign Relations, 2021). Abuja is the capital city, and the largest city is Lagos which is also the most populated (around 1 million) city with street children, followed by Kano, Port Harcourt, and Kaduna majorly (UNICEF, 2018).

As of 2020, about one in every five of the world's out-of-school children are in Nigeria, with many homeless. Currently, about 2.8 million children need education-in-emergencies support in the Northeast due to displacement caused by terrorism (UNICEF, 2022). Many children live on the street because of poverty and derive their existence from petty jobs such as hawking wares or begging. (Alawiye-Adams & Babatunde, 2013). The other factor of street children in northern cities of Nigeria is known to have Almajirai, who are children sent by their Islamic teachers to beg on the streets. This practice is actively encouraged as part of Koranic education in the region. While a small number of Almajirai can also be found in southern Nigeria, their purpose is to assist physically disabled adults, particularly their parents, in begging on the streets (Hansen et al., 2016).

Similar to Ghanaian street children, Nigerian street children also face poverty, risk of substance abuse, child labor, lack of education, and physical, sexual, and mental health issues (Ajiboye & Oladiti, 2008; Aransiola et al., 2009; Nnama-Okechukwu et al., 2023; Dosumu et al., 2016). There is a distressing correlation between street children and child labor, and this issue persists in many countries, including Nigeria (Aransiola, 2013). The prevalence of child labor in Nigeria has been reported to be on the rise. The ILO estimates that as of 2020, there were approximately 15 million child workers in the country.

Overall, poverty, family breakdown, and lack of access to education and healthcare contribute to the high number of street children in Ghana and Nigeria (Ankomah & Omoregie, 2019; Olowa, 2020). The phenomenon of street children in Nigeria represents a complex interplay of ethnic, religious, and nationalistic factors that contribute to their survival. Street children in these countries face numerous challenges, including exposure to violence and exploitation, discrimination, and a lack of necessities such as food and shelter (UNICEF, 2021). Even though the country remarkably set the National Action Plan (NAP) for the elimination of child labor with the International Year for the Elimination of Child Labor (IYECL) (ILO, 2021). Additionally, these children are at risk of being indoctrinated and forced to become child soldiers or, worse, being killed. Unlike Ghana, Nigeria has military training for abducted children, mainly from the streets, for being spies, armed soldiers, and suicide bombers (Wachaya, 2022). Since the involvement of the Nigerian government in child soldiers, the UN stepped up in handover protocols and requested the government to set an example (Becker, 2022). Like Ghana, Nigeria lacks specific legislation to mitigate the prevalence of street children, despite both international and domestic laws pertaining to children's rights. (Fatimayin, 2016).

The federal government of Nigeria works with many NGOs like Child Life-Line (CLL), the Child Welfare League of Nigeria (CWLN), the African Network for the Prevention and Protection Against Child Abuse and Neglect (ANPPCAN), and the Nigerian Network of Non-Governmental Organizations (NNNGO). Aransiola (2013) interviewed the stakeholders of child service. The result of the study states that the stakeholders are incapable of addressing the problems of street children due to inadequate skills and a lack of necessary facilities. Like many other developing countries, Nigeria faces corruption and difficulty implementing the laws, policies, and interventions that protect children.

The UN Child Rights Act of 2003, the African Charter on the Rights and Welfare of the Child from 1990, and subsequent federal children's rights laws passed by the Nigerian federal government provide important protection for children against abuse, neglect, and exploitation. Declaration on Education for All initiative (1990) concentrates on education. However, more targeted measures are necessary to address the specific needs of street children and ensure their rights are upheld (Osaiyuwu et al., 2021).

The support should promote resilience, social cohesion, child protection, education, psychosocial well-being, and livelihood development for the children and their families and communities. Initiatives such as vocational training, skills development, and life skills training can also aid in the children's reintegration into society. Efforts to address the issue include policies and programs established by the government and various organizations, such as UNICEF and Save the Children are still challenging to progress. Overall, the family, society, and government have mostly ignored the Nigerian child on the streets.

COMPARISON WITH WESTERN COUNTRIES

Street children exist in many Western countries, and the number is significantly lower than in Ghana and Nigeria. However, the challenges faced by street children in these countries are similar, such as poverty, family breakdown, and lack of access to education and healthcare (UNICEF, 2012). In addition, street children in Western countries may face challenges related to drug abuse, mental health issues, and involvement in criminal activities (Buckner & Bassuk, 2016). These children may engage in several types of work, such as scavenging for food and recyclable materials, begging, and performing odd jobs to make ends meet. Although street children are often associated with developing countries, they are also a growing concern in developed countries, where poverty, family breakdown, and social exclusion can force children onto the streets. Since the literature does not concentrate more on street children in Western countries, it is difficult to figure out their actual number and condition.

In the United States of America, there are now 1.6 million homeless and runaway children and adolescents. When a youth is forced to be homeless, they risk being involved in risky behaviors such as substance misuse, commercial sexual exploitation, criminal activity, and violent acts. However, street children also exhibit high resilience (Brouillard, 2021). According to OJJDP (2020), Many children living in the street have mental illness, sexually transmitted infections, malnutrition, skin diseases, gastrointestinal disorders, and tuberculosis. Rehabilitating homeless children to a healthy and purposeful existence in the face of such pervasive hazards to mental and physical well-being is challenging. 90% of street children use synthetic drugs, including prescription drugs, alcohol, nicotine, opiates, cannabis, and easily accessible industrial products such as shoe adhesive, according to studies. The report from National Center for Missing & Exploited Children (2020) states it takes about 24 and 36 hours before a minor is involved in sexual activities in exchange for food or sanctuary.

According to the report by another organization, the National Law Center on Homelessness & Poverty, street children in the United States are also more likely to be arrested and incarcerated than their peers, perpetuating the cycle of poverty and homelessness. The problem of street children was common soon after World War II and in the early 1990s and late 1980s. The U.S. government has taken several steps to reduce street children. One of the most important initiatives is the McKinney-Vento Homeless Assistance Act (1987) to address the issue of homelessness among children and youth. This act funds states and local communities to help homeless children and youth access education and other services. The act also requires school districts to provide transportation to homeless children and youth, regardless of their living situation.

Another initiative is the Runaway and Homeless Youth Act (1974) to address the needs of runaway and homeless youth. This act funds various services, including emergency shelters, transitional living programs, and counseling services for runaway and homeless youth. The act also supports street outreach programs to help connect homeless youth with services and resources. Additionally, the U.S. government has established the Interagency Working Group on Youth Programs, a collaborative effort between multiple federal agencies to address the needs of young people, including homeless and runaway youth. The group coordinates services and resources across agencies and identifies best practices for serving this population (youth.gov, n.d.).

Despite these initiatives, the problem of street children in the United States persists. The current issue with Street children is also more likely to experience mental and physical health problems and to be involved in the juvenile justice system. To address this issue, the U.S. government must continue prioritizing funding for programs and services that support homeless and runaway youth. For example, the Los Angeles DCFS foster care system concentrates on housing off the streets to minors than young adults (Ferguson et al., 2008). Apart from the emergency shelters and transitional living programs, the government should handle access to education, healthcare, and social services. Additionally, efforts should be made to address the root causes of homelessness and poverty, including affordable housing, job training, and access to mental health and substance abuse treatment.

Similarly, in Europe, street children are also a growing concern. According to a report by the European Union Agency for Fundamental Rights (2023), there are approximately 1.4 million children at risk of poverty or social exclusion in the European Union. This includes children living on the streets, in overcrowded and inadequate housing, and institutions. The report highlights that street children in Europe face various challenges, including a lack of access to education, healthcare, and social services, as well as discrimination and violence.

The World Bank (2002) states that although the situation of street children in developed countries may be less visible than in developing countries, it is no less severe. The report emphasizes the need for governments to prioritize street children's rights and needs and provide them with access to education, healthcare, and social services. Street children in developed countries face challenges impacting their health, education, and long-term well-being. While the situation of street children may be less visible in developed countries, it is no less severe than in developing countries. Governments and international organizations must work together to address the root causes of homelessness and poverty and to provide street children with the care and protection they need to thrive.

Approaches to addressing the issue of street children vary between Western countries and Ghana and Nigeria. Western countries focus on providing comprehensive support services, such as housing, healthcare, education, and counseling, on helping street children transition out of homelessness (Buckner & Bassuk, 2016). In contrast, in Ghana and Nigeria, efforts focus on providing necessities such as food and shelter and promoting education and vocational training opportunities (Ankomah & Omoregie, 2019; Olowa, 2020). The earlier we engage, the more likely we can increase resilience and reduce exposure. The potential long-term adverse effects of the abovementioned etiological conditions.

CONCLUSION

This chapter has provided insight into street children, including their defining characteristics, reasons for being on the streets, and challenges. The subsequent segments focused on street children in Sub-Saharan countries - Ghana and Nigeria- emphasizing the government and non-governmental organizations' responses to the issue. Both countries have larger population of street children, for example; major cities like Accra of Ghana, with 204,000 street children, and Lagos, Nigeria, with over 100,000 street children (Dankyi & Huang, 2021). Ghana is undergoing significant transformation where their indigenous institutions are transitioning and modernizing (Boakye-Boaten, 2006). However, this transitional phase has created a gap in social responsibility and accountability among individuals, groups, and communities. The difficulty of street children is a reality that should be a concern for all members of society, particularly social advocates and policymakers (Nnama-Okechukwu et al., 2023).

Similarly, Nigeria's governmental institutions are not prepared to handle the growing population of street children, necessitating the proper implementation of the Nigeria Child Rights Act passed in 2003 (Alawiye-Adams & Babatunde, 2013). Such measures could improve the standards of practice in Social Welfare Departments and other government agencies, including the police department.

The next section of the chapter examined the situation of street children in the West, mainly United States, where homelessness is tackled through different approaches, such as Runaway and Homeless Youth Act, DCFS foster care system, and other. Organizations such as missions and permanent supportive housing providers have given shelter for the homeless population in the West. However, despite the billions of dollars spent on combating homelessness, the homeless population continues to rise, indicating a need for continued political action and funding to address the problem. There is a need for concerted efforts from all stakeholders, including government and non-government organizations, to protect vulnerable children (Larkin et al., 2019).

Non-Governmental Organizations (NGOs) have played a vital role in addressing the issue of street children, providing services that local and national governments are unable to afford in both the Sub-Saharan countries and the West discussed in this chapter. However, their programs are more effective on a smaller scale, and reducing the number of street children requires a collective effort. Therefore, it is crucial to approach the issue of street children with involvement of governmental organizations and non-governmental organizations, implement preventative programs and policies, and address the underlying social and economic factors contributing to the problem.

> *"It is not the lack of knowledge or means that is at the root of our most serious social problems. We know what to do and how to do it. What is lacking is the power to effect change."- (Dewees & Klees, 1995).*

REFERENCES

Alawiye-Adams, A. A., & Babatunde, A. (2013). Street Children Phenomenon in Nigeria: The Challenges and Way Forward *SSRN*: https://ssrn.com/abstract=2325114 or http://dx.doi.org/DOI: 10.2139/ssrn.2325114

Ankomah, A. K., & Omoregie, P. (2019). Street children in Ghana: A neglected problem that requires urgent attention. *Journal of Social Science Studies*, *6*(1), 54–70. DOI: 10.5296/jsss.v6i1.14384

Antwi Bosiakoh, T., & Obeng, B. A. (2021). Socio and ethno-cultural embeddedness of transnational Nigerian immigrant entrepreneurs in Ghana. *CMS*, *9*, 55. DOI: 10.1186/s40878-021-00271-z

Aptekar, L. (1994). Street Children in the Developing World: A Review of Their Condition. *Cross-Cultural Research*, *28*(3), 195–224. DOI: 10.1177/106939719402800301

Aransiola, J. O. (2013). Providing Sustainable Supports for Street Children in Nigeria: Stakeholders Challenges and the Policy Options Available. *Advances in Applied Sociology*, *03*, 172–177. DOI: 10.4236/AASOCI.2013.33023

Ayenew, M., Kabeta, T., & Woldemichael, K. (2020). Prevalence and factors associated with substance use among street children in Jimma town, Oromiya national regional state, Ethiopia: A community based cross-sectional study. *Substance Abuse Treatment, Prevention, and Policy*, *15*, 61. DOI: 10.1186/s13011-020-00304-3

BBC. (2019). Nigeria profile - Timeline. BBC News. https://www.bbc.com/news/world-africa-13949550

Beauchemin, E. (1999). *The Exodus: The growing migration of children from Ghana's rural areas to the urban centers*. CAS & UNICEF.

Blum, R. W. (2007). Youth in Sub-Saharan Africa. *The Journal of Adolescent Health*, *41*(3), 230–238. DOI: 10.1016/j.jadohealth.2007.04

Boakye-Boaten, A. (2006). An examination of the phenomenon of street children in selected communities in Accra (Ghana) [Doctoral dissertation, Ohio University*]. OhioLINK Electronic Theses and Dissertations Center*. https://rave.ohiolink.edu/etdc/view?acc_num=ohiou1162599630

Boakye-Boaten, A. (2008). Street children: Experiences from the streets of Accra. *Academia.edu*. https://www.academia.edu/65589458/Street_Children_Experiences_from_the_Streets_of_Accra

Boateng, A., & Dako-Gyeke, M. (2022). Child Labor in Ghana: Current Policy, Research, and Practice Efforts. In Ssewamala, F. M., Sensoy Bahar, O., & McKay, M. M. (Eds.), *Child Behavioral Health in Sub-Saharan Africa*. Springer., DOI: 10.1007/978-3-030-83707-5_13

Briggs, A., Mayhew, H., & Bradley, J. L. (1966). Review of Selections from "London Labour and the London Poor,". *Scientific American*, *215*(1), 123–126. https://www.jstor.org/stable/24930998

Buckner, J. C., & Bassuk, E. L. (2016). Mental disorders, substance abuse, and their comorbidity among homeless youth. In *Handbook of Homelessness in the United States* (pp. 263–277). Springer.

Council on Foreign Relations. (2021). Boko Haram in Nigeria. Council on Foreign Relations. https://www.cfr.org/backgrounder/boko-haram-nigeria

Dankyi E, Huang KY. (2021). Street Children in Ghana's Golden Triangle Cities: Mental Health Needs and Associated Risks. *Child Psychiatry Hum Dev*. 53(4):840-851. DOI: . Epub. PMID: 34350504.DOI: 10.1007/s10578-021-01223-5

Dankyi, E. K. (2022). Children Living on the Street: Current Efforts in Policy Research and Practice in Ghana. In Ssewamala, F. M., Sensoy Bahar, O., & McKay, M. M. (Eds.), *Child Behavioral Health in Sub-Saharan Africa*. Springer., DOI: 10.1007/978-3-030-83707-5_14

Dewees, A., & Klees, S. J. (1995). Social Movements and the Transformation of National Policy: Street and Working Children in Brazil. *Comparative Education Review*, *39*(1), 18.

Dosumu, M., Olumide, A. O., & Omotade, O. O. (2016). Predictors of psychoactive substance use among street children in Ibadan Municipality, Nigeria. *International Journal of Child and Adolescent Health, Suppl.Special Issue: Developmental Issues in Children and Adolescents: Promotion of Positive Youth Development*, 9(2), 195-202. https://login.pvamu.idm.oclc.org/login?url=https://www.proquest.com/scholarly-journals/predictors-psychoactive-substance-use-among/docview/2410492384/se-2

Federal collaboration. Federal Collaboration | Youth.gov. (n.d.). https://youth.gov/feature-article/federal-collaboration

Ferguson, K. M., Dortzbach, K., Dyrness, G. R., Dabir, N., & Spruijt-Metz, D. (2008). Faith-based programs and outcomes for street-living youth in Los Angeles, Mumbai, and Nairobi. *International Social Work*, *51*(2), 159–177. DOI: 10.1177/0020872807085856

Hansen, W. W., Jima, K., Abbas, N., & Abia, B. (2016). Poverty and Economic Deprivation Theory: Street Children, Quranic Schools/Almajirai and the Dispossessed as a Source of Recruitment for Boko Haram and other Religious, Political and Criminal Groups in Northern Nigeria. *Perspectives on Terrorism*, *10*(5), 83–95. https://www.jstor.org/stable/26297656

ILO supports Nigeria's response to Child Labor Emergency. (2021). *Supports Nigeria's Response to Child Labour Emergency.* https://www.ilo.org/africa/about-us/offices/abuja/WCMS_803364/lang--en/index.htm

Larkin, H., Aykanian, A., & Streeter, C. L. (2019). Homelessness Prevention and Intervention in Social Work. doi:DOI: 10.1007/978-3-030-03727-7

McAlpine, K., Henley, R., & Mueller, M.. (2010). A Survey of Street Children in Northern Tanzania: How Abuse or Support Factors May Influence Migration to the Street. *Community Mental Health Journal*, *46*, 26–32. DOI: 10.1007/s10597-009-9196-5

Ministry of Gender. (2015). *Children and Social Protection.* Child and Family Welfare Policy.

Myburgh, C., Moolla, A., & Poggenpoel, M. (2015). The lived experiences of children living on the streets of Hillbrow. *Curationis*, *38*(1), 1274. DOI: 10.4102/curationis.v38i1.1274

Nhapi, T. G., & Agere, L. (2019). Street Children Revisited: Critical Perspectives on Street-Connected Children in a Fragile Zimbabwean Socioeconomic Climate. *Social Development Issues*, *41*(1), 64–82. https://login.pvamu.idm.oclc.org/login?url=https://www.proquest.com/scholarly-journals/street-children-revisited-critical-perspectives/docview/2295417072/se-2

Nigeria agrees to end military detention of children. *Human Rights Watch.* (2023). https://www.hrw.org/news/2022/10/03/nigeria-agrees-end-military-detention-children

Nnama-Okechukwu, C. U., Ebimgbo, S. O., Agha, A. A., & Onalu, C. E. (2023). Vulnerable children aiding visually challenged beggars in Nigeria: Need for social work intervention. *Children & Society*, *37*, 616–633. DOI: 10.1111/chso.12618

Number of children without critical social protection increasing globally. *UNICEF.* (n.d.). https://www.unicef.org/press-releases/number-children-without-critical-social-protection-increasing-globally

Olowa, O. W. (2020). Street children in Nigeria: Challenges and prospects. *Journal of Social and Political Sciences*, *3*(4), 968–974. DOI: 10.31014/aior.1993.03.04.155

OPEC. (2021). Nigeria. OPEC. https://www.opec.org/opec_web/en/about_us/169.htm

Overview. *World Bank.* (2021). https://www.worldbank.org/en/region/afr/overview

Owoaje, E. T., Adebiyi, A. O., & Asuzu, M. C. (2009). Socio-demographic characteristics of street children in rural communities undergoing urbanization. *Annals of Ibadan Postgraduate Medicine*, *7*(1), 10–15. DOI: 10.4314/aipm.v7i1.64055

Sexual Exploitation of Children. (2015). Office of Juvenile Justice and Delinquency Prevention. *Office of Juvenile Justice and Delinquency Prevention.* https://ojjdp.ojp.gov/programs/sexual-exploitation-children

Street children worldwide - abuse, violence, impunity, poverty, addiction & HIV. *Compass Children's Charity.* (2021). https://www.compasschildrenscharity.org.uk/about-us/street-children-worldwide/

The McKinney-Vento homeless assistance act. Institute for Children Poverty Homelessness. (n.d.). https://www.icphusa.org/mkv/

UNICEF. (2012). Children living in the streets. Retrieved from https://www.unicef.org/media/54896/file/UNICE

UNICEF Nigeria, & Nigeria. (2012). *Situation analysis of children and women in Nigeria.* Related UNICEF Websites. https://www.unicef.org/nigeria/reports/situation-analysis-children-and-women-nigeria

Van Blerk, L. (2015). *Growing up on the streets: Building networks of knowledge exchange for delivering impact.* University of Dundee., https://gtr.ukri.org/projects?ref=ES/M006107/1

Wachaya, D., Fandel, G., Byrne, J., Watts, J., Bellinger, F., & Phillips, S. (2022). *Understanding the Nigerian child soldier crisis - Thred Website.* Thred Website. https://thred.com/change/understanding-the-nigerian-child-soldier-crisis/

WBI working papers - World Bank. (n.d.). https://documents1.worldbank.org/curated/en/344301468763803523/pdf/263880WBI0Street0children.pdf

Williams, C. (1993). Who are "street children?" A hierarchy of street use and appropriate responses. *Child Abuse & Neglect*, *17*(6), 831–841. DOI: 10.1016/s0145-2134(08)80013-0

World Atlas. (2021). Ethnic Groups Of Nigeria. *WorldAtlas.* https://www.worldatlas.com/articles/ethnic-groups-of-nigeria.html

World Bank. (2021). Nigeria. *World Bank.* https://data.worldbank.org/country/nigeria

Chapter 7

Exploring the Labeling Theory of Deviance in Barbados:

How Youths' Perceptions of the 'Deviant' Label Is Not Accepted

Nicole Branch-Ellis
Bowie State University, USA

ABSTRACT

This chapter presents findings from a study exploring the extent to which formal interactions with social control agents may propel youth toward delinquent self-perceptions. Using the West Indian island of Barbados as a case study, this research examined the juvenile justice system and juveniles perception of their experiences with the law. This research investigated how youths' exposure to arrest and incarceration affected the likelihood that the juveniles would label themselves negatively, assessed the importance of perceived negative labeling on delinquency, and examined the impact of detention on youths' perceptions of their future possibilities. Findings show that being publicly branded as a deviant does not equate to the acceptance of a deviant label. This research shows that labeling was less likely to be internalized based on the juvenile's social environment; personal, family, and peer history with the law; view of the offenses; personal characteristics and strength; and the practices of social control agents that may acts as a buffer to accepting a deviant label.

DOI: 10.4018/978-1-6684-9343-4.ch007

INTRODUCTION

Little is known about the effects of negative labels on juveniles who have come into conflict with the justice system outside of the United States and Europe. This chapter examines labeling theory's tenets of the etiology of juvenile delinquency by exploring whether youth who come into contact with social control agencies in Barbados are negatively labeled as "delinquent" or "deviant," and the subsequent effects of any such labeling on youth. The purpose here is to determine the extent to which formal interaction with social control agents (in this case, the juvenile justice system comprised of the police, magistrate courts, and correctional institutions) propels juveniles towards delinquent self-perceptions.

Twenty-seven adolescents, 13 females and 14 males, from the Government Industrial School/Secure Residential Facility (GIS/SRF) (formerly named the Government Industrial School in Barbados - GIS) were surveyed. This research (a) documents the offenses committed by girls and boys that placed them in the juvenile detention facility; (b) describes and analyzes the detained youth's perceptions of their experiences with the juvenile justice system, to determine if there is a relationship between the courts' adjudication and the adoption of a deviant self-perception; and (c) discuss the gender-response to youth in conflict with the law. This research revealed two significant findings: (1) even though most of the girls in the system are non-violent offenders, girls are typically incarcerated at an alarmingly higher rate than their male counterparts and (2) contrary to the labeling theory hypothesis, youth in the justice system did not unanimously accept a deviant label because they had been incarcerated.

Notably, it was not until the late 1970s that researchers began to include females in their study samples (Belknap, 2001). Still, there was a point when female delinquents had not been given the same attention as their male counterparts, and everything we "knew" about female delinquency was primarily derived from studies of male delinquency (MacDonald and Chesney-Lind, 2001; Hipwell, Loeber, Stouthamer-Loeber, Keenan, White, and Kroneman, 2002). Now we can say that over the last couple of decades, there have been studies that have progressed our knowledge of gendered pathways and offending (Kruttschnitt, 2016). Akin to the United States, (Espinosa and Sorensen, 2015), adolescent girls have become the fastest-growing segment of the juvenile justice population in Barbados.

According to Sutton and Ruprah (2017), crime rates within the Caribbean have been rising since the 1980s, with almost half of the population (40%) believing that crime is the greatest peril to their country's stability. Despite the growing academic research focused on penal systems in the Caribbean (Bailey & Coore-Desai, 2009; Bergman, Seepersad, Safranoff, & Cafferata, 2020), these efforts have focused on adult incarcerated populations. There has been a limited number of empirical studies on juvenile delinquency, crime, and justice across the Caribbean (Freemon, Nuño, and Katz, 2020). Likewise, there is a shortage of empirical testing of the critical theoretical propositions (Bennett & Lynch, 1996; Birkbeck, 1999; Collins and Stockton, 2018), for instance, the testing of labeling theory in the study of deviance.

AN OVERVIEW OF LABELING THEORY

In the past, juvenile delinquent behavior was largely viewed as the product of the environment or characteristics of individual youths, taking the form of socio-economic hardship and/or behavioral issues in need of treatment or punishment. For this reason, labeling theorists focused their attention on the societal response to deviance. They steered criminological theory away from the juvenile offender and shifted the focus to the juvenile justice system. In so doing, labeling theorists sought to better understand how social control agencies and communities respond to and perpetuate the juvenile's behavior, and how that creates deviance. Labeling, as the name implies, is the formal and informal "application of stigmatizing, deviant 'labels' or tags by society on some of its members" (Akers and Sellers 2009, p.151).

Labeling theory has a long history in juvenile delinquency research. Frederick M. Thrasher's (1927) study of juvenile gangs in Chicago was one of the early examinations of the negative consequences of official labels on delinquents. This was followed by Frank Tannenbaum's study on the "dramatization of evil" in 1938. His premise was that officially labeling a person as "delinquent" may cause that person to become what he has been told he is, much like the "self-fulfilling prophecy" of Robert Merton. Another early proponent of labeling theory is Edwin M. Lemert (1951), who developed the concepts of primary and secondary deviance. His was the first analysis that emphasized "the effects of the social control system on the occurrence and form of deviant behavior and crime". However, it was not until the early 1960s when Howard S. Becker, published his analysis of deviance in his book *Outsiders* (1963) and a journal article entitled *The Other Side*, that he proposed that deviance was fashioned by people with biases against poor and powerless individuals.

The labeling approach has three main assumptions. The tenets of the labeling approach begin with the basic assumption that several factors can influence a juvenile's initial acts of delinquency (known as primary deviance), acts that are so sporadic and incidental that they hold transitory significance to the actor (Scheff, 1966). However, it is society's reaction to the primary acts of delinquency that can place the juvenile in the new status role of "deviant" (Meade, 1974). The fundamental assumption of the labeling theory of deviance is that the negative reactions of members of society expressed towards a first-time offending individual can result in negative self-perceptions, and foster further delinquent involvement, which is known as secondary deviance (Meade, 1974; Adams, Robertson, Gray-Ray, and Ray, 2003). The labeling approach is society's reaction to deviation. Negative stigmatization of juveniles places them at a higher risk of acting in accordance with the "deviant" label (Akers and Sellers 2009, p.155). The final assumption of labeling theory is that the official application of the "delinquent" label is not only dependent on the juvenile's behavior, but also on factors such as the juvenile's age, sex, race, and

Deviance is a social construct – social groups (in particular, social control agencies) define certain actions as deviant, and then stigmatizing sanctions are applied to the "rule breakers," who are labeled, or as Becker (1963) put it, made to feel like "outsiders" to other members of society. This process produces a pattern of deviance. Becker argues that a deviant is "one to whom that label has successfully been applied; deviant behavior is behavior that people so label" (Becker 1963, p. 9). Deviance thus has less to do with the actual act committed by the juvenile than the enforcement of rules and impositions of sanctions for breaking socially defined rules. Lofland (1969, p. 14) has characterized deviance as "the name of the conflict game in which individuals or loosely organized small groups with little power are strongly feared by a well-organized, sizable minority or majority who have a large amount of power".

As Howard S. Becker advised, "students of deviance cannot assume that they are dealing with a homogeneous category when they study people who have been labeled deviant" (1963, p. 9), for not all individuals who have been negatively labeled have committed a deviant act. Likewise, not only are labelers guilty of biased or selective application of laws toward individuals they consider rule-breakers but labeled individuals may also develop a distorted perception of their pre-labeling behavior as deviant because official agents of social control have previously assigned them a role. To labeling theorists, labeled individuals have been victimized by social control agents.

Symbolic Interactionism

Symbolic interactionism offers the theoretical base for labeling theory's explanation of deviant and criminal behavior (Akers and Sellers, 2009; Adams, Robertson, Gray-Ray, and Ray, 2003). The primary tenets of a symbolic interactionist perspective emphasize meanings, and face-to-face interaction through language, gestures, and individual self-identity. In symbolic interactionism, the individual is the unit of analysis. Society is based on the individual – patterns of interaction, competition, deviance, and individual definition of the world. An individual's belief systems, norms, and values are garnered from others, interpreted, and acted upon. Symbolic interactionism is a combination of pragmatism (i.e., the theory of process accepting that reality does not exist in the world, but is created by an individual's actions, which then creates meaning) and Weber's idealism (i.e., the conscious thinking process of individuals as free agents who define aspects of their world).

Labeling theorists view labeled juveniles as people who have experienced some event, endured societal reaction, been publicly labeled a deviant, placed in a deviant role, followed by the development of negative self-perception which reinforces persistent juvenile delinquency and "career" adult criminal involvement. In particular, studies of labeling theory have concentrated on the process of youth adopting the label placed upon them at the formation of secondary deviant behavior. The view of this theory argues that negative self-perception follows rather than leads to delinquency (Shoemaker, 2000, p. 197).

The labeling perspective has also been criticized for theoretical ambiguity on some key concepts and the inability to verify propositions (Adams et al., 2003, p. 172). Research shows that some of its main tenets could not withstand theoretical and empirical examination. Some studies have concluded that formally labeling juveniles had greater reinforced or escalated offending; while others have maintained that formal labeling and sanctions do not influence delinquent careers. There is no consensus on labeling theory. But for all of its shortcomings, labeling theory's assessment of deviance endures because scholars continue to research the causes, effects, and consequences of labeling juvenile delinquents.

THE DIALOGUE ON DELINQUENCY AND CRIME IN BARBADOS

The Caribbean has a small number of detained youth (Freemon, Nuño, and Katz, 2020). According to Deosaran (2010), traditionally, the most common offenses juveniles commit in the Caribbean are behavioral/language problems, vandalism, burglaries, thefts, and drug offenses (transport and peddling). However, in recent years, the Caribbean community has experienced an escalation of violence in schools; including bullying, fights, vandalism, sexual assault, and homicide (Gentle-Genitty, Kim, Yi, Slater, Reynolds, and Bragg, 2017).

At a public meeting, Democratic Labour Party (DLP) member Rasheed Belgrave, an attorney by trade, argued that is unfair to criticize young men for choosing the path of violence without considering the underlying factors that would cause them to engage in such behaviors (Coppin, 2022).

In 2016, an officer with the Royal Barbados Police Force (RBPF) delivered a stern message to a group of campers attending a one-week residential Project S.O.F.T. (Safeguarding Our Future Today) camp. "Consider the consequences of your actions, if you do not want to come face to face with members of the Royal Barbados Police Force and end up being classified as a juvenile delinquent" (Moore, 2018). As a warning, the officer listed several at-risk behaviors that lead to contact with the police - aggressive behavior, violence, acting out sexually, involvement in substance abuse, making suicidal statements, lying, stealing, cheating, running away from home, and patterns of chronic truancy.

In Barbados, there have been growing concerns regarding youth violence and other antisocial behaviors. About 90 percent of juveniles arraigned in juvenile court are charged with drug-related offenses, according to (former) Magistrate of the Juvenile Court Faith Marshall-Harris (The Nation Newspaper, 2008). She stated that drugs are at the root of juvenile offenses. The magistrate identified teenagers 13 to 17 years of age as being the largest group of illegal drug users, primarily marijuana and alcohol. Magistrate Marshall-Harris contended that youth from all strata of society arrested on drug-related charges are represented in juvenile court.

As a result, there has been an outcry for more to be done to combat the perceived rising rate of juvenile delinquency and criminality in Barbados. The community response to this outcry has been to arrest youth for their delinquent and criminal actions. However, the Registrar of the Supreme Court of Barbados and a former magistrate with the Juvenile Court, Barbara Cooke-Alleyne, contended that children in Barbados are given tougher penalties than adults for committing similar offenses (Barbados Government Information Services, 2015). Over the years, the government of Barbados has been criticized for maintaining archaic laws and practices that disregard the country's international treaty obligations.

The Age of Criminal Responsibility, Comparatively

The minimum age of criminal responsibility refers to the youngest age a person can be formally processed in a justice system. For 93 years, the minimum age of criminal responsibility in Barbados was 11 years (the *Juvenile Offenders Act of 1932*, and *the Reformatory and Industrial Schools Act of 1926*) and 18 years the age of majority, the beginning of legal adulthood. However, in 2019, Barbados passed the Juvenile Justice Bill, under this new legislature, the minimum age of criminal responsibility was raised to 12 years. Furthermore, it was declared that children under 14 years old would no longer be confined to a penal institution (Barbados Today, 2019). The Child Justice Bill would replace the *Reformatory and Industrial Schools Act of 1926* law, as the reform is an effort to bring Barbados in compliance with the United Nations rules of children deprived of their liberties.

Comparatively, 24 states in the United States have no minimum age for prosecuting children and there is no state-by-state consensus regarding an appropriate minimum age for juvenile prosecutions. Thus, the state of Florida has set 7 as the minimum age, and New Hampshire and Maryland have declared 13 to be the minimum age of youth court jurisdiction for prosecution (National Juvenile Justice Network, 2023).

Even though, the Juvenile Justice Bill in Barbados has increased the minimum age of criminal responsibility, Barbados' juvenile justice system, though higher than some Caribbean nations - Grenada, Trinidad & Tobago, Antigua & Barbuda, St. Vincent & the Grenadines, Anguilla, Guyana, St. Kitts & Nevis, and Suriname, which range in order from age 7 to 10; and is on par with some of its Caribbean and Latin American neighbors (UNICEF. n.d.); it is still not in line with international best practices. According to The United Nations Committee on the Rights of the Child (UNCRC), over 50 States "have raised the minimum age following the ratification of the Convention, and the most common minimum age of criminal responsibility internationally is 14" (United Nations, 2019, p. 6).

WHAT WE LEARNED ABOUT YOUTH INVOLVED IN THE JUVENILE JUSTICE SYSTEM IN BARBADOS

The question becomes, when using a social context such as that of Barbados, for example, as opposed to the United States or England, would juveniles who have passed through the juvenile justice system have internalized the official label placed upon them by the juvenile justice system, or would they refuse it? Does being processed through the juvenile justice system have a stigmatizing effect as labeling theorists propose? To what extent is society's response to deviant acts mediated by the influence of social factors? And does gender affect the acceptance or refusal of the deviant label?

This research found that, unlike in the United States and Europe, negative labels were less likely to be internalized based on environmental factors, personal characteristics, and the informal practices of social control agents that acted as buffers to the acceptance of a deviant label. This study also found that girls made up forty-two percent of the incarcerated juvenile justice population. Though most of the girls in the system were non-violent offenders, girls were typically incarcerated at a higher rate than their male counterparts.

The Importance of Age

Age is considered an important demographic factor when examining juvenile delinquent behavior. The age of minimum responsibility for which a child may be prosecuted for criminal activity assumes that children of a certain age are competent and responsible enough to be adjudicated in juvenile court. According to Griffin (2003), the majority of states and the District of Columbia hold children 14 years of age and older to be mature enough to be responsible for their offenses and can even be tried as adults in criminal court. Due to this and the middle stage of adolescent development, when it is said that intellectual curiosity develops; 11, 12, and 13-year-old, youth detained at the GIS were excluded from taking part in the survey, instead only 14 to 19-year-old participants were utilized. For this study, the maximum age was determined to be 19 years because a day before their nineteenth birthday is the maximum age youth can be detained in the Government Industrial School.

The largest group of juveniles (48 percent) was 16 years of age. It is supposed that antisocial wrong-doings begin and reach their zenith during the teenage years and promptly deteriorate with the changeover into adulthood. Contact with the police and subsequent arrest of young male and female delinquents was prevalent and as the age-specific self-reported arrest data indicates, there is no difference between females and males. All but one female indicated that they had been arrested before the time that landed them in the detention facility and females just like males had been in conflict with the police from as young as 11 years of age.

Youth Processed Through GIS in Barbados

With permission from the Barbados Ministry of Home Affairs, the Principal of the Government Industrial School made available figures on the number of youth temporarily remanded to and committed for detention to the Government Industrial School and the reasons for their detention. According to the figures obtained from the GIS (see Table 1) between 2001 and 2011, one thousand four hundred and forty-one juveniles (966 males and 475 females) were remanded to the detention facility while pending adjudication by the magistrate in the juvenile court. On average, that was approximately 96 males and 47 females sent to each facility per year; but in actuality, the intake figures for remanded youth look quite different. From 2001, the number of males remanded to the GIS by the court rose from 78 that year to a high of 115 in 2006. From there, the number of males sent to GIS on remand steadily dropped to 76 in 2011. The trend for females had not been so smooth. The number of females remanded to the GIS during the same period fluctuated every year, with a high of 59 in 2001. The year 2010 marked female juvenile remand intake reaching a low in the 20s for the first time in the decade under review. In 2011, the number of females remanded to the GIS by the court was 22.

Table 1. Juveniles remanded and committed to GIS 2001-2011

Years	Remanded		Committed	
	Males	Females	Males	Females
2001	78	59	06	11
2002	78	47	08	11
2003	87	56	21	15
2004	87	54	05	12
2005	102	38	18	06
2006	115	50	15	04
2007	87	49	10	10
2008	94	31	15	09
2009	88	43	15	08
2010	74	26	15	07
2011	76	22	09	06
Total	**966**	**475**	**137**	**99**

The number of juveniles sentenced by the juvenile court to the GIS in the same 10-year span, which witnessed 1441 males and females being remanded to the GIS, was 236. That is 137 males and 99 females. During this time, the largest number of males and females sentenced to the GIS was 21 and 15, respectively, in 2003. The following year GIS opened its doors to the smallest number of male residents in years, five. In 2006, they also received the least amount of girls, four (see Figure 1).

Figure 1. Graphic illustration of juveniles remanded and committed to GIS 2001-2011

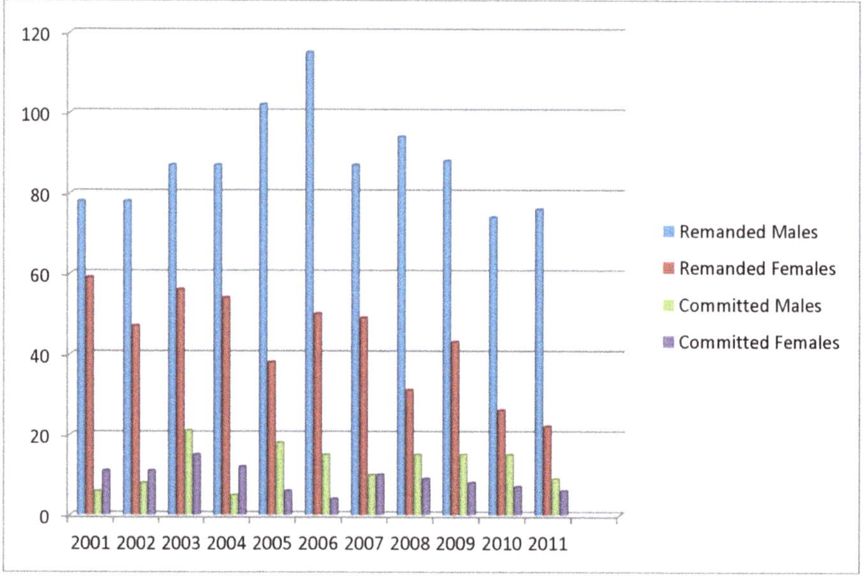

Offenses Juveniles Participated In

Between 2001 and 2011, as Table 2 shows, the bulk of the offenses males were remanded to the GIS for, in descending order included: theft/burglary, wandering, assault/bodily harm, possession of contraband, breaching probation trespassing/ loitering, and wounding. The list of offenses for which the females were remanded to GIS is shorter, but interesting nonetheless. Every year, each of the offenses for which females, in the last ten years have been charged with committing has been in the single digests except one, wandering. The crime of choice for minor females in Barbados seems to be aimlessly walking around unsupervised. This status offense accounts for 284 of the 499 charges against females remanded to GIS in the 10 years under review.

Table 2. Most common offenses for remanded juveniles 2001 – 2011

Offense	Committed	
	Males	Females
Assault/Bodily Harm	127	33
Breach Probation	57	66
Causing Disturbances/Violent Disorder	5	17
Criminal Damage	29	3
Insulting and abusive language	8	7
Living in circumstances	N/A	16
Offensive Weapon	20	5
Refractory Behavior	24	13
Robbery	26	N/A
Possession of a Substance	65	5
Theft/Burglary(males)/Shoplifting (females)	223	10
Threats	37	8
Trespassing/Loitering (males) Trespassing (female)	45	1
Wandering	167	284
Wounding	40	11

The Role of Familial and Community Relationships on the Stigmatizing Effect of Incarceration

The *Juvenile Self-Report Questionnaire* (Branch, 2012), was administered to 27 adolescent participants – 13 females (48.1 percent) and 14 males (51.9 percent) remanded to the Government Industrial School. This survey instrument was designed to examine whether or not the tenets of labeling theory are present in the perspectives of juveniles who had been processed through the juvenile justice system in Barbados. The approach of this exploratory case study analysis offered an alternative method and analysis to the international study of juvenile delinquency that has limited our theoretical understanding of deviance. Branch (2012), used primary data collected from surveys of youth at the Government Industrial School in Barbados in March 2012. The study examined a sample of primarily Black youth ages 14 through 19 years of age.

As indicated by the youth and verified by the official GIS data; juveniles are sentenced to the Government Industrial School for numerous reasons or offenses. To ascertain whether or not the stigmatizing effect of incarceration on juveniles has been weakened because juveniles have relationships or interactions with others who may have been previously arrested, this query was broken down into two parts. To find out if there had been any criminal activities in the youth's environment that did not directly concern them, the respondents were asked if any of their parents, other relatives, friends, or neighbors had been arrested and if any of their parents, other relatives, friends or neighbors had to appear in court on criminal charges. Each relationship was looked at separately.

The respondents revealed that almost half their parents had been arrested and been to court; several of their family members and neighbors had also been arrested and been to court; but almost all of their friends had also been arrested and made a court appearance. Of the twenty-seven youth, only 10 of them indicated that they did not feel stigmatized because of their arrest and only five of those youth had a parent who had also been arrested. However, on the whole, sixteen youths indicated that at some time they felt stigmatized by both their arrest and incarceration. Thus, over half of the sample felt stigmatized by their experiences regardless of having a parent, other relative, friend, or neighbor who had been arrested or gone to court.

When taking the gender of the respondents into account, a few females revealed that they had felt some degree of stigmatization (nine for arrest and seven for sentence to GIS), while some males had, too (eight for arrest and nine for sentence to GIS). Even though these numbers are small and the variation is virtually non-existent the numbers do imply that the female juveniles felt less stigmatized after their initial feeling upon arrest while the males felt more stigmatized by the later incarceration.

The important thing to note about the questions asked of the youth regarding relatives, friends, or neighbors' arrests and court appearances is that we do not know the outcomes of those incidents. We do not know if the charges were dropped or if the relatives, friends, or neighbors went to prison, received probation, or community service. The outcomes may have impacted how youth feel about their arrest and incarceration at GIS. Neighborhood influences are considered to be important drivers of delinquency (Hill & Morris, 2017; Nolterieke, 2020). It is possible, that the positive or negative relationships between the juveniles and their parents/guardians, other family members, peers, and neighbors may be an indicator of the juvenile's participation in delinquent behavior and how they view the social reaction to their behavior. Also, these findings may have been as Hirshfield (2008) noticed in his study, that by the time of a juvenile's first arrest, the youth may already view arrest as a normal part of their community life.

The results were not as expected. In addition, there was not a noticeable difference between male and female respondents.

Juveniles' Perceptions of Being "Cut Off," Stigmatized, and "Deviant"

The youth were asked if they felt cut off from their family and friends because of their incarceration. While placed in the rehabilitative facility, the youth were allowed visitors, letters, and phone calls on a restricted basis, as a means of keeping in contact with life outside of the facility. More than half of the respondents expressed that they had felt disconnected from their loved ones and felt just as detached from their communities, but of that group, only a small number (7) had also felt stigmatized by their family and community. Those who did feel cut off from family and friends expressed feelings of devastation and depression, but here are some articulations in their own words:

> Females:
> "I am unhappy."
> "I miss them badly."
> "I am away from the people that love and try with me."
> "I feel very sad because if I did what I was to do I would be loved."
> Males:
> "I feel cut off because they can only visit me once in three weeks."
> "I feel bad when I cannot see them every day."
> "I feel bad because my family and friends are outside enjoying themselves without me."
> "Some do not visit me"
> "It makes me feel like I want to escape"
> "I am like a bird in a cage I just want to fly again"

Of all the respondents, only one explained his stay in the juvenile detention facility to be beneficial and communicated in a profound way why he did not feel cut off from his family and friends. He stated, "In here was a good thing for me because I could be dead right now." He was referring to the activities he was once involved in.

The youth's feelings of stigmatization by their families and communities, as well as stigmatization because of their arrest and incarceration were also examined to determine if it played a role in whether or not juveniles may identify themselves as "deviant." More youth stated that they never felt stigmatized by their family or the community than youth (6) who revealed that they had felt that way. Interestingly, when they did identify as feeling stigmatized, more youth felt it from their community than their family. Of the fifteen youth, who identified as being deviant, only nine of them indicated that they felt any type of stigmatization due to either their arrest or incarceration. On the whole, only a handful of youth who felt stigmatized by either family or their community or stigmatization because of their arrest or incarceration, also identified with a "deviant" perception of themselves. The juveniles garnered their perception of how they were viewed and ultimately stigmatized from the negative regard they received from both family members and the community.

Reasons youth felt stigmatized by their families:

Females:
"They look down on me."
"They thought wrong about me."
"My mother would exclude me and say she only has one child."
Males:
"They used to tell me that I am foolish."
"That's what my mother tells her friends."
"Some people said I was a criminal"

Reasons youth felt stigmatized by the community are:

Females:
"By verbally abusing and cursing me."
"Everyone used to tell my parents a lot of bad things about me."
"They said I would never make it."
Males:
"They would always say I will end up in the police's hands."
"People always said negative things to me."

Respondents were also asked questions to find out if juveniles who view their friends as "deviant" would also identify themselves as "deviant." Almost all of the youth who thought themselves to be deviant also thought the company they kept to be the same. Over half of the sample identified with the "deviant" label; however, those individuals were primarily female (nine versus six males). Given the responses in the study, it seemed as though females viewed themselves to be deviant because they were having personality and feelings of independence conflicts with their authority figures. Most of the girls who identified as "deviant" conveyed that doing things their way got them into trouble. While the males held their view of deviance in terms of the company they associated with.

Reasons for viewing friends as deviant consist of:

Females:
"They had the same perspective of life as me, to do as I wanted."
"We roll deep."

"I wanted my friends to act like me."
"They looked for trouble."
"I was a gang member and we often looked for fights"
"They did all the same things I did, but they pulled up their socks after I came in."
Males:
"My friends got into a lot of trouble."
"I like the bad boy life."
"I never liked to listen."

Somewhat in line with the present study, are Hirshfield's (2008) findings that youth resisted negative delinquent labels and were mostly interested in shunning the informal labels of their family and friends rather than the formal labels of the juvenile justice system. Reasons for taking on the "deviant" label include:

Females:
"Because I wanted to do as I please."
"I wanted my way to do what I wanted."
"I was rude and disobedient to my family members"
"I like things my way and used to start a lot of fights."
"Most of the time I was in trouble with the law"
"I was never interested in schoolwork. I did all the wrong things, that's what interested me."
Males:
"Because of the friends I hang out with."
"I believed I was a wicked boy."
"They told me I was."

For this category, a lot of nuances were taken into consideration. However, the results were not entirely what were expected. This is largely based on the fact that there are no apparent differences between the male and female respondents, juveniles who felt cut off, stigmatized, or identified themselves as "deviant," and those who did not.

More than half of the juveniles felt disconnected from their families and communities, yet only a small number of juveniles felt stigmatized by their family or community. as a result of, being processed through the juvenile justice system. There is no way to tell if those feeling stigmatized were juveniles with no prior arrest history, but as Paternoster and Iovanni acknowledged, this could be a result of already feeling excluded, "once an actor is excluded from major conventional life situations it is not unreasonable to assume that further exclusion would have little additional meaning" (1989, p. 386).

Labeling, Self-Doubt, and Youth's Aspirations about Their Future

One may imagine that labeling leads to self-doubt about future aspirations. Thus, the juveniles' plans for their lives after they transition out of GIS were examined; about feelings of stigmatization by their family and community, a deviant self-label, and barriers to a successful transition from the GIS.

The juveniles' plans for life after GIS include for the females: enrolling in trade school, community college, or university; and becoming a lawyer, nursing assistant, cosmetologist, and singer. One female stated in specific detail that her plans entail to, "go to college, go to law school in Trinidad, make money, be successful, serve God and support my mother." This same female stated in conversation that she asked the magistrate in court to place her in GIS because it would be easier for her mother. She did not want to give the wrong impression, so she argued that her home environment and her mother were not bad. She insisted that she knew being in the rehabilitative facility would not have been a terrible experience because she would be able to go to school and her mother would not have to pay for meals, uniforms, books, and other expenses. This contrasts with the sentiments of another female who expressed frustration with being confined because as she stated, "You are not allowed to see your young siblings and it's very hurtful to see that we are placed in here for 3-5 years and we never committed a crime, we just left home to maybe cool off."

The male respondents expressed similar goals to the females: to enroll in trade school, community college, or university; become an embalmer, a baker, a landscaper, a fireman, a soldier, a carpenter, and a West Indies cricketer. Only one person, a female, indicated that she did not know what she wanted to do with her life so she would continue to do what she knew, selling marijuana.

Many of the youth stated that there would be no barriers in their path to prevent them from achieving their objectives. But others, more realistically, stated that continued participation in antisocial behaviors and the negative attitudes of others could be hindrances to their good intentions. Equally so, many of the youth admitted that encouragement from both family and the GIS staff would go a long way in providing them with the supportive tools they needed to pursue their ambitions.

> Females:
> "After-care and follow-up care"
> "I need someone to give me that extra push and be there for me."
> Males:
> "Sports"
> "Programs"

The findings in this study illustrate the fact that the impact of a label may differ from one individual to another; thus some scholars (Paternoster and Iovanni, 1989; Bernburg and Krohn, 2003) have argued that the effect of a "deviant" label may depend on the personal characteristics of the youth.

Regardless, some scholars argue that legal processing and sanctions, in particular incarceration, can disrupt "conventional achievements and stigmatize an ever-larger class of individuals" (Apel and Sweeten 2010, p. 448) because stigmatized individuals are looked upon negatively by employers which limits their employment opportunities. As Barry, argues many young people are excluded from higher education, employment, and home ownership because of structural constraints and social inequalities such as lack of qualification for financial support (2010, p. 125).

Therefore, it is interesting that the juveniles in this study linked the support they would need to understand the importance of completing their Caribbean Examination Council (CXC) to be able to do other things in life. In the English-speaking Caribbean, CXC examinations are a milestone, it marks the five-year completion of one's secondary school education. This equivalent to the British O-level examination is also used to determine job qualifications, for employers want to know your numerical grade (1 through 5, with 1 being the best grade); what subjects were taken (e.g. mathematics, English literature, physics, social studies, French, arts and crafts, agricultural science, etc); and whether or not they were at the general or basic proficiency (general is typically preferred).

It has already been established that more youth never felt stigmatized by their family or the community than youth who felt stigmatized; however, over half of the sample identified with the "deviant" label. Interestingly, regardless of stigmatization and taking on the "deviant" label, all but one of the respondents expressed pursuing higher educational and trade school opportunities, legitimate employment, and positive family-oriented goals once they have completed their placement at the Government Industrial School. This indicates that the youth believe in themselves despite their circumstances or they have been told that despite their situations they can achieve or a combination of both. Despite being incarcerated at the island's juvenile detention facility, the youth in this sample were not jaded by their circumstances. For the most part, they were all determined to do better than they had before, to be positive and law-abiding citizens once they re-enter the general population.

This is consistent with research conducted by Unruh, Povenmire-Kirk, and Yamamoto (2009), who found that few incarcerated respondents had anticipated barriers to their educational and employment aspirations as they transitioned to adulthood. In fact, like the present study, the juveniles in the Unruh et al., study expected their future to include: specialized education, skilled work, home ownership, and starting a family. Interestingly, Unruh et al. make the point that for formally incarcerated youth acquiring and sustaining employment is a challenge because they do not normally have prior work history to rely on unless they took part in a work program while incarcerated. To that I say, not many juveniles leave secondary school with prior work experience anyway.

For all juveniles committed to the Government Industrial School, that is all juveniles sentenced to a minimum of 3 years to a maximum of 5 years, they can leave the detention facility and be eligible for a job because they are granted a clean police certificate of character to compliment the CXC qualifications and trade skills they earned while incarcerated. Moreover, employment applications in Barbados do not inquire nor require applicants to state and explain any prior convictions. That is the purpose of the police certificate of character. Knowing this probably equips these young people with confidence, for employers would not refuse employment because of their history since it has been erased. Thus, the deviant label does not hinder securing employment or furthering their education. This practice offers individuals a fresh start by making it possible for them to more easily re-enter society and abstain from deviant or criminal activities.

The majority of studies carried out on delinquency have centered on the family structure. Family structures have been constantly linked to juvenile delinquency; more to the point, family structure has been seen as an important predictive factor of initial and continued juvenile delinquency (Smith and Stern, 1997; Farrington et al., 1986). The reason is, that in society, the relationships between juveniles and their families influence the children's development of antisocial and delinquent behaviors. Therefore, it is likely that negative family relations can influence the deviance.

In an analysis of family disruption on deviance, Kierkus and Baer (2003) examined the impact of familial disruption on delinquent behavior on children's gender. Their findings indicated that the impact of family structure on juvenile delinquency is statistically equal for girls and boys. Thus, the researchers concluded that the effect of family structure on delinquency is unchanged by gender. Likewise, Farrington et al. (1986) contend that weak affectionate relationships (such as parental warmth or intimate communication) between parents and children are associated with delinquency. Adams, Robertson, Gray-Ray, and Ray (2003) found that the informal labeling of parents and peers was a significant predictor of general and serious delinquency. Likewise, Matsueda (1992) concluded from their research that parental labeling was a major predictive variable of delinquency.

As it turns out, children may view themselves negatively when their peer groups and parental figures view and treat them negatively. Thus, positive family relationships may play an influential role in juvenile delinquency and self-identity.

RESPONDENTS' ATTITUDE TOWARDS THE SURVEY

The data collected from the youth was collected in an environment that was familiar to them, classrooms that they routinely used and spent much of their time. The researcher wanted to present as non-threatening, polite, respectful, and encouraging; and could only guess that they came across as honest, trustworthy, engaged, and listening. When interacting with both the female and male juveniles they were all polite and respectful. It was clear that there are institutional rules of conduct, for instance upon a visitor entering a room, all juveniles stood and greeted the researcher with a respectful yet slightly apprehensive "good morning". This was anticipated because the researcher was a stranger, but most importantly a stranger seeking their assistance. It took a lot longer for the boys than the girls to warm up to being interviewed. It could have been because of gender that the girls felt comfortable talking to the researcher about their secondary school experiences, whether the researcher ever got into trouble with the police, what university life is like, the reason for the interest in the research topic, how the research would benefit them, their plans for the future, and their good wishes and their admitted comfort with the researcher. Whilst, the boys wanted to know the age of the researcher, what they did for a living, and provided compliments. This was received as an expression of their youthful curiosity and ability to recognize when an opportunity was at their disposal. It seemed as though they wanted to find out as much from the researcher as they could – to make it a mutually beneficial experience.

Another factor that may have played a role in the females' ease in talking to the researcher was that we were alone for most of the time, whereas with the males an adult female counselor was in the room the entire time and we were periodically joined by her adult male colleague. In the end, the participant's perception of the researcher played a significant role in how honest and forthcoming the youth were. The juveniles were asked to disclose their past deeds; their family life, closeness, and any illegal activities; their arrest history; offense history; and their aspirations amongst other things. They were asked personal and maybe shameful things and the researcher expected, more like hoped, they would reveal this information to her, a stranger. Developing a questionnaire and making reference to the "Government Industrial School" on the instrument gave the youth a feeling that they mattered. One detained female at the GIS facility exclaimed in shock and surprise, "This questionnaire was made for us?" The researcher believed that seeing those words throughout the survey instrument communicated a feeling of importance and that put the participants at ease, to know that something was being done on their behalf. If the participants are comfortable, they are more likely to give forth information more sincerely and freely, and that increases transferability and internal validity for the qualitative and quantitative analyses.

These views were generated from the youth's expressions of gratitude, which were more openly expressed by the females. At the end of the survey, all of the respondents expressed their appreciation for conducting the study, but the females conveyed extra gratitude for the opportunity to be involved in this research and to be able to express their views in hopes that the research would benefit young people to come. As one female articulated, "This [study] may not help us in here right now, but it will help our yout" (West Indian pronunciation of youth). The youth were assured that their viewpoints and concerns would be respected and were thanked by the researcher for the opportunity to meet with them.

THE APPLICABILITY OF THE LABELING THEORY IN BARBADOS

If we accept labeling theory's premises, then we say it is a given, that those who are formally processed through Barbados' juvenile justice system will be officially labeled a "juvenile offenders" (as the title of the 1932 legislative act governing juveniles designates). Applying this argument, then we are also saying that the consequence of being officially labeled a delinquent may cause that person to become what he or she has been told he or she is. Thus, the official label may be the major event that pushes a juvenile to a pathway of blocked opportunities as they transition from adolescence to adulthood. Although the greatest amount of stigmatization comes at the community level, this incarcerated Barbadian juvenile sample does not entirely represent these notions.

Social Class

Twenty-six of the 27 respondents answered, "I don't know" to the household income question on the juvenile questionnaire. Though this high item non-response rate represents a lost opportunity to collect the data on social class needed to test an important argument of labeling theory in the U.S., it also provides another narrative about the social setting on the island.

Labelists typically contend that the effect of formal labeling is dependent upon the race and social class of the offender and that the acceptance of the official label is more consequential for minorities and impoverished individuals. Bernburg and Krohn argue that the labeling of disadvantaged juveniles "is enhanced by the negative stereotypes that are already associated with these youths in the mainstream culture" (2003, p. 1290). However, social class in Barbados does not mirror the U.S. In Barbados, there is a small upper class, a large middle and working class, and a small lower class. This middle class has been socially and politically mobile, attaining a political power that has not been reached by the middle classes in the U.S. Given the challenge of attaining household income from the respondents and the varying ways individuals may interpret their social realities, parent or guardian's occupation may have been a viable index for understanding the socio-economic status of the juveniles in the study.

Disparity Based on Gender

While any number of illegal acts is a cause for concern, it is important to note that fewer than 500 females went before the juvenile magistrate court from 2001 to 2011. The magistrate court, however, sentenced fewer than 100 of them to detention in a juvenile facility. This may be viewed as a good thing. We can surmise that the magistrate believes that the laws of the nation are archaic, and to sentence as many of the juveniles who pass through the courts to a minimum of 3 years or a maximum of 5 years would be harsh. After all, research has suggested that punitive sentencing practices increases recidivism, rather than reduces antisocial or criminal behavior (Wong, Bouchard, Gravel, Bouchard, and Morselli, 2016). Also, given the types of offenses, (for example, wandering and living in circumstances that would expose juveniles to harm or risk), and the close interactive care afforded to the juveniles in conflict with the law, it may not be a stigmatizing label applied to juveniles but a protective label.

With their work in the U.S., Kelly, Loeber, Keenan, and DeLamatre (1997) suggest that the chief delinquency risk factors for males have been poor impulsive control, hyperactivity, aggression, and poor peer relationships. In contrast, the strongest risk factors for females' delinquency have been abuse, victimization, substance abuse, mental health, failure in school, and dysfunctional family. Thus, according to Chesney-Lind and Shelden (1998, p. 92), "it is necessary to begin considering the importance of gender stratification in a patriarchal society."

While the gender gap in remanded youths to the Government Industrial School (GIS) has remained wide, committed youth to the detention facility have been narrowed during the last decade. The closing of the gender gap may be a result of increases in female delinquent or criminal activities or the magistrates have gotten tougher on females. At the same time in the United States, scholars were arguing that the increasing rate of female offending may reflect changes in policies and practices of schools, police, social welfare services, and the juvenile justice system that handles these females (Chesney-Lind and Okamoto, 2001). However, the upsurge in female juvenile offending may not be the sole cause of their increasing rates of arrests. Some have argued that the escalation is linked to the re-labeling of family conflicts (e.g. fights with siblings and parents) as violent offenses, instead of to an actual increase in delinquent behavior among females. There may be a gender bias in the processing of cases involving females, or a failure within the juvenile justice system to acknowledge and comprehend the distinctive developmental concerns or environmental needs of females passing through the system. This is evident in the differing ways males and females view themselves as deviant – males about their peer groups, and females about personality and quest for independence.

Gender has also been extensively examined in juvenile delinquency studies. It is believed that boys are the most perpetrators of illegal activities than girls at any age. This study is no different, according to the findings (see Table 2), males are twice as likely as females to appear before the juvenile court. However, the categories of offenses females are arrested for perpetrating are different from those of males. Furthermore, males have higher numbers of arrests in all crime categories than girls except for wandering and breaching probation. Thus, the offenses in which males and females are overwhelmingly present in juvenile court tell their own story.

To offer some context, Barbadian society is rather patriarchal even though many households are female-headed. Gender is not only limited to traits and behaviors but also encapsulates individuals into cultural ideals and stereotypes that guide how each is viewed. For females more than males, gender can be a restraint on their lives. Males are encouraged to leave the house and those who are seeking male role models tend to spend a lot of time with older males "hanging out on the block;" while females are expected to stay at home and bear the responsibilities of the household duties and caring for their siblings. Females seeking a male role model may also fall victim to older males, nonetheless, both groups of juveniles face the same dangers but it is usually played out in different ways. Males may have older associates who guide them to involvement in thefts, burglary, assault, and drugs (marijuana in particular); whereas, females wander and that is often associated with promiscuity and abuse by older males. Female delinquents are usually associated with an environment of family instability and/or physical and sexual abuse.

These findings could mean that the factors under examination are not necessarily mutually exclusive. We see that some youth feel stigmatized, cut off, and have unfavorable views of others and themselves, but the fact that so many did not feel these ways could be revealing something significant. For some juveniles there may have been just one path to the GIS, for others there may have been numerous pathways to delinquency. These pathways may stem from family fragmentation, exposure to violence in the home or community, substance and alcohol abuse, mental health problems, and violent or non-violent offense patterns. Regardless of the path, for as many juveniles who view themselves negatively, there are an equal number of their counterparts who do not view themselves in the same light. In addition to positive family bonds, these juveniles could be reporting high self-esteem and personal resilience levels that this study did not account for. The juveniles do not feel overwhelmingly stigmatized because of their arrest, incarceration, or by their families.

What is more, the juveniles are essentially split down the middle on their feelings of self-deviance. Incarceration is usually associated with the notion of being a disappointment, not a success. However, regarding their plans for the future, the juveniles believed that their education and becoming gainfully employed were opportunities within their grasp. All but one person had communicated a law-abiding future for themselves as they transitioned out of the Government Industrial School and onto adulthood and what is more, few juveniles anticipated barriers to their goals.

Labeling theory does not argue that once all youth come into contact with social control agencies subsequent deviant behavior will take place. The perspective simply seeks to illustrate the circumstances under which a youth's deviant orientation may produce labels, which may encourage additional delinquent involvement, or not, as in the case of this Barbadian sample.

The Role of Culture

In the 21st century, we still have not solved the problem of juvenile delinquency. This may be because we still do not understand how youths who commit delinquent acts and more serious offenses think and subsequently behave. In Barbados and abroad, there has been a wave of panic over the growth of delinquency and crime committed by juveniles. Even though the concern over juveniles' involvement in delinquency and crime is justified, it has been inflated by a few events around the world. As a result, the actions of the most serious offenders have created a fear of youth, even those who engage in status offenses.

Juvenile delinquency and crime in the U.S. seem to reflect a few highly dramatic crimes rather than statistical increases in delinquencies or crimes with the mass shooting at the Columbine High School by two teenagers in Colorado; the D.C. sniper shootings by a teenager and his adult accomplice; and the shootings in Red Lake, Minnesota where a teenager killed nine people and himself. England, too, has had a wave of violent youth crimes – the murder of a 2-year-old by two 10-year-old boys and the torture, sexual humiliation, and attempted murder of 9 and 11-year-old boys by 10 and 12-year-old brothers. Over the years, juvenile offending has been hyped and over-sensationalized, and the incidence of offending has been distorted.

As in the U.S. and England, juvenile delinquency and offending in Barbados have come into the limelight of the media, communities, and political discussions. For some, juvenile delinquency reflects the influence of popular culture, the deterioration of the family, and loose morals. Newspaper headlines reading: "Attorney General: time to halt crime," "AG youth crime concern," "Firm hand needed for problem kids," "Open eyes to sources of indiscipline," "Reform needed," "Gangs in school," and "Magistrate: Drug prevalence in youth a concern" argue youths of today are out of control and in dire need of discipline or rehabilitation. In Barbados, politicians have publicly urged parents, families, and community members to work together to help reduce youth involvement in drugs, crime, and other forms of delinquency.

The juvenile court, under the umbrella of the juvenile justice system, has official responsibility for juvenile offenders on the island. Thus, juveniles arrested for violent, nonviolent, and status offenses are tried and sentenced in juvenile courts under a more informal process than adult offenders. However, although the informal process is intended to be more lenient towards youths, then Acting Prime Minister of Barbados and Minister of Home Affairs, Freundel Stuart argued that the island's juvenile justice system is far too retributive. In his view, the system seeks revenge rather than rehabilitation in that it does not promote probation, community service, and other forms of correctional alternatives to incarceration (Austin 2009). He argues that alternate options to incarceration should be employed, and that non-custodial or community corrections alternatives would keep offenders in the community by building ties to family, employment, and other normal sources of stability and success. He has stated that "the Caribbean needs to focus its efforts on the rehabilitation and reintegration of juvenile offenders back into society" (Austin, 2009).

This claim that Barbados' juvenile justice system is not rehabilitating youth who come into conflict with the law and that the juvenile justice system is not effectively reintegrating juveniles back into society, suggests a possible disconnect between what the community knows and what is being accomplished. From the findings in this study, we see that the type of offenses and severity of crime in Barbados are different from the U.S. and England. This draws attention to two distinctions that affect labeling in Barbados: (1) the laws governing juveniles and (2) the practices of social control agents overseeing the juveniles. This reinforces the fact that deviance is a social construct that is relative to culture, circumstances, and the actor.

What labeling theory does not account for is that differing cultural settings may reveal behaviors that are not collectively endorsed, practiced, or enforced as deviant. For example, in Barbados, juveniles, especially females, are sentenced to the GIS for a minimum of 3 years and a maximum of 5 years, for living in circumstances that would expose them to harm or risk and wandering; yet, in the U.S. those would not justify institutionalizing a juvenile in a detention facility. One has to question the nature of such 'offenses;' exactly how offensive these 'offenses' are to the Barbadian people; why are they offensive; and how the severity and type of offense affects those being labeled. These are cultural distinctions in laws and practices not specified by labeling.

Impact of Formal vs. Informal Sanctions in Large-Scale vs. Small-Scale Societies

Typically, the larger a study's sample size, the more significant and reliable the findings. The sample size used in this study may be relatively small, but it should be viewed in its appropriate context, like the Rubin's vase. This image can switch between two black faces looking at one another on a white background, and a white vase on a black background. The overall numbers on the island are low. The Barbadian population of just over a quarter million people has had a committed juvenile population of less than one percent in the last 10 years. That is a commendable feat considering that the aim of any developed country should be to reduce the institutionalization of juveniles. Keeping in mind that juveniles are sentenced to the GIS for three to five years, every year, the number of youth committed to GIS is low. From 2001 to 2011, 137 males and 99 females were sentenced to the GIS by the juvenile court for a minimum of 3 or a maximum of 5 years incarceration. That is only 16 percent of the 1441 juveniles remanded to the GIS while awaiting adjudication in the juvenile court (see Figure 1).

Juvenile volunteers for this study were solicited from both Government Industrial School facilities. Taking the total number of juveniles committed to the GIS from 2001 to 2011, a statistical formula (Dillman, 2007) determined that 27 percent (± 10% sampling error and 95% confidence level) of the GIS committed population would be a suitable sample size. This study sampled 11 percent of the 236 youth committed in the last decade. During this time, the number of juveniles committed to the correctional facility has fluctuated with intake numbers as high as 21 males and 15 females in 2003, and numbers as low as five males in 2004 and four females in 2006. But also, during this time, committal sentences were vacated. Given the unknown number of youth monthly, weekly, and daily committed to GIS, the mathematical odds may be closer to the determined sample size of 27 percent than the 11 percent based on the known number of committed youth in 10 years.

In *Urbanism as a way of life*, Wirth (1930) argued that when populations grow too large, systems have to formalize sanctions to maintain order. "Formal controls are instituted to counteract irresponsibility and potential disorder. Without rigid adherence to predictable routines a large compact society would scarcely be able to maintain itself" (1930:38). The findings of the present study, particularly the acceptance or refusal of a deviant identity raise questions about the fluidity of deviant labels assigned by social control agents. This can be discussed in the context of Tönnies' (1887) distinctions between rural and urban communities, known as Gemeinschaft and Gesellschaft. In Gemeinschaft communities, social bonds are based on kinship and friendship. These communities are characterized by their small-scale, intimate communities with a strong sense of consensus, tradition, and informality. Gesellschaft communities are the opposite: they are large-scale societies that function on an impersonal and formal level, dependent upon the specialized skills of the people.

In the U.S., the general population and the sub-population of juvenile offenders are so large that they are treated with rigid formal sanctions and procedures that help to maintain order. They represent the quintessential Gesellschaft society. As previously explained, two types of labeling can take place. Formal and informal deviant 'labels' can have differing effects on juveniles. The labeling approach contends that formal interaction with social control agents pushes individuals towards delinquent self-concepts. Labelists argue that juveniles' perceptions of their "deviant" self-concept are heightened or created by their contact with the juvenile justice system, and social control agencies. The position of the labeling theory of deviance is that a juvenile formally processed through a juvenile justice system is officially labeled a "juvenile offender." Accepting this argument implies that being officially labeled as a delinquent may cause juveniles to conjure self-fulfilling prophecies that would reinforce their delinquency. This implies that the way juveniles feel about themselves and behave depends upon how people respond to them.

Though Barbados is non-rural, it does have characteristics of the Gemeinschaft community. In Barbados, officials, even police officers, take on the role of social workers to assist the juveniles they serve. Barbados has a functioning juvenile justice system, but it is relatively small compared to the U.S. and the U.K. Thus, officials can exercise informal social control while enforcing formal sanctions. In this Gemeinschaft-type community, labels can become fluid. Labeling theory fails to account for the fact, that people can, re-label themselves. Thus, labels are not static but are dynamic.

In Barbados, there are laws in place to govern youthful offenders, yet we see from the findings that social control agents have face-to-face relations with juveniles under their care. In this type of intimate setting, the lines between formal and informal controls become blurred by the face-to-face interaction between social control agents and juveniles. This type of face-to-face interaction has developed into a relationship that many juveniles at the GIS have grown to depend upon for support. The perceived positive reinforcement that the juveniles receive from the social control agents may make it more difficult for juveniles to internalize the formal label of deviance automatically entailed by being processed through the juvenile justice system. Because of the small numbers of juveniles served in all branches of the juvenile justice system, and the face-to-face relations make it possible, these settings operate at a more personal and informal level and permit more informal social control.

Lofland (1969) argues that the acceptance or refusal of a deviant self-identity depends upon (1) disorientation – the ability to cope with life's situations; (2)

affective bonds with others – positive emotional attachments to conventional and deviant others; and (3) congruence between actor's and others' cognitive categories – use of similar verbal language to describe the deviant identity between labeler and labeled individual (1969:177-205). Though few labelists expanded upon Lofland's argument, this study found that the factors he cites, together with personal characteristics and the blurring of formal and informal controls in face-to-face interactions between social control agents and juveniles, may explain why some juveniles feel stigmatized and accept the deviant label while others do not. With a juvenile justice system established to separate juveniles from adults on the assumption that youths should be treated differently than adults, it can be assumed that many of these juveniles believe that they have redeeming qualities that can still be corrected because importance is placed on their educational, life skills, and social development. In such an environment, juveniles may be less likely to internalize a deviant label, because they are given opportunities to counter the formal label. This is significant because most studies examine either formal or informal labeling, and few examine the interaction of formal and informal labeling and how each may vary across cultural settings or countries.

Suitability of Labeling Theory in Barbados

As a process-oriented approach, the labeling theory of deviance "has shifted the focus of investigation and analysis from the etiology of deviant behavior to the process whereby individuals come to occupy deviant roles or enter deviant careers" (Ageton & Elliott 1974). Though the labeling theory of deviance has not been discredited, by the 1980s, critics had abandoned the theory, citing poor reasoning and misrepresented hypotheses. But Schur (1971) has argued that labeling theory has been misunderstood, over-simplified, and unfairly criticized. Paternoster and Iovanni, acknowledged that the move to discount labeling theory was premature because the bulk of the studies purporting to examine the theory did not provide valid tests of labeling (1989:384).

The review of the literature and the analysis of the findings of this study confirm the challenges of pinpointing the exact role that the juvenile justice system performs as a labeling agent. Defending labeling theory is difficult because it is hard to separate the effects of labeling by social control agents (formal interactions) from the other effects taking place in the lives of juveniles as a result of their interactions with their communities, peers, and families (informal interactions). However, I accepted this challenge and examined the effect of the justice system on juveniles by focusing on the classical labeling tenets of Tannenbaum (1938), Lemert (1951), and Becker (1963).

This chapter asks how the findings on a small juvenile sample from Barbados affect a 60-year-old theory of deviance. To labeling theorists, deviance is an accidental side-effect of society's attempt at social control. Central to labeling theory is the change that should take place in juveniles' self-concept, role, and behavior after they have been labeled. However, the negative effects of labeling were not the same as labeling tends to find in the U.S.

Think of the Rubin's vase, labeling seems similar, as it looks significantly different in different social settings, in this case, countries. Labeling theory has primarily been examined in the United States and thus has been tested on the standards of American legislation and procedures. This study has identified four differences between the cultural landscape and social practices of Barbados and the United States that may help answer why this sample of juveniles did not produce findings in line with the predictions of labeling and stigmatizing theories tested in the U.S.

CONCLUSION

The research questions and hypotheses used here were developed from the tenets of the labeling theory of deviance. Some observations of the theory that holds with juveniles in the U.S. were not as applicable to juveniles in Barbados. The present study shows that being publicly branded as a deviant does not equate to the acceptance of a deviant label and that labels seem to be less stigmatizing in Barbados. This differs from the predictions of labeling theory in that labeling in Barbados seems to be less an individual internalization of societal characterizations as deviant, and more a collective, cultural expectation of what is normal.

While scholars battle over the effects of race and social class on labeling, this sample of juveniles in Barbados, showed that the acceptance of the "deviant" label may have been contingent on personal factors other than race and social class, including the juvenile's social environment, personal, family, and peer history with the law; their views of the offenses against them; and their character and strength. This research shows that the impact of a label may be damaging to certain juveniles based on personal characteristics and strengths, but also the practices of social control agents might buffer acceptance of a deviant label. The nature of Barbados' social structure, including its laws, programs, and the low levels of offenses committed, might make it less likely that labeling will be as stigmatizing and as likely to be internalized.

While these results may not be generalizable to other countries, they illustrate that each society has unique laws, behaviors, and practices and that theoretical expectations found in other settings may not be as applicable to other settings. The conditions of labeling have to be in place for the theory to hold. This study shows the importance of talking directly to juvenile informants to get their views in their own words without relying solely on quantitative analyses to examine labeling. An integrated analysis is more appropriate for the labeling theory of deviance. These findings are significant for informing the theoretical development of deviance.

REFERENCES

Adams, M. S., Robertson, C. T., Gray-Ray, P., & Ray, M. C. (2003). Labeling and delinquency. *Adolescence, 38*(149), 171–186.

Ageton, S. S., & Elliott, D. S. (1974). The Effects of Legal Processing on Delinquent Orientations. *Social Problems, 22*(1), 87–100.

Akers, R., & Sellers, C. (2009). *Criminological theories: Introduction, evaluation, and application* (5th ed.). Oxford University Press.

Apel, R., & Sweeten, G. (2010). The Impact of Incarceration on Employment during the Transition to Adulthood. *Social Problems, 57*(3), 448–479.

Austin, A. E. (2009). Cognitive apprenticeship theory and its implications for doctoral education: A case example from a doctoral program in higher and adult education. *The International Journal for Academic Development, 14*(3), 173–183.

Bailey, C., & Coore-Desai, C. (2009). Offender abuse history: Findings from Her Majesty's Prison, Barbados. Caribbean Journal of Criminology and Public Safety, 14(1–2), 49–80. https://sta.uwi.edu/conferences/09/salises/documents/C%20Bailey.pdf

Barbados Government Information Services. (2015). *Reforming juvenile laws in Barbados.* Retrieved May 25, 2023 Reforming Juvenile Laws In Barbados | GIS (gisbarbados.gov.bb)

Becker, H. S. (1963). *Outsiders: Studies in the Sociology of Deviance.* Free Press.

Bennett, R. R., & Lynch, J. P. (1996). Towards a Caribbean criminology: Prospects and problems. *Caribbean Journal of Criminology and Social Psychology, 1*(1), 8–37.

Bergman, M., Seepersad, R., Safranoff, A., & Cafferata, F. (2020). *Regional comparative report: Survey of individuals deprived of liberty: Caribbean 2016-2019.* Inter American Development Bank., DOI: 10.18235/0002651

Bernburg, J. G., & Krohn, M. D. (2003). Labeling, Life Chances, and Adult Crime: The Direct and Indirect Effects of Official Intervention in Adolescence on Crime in Early Adulthood. *Criminology, 41*(4), 1287–1318.

Birkbeck, C. (1999). By your theories you shall be known: Some reflections on Caribbean criminology. *Caribbean Journal of Criminology and Social Psychology, 4*(1), 1–31.

Branch, N. T. (2012). *Reconsidering Labeling Theory: A Case Study of Juvenile Delinquency in Barbados*. Howard University.

Chesney-Lind, M., & Okamoto, S. K. (2001). Gender Matters: Patterns in Girls' Delinquency and Gender Responsive Programming. *Journal of Forensic Psychology Practice*, *1*(3), 1–28.

Chesney-Lind, M., & Sheldon, R. G. (1998). *Girls, Delinquency and Juvenile Justice*. Wadsworth Publishing Co.

Collins, C. S., & Stockton, C. M. (2018). The Central Role of Theory in Qualitative Research. *International Journal of Qualitative Methods*, *17*(1). Advance online publication. DOI: 10.1177/1609406918797475

Coppin, J. (2022). *Examine root causes of violence among youth*. The Nation News. Retrieved May 27, 2023 https://www.nationnews.com/2022/09/26/examine-root-causes-violence-among-youth/

Deosaran, R. (2010). *Caribbean Encyclopedia of Crime and Punishment*. Sage Publication.

Dillman, D. A. (2007). *Mail and internet surveys: The Tailored Design Method 2007 update with new internet, visual, and mixed-mode guide*. John Wiley & Sons, Inc.

Espinosa, E., & Sorensen, J. (2015). The influence of gender and traumatic experiences on length of time served in juvenile justice settings. *Criminal Justice and Behavior*.

Farrington, D. P., Ohlin, L. E., & Wilson, J. Q. (1986). *Understanding and Controlling Crime*. Springer-Verlag.

Freemon, K., Nuño, L., & Katz, C. (2020). The status of youth incarceration in the Caribbean. *Caribbean Journal of Criminology*, *2*(1), 48–74.

Gentle-Genitty, C., Kim, J., Yi, E.-H., Slater, D., Reynolds, B., & Bragg, N. (2017). Comprehensive assessment of youth violence in five Caribbean countries: Gender and age differences. *Journal of Human Behavior in the Social Environment*. Advance online publication. DOI: 10.1080/10911359.2016.1273811

Griffin, P. (2003). *Trying and sentencing juveniles as adults: An analysis of state transfer and blended sentencing laws. Pitts-burgh*. National Center for Juvenile Justice.

Hill, S. M. & Morris, P. K. (2017). Drug Trafficking and Gang Violence in the Caribbean. *Crime, Violence and Public Safety in the Caribbean*, 52-75. https://doi.org/DOI: 10.4324/9781315525778-3

Hipwell, A., Loeber, R., Stouthamer-Loeber, M., Keenan, K., White, H. R., & Kroneman, L. (2002). Characteristics of girls with early onset disruptive and antisocial behaviour. *Criminal Behaviour and Mental Health*, *12*, 99–118.

Kelly, B. T., Loeber, R., Keenan, K., & DeLamatre, M. (1997). "Developmental Pathways in Boys' Disruptive and Delinquent Behavior". *Juvenile Justice Bulletin*. Retrieved December 11, 2010 (https://www.ncjrs.gov/pdffiles/165692.pdf)

Kierkus, C. A., & Baer, D. (2003). Does the Relationship Between Family Structure and Delinquency Vary According to Circumstance? An Investigation of Interaction Effects. *Canadian Journal of Criminology and Criminal Justice*, *45*(4), 405–429.

Kruttschnitt, C. (2016). The politics and place of gender in research on crime. *Criminology*, *42*(2), 307–336.

Lemert, E. M. (1951). *Social Pathology*. McGraw-Hill.

Lofland, J. (1969). *Deviance and identity*. Prentice-Hall.

MacDonald, J., & Chesney-Lind, M. (2001). Gender bias and juvenile justice revisited: A multiyear analysis. *Crime and Delinquency*, *47*, 173–195.

Matsueda, R. L. (1992). Reflected appraisals, parental labeling, and delinquency: Specifying a symbolic interactionist theory. *American Journal of Sociology*, *97*(6), 1577–1611. DOI: 10.1086/229940

Meade, A. C. (1974). The labeling approach to delinquency: State of the theory as a function of method. *Social Forces*, *53*(1), 83–91.

Moore, R. S. (2018). The touchy topic of juvenile delinquency. The Barbados Advocate. Retrieved April 15, 2023 The touchy topic of juvenile delinquency | Barbados Advocate

National Juvenile Justice Network. (2023). *Raising the Minimum Age for Prosecuting Children.* Retrieved May 16, 2023 Raising the Minimum Age for Prosecuting Children (njjn.org)

Nolterieke, L. (2020). Delinquency in the Caribbean: Stakeholder perceptions of root causes. Honors Theses, University of New Heaven. https://digitalcommons.newhaven.edu/honorstheses/31

Paternoster, R., & Iovanni, L. (1989). The labeling perspective and delinquency: An elaboration of the theory and assessment of the evidence. *Justice Quarterly*, *6*(3), 359–394.

Scheff, T. J. (1966), 1984 2nd ed., 1999 3rd ed. Being mentally ill: A sociological theory. Aldine, Chicago

Schur, E. M. (1971). *Labeling Deviant Behavior: Its Sociological Implications*. Harper & Row.

Shoemaker, D. J. (2000). *Theories of delinquency: An examination of explanations of delinquent behaviour* (4th ed.). Oxford University Press.

Smith, C. A., & Stern, S. B. (1997). Delinquency and Antisocial Behavior: A Review of Family Processes and Intervention Research. *The Social Service Review, 71*, 382–420. DOI: 10.1086/604263

Sutton, H., & Ruprah, I. J. (2017). *Restoring paradise in the Caribbean: Combatting violence with numbers*. Inter-American Development Bank.

Tannenbaum, F. (1938). *Crime and the community*. Ginn and Company.

The Nation Newspaper. (2008). *Gone to pot*. Retrieved September 30, 2009 (http://archive.nationnews.com/archive_detail.php?archiveFile=2008/January/28/LocalNews/52442.xml&start=0&numPer=20&keyword=Gone+to+Pot&sectionSearch=&begindate=1%2F1%2F2008&enddate=4%2F28%2F2010&authorSearch=&IncludeStories=1&pubsection=&page=&IncludePages=1&IncludeImages=1&mode=phrase&archive_pubname=Daily+Nation%0A%09%09%09)

Barbados Today (2019). *Cabinet approves new Juvenile Justice Bill* Retrieved May 25, 2023 Cabinet approves new Juvenile Justice Bill - Barbados Today

Tönnies, F. 1887. "Community and Society." Pp. 16-22 in *The Urban Sociology Reader*. Jan Lin and Christopher Mele (Eds.). London: Routledge.

UNICEF. n.d. Legal minimum ages and the realization of adolescents' rights. Retrieved May 16, 2023 PDF Minimum age for criminal responsibility.pdf (unicef.org)

United Nations. (2019). Convention on the Rights of the Child. Retrieved May 17, 2023 from General comment No. 24 (2019) on children's rights in the child justice system | OHCHR

Unruh, D., Povenmire-Kirk, T., & Yamamoto, S. (2009). Perceived Barriers and Protective Factors of Juvenile Offenders on their Developmental Pathway to Adulthood. *Journal of Correctional Education, 60*(3), 201–224.

Wirth, L. 1930. "Urbanism as a Way of Life." Pp. 32-41 in *The Urban Sociology Reader*. Jan Lin and Christopher Mele (Eds.). London: Routledge.

Wong, J. S., Bouchard, J., Gravel, J., Bouchard, M., & Morselli, C. (2016). Can at-risk youth be diverted from crime? A meta-analysis of restorative diversion programs. *Criminal Justice and Behavior*, *43*(10), 1310–1329. DOI: 10.1177/0093854816640835

Chapter 8
Comparative Analysis of Diversion Programs for Children in Kenya and Tanzania

Antony Wando Odek
St. Paul's University, Kenya

Victor Wakumile Ndururu
Independent Researcher, Kenya

Terry Odhiambo
United States International University-Africa, Kenya

Jane Gift Akinyi
Catholic University of Eastern Africa, Kenya

ABSTRACT

This chapter presents a comparative analysis of juvenile justice systems in Kenya and Tanzania, with a focus on the implications of diversion programs on child development. Although both countries emphasize rehabilitation over punitive measures, significant gaps in aligning with international standards remain. Through an analysis of secondary data from legislative documents, policy reports, and case studies, the chapter highlights Kenya's structured interventions and their implementation challenges, as well as Tanzania's community-based approach, which lacks detailed guidelines. The study concludes with recommendations for developing training programs, addressing resource limitations, and enhancing research to foster evidence-based improvements in both systems.

DOI: 10.4018/978-1-6684-9343-4.ch008

1. INTRODUCTION

Youth are a nation's future assets, but they face current concerns such as drug usage and criminal activity. As a result, every jurisdiction in the world is dealing with the issue of juvenile delinquency, which refers to children' behaviours that deviate from criminal law standards and has far-reaching consequences for society and economic growth (Sarwanto, 2023). Juvenile delinquency has become a major issue during the last decade. From 2009 to 2019, juvenile crime rates increased noticeably in many regions (Feld, 2019).

According to a United Nations Office on Drugs and criminality (UNODC) report (quoted in Young & Giller, 2021, p.3), adolescent criminality in Europe increased by 2.6% in 2021, compared to 1.7% the previous year. Similarly, other regions saw various rates of growth: South East Asia by 0.7%, Latin America by 3.9%, and North America by 1.8%. The unusually high proportion of youth crime in Latin America has been related to the drug economy that exists in countries such as Mexico and Colombia (Bagley & Rosen, 2017). The drug trade provides both motive and means for youngsters to engage in illegal activity, resulting in much higher crime rates in these areas.

Juvenile delinquency is also a big concern in Africa, with an increasing number of young people getting involved in illegal activities. Juvenile delinquency has increased dramatically in Africa's quickly developing countries, including Ghana, Kenya, and Nigeria. According to UNIHABITAT, a shortage of employment prospects encourages many young people to engage in illegal activities in order to survive (Young & Giller, 2021). Between 2007 and 2019, juvenile criminality in Africa rose from 3.2% to 5.7% (Walker & Maddan, 2019). This figure emphasises the important need for tailored interventions that not only dissuade criminal behaviour but also help young offenders recover and successfully reintegrate into their communities.

However, effectively tackling juvenile crime requires a balanced approach that combines punitive measures with rehabilitative initiatives aimed at encouraging the development and successful reintegration of young offenders into society. International human rights law recognises the need of treating child criminality differently than adult crime. It is also widely acknowledged that this alternative strategy should prioritise rehabilitation, restoration, and diversion away from the conventional criminal system as much as possible (Dean, 2018)

In this context, diversion programs play a crucial role by steering juveniles away from formal judicial proceedings and towards rehabilitation-focused initiatives. Diversion programs encompass a wide range of components and general interventions, including recreation, advocacy, resource brokerage, vocational or educational training, and group or individual counseling (Chanila et al., 2024). In many countries, diversion is now the main method of dealing with children who are in conflict with the law for the first time and who committed a non-violent offence (Casey, 2019). Diversion measures are also increasingly used for children who are repeat offenders, known as recidivists, and/or those who have committed more serious offences.

Diversion is commonly practiced in the Eastern and Southern African region, where it has increasingly been recognized as an effective and efficient measure to respond to a child's offending behaviour and to prevent repeat offences (Atilola et al., 2020). Increasingly, countries have begun to incorporate provisions on diversion into child justice legislation and frameworks, empowering police officers, prosecutors and/or judges to divert children in conflict with the law when appropriate. In the absence of legislative amendments pertaining to diversion, some countries rely on existing prosecutorial discretion to implement diversion programmes and activities. In South Africa, for example, diversion was introduced in the early 1990s through the issuance of a practice directive to public prosecutors on the exercise of their authority to withdraw charges in cases when prosecution was deemed unnecessary to the public interest (Cameron, 2020). The success of these early efforts paved the way for diversion to be made the cornerstone of the country's 2009 child justice legislation. Studies have found that diversion programs for youth are significantly more successful than traditional juvenile justice systems in reducing recidivism, with programs focusing on medium to high-risk youth being more effective than those targeting low-risk offenders (NeMoyer et al., 2020).

Despite the establishment of comprehensive legal frameworks governing youth justice in Africa, including Kenya and Tanzania, significant challenges hinder effective implementation, as highlighted by the National Crime Research Centre (National Crime Research Centre, 2023). Issues such as compliance, officer training, inadequate infrastructure, and the relevance of rehabilitation programs persist, with studies by Kadilu (2017) and Mensa-Bonsu (n.d.) pointing to minimal operationalization of juvenile rights and the ineffectiveness of diversion programs due to resource limitations. While these studies provide valuable insights into legal and institutional challenges, they do not conduct a comparative analysis between Kenya and Tanzania. Furthermore, they fail to evaluate the legal provisions governing diversion and rehabilitation, analyze available rehabilitation programs, or identify best practices and challenges in balancing these approaches.

In response to these existing gaps, this study focuses on Kenya and Tanzania, two neighboring countries with distinct yet comparable systems of juvenile justice. By examining their approaches to diversion and rehabilitation, the research aims to identify lessons and best practices that can inform policy and practice across the region. Understanding the implementation of various responses to youth crime, including diversion programs, is fundamental to formulating more effective strategies and enhancing juvenile justice systems in both contexts. This comparative analysis will contribute to a deeper understanding of how to address the challenges faced by each country, ultimately fostering more effective juvenile justice practices.

2. STATEMENT OF THE PROBLEM

The operation of a juvenile justice system is a significant indicator of a country's commitment to protecting children's rights, providing a framework for analysing societal responses to juvenile delinquency that balance punitive measures and rehabilitative efforts. In Kenya, it is estimated that 130 out of every 100,000 children pass through the criminal court system on a daily basis, with 30 of those youngsters committing crimes and offences punishable by law(Kenya National Bureau of Statistics, 2021). While exact numbers are not readily available in Tanzania, issues such as insufficient legislative frameworks, budget constraints, and limited access to rehabilitation programs all have a substantial impact on the functioning of the juvenile justice system.

Despite efforts from both countries, there is a significant gap in detailed, comparative evaluations of juvenile diversion programs. This lack of analysis restricts our understanding of how various interventions affect the rehabilitation and reintegration of juvenile offenders. This study seeks to close this gap by assessing the developmental effects of diversion programs in Kenya and Tanzania, identifying best practices, and making recommendations for improving rehabilitation efforts. By focussing on these two neighbouring nations, the research will provide useful insights that can be used to inform policy and practice, resulting in a more effective and equitable juvenile justice system in the region.

3. OBJECTIVES OF THE STUDY

i. To evaluate the legal provisions governing the diversion and rehabilitation of juvenile offenders in Kenya and Tanzania.
ii. To analyze the types of rehabilitation programs available for juvenile offenders in both countries.
iii. To identify best practices and challenges in balancing diversion and rehabilitation

4. LITERATURE REVIEW

This study compares diversion programs for children in Kenya and Tanzania using published and unpublished studies, government papers, and media sources. A potential drawback of the analysis is the scarcity of comprehensive research available, which is similar to issues seen in other domains. This scarcity restricts the depth of critique feasible and indicates knowledge gaps that the study intends to fill by synthesizing existing material and recommending areas for future research. Furthermore, while the focus in Kenya and Tanzania remains on juvenile justice and rehabilitation, broader societal settings and resource allocation objectives must be considered, as these can have a substantial impact on the effectiveness of diversion programs. Understanding these context-specific factors is critical for evaluating the legal frameworks, rehabilitation techniques, and developmental outcomes for juvenile offenders in each country. This comparative research aims to provide significant insights into enhancing diversion programs and obtaining better outcomes for children involved in the court system by analyzing existing evidence while accounting for contextual effects.

This section delves into the theoretical foundations of juvenile justice in order to contextualize diversion programs, offering a global overview of tactics as well as a regional perspective on the unique issues faced in Sub-Saharan Africa, specifically Kenya and Tanzania. An examination of published and unpublished studies, government papers, and media stories reveals a key limitation: a lack of extensive research, which limits critical depth and emphasizes information gaps that this study aims to fill. Consider broader socioeconomic circumstances and resource allocation, as these issues have a considerable impact on the effectiveness of diversion programs. This comparative analysis seeks to improve diversion programs and outcomes for children in the criminal justice system by synthesizing existing literature and contextual effects.

4.1 Understanding of Juvenile Justice

Juvenile delinquency refers to crimes committed by minors, and definitions differ by jurisdiction due to the lack of a standardised global framework. A juvenile is commonly described as someone over the minimum age of criminal responsibility, which spans from 6 to 18 years, but under 18, with the United Nations defining youth as anyone aged 15 to 24 (Young et al., 2017). Diversion programs strive to divert young offenders away from formal court systems and towards rehabilitative choices, aiming to limit the negative effects of jail while promoting better outcomes such as reduced recidivism and improved academic achievement (Bynum & Thompson, 1996).

Despite their potential benefits, diversion programs' performance varies, owing to a lack of frequent evaluation and the variability of program design and target demographics (Dean, 2018; Mears et al., 2016). While community-based programs have proven effective in reducing recidivism when tailored to specific needs, the lack of standardisation makes comparisons between programs difficult. A comparative examination of diversion programmes in Kenya and Tanzania is required to understand how different methodology and legislative frameworks affect effectiveness, allowing for the identification of best practices and areas for development in juvenile justice systems (UNODC, 2018).

4.2 Theoretical Framework

This study is anchored in Labeling Theory, Differential Association Theory, Restorative Justice Theory (RJT), and Social Learning Theory. These theoretical models enrich the comparative analysis of diversion programs in Kenya and Tanzania, guiding the development of culturally relevant strategies that address youth offending and promote rehabilitation while reducing recidivism among juvenile offenders.

4.2.1 Labelling Theory

Labelling Theory, proposed by Howard Becker (1963) and refined by John Lundman (1993), emphasizes the negative consequences of subjecting children and young people (CYP) to formal legal proceedings for minor offences. According to this idea, labelling these individuals as "offenders" can lead to stigmatization and alienation, eventually resulting in a self-fulfilling prophesy in which labelled juveniles acquire a "deviant identity" (Case & Haines, 2021). According to research, CYP who have been identified by the criminal justice system are more likely to reoffend than those who go undetected, emphasizing the risks of heightened attention and surveillance that comes with such labelling (McAra & McVie, 2018). This notion is critical in the context of diversion programs because it emphasizes the importance of dealing with small offences outside of formal institutions in order to avoid reinforcing bad pathways.

When examining diversion programs in Kenya and Tanzania, the implications of Labelling Theory become very important. Both countries have built legal systems to govern juvenile offenders, with a focus on rehabilitation. However, the potential negative consequences of labelling must be carefully considered while designing and implementing these initiatives. Policymakers can reduce stigma by ensuring that diversion schemes are accessible and effective, while still maintaining their legal commitments to protect young offenders' rights. Recognizing the consequences of labelling can help lead the creation of more inclusive and successful diversion initiatives that are consistent with international best practices, resulting in better outcomes for CYP.

Research supports the issues stated by Labelling Theory by indicating that labelling can lead to a "correctional spiral," in which being identified as an offender increases the chance of reoffending (Goldson, 2015). While Goldson's arguments lack empirical proof, other research back up the negative impact of labelling on recidivism rates (McAra & McVie, 2018). Hart (2014) emphasizes the difficulty of providing support to CYP without identifying them as criminals, stating that the emphasis on victim justice frequently overshadows the child's needs and the stigmatizing implications of labelling. This highlights the significance of developing diversion programs that priorities rehabilitation while avoiding the negative consequences of labelling.

The voluntary character of many diversion programs represents a viable method to minimizing the impacts of labelling. Robin-D'Cruz (2019) observes that a considerable proportion of these programs (70%) demand the young person's consent for participation, distinguishing them from statutory supervision. This voluntary part is critical for minimizing stigma and instilling a sense of agency in CYP. By framing diversion as a voluntary decision rather than a punitive punishment, programs can maximize their therapeutic potential while preserving the dignity of young offenders. Despite advances, Robin-D'Cruz emphasises the need for additional adjustments to ensure that diversion strategies properly decrease labelling hazards while maximising rehabilitative benefits. This factor is critical for comparing diversion programs in Kenya and Tanzania, where good implementation has a major impact on youth outcomes.

4.2.2 Differential Association Theory

Differential Association Theory, first articulated by Edwin Sutherland and later expanded by researchers such as Cressy (1952), provides a fundamental paradigm for understanding the dynamics of youth involvement in the youth justice system. According to this hypothesis, young people frequently develop antisocial attitudes and behaviours as a result of their interactions with peers and adults in their environment. This theory makes the essential assumption that criminal behaviour is learnt through social contacts, in which juveniles internalise the beliefs and conventions of those with who they associate.

Research supports this viewpoint, demonstrating that exposure to seasoned criminals can have a criminogenic effect, raising the chance of recidivism among youth (Loeb et al., 2015). Such findings highlight the potential risks of exposing young people to the YJS, where negative peer pressures can reinforce criminal behaviour rather than aid effective rehabilitation.

Diversion programs are a proactive approach for limiting youth contact with the formal judicial system, hence lowering the chance of antisocial behaviour associated with delinquency. By diverting young offenders away from punishing judicial processes, these programs promote good social relationships with mentors, peers, and community resources, encouraging prosocial behaviour. This is consistent with Differential Association Theory, which emphasises the importance of good peer influences in reducing criminal behaviour. By providing conditions that promote healthy growth, diversion strategies assist adolescents in avoiding bad influences that may lead to further criminal action.

In the context of a comparative comparison of diversion programs in Kenya and Tanzania, the theory emphasises the relevance of interventions that restrict young exposure to negative peer influences in the juvenile justice system. Policymakers can create more effective diversion programs that reduce recidivism while also supporting youth development by focusing on peer dynamics and creating good social connections. This approach is consistent with broader efforts to develop healthier communities and improve juvenile justice outcomes.Bottom of Form

4.2.3 Restorative Justice Theory (RJT)

Restorative Justice Theory (RJT), developed by Howard Zehr in 1990, advocates for a paradigm shift in how justice is perceived, emphasizing the repair of harm caused by criminal behavior rather than merely punishing offenders. RJT posits that crime is a conflict between individuals, not just a violation of state laws, and encourages the involvement of all stakeholders, victims, offenders, and the community, in the resolution process. This inclusive approach fosters dialogue, understanding, and healing, allowing offenders to take responsibility for their actions and their consequences (Zehr & Mika, 1998).

In the context of Kenya and Tanzania, applying RJT principles can enhance legal frameworks governing diversion and rehabilitation for juvenile offenders. By integrating restorative concepts into legislation, both countries can create environments that prioritize accountability and communal responsibility, facilitating cooperation among community members in crime prevention and offender rehabilitation. Aligning diversion programs with RJT can significantly improve their effectiveness in reducing recidivism by addressing the specific needs of juvenile offenders and fostering personal growth (Umbreit, 1994). Implementing RJT in these nations leads to culturally relevant interventions that resonate with local values, promoting a compassionate and constructive response to crime, ultimately contributing to safer and more resilient communities (Zehr, 1990).

4.2.4 Social Learning Theory

Social Learning Theory, developed by Albert Bandura (Grusec, 1992), posits that individuals learn behaviors, attitudes, and their consequences primarily through observation and imitation of others in their social environment. Bandura identifies several key assumptions that underpin this theory, which are crucial for understanding its application in juvenile rehabilitation and diversion programs. One primary assumption of Social Learning Theory is that behavior is learned through observational learning, meaning that individuals can acquire positive behaviors by watching mentors or peers who model constructive actions. In the context of diversion programs for juvenile offenders, this suggests that exposure to positive role models can significantly influence behavior. For example, when a young offender observes a peer successfully reintegrating into society after participating in a diversion program, they may be motivated to emulate that behavior. Bandura's Bobo doll experiment underscores the powerful impact that role models can have, highlighting the importance of incorporating positive figures in rehabilitation initiatives to foster better behavioral outcomes (Grusec, 1992).

Another key assumption is the significance of reinforcement and punishment in shaping behavior. Bandura posits that behaviors associated with positive outcomes are more likely to be imitated, while those linked to negative consequences are less likely to be adopted (Grusec, 1992). In diversion programs, consistently reinforcing positive behaviors, through praise, rewards, or opportunities for personal growth, can enhance the effectiveness of rehabilitation. Additionally, the concept of self-efficacy, or an individual's belief in their ability to succeed, plays a critical role in this context. By fostering self-efficacy through skill-building, achievable goals, and supportive environments, diversion programs can empower young offenders to take ownership of their rehabilitation journey, increasing the likelihood of positive outcomes and reducing recidivism (Grusec, 1992).

While Social Learning Theory offers useful insights into the design of diversion programs for juvenile offenders in Kenya and Tanzania, it has limitations, such as the potential failure to account for the complex interplay of individual, environmental, and situational factors that influence behaviour (Akers et al., 1998). Furthermore, much of the research supporting the hypothesis comes from controlled laboratory settings, which may not accurately reflect the circumstances faced by juvenile offenders (Miller & Prinz, 1990). Nonetheless, the theory emphasises the significance of good role models and reinforcement tactics in rehabilitation program design, arguing for environments that model and encourage positive behaviours. Effective diversion programs should encourage mentorship and community involvement to create constructive social relationships among juvenile offenders, in line with the larger goals of rehabilitative justice systems. To address concerns about public safety and serious offenders, theoretical frameworks such as Restorative Justice Theory must be integrated to ensure appropriate supervision while maintaining the supportive elements of Social Learning Theory that foster accountability and self-awareness, thereby improving rehabilitation outcomes and contributing to safer communities.

Overall, the relevance of these theoretical frameworks in evaluating legal provisions, analyzing rehabilitation programs, and identifying best practices in Kenya and Tanzania is profound. By grounding their approaches in Restorative Justice, Social Learning Theory, and Labeling Theory, policymakers and practitioners can create a more effective juvenile justice system. These frameworks offer insights into developing legal provisions that prioritize rehabilitation, designing programs that utilize positive role models, and addressing the complexities of balancing diversion with community safety. As both countries continue to address the challenges within their juvenile justice systems, incorporating these theoretical perspectives can lead to more informed decision-making and improved outcomes for young offenders.

4.3 Global Overview of Juvenile Diversion Programs

Diversion programs, which prioritise rehabilitation over punitive measures, have grown in popularity around the world as an important tool for combating adolescent delinquency. Countries including the United States, the United Kingdom, Canada, Australia, and the Netherlands have established successful diversion programs aimed at rehabilitating first-time and nonviolent child offenders. Diversion programs originated in the United States in the 1960s and 1970s, spearheaded by the President's Commission on Law Enforcement and Administration of Justice (Gibbons & Blake, 1976). While there are no national guidelines for these programs, they have increased in popularity due to their ability to provide personalised solutions to the needs of specific groups, such as adolescents or people suffering from mental illnesses (Ozturk et al., 2022). These programs have proven effective at reducing recidivism and the costs associated with incarceration.

England has a long legal history in juvenile justice, with its approach balancing welfare and crime control measures. The country's juvenile justice system evolved significantly from the 19th century, starting with the Industrial School Act of 1866, which dealt with vagrant children, and advancing to the Children and Young Person Act of 1969, which prioritized the care and protection of young offenders (Thorpe et al., 2024). The Crime and Disorder Act of 1998 included various amendments that emphasised early intervention and community-based solutions to prevent youth offending and recidivism. A distinguishing feature of England's system is its multi-agency framework, represented by Youth Offending Teams (YOTs), which are made up of specialists from many sectors that collaborate to give comprehensive support.

This approach prioritises diversion from formal justice at various stages, giving juvenile offenders access to rehabilitative and restorative justice choices.

Canada's experience with diversion programs has been properly integrated into the youth justice system. The Young Criminal Justice Act (YCJA) of 2003 established the legal basis for extrajudicial measures, allowing teenage offenders to participate in rehabilitation through community service, counselling, and educational programs. These approaches have resulted in considerable reductions in youth incarceration and recidivism rates (Corrado et al., 2015). However, the success of Canada's diversion programs differs by province due to inequalities in resources and community services emphasising the importance of equitable access to support mechanisms for young offenders (Pappas & Dent, 2023). In New Zealand, young offenders can be diverted to restorative interventions at the police or court level. Police diversion arises after a suspect has been apprehended but before prosecution, and it can take several forms, ranging from an advisory not to repeat their crimes to arrest and court proceedings (Barretto et al., 2018). As a result, the process diverts the perpetrator who might otherwise face legal proceedings.

Diversion strategies are also gaining traction in Asia, but comprehensive implementation is difficult. To reintegrate juvenile criminals into society, diversion programs in Japan emphasize rehabilitation, which frequently includes family and community assistance. Similarly, South Korea's diversion strategies prioritize reconciliation through mediation between offenders and victims (McAra & McVie, 2018). However, due to insufficient resources, countries such as Indonesia and the Philippines fail to implement juvenile justice reforms consistently. Recent reforms in these countries, aided by non-governmental organizations (NGOs), are beginning to close these gaps, expanding the reach of youth diversion efforts (UNICEF, 2019).

The preceding perspective on diversion programs teaches vital lessons for emerging countries. The accomplishments of countries such as Canada and the Netherlands underscore the necessity of community-based rehabilitation, whilst the obstacles faced by Southeast Asian countries emphasize the need for enough resources and continuous enforcement. These examples serve as templates for customizing diversion strategies to local situations, providing insights into how to rehabilitate young offenders without overburdening formal legal systems. Adapting these ideas allows developing regions to reconcile the requirement for public safety with the rehabilitation of juvenile offenders, resulting in more sustainable outcomes.

4.4 Regional Perspective: Juvenile Justice in Sub-Saharan Africa

Juvenile justice systems in Sub-Saharan Africa have considerable challenges, especially in quickly growing countries where socioeconomic factors like unemployment and poor educational opportunities are directly connected to increased adolescent crime rates (Young & Giller, 2021). According to a United Nations Children's Fund (UNICEF, 2023) research, many countries in the region are gradually implementing diversion mechanisms into their child justice legislation. This change allows police officers, prosecutors, and judges to divert minors who are in trouble with the law when appropriate. While these legal amendments indicate progress, their successful implementation is frequently delayed by a lack of funds and training for people in charge of carrying out these programs (Walker & Maddan, 2019). This disconnect between policy and practice raises serious concerns regarding the viability and efficacy of diversion programs, as well as their potential effects on adolescent rehabilitation.

In South Africa, the Child Justice Act of 2008 prioritizes diversion and restorative justice in dealing with juvenile offenders, with the goal of holding children accountable while avoiding punitive measures (Murhula & Singh, 2019). The Act, influenced by the African ideal of Ubuntu, aims to protect the dignity of child offenders while also promoting reconciliation. South Africa has increased the minimum age of criminal responsibility to ten years, which is greater than in many other African countries but still lower than international norms (Milner, 2024). The Act reflects the country's long-standing commitment on reconciliation following apartheid.

In Zambia, customary law is central to the justice system, with traditional courts led by chiefs and elders emphasizing accessibility and restorative methods (Clifford, 2024). However, the system has been criticized for gender bias, limited funding, and a lack of formal legal status Despite these limitations, customary law has the potential to be modified and integrated into modern human rights norms (Diala & Kangwa, 2019). A hybrid strategy that combines customary and formal systems could increase its effectiveness.

Other African countries, notably Uganda, South Sudan, and the Kingdom of Lesotho, are gradually embracing diversionary techniques based on traditional methods for settling disputes. In Uganda, for example, village courts play an important role in promoting reconciliation and restorative justice. Instead of punishing young offenders, these community-based programs seek to repair harm and restore connections. Similarly, in Lesotho, grassroots initiatives such as child justice committees promote culturally appropriate restorative processes that empower local communities. While these systems prioritizes children's rights and offer opportunities for rehabilitation, restorative methods are rarely extended to adult offenders . This difference indicates a substantial inequality in the criminal justice system, as adults are frequently subjected to punitive measures without the possibility of rehabilitation through restorative techniques (Robinson, 2009). This mismatch puts into question the general fairness and effectiveness of justice systems that do not use restorative principles uniformly across age groups.

Despite increasing support for restorative justice in African juvenile justice systems, there is a considerable gap in empirical research on how diversion programs are administered in various socioeconomic and legal situations, notably in East Africa. Much emphasis has been placed on Western legal frameworks, which can eclipse the importance of traditional African customary rules in providing restorative justice. Furthermore, the cohabitation of multiple legal systems, known as legal pluralism, is little understood, particularly in terms of how it affects juvenile crime rates, rehabilitation outcomes, and the efficacy of diversion programs. In Kenya and Tanzania, where both formal and customary legal systems play key roles, there is a paucity of detailed analysis of how these systems interact to handle juvenile justice challenges.

Given this backdrop, the current study seeks to address a crucial research vacuum by conducting a comparative analysis of diversion programs for children in Kenya and Tanzania. Although diversion and restorative justice have gained popularity in Sub-Saharan Africa, there is little empirical study on how these principles are applied in varied socioeconomic and legal contexts in East Africa. This study will uncover best practices and potential gaps in how restorative justice is handled by comparing Kenya's and Tanzania's approaches, notably in terms of adolescent crime rates and rehabilitation outcomes. Furthermore, the study will look into how combining old customary rules with modern legal systems might improve the inclusivity and effectiveness of diversion programs. This study aims to justify the need for a more in-depth understanding of these approaches, providing policymakers and practitioners with vital insights into improving rehabilitation and reducing youth recidivism in East Africa.

4.5 Legal Provisions Governing Juvenile Diversion and Rehabilitation in Kenya and Tanzania

The legal and policy framework for diversion in Kenya is shaped by various international and regional conventions, as well as domestic legislation aimed at protecting children's rights. Key instruments include the United Nations Convention on the Rights of the Child (UNCRC), which Kenya ratified in 1990, the African Charter on the Rights and Welfare of the Child (ACRWC), and several International Labour Organization (ILO) conventions. These frameworks call for the protection of children from harmful practices such as child labor, exploitation, and abuse. Domestically, the Children's Act, enacted in 2001, integrates the principles of the UNCRC and ACRWC, ensuring the best interests of the child are paramount in any legal or administrative action concerning them. This Act guarantees a child's right to essential services such as healthcare, education, and protection.

Kenya has made significant efforts to align its policies with the legal frameworks protecting children's rights. Initiatives like the National Policy on Orphans and Vulnerable Children, the Draft Child Labour Policy, and the Adolescent Reproductive Health and Development Policy have been introduced to address specific child-related issues. However, some policies remain drafts, and there is still a gap in fully finalizing and implementing these frameworks. Although the current Constitution does not explicitly address child rights, the Draft Constitution highlights the child's best interests as paramount. Similarly, the Children's Act under Section 4(2) ensures that child-related decisions by courts or institutions prioritize the child's well-being.

In terms of diversion, the framework in Kenya has largely relied on goodwill and existing child protection provisions, with initiatives like police training on child rights and the establishment of child protection units. However, diversion is not yet fully embedded in law, and much of its application is informal. The proposed Children's Law (Amendment Bill) 2007 seeks to formally incorporate diversion provisions into the Children's Act, marking a significant step toward making the justice system more child-friendly. Until the Bill is passed, diversion remains a practice supported by the justice system's goodwill, but its full legal backing is still pending.

Both Kenya and Tanzania have established legal frameworks intended to support the diversion and rehabilitation of juvenile offenders. In Kenya, the *Children Act of 2001* provides guidelines for rehabilitative measures, emphasizing the need for diversion away from formal judicial proceedings (Atilola, 2020). Similarly, Tanzania's *Law of the Child Act of 2009* aims to prioritize rehabilitation over punitive measures. However, despite these legal provisions, the practical application of diversion programs often falls short. Atilola (2020) highlights the inconsistencies in implementing these laws, particularly in rural and under-resourced areas where support systems are limited.

4.6 Conclusion of the Literature Review

The literature highlights the value of rehabilitative measures such as restorative justice for juvenile offenders, citing successful instances from the United States, Canada, and South Africa. In contrast, Kenya and Tanzania confront difficulties in conducting successful diversion programs due to limited resources and uneven enforcement, particularly in rural areas. Although legal frameworks exist, such as Kenya's Children Act and Tanzania's Law of the Child Act, considerable gaps in policy and practice persist, with cultural and socioeconomic considerations being overlooked. This study aims to conduct a comparative analysis of diversion programs in both nations, evaluating their effectiveness and suggesting best practices for improving rehabilitation outcomes for young offenders.

5. METHODOLOGY AND DATA

A qualitative methodology was used to meet the study's aims, with an emphasis on document studies and alternative assessments. This strategy makes use of existing records, such as academic research and government documents, to provide insights into settings and groups that would otherwise be unobservable (Johnson et al., 2020). These sources, which were generally accessible and accurate, provided a solid framework for the research, allowing for a thorough examination of Kenya and Tanzania's diversion programs for juvenile offenders.

The qualitative methodology is ideal for this comparative research for two reasons. First, the literature study allowed researchers to get a thorough understanding of the socioeconomic dynamics unique to Kenya and Tanzania, particularly the existing diversion programs. This aided in identifying the distinguishing features of each country's approach to juvenile justice, as well as the larger socioeconomic context in which these programs function. Second, document analysis enabled the evaluation of nuanced societal interactions and behaviours within the broader social environment (Creswell & Báez, 2020). This enabled an investigation into how societal attitudes and cultural norms influence the implementation and efficacy of diversion programs in both countries.

Existing sources vary in their value according to accessibility and accuracy. Documents gave useful information about the culture of institutions and diversion program participants, which helped to develop relevant evaluation questions. Existing records were used to make comparisons, such as comparing project participants to applicants, contrasting project proposals with implementation records, and analysing institutional policies and program descriptions before and after interventions were implemented (Aspers & Corte, 2019). Despite potential issues with document accuracy, completeness, and authenticity, the qualitative technique was acceptable for this exploratory study, given the scarcity of past research on juvenile diversion programs in Kenya and Tanzania.

6. FINDINGS AND DISCUSSIONS

6.1 Legal Provisions

Both Kenya and Tanzania have created legal frameworks to oversee their juvenile justice systems, but each faces unique obstacles in efficiently enforcing their laws. Kenya's Children Act 2001, which was updated in 2021, represents a substantial shift towards a rehabilitative rather than punitive approach to juvenile justice. This legislation places a major emphasis on diversion, which is a technique that addresses juvenile offences by providing alternative rehabilitative measures prior to the formal filing of charges. According to Muema et al.(2023), Kenya's legal framework incorporates a diverse range of diversion methods, displaying a comprehensive approach that addresses all sorts of offences, including serious and recurrent offences. The Act requires that diversion be explored for juvenile offenders at the outset of court proceedings, emphasising a proactive approach to preventing future delinquency and reducing the societal stigma associated with criminal behaviour.

Kenya's approach to diversion demonstrates its dedication to early intervention and rehabilitation. The legal system seeks to facilitate juveniles' reintegration into society by providing structured diversion choices such as community service, counselling, and other rehabilitation programs, in addition to holding them accountable for their behaviour. This strategy not only conforms with international standards promoting children's rights and welfare, but it also reflects a larger social purpose of encouraging positive outcomes for young offenders. The emphasis on early intervention is critical because it aims to address underlying issues that contribute to juvenile delinquency and lower the chance of future criminal behaviour.

Despite the strong legislative structure and progressive policies, Kenya confronts difficulty in effectively implementing its juvenile justice legislation. These issues include ensuring that diversion policies are applied consistently throughout regions, as well as addressing logistical and resource constraints that may limit the availability and quality of rehabilitative treatments. Furthermore, the transition from punitive to rehabilitative techniques necessitates continuing cooperation and coordination across stakeholders, including law enforcement, the judiciary, social services, and community organisations. While Kenya's Children Act 2001 represents a substantial step forward in juvenile justice reform, particularly in terms of diversion and early intervention, more work is needed to improve implementation and solve existing issues. Kenya may strengthen its juvenile justice system even further by improving coordination, expanding resources, and refining operational processes, resulting in better results for Juvenile delinquents

Tanzania's law provisions for diversion programs for juvenile offenders appear to be less explicit and more difficult to implement than Kenya's. Tanzania's legal framework contains the Law of the Child Act, R.E. (2019), and other related laws that are consistent with international treaties such as the Convention on the Rights of the Child (CRC). However, unlike Kenya, Tanzania's rules and regulations do not explicitly promote diversion as a major technique for dealing with juvenile offences. Table 1 compares the variations and similarities in the legal provisions governing diversion in Tanzania and Kenya.

Table 1 . Comparison between legal provisions guiding diversion in Tanzania and Kenya

Aspects	Kenya	Tanzania
Legal Framework	-Children Act 2001, revised in 2021 and enacted in 2022 -Diversion Guidelines and Explanatory Notes (2019) - Diversion Policy (2019)	-Law of the Child Act, R.E. (2019) -Law of the Child Act CAP 13 -Law of the Child (Juvenile Court) Rules (2016) -Tanzania Police Force, Police General Orders -National Guideline for Implementation of Community Rehabilitation Programme (2019)
International Alignment	Aligns with international standards and CRC	Aligns with international conventions like CRC and African Charter
Minimum age of criminal responsibility:	12 years	10 years, 12 for sexual offences
Decision-making authority	Any authorized officer or Judicial Officer including public prosecutors	
Emphasis	Reformative approach, rehabilitation, early intervention	Best interest of the child, rehabilitation, child-friendly procedures
Types of offences eligible for diversion:	Criminal offences	All non-predicate or serious offences
Diversion Measures	Advocates for diversion before charges, structured levels	Limited explicit mention of diversion, reactive approach
Implementation Challenges	Effective implementation challenges noted	Limited operationalization, gaps in child protection
Coordination and Development	Ongoing development of operational rules	Calls for comprehensive reforms, integration of community-based solutions
Criticism and Gaps	Lack of comprehensive diversion options, reliance on international instruments	Lack of child-friendly procedures, persistence of corporal punishment
Stakeholder Support	Strong support for diversion among stakeholders	Calls for reforms, integration of preventive measures

This table highlights the differences and similarities in the legal frameworks, implementation challenges, and stakeholder support for juvenile diversion in Kenya and Tanzania, identifying areas for potential improvement and reform in both countries.

One notable difference highlighted in the table is that Kenya's Children Act 2001, revised in 2021, specifically mandates the consideration of diversion for all types of offenses, including severe and repeat offenses. This proactive approach allows for the early intervention and rehabilitation of juvenile offenders before formal charges are filed, aiming to prevent further delinquency and reduce the stigma associated with criminal behavior. In contrast, Tanzania's approach to juvenile justice, as indicated in the table, appears more reactive and less focused on structured diversion options.

Tanzania's legal framework does not provide as comprehensive a set of guidelines and policies explicitly dedicated to diversion programs compared to Kenya. Kenya has detailed Diversion Policy (2019), which provide specific guidance on the implementation of diversion measures. These documents likely contribute to a more structured and consistent application of diversion practices across different regions in Kenya.

Similarly, Tanzania's juvenile justice system faces substantial challenges that hinder its effectiveness in safeguarding children in conflict with the law. As indicated in the table, one of the primary issues is the limited operationalization of legal provisions across different regions. This inconsistency leads to unequal access to justice for juvenile offenders, depending on where they are located and the resources available locally. The lack of a strong emphasis on diversion programs exacerbates these challenges. Diversion, which offers alternative paths to rehabilitation and reintegration outside of traditional judicial processes, is underutilized in Tanzania. This omission overlooks an opportunity to address juvenile offenses early and effectively, potentially reducing recidivism rates and promoting positive outcomes for young offenders (Bakta, 2016).

Moreover, Tanzania's juvenile justice system suffers from gaps in child protection and inconsistencies in the treatment of juvenile offenders. Kadilu (2017) underscores the need for urgent reforms to standardize child-friendly practices and eliminate punitive measures like corporal punishment. These reforms are essential to bring Tanzania's approach in line with international standards that prioritize the best interests of the child and rehabilitation over punishment. Anderson's (2012) analysis further reveals systemic issues, such as the lack of coordination among judicial institutions, social welfare officers, families, and communities. This fragmentation impedes effective case management and support provision for juvenile offenders throughout their legal proceedings and rehabilitation processes.

Overall, while the two countries share common goals of aligning their juvenile justice systems with international standards and promoting rehabilitation, they differ in the specificity and implementation of their legal frameworks, particularly regarding diversion programs and the types of offences eligible for diversion. Kenya's approach is more structured and proactive in implementing diversion before charges, whereas Tanzania faces challenges in operationalizing diversion and ensuring consistent implementation of juvenile justice principles. The countries need ongoing reforms to improve their juvenile justice systems and protect juvenile offenders' rights and welfare.

6.2 Types of Rehabilitation Programs

Rehabilitation within juvenile justice systems is theoretically vital for correcting young offenders' behavior and promoting their successful reintegration into society (Aazami et al., 2023). Both Kenya and Tanzania emphasize rehabilitation in their juvenile justice frameworks, though their strategies and implementation differ, reflecting distinct societal contexts and challenges.

In Kenya, rehabilitation programs prioritize culturally rooted interventions, often incorporating community elders in counseling efforts. This approach resonates with local values, fostering both rehabilitation and the reinforcement of positive cultural norms. According to Karanja (2021), community-based interventions involving elders in counseling sessions have demonstrated positive outcomes, reducing recidivism rates and strengthening social cohesion. Additionally, vocational training in Kenya often targets sectors aligned with the country's economic needs, such as agriculture and technology. Programs like the "Youth Empowerment Program" provide hands-on training that has led to a measurable decrease in recidivism rates, equipping juveniles with skills that enhance their employability (Mutua, 2022). The integration of practical skill-building into rehabilitation efforts reflects the economic landscape of Kenya and its focus on sustainable employment for reintegrating offenders.

In contrast, Tanzania employs a community-based approach that leverages familial and social structures to support rehabilitation. Programs actively engage families and local leaders, fostering a collective sense of responsibility for juvenile offenders (Sigonda, 2000). This approach acknowledges the influence of familial and communal relationships in shaping juvenile behavior, emphasizing social reintegration over punitive measures. Moreover, vocational training in Tanzania frequently incorporates local crafts and trades, encouraging pride in cultural heritage while providing practical skills. Evaluations show that juveniles who participate in community-based skill-building workshops experience lower reoffending rates and improved social integration (Sigonda, 2000). Tanzania's focus on using local traditions as a foundation for rehabilitation mirrors the country's broader socio-cultural priorities.

Despite these efforts, both countries face significant challenges that undermine the effectiveness of their rehabilitation programs. In Kenya, underfunding poses a major issue. The Kenya National Commission on Human Rights (2020) reported that less than 10% of the juvenile justice budget is allocated to rehabilitation programs, resulting in limited resources and a reduced scope of services. This funding gap affects the availability and quality of programs, making it difficult to maintain consistent rehabilitation efforts across the country. Similarly, in Tanzania, bureaucratic inefficiencies and inadequate training for personnel hinder the implementation of effective rehabilitation services. This lack of capacity not only limits access to essential services but also compromises the quality of care provided to juvenile offenders.

In terms of legal frameworks, Kenya's Children Act (2001, revised in 2021) provides a comprehensive set of diversionary measures aimed at promoting accountability and facilitating successful reintegration. These measures include restorative justice practices such as requiring unconditional apologies to victims and promoting restitution or compensation (Muema et al., 2023). Kenya's focus on individualized approaches, such as community service, vocational training, and counseling, demonstrates a commitment to reducing recidivism through targeted rehabilitation efforts. The emphasis on vocational training, counseling for substance abuse, and supervision by children's officers reflects Kenya's holistic approach to addressing the underlying causes of juvenile delinquency.

On the other hand, Tanzania's legal framework under the Law of the Child Act (2019) focuses heavily on community-based rehabilitation, emphasizing psychosocial care, life skills training, and family reintegration (Casey, 2019). However, Tanzania's framework lacks the detailed diversionary measures found in Kenya's legal system, which can lead to inconsistencies in implementation. Despite this, Tanzania's reliance on local resources and communal engagement offers a culturally relevant approach to juvenile justice that aligns with the country's broader social structures.

Both countries, despite their rehabilitation-focused frameworks, continue to face challenges in implementation. In Kenya, inconsistent application of diversionary measures across regions and insufficient resources hinder the full realization of the Children Act's objectives. Tanzania, with its more localized approach, struggles with disparities in program effectiveness due to varying regional contexts and limited resources.

6.3 Best Practices and Challenges

Balancing diversion and rehabilitation in Kenya and Tanzania poses both opportunities and challenges within their respective juvenile justice systems. In Kenya, the Children Act 2001, revised in 2021, exemplifies a proactive approach emphasizing rehabilitation through a variety of diversionary measures aimed at juvenile offenders. These measures include restorative practices such as apologies to victims and community service, alongside counseling, vocational training, and supervision by children's officers (Muema et al., 2023). By focusing on these interventions, Kenya seeks to address the underlying causes of juvenile delinquency and promote positive behavioral change, thus aligning with international best practices that prioritize rehabilitation over punitive measures.

However, Kenya faces challenges in effectively implementing these diversionary measures across all regions and consistently for all types of offenses. The system's capacity to provide adequate resources, including trained personnel and rehabilitation facilities, remains uneven, impacting the quality and accessibility of these programs (UNICEF, 2019). Moreover, there is a need for greater coordination among stakeholders involved in the juvenile justice process to ensure that diversion programs are applied consistently and effectively.

In Tanzania, while legal provisions like the Law of the Child Act R.E. (2019) and related guidelines emphasize rehabilitation and child-friendly procedures, the implementation of diversionary measures presents significant challenges. The focus on community rehabilitation services, counseling, and life skills programs demonstrates an intent to rehabilitate juvenile offenders and reintegrate them into society (URT, 2019). However, the actual operationalization of these programs varies widely across regions, leading to inconsistencies in treatment and outcomes for juvenile offenders (Kadilu, 2017).

Tanzania also grapples with systemic issues such as the persistence of punitive measures like corporal punishment and insufficient resources allocated to juvenile justice programs (Bakta, 2016). These challenges hinder the effective implementation of diversionary approaches and undermine efforts to prioritize rehabilitation over punishment. Moreover, the lack of comprehensive data and monitoring mechanisms further complicates efforts to evaluate the impact and effectiveness of diversion programs in Tanzania (Anderson, 2012).

In both countries, addressing these challenges requires sustained efforts to enhance the capacity and coordination of juvenile justice systems. Strengthening institutional frameworks, increasing resource allocations, and improving training for personnel involved in juvenile rehabilitation are crucial steps towards achieving a balanced approach that effectively integrates diversion and rehabilitation practices. By learning from international best practices and committing to continuous improvement, Kenya and Tanzania can advance their juvenile justice systems to better serve the rehabilitation needs of young offenders while promoting community safety and welfare.

7. CONCLUSIONS AND RECOMMENDATIONS

The analysis finds that Kenya and Tanzania have made great progress in aligning their juvenile justice systems with international standards. Kenya's juvenile justice system takes a proactive approach to diversion and rehabilitation. This legal framework requires the consideration of diversion for all sorts of offences and includes extensive recommendations for execution. Kenya seeks to treat juvenile delinquency holistically by emphasising early intervention and rehabilitation through structured programs such as community service, counselling, and vocational training. Tanzania's legal laws, while consistent with international norms, place little focus on structured diversion programs. Tanzania's approach is more focused on community-based rehabilitation, indicating a reactive position in comparison to Kenya.

Kenya's juvenile offender rehabilitation programs are also distinguished by a holistic approach and a wide range of interventions adapted to individual requirements. These programs seek not just to address the underlying reasons of delinquency, but also to assist successful reintegration into society. Tanzania's approach, on the other hand, focusses on community-based services and life skills training, but lacks the specificity and consistency seen in Kenya's rehabilitation initiatives. This distinction complicates delivering uniform outcomes across areas and guaranteeing successful rehabilitation for all juvenile offenders.

Finally, the study reveals that both countries face obstacles in implementing effective diversion and rehabilitation techniques within their juvenile justice systems. Kenya faces difficulties such as varying diversion practices and limited resources, needing stronger stakeholder collaboration. Similarly, Tanzania has discrepancies in implementing legislative rules, insufficient resources, and systemic difficulties such as the permanence of punitive actions.

Based on the highlighted difficulties and conclusions of Kenya and Tanzania's juvenile justice systems, below are three major recommendations:

1. Kenya and Tanzania should create comprehensive training programs for court officers, law enforcement, social workers, and other stakeholders in juvenile justice. These programs should prioritise understanding and implementing diversion programs. Training sessions should emphasise the significance of early intervention, identifying appropriate diversion options, and consistently applying diversion procedures across all areas and types of offences. By providing professionals with the appropriate skills and information, both countries can ensure that diversion programs are used effectively to rehabilitate adolescents in conflict with the law.
2. Addressing funding restrictions is critical for extending and improving diversion programs in both nations. Kenya should provide adequate funding to establish and sustain a variety of diversion programs such as community service, counselling, and vocational training. This includes investing in the infrastructure, staff, and resources required to provide these services successfully. Similarly, Tanzania should expand financing for community-based rehabilitation services and strengthen infrastructure to enable distinct diversion programs in various

locations. By increasing budget allocation, both countries can improve their ability to provide comprehensive and effective diversionary strategies suited to the requirements of juvenile offenders.

3. Kenya and Tanzania should prioritise research and collaborate with academics and international organisations to promote evidence-based practices in juvenile justice. Regular reviews and assessments of diversion programs are required to determine their efficacy in reducing recidivism and fostering positive outcomes for children. Both countries may learn from one another and adopt new approaches to improving their juvenile justice systems by sharing findings and best practices via regional and international networks. This collaborative initiative will promote continual development and alignment with international standards for diversion and rehabilitation of children involved in the criminal system.
4. To extend and improve diversion programs, both Kenya and Tanzania must address resource constraints by giving adequate funds to provide a variety of diversion options, such as community service, counselling, and vocational training. Kenya should invest in required facilities, personnel, and materials, whereas Tanzania should enhance financing for community-based rehabilitation and infrastructure improvements to support regionally unique initiatives. Both countries should prioritise research and engagement with academic institutions and international organisations to develop evidence-based juvenile justice practices. Regular reviews, exchanging findings, and learning from one another will help to develop juvenile justice systems, line with worldwide norms, and improve rehabilitation outcomes for juvenile offenders.

REFERENCES

Aazami, A., Valek, R., Ponce, A. N., & Zare, H. (2023). A Systematic Assessment of Risk and Protective Factors and Interventions to Reduce Juvenile Delinquency. *Soc. Sci.*, *12*, 474.

Akers, J. F., Jones, R. M., & Coyl, D. D. (1998). Adolescent friendship pairs: Similarities in identity status development, behaviors, attitudes, and intentions. *Journal of Adolescent Research*, *13*(2), 178–201.

Aspers, P., & Corte, U. (2019). What is qualitative in qualitative research. *Qualitative Sociology*, *42*, 139–160.

Atilola, O., Abiri, G., & Ola, B. (2020). Psychiatric morbidity among adolescents and youth involved with the juvenile justice system in sub-Saharan Africa: Systematic scoping review of current studies and research gaps. *International Journal of Law and Psychiatry*, *73*, 101633.

Bagley, B. M., & Rosen, J. D. (2017). *Drug trafficking, organized crime, and violence in the Americas today*. University Press of Florida.

Bakta, S. (2016). *A critical examination of the child justice system in mainland Tanzania*. South Africa: Doctorate thesis, University of Cape Town.

Barretto, C., Miers, S., & Lambie, L. (2018). The views of the public on youth offenders and the New Zealand criminal justice system. *International Journal of Offender Therapy and Comparative Criminology*, *62*(1), 129–149.

Becker, H. S. (1963). *Outsiders: Studies in the sociology of deviance*. Free Press Glencoe.

Bynum, J. E., & Thompson, W. E. (1996). *Juvenile delinquency: A sociological approach* (3rd ed.). Allyn & Bacon.

Bynum, W. E., & Thompson, J. E. (1996). *Juvenile delinquency: A sociological approach*. Allyn and Bacon.

Cameron, E. (2020). The crisis of criminal justice in South Africa. *South African Law Journal*, *137*(1), 32–71.

Case, S., & Haines, K. (2021). Abolishing youth justice systems: Children first, offenders nowhere. *Youth Justice*, *21*(1), 3–17.

Casey, S. (2019). *Diversion of Children in Conflict with the Law: International Models and Best Practices*. UNICEF ESARO.

Chanila, D. S., Mohamed, F., & Pittman, S. (2024). Re implementation of the diversion program in juvenile justice administration in Dar es salaam, Tanzania: Benefits and challenges. *Institute of Social Work Journal*, *3*(1), 1–32.

Clifford, W. (2024). Zambia. In *African Penal Systems* (pp. 237–258). Routledge.

Corrado, D., Wichter, T., Link, M. S., Hauer, R., Marchlinski, F., Anastasakis, A., & Calkins, H. (2015). Treatment of arrhythmogenic right ventricular cardiomyopathy/dysplasia: An international task force consensus statement. *European Heart Journal*, *36*(46), 3227–3237.

Creswell, J. W., & Báez, J. C. (2020). *30 essential skills for the qualitative researcher*. Sage Publications.

Dean, J. (2018). *The use of diversion in juvenile justice settings in Australia with particular focus on the state of Victoria.* Retrieved August 2024, from Institute for Criminal Justice Reform: http://icjr. or. id/wp-content/uploads/2018/05/The-Use-of-Diversion-in-Juvenile-Justice-Diala, A. C., & Kangwa, B. (2019). Rethinking the interface between customary law and constitutionalism in sub-Saharan Africa. *De Jure Law Journal*, 52(1), 189-206.

Feld, B. C. (2019). *The evolution of the juvenile court: Race, politics, and the criminalizing of juvenile justice* (Vol. 4). NYU Press.

Gibbons, D. C., & Blake, G. F. (1976). Evaluatin the Impact of Juvenile Diversion Programs. *Crime and Delinquency*, *22*(4), 411–420.

Goldson, B. (2015). Child criminalisation and the mistake of early intervention. *Criminal Justice Matters*, *102*(1), 27–28.

Grusec, J. E. (1992). Social learning theory and developmental psychology: The legacies of Robert Sears and Albert Bandura. *Developmental Psychology*, *28*(5), 776–786.

Hart, D. (2014). *Pre-court arrangements for children who offend.* National Association for Youth Justice.

Johnson, J. L., Adkins, D., & Chauvin, S. (2020). A review of the quality indicators of rigor in qualitative research. *American Journal of Pharmaceutical Education*, *84*(1), 7120.

Kadilu, M. (2017). *Protecting the rights of detained juvenile delinquents: Tanzania's compliance with international standards.* India: Phd Thesis, Acharya Nagarjuna University.

Kenya National Bureau of Statistics. (2021). *Economic Survey Report*. Government Printers.

Loeb, R. C., Waung, M., & Sheeran, M. (2015). Individual and familial variables for predicting successful completion of a juvenile justice diversion program. *Journal of Offender Rehabilitation, 54*(3), 212–237.

Lundman, R. J. (1993). *Prevention and control of juvenile delinquency*. Oxford University Press.

McAra, L., & McVie, S. (2018). Transformations in youth crime and justice. In Goldson, B. (Ed.), *Juvenile Justice in Europe: Past, Present and Future. Abingdon* (pp. 74–103). Routledge.

Mears, D. P., Kuch, J. J., Lindsey, A. M., Siennick, S. E., Pesta, G. B., Greenwald, M. A., & Blomberg, T. G. (2016). Juvenile court and contemporary diversion. *Criminology & Public Policy, 15*(3), 953–981.

Mensa-Bonsu, M. A. (n.d.). The Trouble with Judicial Amendments: Lessons from Ghana.

Miller, G. E., & Prinz, R. J. (1990). Enhancement of social learning family interventions for childhood conduct disorder. *Psychological Bulletin, 108*(2), 291.

Milner, A. (2024). *African penal systems*. Taylor & Francis.

Muema, F. M., Nyangwencha, S. K., & Njoroge, M. (2023). *Perceptions of Justice Involved Children on the Child Justice System in Nairobi County*. The University Journal.

Murhula, P. B., & Singh, S. B. (2019). A critical evaluation of the literature on the rehabilitation technique for offenders in South Africa. *African Journal of Criminology and Justice Studies, 12*(1), 12.

National Crime Research Centre. (2023). *Efficacy and adequacy of criminal Justice agencies in Kenya: the case of children in conflict with the law*. NCRC.

NeMoyer, A., Gale-Bentz, E., Goldstein, N. E., & Pema Harvey, L. (2020). Factors associated with successful completion of a community-based, postarrest juvenile diversion program and subsequent rearrest. *Crime and Delinquency, 66*(5), 603–626.

Ozturk, B., Bell, A., McLeod, D., & Gentzler, R. (2022). Criminal justice diversion and the importance of program retention. *Journal of Forensic Social Work, 6*(1), 43–56.

Pappas, L. N., & Dent, A. L. (2023). The 40-year debate: A meta-review on what works for juvenile offenders. *Journal of Experimental Criminology*, *19*(1), 1–30.

Penal Reform International. (2013). *UK Aid The Minimum Age of Criminal Responsibility (Justice for Children Briefing No. 4)*. Penal Reform International.

Robin-D'Cruz, C. (2019). *Mapping youth diversion in England and Wales.* Retrieved August 2024, from https://justiceinnovation.org/portfolio/mapping-youth-diversion

Robinson, W. S. (2009). Ecological correlations and the behavior of individuals. *International Journal of Epidemiology*, *38*(2), 337–341.

Sarwanto, A. (2023). The Phenomenon of Juvenile Delinquency that Occurs in the Era of Globalization. *The Easta Journal Law and Human Rights*, *1*(02), 45–50.

Sigonda, G. G. G. (2000). *The Impact of Infrastructural Projects on the Environment in Tanzania: The Case of Mindu Dam*. The University of Manchester.

Thorpe, D. H., Smith, D., Green, C. J., & Paley, J. H. (2024). *Out of care: The community support of juvenile offenders*. Taylor & Francis.

Umbreit, M. S. (1994). Crime victims confront their offenders: The impact of a Minneapolis mediation program. *Research on Social Work Practice*, *4*(4), 436–447.

UNICEF. (2023). *Diversion of Children in Conflict with the Law in Eastern and Southern Africa Diversion programmes in the Eastern and Southern Africa Region: Best practices, opportunities and challenges.* UNICEF.

United Nations Office on Drugs and Crime. (2018). *Introductory handbook on the prevention of recidivism and the social reintegration of offenders.* Retrieved July 2024, from. https://www.unodc.org/documents/justice-and-prison-reform/18-02303_ebook.pdf

Walker, J. T., & Maddan, S. (2019). *Statistics in criminology and criminal justice*. Jones & Bartlett Learning.

Young, H., & Giller, C. (2021). Juvenile Delinquency in the United States of America. *Journal of Sociology, Psychology &. Religious Studies*, *3*(4), 1–7.

Young, S., Greer, B., & Church, R. (2017). Juvenile delinquency, welfare, justice and therapeutic interventions: A global perspective. *BJPsych Bulletin*, *41*(1), 21–29.

Zehr, H. (1990). *Changing lenses: A new focus for crime and justice*. Herald Press.

Zehr, H., & Mika, H. (1998). Fundamental concepts of restorative justice. *Contemporary Justice Review*, *1*, 47–55.

KEY TERMS AND DEFINITIONS

Comparative Analysis: This is a method of assessing the similarities and differences between diversion programs for juvenile offenders in Kenya and Tanzania. It entails assessing how each country's legal frameworks, rehabilitation programs, and issues align with or differ from one another in order to discover best practices and opportunities for development.

Diversion Programs: These are structured interventions that aim to move juvenile offenders away from formal court processes and towards rehabilitative options. The goal is to keep juveniles out of the formal judicial system by providing programs such as counselling, education, and community service that focus on behaviour correction and reintegration into society.

Juvenile Delinquency: This refers to criminal or deviant behaviour committed by minors (children under the age of 18) that violates legal or societal norms.

Juvenile Justice: This refers to the legal framework and procedures in place to deal with minors who participate in criminal activity. The juvenile justice system emphasises accountability while also focussing on rehabilitation and reintegration into society. In Kenya and Tanzania, juvenile justice policies seek to protect the rights of young offenders while also supporting their development.

Legal Provisions: These are the precise laws and rules that govern how juvenile offenders are handled by the court system. In this context, legal provisions relate to legislation in Kenya and Tanzania

Qualitative Methodology: This is the research approach used to gather in-depth, non-numerical data from sources like policy reports, case studies, and legislative documents. In this study, qualitative methods help analyze and compare the legal frameworks and rehabilitation strategies for juveniles in Kenya and Tanzania, focusing on their developmental and social implications.

Rehabilitation Programs: These are structured efforts that help juvenile offenders rectify their behaviour and reintegrate into society in a positive and constructive way. Rehabilitation programs in Kenya and Tanzania frequently emphasise community-based efforts, educational opportunities, vocational training, and psychological assistance in order to reduce recidivism.

Chapter 9

Challenges in Safeguarding Childrens' Rights in Kenya's Criminal Justice System:

A Prosecuter's View

Michael Kipkemei Sang
https://orcid.org/0009-0009-0086-5323
Office of the Director of Public Prosecutions, Kenya

ABSTRACT

This paper examines the practical challenges of safeguarding children's rights within Kenya's criminal justice system, focusing on gaps in legal representation, professional training, privacy protections, and support systems for vulnerable groups such as child parents, victims, and youth offenders. Drawing on lessons from jurisdictions like South Africa, Canada, the United Kingdom, and the United States, the paper offers actionable recommendations to strengthen Kenya's child justice framework. These include ensuring continuous legal assistance, enhancing accessibility of information, implementing individualized assessments, and safeguarding children's privacy in criminal proceedings. The study advocates for a child-centered, rights-based approach to justice that prioritizes rehabilitation and reintegration over punitive measures, aiming to align Kenya's practices with international standards and best practices.

DOI: 10.4018/978-1-6684-9343-4.ch009

1. INTRODUCTION

The protection of children's rights within the criminal justice system is a cornerstone of any society committed to justice and human dignity (Viola, 2009). In Kenya, the legal and policy frameworks for safeguarding the rights of children in conflict with the law are extensive, including the Constitution, the Children Act, and the Legal Aid Act. However, significant gaps persist in the practical implementation of these safeguards, leaving many children vulnerable to systemic failures and injustices (Viola, 2009). This paper critically examines the challenges and proposes reforms to ensure the realization of children's rights within Kenya's criminal justice system, drawing on comparative lessons from jurisdictions such as South Africa, Canada, the United Kingdom, and the United States.

Children in conflict with the law face unique vulnerabilities arising from their developmental stage, dependence on adults, and limited understanding of legal processes (Viola, 2009). Issues such as inadequate legal representation, lack of child-friendly procedures, breaches of privacy, and insufficient support systems exacerbate these vulnerabilities. Additionally, challenges such as youth radicalization, stigmatization of offenders, and the systemic neglect of vulnerable groups like child parents and victims further highlight the urgent need for reform (Viola, 2009).

This paper adopts a multi-dimensional approach to identify and address these challenges. It explores the statutory and policy frameworks currently in place, highlighting gaps and inconsistencies in their application. Practical challenges such as limited access to legal assistance, insufficient professional training, and weak privacy protections are analyzed in depth. Drawing lessons from jurisdictions with progressive child justice systems, the paper offers actionable recommendations, including ensuring continuous legal assistance, conducting individual child assessments, enhancing the accessibility of legal information, and protecting children's privacy.

By advocating for a child-centered and rights-based approach, this paper underscores the importance of aligning Kenya's criminal justice practices with international standards and best practices. Only by addressing these critical gaps can Kenya create a justice system that truly upholds the rights and dignity of children, fostering their rehabilitation and reintegration into society.

2. LEGAL AND POLICY FRAMEWORK OF CHILDREN'S RIGHTS IN KENYA'S CRIMINAL JUSTICE SYSTEM

This section sets out the current statutory and policy framework for the protection of the rights of children in conflict with the law.

2.1 Statutory Framework

2.1.1 Children Act, 2022

The **Children Act, 2022** provides a robust statutory framework for safeguarding the rights of children in conflict with the law within Kenya's criminal justice system. Key provisions relevant to the study include:

- **Best Interests of the Child**.

Section 8 establishes that the best interests of the child shall be the primary consideration in all matters involving children. This principle underpins the entire statutory framework (Children Act 2022, s. 8).

- **Rights of Children in Conflict with the Law**.

Section 26(7) of the Children Act, 2022 emphasizes that detention of children must be a measure of last resort and for the shortest appropriate period, in line with constitutional principles. Section 26(2) of the Act requires that children deprived of liberty be held separately from adults, with facilities appropriate to their age and needs (Children Act 2022, s.26(2)).

- **Diversion Mechanisms**.

Part XV introduces a diversion framework aimed at rehabilitating children and keeping them out of the formal justice system. Section 226 outlines the objectives of diversion, including reducing stigmatization and recidivism (Children Act 2022, s.226). **Section 230** of the Act provides levels of diversion interventions, while **Section 231** empowers courts to apply diversionary measures.

- **Procedural Rights**.

Section 220 of the Children Act, 2022 guarantees a child offender the right to be heard and to legal assistance. Section 243 requires proceedings involving child offenders to adopt child-friendly procedures to ensure their participation and protection.

- **Detention Standards**.

Sections 26(3) and 26(6) of the Children Act, 2022 mandate that children with disabilities or other special needs receive accommodations that meet their personal needs during detention.

- **Specialized Institutions**.

Section 77 of the Children Act, 2022 establishes remand homes for the temporary care of children in conflict with the law, and Section 78 provides for rehabilitation schools for corrective measures, emphasizing education and reintegration.

2.1.2 Legal Aid Act, 2016

The Legal Aid Act, 2016 is a significant statutory framework that promotes access to justice for vulnerable groups, including children in conflict with the law (Legal Aid Act, 2016). Relevant provisions include:

- **Right to Legal Representation**.

Section 36(1)(b) of the Legal Aid Act, 2016 explicitly recognizes children as eligible for legal aid services, ensuring they receive state-supported legal representation (Legal Aid Act 2016, s.36(1)(b)). Section 43(3) mandates courts to ensure unrepresented children in proceedings under the Children Act or other laws are provided with legal representation by the National Legal Aid Service (NLAS).

- **Institutional Responsibility**.

Section 7(1)(f) of the Legal Aid Act, 2016 tasks the NLAS with facilitating legal representation for indigent children in conflict with the law. Section 7(1)(k) of the Act mandates the NLAS to promote legal literacy and educate vulnerable groups, including children, on their rights (Legal Aid Act 2016, s.7(1)(k)).

- **Support for Children in Custody**.

Section 42(1) of the Legal Aid Act, 2016 requires officers in charge of children's remand homes or other places of lawful custody to inform children of their right to legal aid and facilitate applications for such aid.

- **Criteria for Legal Aid**.

Section 36(4) of the Legal Aid Act, 2016 stipulates that the NLAS must ensure resources are allocated to cases where the cost is justified by the seriousness and importance of the proceedings. For children, this underscores prioritizing cases involving potential significant harm or loss of rights (Legal Aid Act 2016, s.36(4)).

- **Legal Awareness and Education**.

Section 7(1)(k) of the Legal Aid Act, 2016 includes the mandate to raise awareness about the legal rights of children, equipping them to understand and assert their rights effectively.

- **Alternative Dispute Resolution (ADR)**.

Section 39 of the Legal Aid Act, 2016 highlights ADR as a means to resolve disputes, which can benefit children by providing less adversarial and more rehabilitative approaches (Legal Aid Act 2016, s.39)

2.1.3 Penal Code (Cap. 63)

The Penal Code provides critical statutory provisions relevant to safeguarding the rights of children in conflict with the law, particularly regarding age-appropriate criminal responsibility and procedural protections (Penal Code (Cap. 63)). Key sections include:

- **Immature Age and Criminal Responsibility**.

Section 14(1) of the Penal Code establishes that a child under the age of eight years is not criminally responsible for any act or omission (Penal Code, s. 14(1)). Section 14(2) provides that children aged between 8 and 12 years are presumed incapable of criminal intent unless proven that they had sufficient capacity to understand the act and its consequences.

- **Detention and Sentencing**.

Section 18 of the Penal Code regulates the use of force in effecting arrests, emphasizing proportionality and necessity, which is particularly relevant when dealing with children. Section 25 prohibits the imposition of the death penalty on offenders who were below 18 years at the time of the commission of the offense (Penal Code, s.25)

- **Offenses Specific to Children.**

Section 146 of the Penal Code addresses the protection of children with mental illnesses from exploitation, particularly in offenses related to morality. Section 174 criminalizes child stealing, highlighting the special protection accorded to children under the law (Penal Code, s.174).

- **Safeguards Against Abuse.**

Section 242A of the Penal Code prohibits the supply of harmful substances to children, ensuring their protection from criminal exploitation and harm.

- **General Duties.**

Section 216 of the Penal Code underscores the responsibility of persons in charge of a child to provide necessaries of life, failure of which is a punishable offense.

2.1.4 Criminal Procedure Code (Cap. 75)

The Criminal Procedure Code (CPC) outlines the procedural safeguards for children in conflict with the law (Criminal Procedure Code (Cap. 75)). Key provisions include:

- **Bail Provisions.**

Section 123 of the Criminal Procedure Code establishes the right to bail, emphasizing that bail should be granted to child offenders unless there are compelling reasons to deny it.

- **Protection of Identity.**

Section 77 of the Criminal Procedure Code mandates open court proceedings but allows for closed sessions in cases involving children to protect their identities and interests.

- **Right to Legal Representation.**

Section 193 of the Criminal Procedure Code upholds the right of all accused persons, including children, to legal representation (Criminal Procedure Code, s.193).

- **Reconciliation**.

Section 176 of the Criminal Procedure Code promotes reconciliation, an integral principle for handling juvenile offenders.

2.2 Policy Framework

2.2.1 National Strategy on Justice for Children 2023-2028

The National Strategy on Justice for Children (2023-2028) is a comprehensive framework developed by Kenya's National Council on the Administration of Justice (NCAJ) to enhance the administration and access to justice for children (National Strategy on Justice for Children, 2023-2028). Launched in July 2024, this strategy underscores the country's commitment to safeguarding children's rights within the justice system (National Strategy on Justice for Children, 2023-2028).

Key Objectives include:

- Coordinated Approach: Ensure a coordinated, efficient, effective, and consultative approach in the administration of justice for children in Kenya.
- Stakeholder Empowerment: Empower stakeholders to prevent violence against children and ensure timely responses, promoting child participation towards a child-friendly justice system that is well-resourced.
- Strengthened Coordination: Enhance coordination among NCAJ and relevant stakeholders to promote, protect, and improve access to justice for children in both formal and informal sectors.
- Monitoring and Evaluation: Establish a monitoring, evaluation, learning, and budgeting framework for the child justice system (National Strategy on Justice for Children, 2023-2028).

Strategic Focus Areas include:

- Child-Friendly Facilities: Develop and maintain facilities that cater specifically to the needs of children within the justice system.
- Training of Justice Actors: Provide specialized training for justice actors to handle children's cases with sensitivity and expertise.
- Resource Allocation: Advocate for increased budgetary allocations to support the effective implementation of child justice initiatives.
- Community Engagement: Foster partnerships with communities, civil society organizations, and development partners to create a holistic child-friendly justice sector (National Strategy on Justice for Children, 2023-2028).

The strategy also emphasizes the importance of addressing systemic issues such as abuse, neglect, and exploitation, recognizing these as societal failures that hinder national progress. By implementing this strategy, Kenya aims to transform how society and the justice system interact with and protect children, ensuring their rights are upheld and their well-being prioritized (National Strategy on Justice for Children, 2023-2028).

2.2.2 The Child Justice Strategy

The Child Justice Strategy is a pivotal component of Kenya's policy framework aimed at safeguarding children's rights within the criminal justice system. This strategy outlines a comprehensive approach to prevent children from coming into conflict with the law and to protect those who do (National Strategy on Justice for Children, 2023-2028).

Strategic Objectives of the Child Justice Strategy include:

- Prevention: Implement measures to prevent children from engaging in activities that may lead to legal conflicts.
- Protection: Ensure that children who come into contact with the law are treated with dignity and their rights are upheld throughout the judicial process.
- Rehabilitation: Focus on rehabilitative measures rather than punitive actions, aiming to reintegrate children into society as responsible individuals.
- Coordination: Enhance collaboration among various stakeholders, including government agencies, non-governmental organizations, and the community, to create a cohesive child justice system (National Strategy on Justice for Children, 2023-2028).

The strategy emphasizes the importance of a child-friendly justice system that is well-resourced and capable of addressing the unique needs of children. It also highlights the necessity for increased budgetary allocations to support child justice initiatives, as underscored by Chief Registrar of the Judiciary, Winfridah Mokaya, during the launch of the National Strategy on Justice for Children 2023-2028 (The Judiciary, 2024).

2.2.3 A Prosecutor's Guide to Children in the Criminal Justice System

The Prosecutor's Guide to Children in the Criminal Justice System is a comprehensive manual developed by Kenya's Office of the Director of Public Prosecutions (ODPP) to assist prosecutors in handling cases involving children (Office of the

Director of Public Prosecutions, 2020). Recognizing the complexities and sensitivities inherent in such cases, the guide aims to ensure that children's rights are upheld throughout the judicial process (Office of the Director of Public Prosecutions, 2020).

Key Objectives include:

- Enhance Awareness: Increase understanding among prosecutors regarding the rights of children in conflict with or in contact with the law.
- Provide Practical Framework: Offer clear guidelines to ensure that prosecutorial decisions and actions are in the best interests of the child (Office of the Director of Public Prosecutions, 2020).

The guide emphasizes several fundamental principles:

- Best Interests of the Child: Ensuring that all actions and decisions prioritize the child's welfare.
- Right to Representation: Guaranteeing that children have access to legal aid and assistance.
- Protection from Torture: Safeguarding children from any form of torture or degrading treatment.
- Participation and Right to Be Heard: Allowing children to express their views in matters affecting them.
- Deprivation of Liberty as a Last Resort: Ensuring that detention is used only when absolutely necessary.
- Promotion of Dignity and Worth: Treating children with respect and recognizing their inherent value.
- Protection from Discrimination: Ensuring equal treatment for all children, regardless of background.
- Right to Privacy: Protecting the confidentiality of children's information.
- Parental Care and Participation: Involving parents or guardians in the judicial process concerning their children (Office of the Director of Public Prosecutions, 2020).

Launched in November 2021, the guide serves as a practical tool for prosecutors, aiming to minimize discrimination and undue stress for children within the criminal justice system. It underscores the necessity for a child-friendly approach, ensuring that the judicial process is sensitive to the unique needs of children (Office of the Director of Public Prosecutions, 2020).

3. PRACTICAL CHALLENGES OF SAFEGUARDING CHILDREN'S RIGHTS IN KENYA'S CRIMINAL JUSTICE SYSTEM

This section identifies selected issues that are used to highlight the practical Challenges that face prosecutor and other criminal justice stakeholders.

3.1 Representation and Participation of Children in Criminal Proceedings

Ensuring the effective representation and participation of children in Kenya's criminal justice system presents several practical challenges for prosecutors and other stakeholders.

Many children lack access to adequate legal representation due to financial constraints and a shortage of child-focused legal aid services. While the National Legal Aid and Awareness Programme (NALEAP) provides assistance, its reach is limited, leaving many children without proper legal support (Oduor & Nyaata, 2022).

A significant number of legal practitioners are not sufficiently trained in child rights and child-friendly legal procedures. This gap can lead to inappropriate handling of cases involving children, potentially compromising their rights and well-being (Oduor & Nyaata, 2022).

Many courtrooms lack facilities and procedures tailored to the needs of children, making the legal process intimidating and inaccessible. The absence of child-friendly environments can deter children from effectively participating in proceedings (Oduor & Nyaata, 2022).

Cultural norms and societal attitudes often discourage children from speaking out or participating in legal matters, especially in cases involving family members or authority figures. This reluctance can hinder the pursuit of justice and the protection of children's rights (Oduor & Nyaata, 2022).

Many children are unaware of their legal rights and the mechanisms available to protect them. This lack of awareness impedes their ability to seek representation and participate meaningfully in legal proceedings (Oduor & Nyaata, 2022).

Prolonged legal processes can be particularly detrimental to children, causing unnecessary stress and potentially violating their right to a speedy trial. Delays may result from systemic inefficiencies or a backlog of cases (Oduor & Nyaata, 2022).

There is a scarcity of support services, such as counseling and psychological assistance, for child victims and offenders. The lack of these services can affect their ability to participate effectively in proceedings and recover from trauma (Oduor & Nyaata, 2022).

3.2 Children Who are Vulnerable Victims and Witnesses

Safeguarding the rights of vulnerable child victims and witnesses within Kenya's criminal justice system presents several practical challenges:

Many child victims and witnesses lack access to essential support services, such as counseling and psychological assistance. This deficiency can impede their ability to participate effectively in legal proceedings and recover from trauma (Kiniti, 2013).

A significant number of legal practitioners are not adequately trained to handle cases involving vulnerable children. This gap can lead to inappropriate questioning and handling, potentially causing further distress to the child (Kiniti, 2013).

Many courtrooms are not equipped to accommodate the needs of child victims and witnesses, making the legal process intimidating and inaccessible. The absence of child-friendly environments can deter children from effectively participating in proceedings (Kiniti, 2013).

Cultural norms and societal attitudes often discourage children from speaking out or participating in legal matters, especially in cases involving family members or authority figures. This reluctance can hinder the pursuit of justice and the protection of children's rights (Kiniti, 2013).

Children may fear retaliation from perpetrators, especially in cases involving organized crime or familial abuse. This fear can discourage them from testifying or cooperating with legal authorities (Kiniti, 2013).

Prolonged legal processes can be particularly detrimental to child victims and witnesses, causing unnecessary stress and potentially violating their right to a speedy trial. Delays may result from systemic inefficiencies or a backlog of cases (Kiniti, 2013).

Existing legal frameworks may not provide sufficient protection for vulnerable child victims and witnesses, leading to gaps in their protection and support during legal proceedings (Kiniti, 2013).

3.3 Children Who are Vulnerable Offenders

3.3.1 Child Parents – Republic v BC [2022] KEHC 17153 (KLR)

The case of *Republic v BC* highlights critical challenges in handling child parents as offenders within Kenya's criminal justice system. The judgment, delivered by Justice Matheka, underscores systemic gaps and the need for child-centered approaches in such cases (*Republic v BC*, 2022).

The subject, a 17-year-old child, was charged with the murder of her firstborn child. She was a survivor of early childhood trauma, having been married at 15 and subsequently abandoned by her husband while pregnant with her second child. The child experienced neglect and abuse, which led to psychological distress and the tragic circumstances surrounding the case (*Republic v BC*, 2022).

The judgment criticized the police and prosecution for focusing solely on the crime without investigating the surrounding issues of child marriage and defilement (*Republic v BC*, 2022, paras 22-23).

There was no compliance with Section 218 of the Children Act, 2022 which mandates police to notify the Secretary of Children Services and facilitate a social inquiry report within 24 hours of arrest (*Republic v BC*, 2022, para 10). This failure denied the subject critical protections and assessments meant to safeguard her welfare.

The court emphasized that child offenders are often children in need of care and protection, as recognized under Section 144 of the Children Act (*Republic v BC*, 2022, para 1). The court noted the importance of balancing criminal proceedings with measures to address the child's welfare and rehabilitation needs (*Republic v BC*, 2022, paras 6-7).

The court accepted a plea agreement, reducing the charge to manslaughter. This approach considered the subject's mitigating circumstances, including her psychological trauma and victimization (*Republic v BC*, 2022, paras 15-18).

The court employed restorative justice measures, including probation, counseling, and vocational training, as stipulated under Section 239(1) of the Children Act (*Republic v BC*, 2022, paras 29-31).

The subject was committed to the SGP Hostel for rehabilitation, with provisions for counseling, psychological support, and medical care during her pregnancy (*Republic v BC*, 2022, para 35).

The court identified various challenges:

- Inadequate Coordination: Lack of coordination between child protection agencies, as evidenced by the delayed and incomplete submission of reports from the Directorate of Children Services and Probation Services (*Republic v BC*, 2022, paras 19-20).
- Systemic Gaps in Justice Agencies: Insufficient awareness and implementation of child protection laws by justice stakeholders (*Republic v BC*, 2022, para 11).
- Neglect of Gender-Based Violence Context: The court highlighted the failure to address the defilement and child marriage aspects of the case, reflecting systemic insensitivity to the vulnerabilities of child parents (*Republic v BC*, 2022, paras 23-24).

This judgment illustrates the importance of adopting a holistic and child-sensitive approach to justice for vulnerable child parents.

3.3.2 Youth Sexual Offenders

Addressing the rights of youth sexual offenders within Kenya's criminal justice system presents multifaceted challenges that require a delicate balance between accountability, rehabilitation, and safeguarding the rights of the young individuals involved (Musiega, 2021).

Youth sexual offenders often face significant societal stigma, which can impede their reintegration into the community. This stigmatization may lead to isolation, hindering rehabilitation efforts and increasing the risk of recidivism (Musiega, 2021).

There is a scarcity of specialized rehabilitation programs tailored to the unique needs of youth sexual offenders. Existing facilities may lack the resources and trained personnel necessary to address the psychological and behavioural aspects of sexual offending among youths (Musiega, 2021).

The criminal justice system often grapples with balancing the need for accountability with the rights of juvenile offenders. Ensuring fair trials, appropriate sentencing, and access to legal representation are critical yet challenging aspects (Musiega, 2021).

Judicial officers, prosecutors, and law enforcement personnel may lack specialized training in handling cases involving youth sexual offenders. This deficiency can lead to inappropriate handling of cases, potentially infringing on the rights of the offenders and victims alike (Musiega, 2021).

There is a notable lack of comprehensive support systems, including counseling and family therapy, which are essential for the rehabilitation of youth sexual offenders. The absence of such support can hinder the offender's ability to reform and reintegrate into society (Musiega, 2021).

Community attitudes towards youth sexual offenders can be punitive rather than rehabilitative. Engaging communities in the rehabilitation process is crucial, yet challenging, due to prevailing negative perceptions (Musiega, 2021).

3.4 Privacy Rights of Children in the Criminal Justice System

Safeguarding the privacy rights of children within Kenya's criminal justice system is essential to protect their dignity and promote their rehabilitation (Nkirote, 2016). However, several practical challenges impede the effective protection of these rights:

While the Constitution of Kenya and the Children Act provide for the protection of children's privacy, there are gaps in implementation and enforcement. For instance, the Children Act mandates that proceedings involving children be conducted in camera to protect their identities, but this is not consistently applied (Nkirote, 2016).

Instances of media outlets publishing information that could lead to the identification of child offenders or victims are not uncommon. This exposure can lead to stigmatization and psychological harm, undermining the child's right to privacy (Nkirote, 2016).

The rise of digital technologies has introduced new challenges in protecting children's privacy. Inadequate data protection measures can lead to unauthorized access and misuse of children's personal information. The Communications Authority of Kenya has recognized these risks and developed draft Industry Guidelines for Child Online Protection and Safety to address them (Nkirote, 2016).

There is a general lack of awareness among law enforcement officers, judicial personnel, and the public regarding the importance of maintaining the confidentiality of children's information. This ignorance can result in unintentional breaches of privacy (Nkirote, 2016).

Many legal practitioners are not adequately trained in handling cases involving children, leading to potential breaches of privacy during legal proceedings. The Office of the Director of Public Prosecutions has developed a Prosecutor's Guide to Children in the Criminal Justice System to address this issue, emphasizing the protection of children's privacy rights (Nkirote, 2016).

3.5 Youth Radicalized by Extremist Content

Addressing the issue of youth radicalization by extremist content within Kenya's criminal justice system presents several practical challenges:

The proliferation of internet access has facilitated the spread of extremist ideologies among Kenyan youth. Extremist groups utilize social media platforms to disseminate radical content, making it challenging for authorities to monitor and counteract these influences effectively (Mudeizi, 2022).

High unemployment rates and economic disparities make youth more susceptible to radicalization. The lack of economic opportunities can lead to frustration and a sense of marginalization, which extremist groups exploit to recruit young individuals (Mudeizi, 2022).

There is a scarcity of specialized rehabilitation programs tailored to the unique needs of radicalized youth. Existing facilities may lack the resources and trained personnel necessary to address the psychological and ideological aspects of radicalization among youths (Mudeizi, 2022).

The criminal justice system often grapples with balancing the need for accountability with the rights of juvenile offenders. Ensuring fair trials, appropriate sentencing, and access to legal representation are critical yet challenging aspects (Mudeizi, 2022).

Judicial officers, prosecutors, and law enforcement personnel may lack specialized training in handling cases involving radicalized youth. This deficiency can lead to inappropriate handling of cases, potentially infringing on the rights of the offenders and victims alike (Mudeizi, 2022).

There is a notable lack of comprehensive support systems, including counseling and family therapy, which are essential for the rehabilitation of radicalized youth. The absence of such support can hinder the offender's ability to reform and reintegrate into society (Mudeizi, 2022).

Community attitudes towards radicalized youth can be punitive rather than rehabilitative. Engaging communities in the rehabilitation process is crucial, yet challenging, due to prevailing negative perceptions (Mudeizi, 2022).

4. PROPOSALS FOR STRENGTHENING CHILDREN'S RIGHTS IN KENYA'S CRIMINAL JUSTICE SYSTEM: COMPARATIVE LESSONS

This section borrows lessons from the experiences of comparative jurisdictions and uses them to makes specific proposals for strengthening children's rights in the criminal justice system of Kenya.

4.1 Continuous and Effective Legal Assistance

Ensuring continuous and effective legal assistance for children in conflict with the law is crucial for safeguarding their rights within the criminal justice system (Prinsloo, 2008). Examining South Africa's approach provides valuable insights for enhancing Kenya's legal framework.

4.1.1 South Africa

South Africa's legal system offers robust provisions for legal assistance to children:

- Automatic Legal Aid Provision: Children accused of criminal offenses are entitled to automatic legal representation without the need to prove financial incapacity. This ensures that all children, regardless of their economic status, have access to legal counsel (Prinsloo, 2008).
- Specialized Legal Aid Units: The Legal Aid Board (LAB) has established dedicated units focusing on children's cases, providing specialized representation in criminal courts and children's courts (Prinsloo, 2008).
- Child-Friendly Legal Procedures: The Child Justice Act mandates that legal proceedings involving children be conducted in a manner that is understand-

able and accessible to them, promoting their active participation (Prinsloo, 2008).

4.1.2 Lessons for Kenya

To strengthen children's rights within its criminal justice system, Kenya can adopt the following measures:

- Automatic Entitlement to Legal Aid: Implement policies ensuring that all children accused of criminal offenses receive free legal representation without the need to demonstrate financial need. This aligns with international standards and promotes equitable access to justice.
- Establishment of Specialized Legal Aid Units: Create dedicated units within the National Legal Aid Service focusing on children's cases, staffed with professionals trained in child rights and juvenile justice.
- Training for Legal Practitioners: Provide continuous training for legal practitioners on child-friendly legal procedures and the unique needs of child clients to ensure effective representation.
- Public Awareness Campaigns: Conduct campaigns to inform the public, especially children and their guardians, about the availability of legal aid services and the rights of children within the justice system.

4.2 Mandatory and Continuous Professional Training

Ensuring that government personnel involved with children in conflict with the law receive continuous professional training is crucial for safeguarding children's rights within the criminal justice system (Kilkelly, 2008). Examining the United States' approach offers valuable insights for enhancing Kenya's legal framework.

4.2.1 United States

In the United States, several initiatives focus on the continuous training of professionals handling juvenile cases:

- Office of Juvenile Justice and Delinquency Prevention (OJJDP): The OJJDP provides extensive training and technical assistance to juvenile justice practitioners, emphasizing best practices and standards in juvenile justice (Kilkelly, 2008).

- National Training and Technical Assistance Center (NTTAC): NTTAC connects practitioners with resources and training opportunities, promoting the use of evidence-based practices in juvenile justice (Kilkelly, 2008).
- Specialized Training Programs: Various programs offer specialized training for law enforcement, prosecutors, and judges on interacting with child defendants, focusing on trauma-informed care and adolescent development (Kilkelly, 2008).

4.2.2 Lessons for Kenya

To strengthen children's rights within its criminal justice system, Kenya can adopt the following measures:

- Establish a National Training Framework: Develop a centralized framework for the continuous training of all professionals involved in juvenile justice, including law enforcement, judiciary, and social workers.
- Implement Mandatory Training Modules: Introduce compulsory training modules focusing on child psychology, rights of the child, and child-friendly communication techniques for all personnel interacting with child defendants.
- Create Specialized Units: Establish specialized units within law enforcement and the judiciary dedicated to handling juvenile cases, staffed by personnel with advanced training in child rights and juvenile justice.
- Foster Interagency Collaboration: Encourage collaboration between various agencies to share best practices, resources, and training opportunities, ensuring a cohesive approach to juvenile justice.
- Monitor and Evaluate Training Programs: Implement mechanisms to assess the effectiveness of training programs regularly, allowing for continuous improvement and adaptation to emerging challenges.

4.3 Individual Child Assessments

Implementing timely and effective individual assessments for children in conflict with the law is crucial for safeguarding their rights and promoting their well-being within the criminal justice system (Gilliss, 2023). Examining Canada's approach provides valuable insights for enhancing Kenya's practices in this area.

4.3.1 Canada

In Canada, individual assessments of children in conflict with the law are integral to the justice process:

- Comprehensive Evaluations: Assessments encompass the child's psychological, social, and familial circumstances to inform judicial decisions. These evaluations are conducted by trained professionals, including social workers and psychologists, ensuring a holistic understanding of the child's situation (Gilliss, 2023).
- Child and Guardian Involvement: The assessment process actively involves the child and their guardians, ensuring that their perspectives and needs are considered. This participatory approach aligns with the principles of the United Nations Convention on the Rights of the Child, emphasizing the child's right to be heard in matters affecting them (Gilliss, 2023).
- Mandatory Reporting Obligations: Professionals conducting assessments are legally obligated to report any reasonable grounds to suspect that a child is at risk of abuse or neglect. This duty to report is enshrined in provincial legislation, such as Ontario's Child, Youth and Family Services Act, ensuring that protective measures are promptly initiated when necessary (Gilliss, 2023).

4.3.2 Lessons for Kenya

To strengthen the protection of children's rights within its criminal justice system, Kenya can adopt the following measures:

- Establish Standardized Assessment Protocols: Develop and implement standardized protocols for conducting individual assessments of children in conflict with the law. These protocols should ensure comprehensive evaluations that consider the child's psychological, social, and familial contexts.
- Ensure Active Participation: Guarantee that children and their guardians are actively involved in the assessment process. This involvement respects the child's right to participate in decisions affecting them and ensures that their voices are heard.
- Mandate Reporting Duties: Legislate mandatory reporting obligations for professionals conducting assessments. When there are reasonable grounds to believe that a child is at risk of abuse or neglect, these professionals should be required to report such concerns to the appropriate authorities promptly.
- Provide Specialized Training: Offer specialized training for professionals responsible for conducting assessments to equip them with the necessary skills and knowledge to perform thorough and sensitive evaluations.
- Monitor and Evaluate Assessment Practices: Establish mechanisms to monitor and evaluate the effectiveness of assessment practices regularly. This continuous evaluation will facilitate improvements and adaptations to emerging challenges.

4.4 Greater Accessibility of Information

Ensuring that children involved in the criminal justice system can access and comprehend information is crucial for safeguarding their rights and promoting their active participation in legal proceedings (Cunneen et al., 2018). Examining the United Kingdom's approach offers valuable insights for enhancing Kenya's practices in this area.

4.4.1 United Kingdom

The UK has implemented several measures to make legal information more accessible to children:

- Child-Friendly Communication: Legal practitioners are trained to use language that is appropriate for the child's age and understanding, ensuring that children can grasp the proceedings and their rights (Cunneen et al., 2018).
- Specialized Support Services: The UK provides intermediaries and advocates who assist children in understanding legal processes and expressing their views effectively (Cunneen et al., 2018).
- Educational Resources: Governmental agencies have developed materials, such as guides and videos, tailored to children to explain legal procedures and their rights within the justice system (Cunneen et al., 2018).

4.4.2 Lessons for Kenya

To enhance the accessibility of information for children in its criminal justice system, Kenya can consider the following measures:

- Develop Child-Friendly Materials: Create informational resources, including brochures, videos, and interactive tools, that explain legal processes and rights in simple, age-appropriate language.
- Implement Training Programs: Provide training for legal practitioners, law enforcement officers, and judicial personnel on effective communication strategies with children, emphasizing the use of clear and understandable language.
- Establish Support Mechanisms: Introduce roles such as child advocates or intermediaries who can assist children in navigating the legal system, ensuring they understand proceedings and can express their views.

- Leverage Technology: Utilize digital platforms to disseminate information and educational content, making it more accessible to children and their guardians.
- Engage in Community Outreach: Conduct awareness campaigns and workshops within communities to educate children and their families about their rights and the legal processes affecting them.

4.5 Protection of Children's Privacy in Criminal Proceedings

Protecting children's privacy in criminal proceedings is essential to uphold their dignity and promote their rehabilitation (Lacombe, 2017). Examining Canada's approach offers valuable insights for enhancing Kenya's practices in this area.

4.5.1 Canada

In Canada, several measures are in place to safeguard the personal information of children involved in criminal proceedings:

- Youth Criminal Justice Act (YCJA): This legislation includes provisions that restrict the publication of any information that could identify a young person involved in criminal proceedings, thereby protecting their privacy and facilitating their reintegration into society (Lacombe, 2017).
- Anonymity in Court Records: Court records involving minors are typically anonymized, and access is limited to authorized individuals, ensuring that sensitive information is not disclosed publicly (Lacombe, 2017).
- Data Protection Regulations: Agencies handling personal information of children are required to implement strict data protection measures, considering the sensitivity and vulnerability of minors (Lacombe, 2017).

4.5.2 Lessons for Kenya

To strengthen the protection of children's privacy in criminal proceedings, Kenya can consider the following measures:

- Enact Comprehensive Legislation: Develop laws that explicitly prohibit the publication of identifying information of minors involved in criminal cases, similar to Canada's YCJA.
- Implement Anonymity Protocols: Ensure that court records and legal documents involving children are anonymized, and access is restricted to authorized personnel only.

- Strengthen Data Protection Policies: Mandate that all agencies handling children's personal information adopt robust data protection measures, taking into account the specific needs and vulnerabilities of minors.
- Provide Training for Legal Practitioners: Offer specialized training to legal professionals on the importance of maintaining confidentiality and the ethical handling of sensitive information related to children.
- Raise Public Awareness: Conduct campaigns to educate the media and the public about the legal restrictions and ethical considerations regarding the disclosure of information about minors in criminal proceedings.

5. CONCLUSION

The effective protection of children's rights within Kenya's criminal justice system is not merely a legal obligation but a moral imperative that reflects the nation's commitment to justice and the rule of law. Despite the robust statutory and policy frameworks, the practical challenges identified in this paper—ranging from inadequate legal representation and systemic gaps in privacy protections to the stigmatization of vulnerable child offenders—underscore the urgent need for comprehensive reform.

Drawing on comparative lessons from jurisdictions such as South Africa, Canada, the United Kingdom, and the United States, this paper highlights actionable pathways for strengthening children's rights. Recommendations such as ensuring continuous and free legal assistance, mandatory professional training, implementing individualized child assessments, enhancing accessibility of information, and safeguarding children's privacy in criminal proceedings are critical for aligning Kenya's criminal justice system with international standards and best practices.

A justice system that prioritizes the best interests of the child must go beyond punitive measures to focus on rehabilitation, reintegration, and protection. By adopting these proposals, Kenya can not only bridge the gaps in its legal and institutional frameworks but also set a benchmark for the region in advancing children's rights. The transformative potential of these reforms lies in fostering a child-centered justice system that ensures no child is left vulnerable to systemic failures. In doing so, Kenya will take a significant step toward realizing the constitutional promise of justice for all, especially for its most vulnerable citizens—its children.

REFERENCES

Children Act, 2022

Criminal Procedure Code (Cap. 75)

Cunneen, C., Goldson, B., & Russell, S. (2018). Human rights and youth justice reform in England and Wales: A systemic analysis. *Criminology & Criminal Justice*, *18*(4), 405–430.

Gilliss, S. (2023). *Children's Rights Awareness, Rights-Informed Practices and Child-Friendly Justice in a Secure Custody Facility in Canada* (Doctoral dissertation, Université d'Ottawa/University of Ottawa).

Kilkelly, U. (2008). Youth justice and children's rights: Measuring compliance with international standards. *Youth Justice*, *8*(3), 187–192.

Kiniti, J. W. (2013). *The Criminal Justice Process: the Enforcement of Rights of the Children in Kenya* (Doctoral dissertation, University of Nairobi).

Lacombe, É. F. (2017). Prioritizing children's best interests in canadian youth justice: Article 3 of the un convention on the rights of the child and child-friendly alternatives. *Windsor Yearbook of Access to Justice*, *34*(2), 209–233.

Legal Aid Act, 2016

Mudeizi, H. M. (2022). *Determinants of Children's Rights Violations in Prosecution: A Case of Nairobi City County, Kenya* (doctoral dissertation, kenyatta university).

Musiega, R. (2021). *Enhancing Child Justice in Kenya: an Appraisal of the Implementation of the Rights of Child Offenders* (Doctoral dissertation, University of Nairobi).

National Strategy on Justice for Children 2023-2028

Nkirote, K. J. (2016). *An Analysis of The Adequacy of The Legal Framework in Protecting The Rights Of Child Offenders in Kenya* (Doctoral dissertation, University Of Nairobi).

Oduor, A. J., & Nyaata, V. M. (2022). A survey of children's rights in the juvenile justice system in Kenya. [JLJ]. *Journal of Law and Jurisprudence*, *1*(1), 1–7.

Office of the Director of Public Prosecutions (2020) 'A Prosecutor's Guide to Children in the Criminal Justice System'

Penal Code (Cap. 63) Laws of Kenya

Prinsloo, J. (2008). In the best interest of the child: The protection of child victims and witnesses in the South African Criminal Justice System. *Child Abuse Research in South Africa*, *9*(2), 49–64.

Republic v BC [2022] KEHC 17153 (KLR)

The Judiciary. (2024) 'CRJ Mokaya underscores need for increased budgetary allocation for Child Justice Sector' available at https://judiciary.go.ke/crj-mokaya-underscores-need-for-increased-budgetary-allocation-for-child-justice-sector/

Viola, M. W. (2009). The protection of rights of juveniles in the criminal justice system in Kenya.

Chapter 10

The Legal Dilemma in the Implementation of Laws Against Drug Abuse Among Street Children in Nairobi, Kenya

Terry Jeff Odhiambo
https://orcid.org/0000-0003-1102-6612
United States International University-Africa, Kenya

Solomon Koyi
Alupe University College, Kenya

Anthony Odek
St. Paul's University, Kenya

ABSTRACT

According to the Consortium of street children, there are about 60,000 street children in the country. While on the streets, these children are exposed to a hard life with drug abuse. This scenario puts them in a conflict situation with law enforcement. Drug abuse is criminalized in Kenya through the Narcotic Drugs and Psychotropic Substances Act (1994) and other legal frameworks. The study's objectives were to establish the legislative framework to curb drugs among street children and explore the challenges these laws face. The study adopted a Case Study design in which Nairobi, Kenya's capital, was the case study. Sampling was stratified among the 17 sub-counties in the city, and each had an equal representation of 4, making a total of 68 respondents. The target population consisted of social workers, law enforcers

DOI: 10.4018/978-1-6684-9343-4.ch010

(particularly in the children's department), and administrators such as chiefs and Sub County commissioners. Data was collected using KIIS (Key Informant Interviews), document analysis, and desktop review.

1. INTRODUCTION

According to the National Census Street families Report (2018), Kenya has a total of 46, 639 persons living on the streets. Out of these, a majority of them are aged between 10-34 years and the highest concentration is in Nairobi, Mombasa and Uasin Gishu counties. A majority of them are males 972.4%) and those aged 19-34 followed by children below 19 years who were at 19,752. In Nairobi, it was established that there were 15,337 people living on the streets while in Mombasa they were 7,529, Kisumu 2,746, Uasin Gishu 2,147 and Nakuru 2005 (National Census for Street Families Report, 2018).

The numbers keep on rising day by day because of several factors such as poverty at family level, death of parents, separation or divorce of parents, abandonment, parents living on the streets, mistreatment by parents or relatives, tribal displacement, inadequate food at home, influence of friends, getting lost while travelling, lack of school fees, fear of being reprimanded and an illusion of freedom while living on the streets. Over the years, efforts have been fronted by the government and non-governmental organizations to address the issue. For example, in 2002, when the NARC government took over, the Ministry of Local Government then embarked on a rehabilitation program for street children in collaboration with the National Youth Service (NYS). This led to offering of informal education, training as well as giving some of them an opportunity to go back to school. This program saw 6,000 ex-street children being enrolled in different primary schools across the country (Morangi, 2013).

While on the streets, one of the things that these children engage in is drug abuse (Obondo, 2020). The most abused drugs by the street children in Nairobi are hydrocarbons, tobacco, alcohol, cannabis and *Khat*. In an attempt to curb this menace, the Kenyan Criminal Justice System has been reactionary. The US Department of Justice (2021), notes that on many occasions, the criminal justice system demonstrate brutal attitudes towards street children. These children are subjected to corporal punishment, incarceration with adults and disregard to their welfare. This, in itself raises questions as to what extent should the criminal justice system go in implementing laws on drug abuse among street children. It is against this background that the study sought to establish the legal dilemma faced by the criminal justice system in balancing the intentions of the law against drug abuse while at the same time adhering to the laws on the rights of the children living on the streets.

1.1 Statement of the Problem

Drug abuse is a serious crime in Kenya. According to NACADA laws which guide Kenya in terms of drug abuse are both international and domestic. Internationally, Kenya is a signatory to the convention on Narcotic Drugs (1961), the Convention on Psychotropic Substance (1971) and the United Nations Convention against illicit traffic in narcotic drugs and substances. Locally, laws governing drug abuse include: the Narcotic drugs and Psychotropic Substance Act and the National Authority for the Campaign against Alcohol and Drug Abuse Act (2022). At the same time, the constitution of Kenya mandates county governments to develop laws on control of drugs within their respective counties.

Similarly, there are also laws which protect the rights of children regardless of their background or any other reason. What this implies is that as much as the children living on the streets are prone to drug abuse hence breaking the laws on drug abuse, they are also protected by other laws such as the Convention on the rights of the children, Children's Act 2022 as well as the Convention on the Rights of the Child, the Children's Act 2022, and the Constitution of Kenya (2010). Therefore, the criminal justice system, notably the law enforcement agencies at both county level and the Police as well as the judiciary are faced with legal dilemma in balancing the two sets of laws as far as dealing with drug abuse among the children living on the streets. This therefore formed the gist of this study.

1.2 Objectives

The study was guided by two objectives namely:

1. To establish the legal frameworks in place to address drug abuse among street children
2. To examine the challenges faced in the implementation of the laws on drug abuse among street children

2. LITERATURE REVIEW

Drug abuse is a criminalized offence under Kenyan laws. According to the KNBS (2018), there are 5,397 persons in prisons for drug related offences. Out of these, 5,243 are male while 154 are female. Children who are serving sentences related to drug abuse total 7.9% of those in prison. According to the KHRC (2018), one of the challenges which has impeded successful implementation of laws on drug abuse is a punitive legal regime. Oblivious of the fact that drug abuse is a phenomenon that needs a psycho social approach, the Ministry of Interior favors arrest and jailing of the victims instead of committing them to rehabilitation. The end result has been that on one hand, the social workers who are supposed to offer rehabilitation services have been discouraged by this approach. At the same time, this approach has occasioned a cat and mouse game between the drug abusers on one hand and the enforcement agencies on the other. The KCHR (2018) report recommends that there should be massive sensitization of the law enforcers on the rights of the victims, especially the young victims because the same laws also protect these children.

Children are often pushed to the streets because of many reasons, some of which are beyond their control. From this angle therefore, they are largely victims of circumstance. Sitienei (2020) examines the motivating factors for the choice to be in the streets as microsystem, mesosystem, exosystem, macrosystem and chrolosystem. Each system contributes to the development of children and their choice to live in the streets. According to Swick and Williams (2006), microsystem entails the most immediate physical, social and psychological environment. This provides children living on the streets with painful memories due to experiences that made them escape to the street. On the other hand, the mesosystem ought to provide a supportive environment to the child. If this fails, it drives the child to seek alternative survival route. The Macro system here entails the overall social context which includes the legal system as well as the broad social approach to the street children phenomenon. Lastly, the chronosystem entails the dimensions of time-as they grow older, they react differently to environmental changes which can influence them.

The deduction from this theoretical lens is that for the legal system to effectively and efficiently work, they should be alive to the fact that these children are victims of the social and psychological products within their context. As such, the approach towards dealing with juvenile delinquency should entail a delicate balancing act that on one hand seeks to curb drug abuse but on the other hand acknowledging the social, economic, psychological and environmental context and thus originate pragmatic measures that are alive to these factors.

3. METHODOLOGY

This study adopted a Case Study Design with the focus on Nairobi city which is Kenya's capital and has the registered the highest number of street children in the whole country. The target population entailed the law enforcement officers, administrators, social workers as well as ward administrators. In total, a sample of 68 was targeted using stratified sampling spread across the 17 sub counties in Nairobi City County. Each sub county produced 4 respondents. Data was collected mainly through interviews, document analysis and secondary sources which entailed laws governing drugs and children as well as newspaper commentaries and reviews. Analysis was qualitative in which the collected data was categorized into themes which were based on the objectives. Analysis entailed narration, excerpts as well as quotations.

4. FINDINGS AND DISCUSSIONS

4.1 Legal Framework on drugs and its Implementation on Street Children

The Kenyan Constitution (2010) provides for the incorporation of treaties and conventions into the Kenyan domestic laws. This is provided for in Section 2(6). Therefore, based on this, three conventions namely the Convention on Narcotic Drugs in 1961, Convention on Psychotropic Substances in 1971 and the United Nations Convention against Illicit traffic of drugs are part of the domiciled laws that address drug abuse. The single Convention on Narcotic drugs is aimed at combating drug abuse through a coordinated international action. This treaty thus obliges the signatory countries to limit the possession, use, trade, manufacture of drugs as well as combat international drug trafficking. The convention was ratified by 186 parties and Kenya is among them.

The Convention of Psychotropic Substances 1971 also forms part of the legal regime against drug abuse in Kenya. This Convention was ratified in 1971 and it cautions states against tolerating drug abuse and drug trade related activities as it undermines the legitimate economies and threaten the stability, security and stability of sovereign states. Of particular importance is that the Convention cautions states against allowing children to possess or indulge in drugs as follows:

'Children are used in many parts of the world as an illicit drug consumers market and for purposes of illicit production, distribution and trade in narcotic drugs and Psychotropic substances, which entails a danger of inculcable gravity. UN, 1971

Article 3 of the Convention requires nations to bas possession of drugs for personal use and urges them to criminalize the possession, purchase of cultivation of narcotic drugs or psychotropic substances for consumption.

The last international convention that Kenya is obliged to in terms of drug abuse control is the United Nations Convention against traffic of illicit drugs in 1988. It provides for international cooperation in extradition of drug traffickers and controlled deliveries of drugs. What comes out is that these international treaties place on Kenya a firm obligation to ensure that drug abuse and trafficking is criminalized. It thus does not occur as a coincidence when firm criminal justice system is embraced by Kenya in combating the drug menace.

On the domestic scene, the first law which governs drug abuse is the Narcotic Drugs and the Psychotropic Act. The main section of the act that addresses itself to drug abuse is section 5(1) b and d which states that:

Any person who without lawful and reasonable excuse is found smoking, sniffing or otherwise any narcotic drug or psychotropic substance shall be guilty of an offence and shall be liable to a fine of two hundred and fifty thousand shillings or imprisonment for a term not exceeding ten years or both.

Secondly, the NACADA Act 2012 is also another legal instrument that guides the fight against drug abuse. The Act establishes a national authority that is aimed at not only carrying out public education on alcohol and drug abuse, but also coordinating public participation in the control of drugs, facilitating inter agency collaboration, monitoring and surveillance, research and publication on drug abuse and assist county governments in developing and implementing policies aimed at drug abuse (Kenya Law, 2022).

The last legal framework that guides the fight against drugs and drug abuse touches on the mandate of the County governments as enshrined in the fourth schedule function 13 on controlling of drugs and pornography. This function has given county governments a wide berth in dealing with drugs and drug abuse, particularly among children. For example, using this same law, Kinyanjui (2021) reports that the county government of Nairobi allocated 40 million to rescue, rehabilitate and reintegrate street children and other vulnerable children in Nairobi. Therefore, what comes out is that there is abundance of both national and international legal framework on the issue of drugs and drug abuse. The biggest question is whether these laws are alive to the rights, plight and context of these children or not.

4.2 Legal Framework on Children's Rights and its implementation

Children have a prominent place in both international conventions and domestic laws. The Rights of children are safeguarded in the following legal instruments; Convention on the Rights of the child, the Children's Act (2022) and the Constitution of Kenya 2010. The Convention on the Rights of the child is an international convention which was adopted on 20th November 1989 under the General Assembly resolution 44/25 (UNHR, 2020). It binds signatory states to prevent the discrimination of the child based on anything and to take measures to ensure that the child is protected against any form of discrimination or punishment. The Convention also binds signatory countries to undertake to ensure that child is part is put first in any matter involving them including courts of law. For example, states are obliged in Article 9 to ensure that a child shall ot be separated from his/her parents against their will, except when competent authorities subject to judicial review determine in accordance with the law, that such separation is necessary.

Locally, the Children's Act No. 8 of 2001 which was later repealed expressly provided for parental responsibility, fostering, adoption and protection of children. If this was to occur, then cases of children living on the streets would not exist. It also provided for the implementation and giving effect to the principles governing the rights of the child and also the African Charter on the Rights and welfare of the child (Children's Act No.8 of 2001). Perhaps the most progressive legal development as far as the rights of the children are concerned in Kenya is the Constitution of 2010. Article 53 recognizes the right of all children to be protected from abuse, neglect, harmful cultural practices, all forms of violence, inhumane treatment and punishment and hazardous or exploitative labor. It therefore behooves on the criminal justice system as well as related agencies to execute law in a manner which is in the best interest of the child. Street children fall under the category of children and as such are supposed to be covered by this legal framework.

4.3 Legal Dilemma in implementing laws on drugs abuse

The first challenge relates to the full implementation of the international Covenants on drugs domestically. For example, when the state binds itself to these conventions to curtail drugs and substance abuse, there exist no formulae in these conventions that provided how to have exemptions, particularly of children living on the streets accused of dealing with drugs or how to deal with them while respecting their rights. This lacuna leaves the criminal justice system with no other option than to handle these children as any other adult drug abusers. In so doing, they end up violating the Rights of these children. For example, US Department of Justice (2021) cites cases where street children who are found engaging in drugs face brute force under the hands of the law enforcers (County and Police). They are reported to have been harassed and beaten by police officers. Police roundups are often conducted with brute force and with little regard for children's rights and welfare hence contravening both local n and international provisions of Children's laws hence putting them in a dilemma. This scenario was well articulated by one of the informants:

We, as law enforcers, work with orders and if we are to deal with drug abuse, it does not matter who is abusing drugs as long as we get hold of the person. The children living in the streets even do not have identification documents so it becomes hard to know their exact age. (Key informant, Kamukunji).

Secondly, the other dilemma faced by the criminal justice system in implementing laws on drugs among street children is that of moral legitimacy. The same government which is a signatory to international Conventions on the rights of the child which binds it to put in place mechanisms for the protection of the child is the one that is criminalizing them because of abusing drugs. From this perspective, the government can be rightly accused of giving rise to the street children's menace because of its action or inaction. It therefore becomes a double edged sword for the government to occasion the problem by not ensuring the covenants of the Children's rights are fully implemented and at the same time subjecting them to the punitive laws on drug abuse by virtue of living on the streets.

Thirdly, the manner in which cases involving children living on the streets, especially those accused of drug abuse, also generates more questions than answers. According to the US Department of Justice (2021), despite the requirement that children's cases be heard in special juvenile courts, such cases have often been tried in regular courts along with adults where the children are denied special protection as enshrined in the law as established. In other cases, street children accused of drug abuse are committed in the same detention facilities as adults and such actions justified on the basis that they do not have documentation to prove that they are underage. These particular examples serves to prove that there is indeed a legal dilemma that the criminal justice system face in implementing the laws that seek to curb drug abuse among street children.

CONCLUSION

This study concludes that there is a lack of coherence in the implementation of laws addressing drug abuse among street children, primarily due to the failure to balance drug control measures with child protection laws. This inadequacy has worsened the situation, leaving street children at a disadvantage. On one hand, government agencies have, whether by design or neglect, failed to uphold their mandate to protect children's rights, thereby contributing to the street children crisis. On the other hand, the same government has enacted punitive laws that criminalize these children, effectively punishing them for circumstances created by its own actions and inactions.

Recommendations

The study recommends the following:

- A National Street family Act be in place to synchronize the laws on Children's Rights and Drug abuse
- A Street families Rehabilitation Fund be put in place to cater for the welfare of the children appropriately

- Sensitization of the various government agencies on the rights and obligations of the state
- A holistic approach combining social, psychological, economic facets to the problem of curbing drug abuse among street children.

REFERENCES

Kenya Law. (2022). *National Authority for the Campaign Against Alcohol and Drug Abuse Act*. Kenyalaw.org. https://new.kenyalaw.org/akn/ke/act/2012/14/eng@2022-12-31

KHRC KBS. (2018). The Economic Survey. KNBS Sitienei. Life Experiences of children living on the streets in Kenya. Journal of Child and Adolescent trauma]. *E (Norwalk, Conn.)*, •••, 92020.

National Census Street Families Report (2018). Street families rehabilitation fund. Ministry of Labor and Social Protection

Morangi, R. (2013). Effectiveness of street children intervention in Eldoret. *International Journal of Smart Technologies*, *6*, 14.

Obondo, A., & Pthieno, J. (2020). Patterns of Substance abuse among Kenyan Street Children. *AJOL. VOl*, *12*, 2.

Swick, K. J., & Williams, R. D. (2006). An analysis of Bronfenbrenner's bio-ecological perspective for early childhood educators: Implications for working with families experiencing stress. *Early Childhood Education Journal*, *33*(5), 371–378.

United Nations (2020) Single Convention on Narcotic Drugs The Kenyan Constitution (2010) Kinyanjui. M 92021) City Hall to spend 40 million to rehabilitate street children. *The Star. April 2021* Children's Act No. 8 of 2000

US Department of Justice. (2021). *Juvenile Injustice: Police Abuse and Detention of Street children in Kenya. USDJ KNCHR (2018).* Human Rights and Drug Abuse.

Chapter 11
Children of Somalia

Vineeth Vijayan
Prairie View A&M University, USA

ABSTRACT

Children in Somalia confront several challenges, including being exposed to many types of criminality and violence. Due to decades of violence and instability, Somalia's legal system has been disrupted, leaving a dearth of institutions and legal protections to protect children. The protection of children in Somalia has been demanded by the UN, especially in light of the country's current 15-year-old criminal responsibility age. Also, Somalia's courts and jails are not set up to meet the needs of young victims or offenders. Street children and child soldiers are particularly vulnerable to abuse and exploitation, with many facing re-victimization by the government. In general, Somalia's children are in terrible condition, and immediate action is required to guarantee that their rights are upheld and that they may lead secure lives. The building of a strong legislative framework in Somalia that can adequately meet children's needs and stop further harm to this vulnerable group requires the cooperation of the international community.

INTRODUCTION

Somalia is located on the East African coast, on the outskirts of the Somali Peninsula, also known as the Horn of Africa. The Gulf of Aden borders it on the North and the Indian Ocean on the east. It has around 11.3 million in the population (July 2018 est) with 2.08 population growth. Somalia's ethnic Somalis make up 95 percent of the population, and associations with the small percentage of Arabs, Indians, Pakistanis, Asians, Europeans, and mixed groups who live there are mostly peaceful.

The Somali Republic was established in 1960 when southern Italian Somalia and northern British Somaliland combined. In the new political system, the South gained

DOI: 10.4018/978-1-6684-9343-4.ch011

significant control over the underdeveloped North. Regional rivalries influenced clan politics in a big way. The renowned Isaaq clan, once the majority in Somaliland, has become an ethnic minority. The Darood clan, which had previously been a minor player in the North, reunited with Darood from the South to form a new solid force. Since the clans allied themselves with rival political forces, the electoral structure became fractious (Metz, 1992).

During the early 1990s clan wars, northern Somalia proclaimed itself the independent Somaliland Republic, named former Somali Prime Minister Muhammad Ibrahim Egal as its president, wrote a constitution, established an assembly and governmental structures, and started to act effectively independently of the warring South. The Somaliland Republic continues to declare independence despite not being recognized as a separate nation. During the 1990s, members of the Murjateen clan in northeastern Somalia formed their own government, naming their territories Puntland. Still, they promised to return to Somalia if a central government was established (Countries and their cultures, 2009.).

Somalia has a significantly younger population, with 44% under 14. Somalia faces a significant challenge in facilitating future generations due to an inadequate educational system and a high unemployment rate, especially among the younger population. Somali civilians have been subjected to extreme violence as a result of ongoing military conflict, instability, a lack of state support, and recurring humanitarian crises. There are approximately 2.6 million internally displaced people (IDPs) in the country, many of whom are living in poverty and at risk of violence (Human Rights Watch, 2020).

Child recruitment is a serious crime that continues to claim the lives of an estimated 200,000–500,000 children worldwide (BENREY, 2016). According to Singer, children make up 40% of the world's military forces, including national armies, terrorist factions, and non-state armed opposition organizations, and they fight in 75% of global wars (Singer, 2006).

CRIME AGAINST CHILDREN

Considering the situation at the ground level, it is difficult to get accurate statistics and information regarding the crime committed against children. Child exploitation was committed by all Somali parties to the conflict, including murders, maiming, and the recruiting and use of child soldiers. In 2018, the United Nations reported more incidents of enlisted children being used as soldiers in Somalia than anywhere else. In 2019, Al-Shabab continued its violent child recruitment program, threatening communities that refused to hand over their children ("Briefing to the Security Council on the humanitarian situation in Somalia," 2019).

Conflict, migration, starvation, and disease remain constant problems for Somalia's children. The death rates for children and mothers are among the worst in the world. One of every seven children dies before age five, often from preventable diseases, and a polio epidemic is still a possibility. Just four out of ten children attend school, and militia groups recruited nearly 800 children last year ("Background note on Somalia's ratification of the convention on the rights of the child," 2015). Thousands of Somali children under 18 have been recruited, frequently illegally, by the Islamist armed group Al-Shabab during the last decade, with many serving as front-line soldiers (Bader & Wabwire, 2018).

The number of former CAAFG who survived or were liberated by armies shows that participating in military wars and witnessing massacres, murders, civilian beheadings, bombings, and other manifestations of overt brutality are traumatizing events that leave physical and emotional wounds long after these children have stopped participating (Schauer & Elbert, 2010).

Harmful practices against girls are popular, including child marriage and female genital mutilation (FGM). According to government statistics, Somalia has the highest prevalence rate of FGM in the country, at 99 percent. Somali children are also often coerced into early marriages, with 34% of girls marrying before the age of 18 and 16% marrying before the age of 15 (Pandian, 2020). Girls are subjected to the most extreme method of the procedure, infibulation. Religion, history, and sexual morality play a role in the exercise. Although government and Islamic leaders' educational and awareness drives aimed at ending the ritual, there is little to indicate that this will improve in the immediate future. Around 1,442 boys and 53 females, some as young as 8, were recruited and used. The largest attacker, Al-Shabaab (1,169), was followed by government security forces, including the Somali Police Force (100). Three hundred children were used as escorts, border guards, and maintenance staff, while 269 were used as soldiers (Regilme, S., & Spoldi, E. 2021).

LEGAL SYSTEM AND LEGAL PROVISIONS

Somalia had four legal traditions when it gained independence: English common law, Italian law, Islamic sharia or religious law, and Somali customary law (traditional rulers and sanctions). Since 1960, the challenge has been to unify this disparate legal inheritance into a single system. A uniform penal code, a code of criminal court rules, and a centralized judicial organization were all implemented in the 1960s. The Italian system of judicial rulings has been preserved based on the implementation and interpretation of the legal code. The courts also used the

English common law and doctrines in matters not governed by legislation (Metz, 1992). The people of Somalia ratified a Constitution, which had been drafted in 1960, in a popular referendum on June 20, 1961.

Somalia's last functional central government was overthrown in 1991, and the resulting instability has enabled pirates and Islamist groups to plot attacks worldwide to establish bases in the country. Somalia has been ravaged by two decades of violence, and al-Qaeda affiliates control many territories. In 2012 the Somalian constitution was revised, and the Provisional Constitution of the Federal Republic of Somalia became the main law among Somalis. It serves as the legal basis for the Federal Republic's existence as well as a source of legal authority. It establishes citizens' rights and responsibilities, as well as the government's framework (Harper, 2021). Paragraph three of the new constitution specifies that the constitution promotes human rights. Children are dealt with in a different subsection, which specifies that children have the right to be protected from neglect and mistreatment and public legal aid where possible. In terms of education, paragraph 30 states that every Somali resident has the right to a free high school education.

Article 28 talks about family care in which 28(2) states that Mother and child care is a legal duty of the State, and 28(3) describes that Every child has the right to care from their parents, including education and instruction. In instances where this care is unavailable from the family, others must provide it. This right applies to street children and children of unknown parents, the rights of whom the State has a particular duty to fulfill and protect ("Provisional Constitution 2012", 2012).

Article 29 describes the rights of children. 29(1) Every child has the right to a good and righteous name and a nationality from birth. 29(2) Every child has the right to be protected from mistreatment, neglect, abuse, or degradation. 29(3) No child may perform work or provide services unsuitable for the child's age or create a risk to the child's health or development in any way. 29(4) Every child may be detained only as a last resort, for a limited time, under inappropriate conditions, and must be detained separately from adults, with the exception of the child's immediate family. The child's immediate family must be informed of the child's detention as soon as practicable. 29(5) Every child shall have the right to legal aid paid for by the State if the child might otherwise suffer injustice. 29(6) Every child has the right to be protected from armed conflict and not to be used in armed conflict. 29(7) In every matter concerning a child, the child's best interests are paramount. 29(8) In this article, the word 'child means a person under 18 years of age ("Provisional Constitution 2012", 2012).

Article 30 describes the right to education. They have mainly mentioned about article 30(1). Education is a basic right for all Somali citizens. 30(2) Every citizen shall have the right to free education up to secondary school. 30(3) The State shall give priority to the development, expansion, and extension of public education ("Provisional Constitution 2012", 2012).

Somaliland established a juvenile justice law in 2007, which mainly focused on protecting the rights of children in accordance with the International Child Right Conventions and International Human Rights Law and in a manner consistent with Somaliland's cultural and Islamic values and on establishing humane and fair justice system for children ("Juvenile Justice Law," 2007).

Since 2007, Somaliland has had a Criminal Justice Law in place, but it is not yet fully operational and plans to develop a juvenile justice system are underway. Somaliland enacted a juvenile justice bill in 2007 but has yet to put it into effect due to budgetary pressures and a lack of understanding of the law by the responsible agencies and their employees. The age of criminal responsibility is set at 15, and penalties must be proportionate to the child's situation and the gravity and extent of the offense. It bans corporal punishment, life imprisonment, and the death penalty and sets a maximum sentence of 15 years. The bill also establishes safeguards for the child's record and guarantees consistent child participation and child rights during proceedings. The bill mainly focused on the establishment of children's courts, children's pre-trial detention centers, and children's rehabilitation centers ("Failing law leaves children unprotected in Somaliland," 2011). Puntland is now working on a juvenile justice bill. Children are easily oppressed and abused because they have limited access to justice, and violators are not held accountable due to weak law enforcement. There are also a variety of competing justice systems which is federal, religious, and conventional – that operate counter to one another ("Juvenile Justice - Somalia," n.d.).

United Nations

The United Nations was formed In 1945 as a successor to the League of Nations, an international association of countries formed to foster international peace, security, and cooperation. It plays a key role in many conflicts and fights between nations and organizations. The United Nations is part of the United Nations system, with several grants, programs, and specialist departments, each with its own mission, administration, and budget. (United Nations, 2021).

Hassan Sheikh Mohamud, the President of Somalia, signed the Convention on January 20, 2015, after the Somali Parliament ratified it by 140 votes to one abstention on December 13, 2014. As a result of the ratification, Somali children now have constitutionally enforceable rights, with the CRC establishing a mechanism for the government to promote and safeguard those rights. Although the CRC is a compilation of universally agreed non-negotiable principles and commitments that include safeguards and security for children's rights, its three Optional Protocols deal with protecting children from slavery, exploitation, and child pornography; banning their recruitment in military conflict; and encouraging children to submit concerns to the UN if their rights are violated ("UN lauds Somalia as country ratifies landmark children's rights treaty," 2015). The Somali government must align its laws, policies, and practices with the CRC's standards. The ratification lays the groundwork for the government's scheme growth and capacity building ("Background note on Somalia's Ratification of the Convention on the Rights of the Child," n.d.)

United Nations Assistance Mission in Somalia is another UN system that is organized to deal with issues in Somalia. The mission of UNSOM covers the protection of children harmed by armed conflict, as well as assisting Somalia in preventing and ending significant child rights abuses committed by conflict parties, with an emphasis on improving the execution of the Government Action Plans on Children and Armed Conflict (CAAC), which were signed in 2012 ("Child Protection," n.d.).

UNSOM's **Child Protection Unit (CPU),** part of the Human Rights and Protection Group (HRPG), is in charge of carrying out the mandate on child protection. CPU co-chairs the Country Task Force on Monitoring and Reporting (CTFMR), a framework established by the UN Security Council's Resolution 1612 (2005) to track and report the six grave violations of children's rights. The six grave violations are killing and maiming of children, recruitment and use of children, Rape and other forms of sexual violence against children, abduction of children, attacks on schools and hospitals, and Denial of humanitarian access for children. The Child Protection Unit collaborates with government institutions such as the Ministry of Defense, the Ministry of Women and Human Rights Development, the National Intelligence and Security Agency, the Somali National Army, and a number of foreign and UN agencies, funds, and programs ("Child Protection," n.d.).

AGE OF CRIMINAL RESPONSIBILITY

Several laws define differing ages for child protection, which causes confusion and prohibits children from taking advantage of the available safeguards (Unicef, 2016). According to Section 59 of the Penal Code of 1962, the legal age of criminal liability is 14 years. A child between the ages of 14 and 18 is considered not to be legally liable for his or her acts until it can be shown that he or she has the capacity to comprehend the actions. Section 60 further specifies that the maximum sentence for a conviction and imprisonment is five years. Minors under 18 who commit an offense are remanded in institutions apart from adults and granted moral rehabilitation, according to Section 137 of the Penal Code of 1962 ("Somalia: Penal Code," 1962). Children in Somalia are described as those 18 or younger, even though laws in other regions make the age of maturity 15 years old. From the age of 15, children are now criminally liable. Except where children commit heinous offenses, international law mandates that they be treated differently than adults, with better care and rehabilitation given priority over imprisonment (Bader & Wabwire, 2018).

The Juvenile Courts and Reformatories Law also establishes provisions to ensure the child's best interests. However, this rule contrasts with the interim constitution, which describes a child as anyone under 18. (United Nations, 2024).

COURTS

Children in Somalia are trailed under different under different laws. Due to the overlapping status of the age of responsibility or maturity, it is difficult to identify the court systems for the children. Even though there are laws stating children who are part of militia groups who might have committed serious offenses should be trialed according to the juvenile justice standards. Although criminal prosecution of children is uncommon in Somalia, Human Rights Watch discovered that the authorities use an outdated legal structure to prosecute children in military courts as adults for security offenses, even solely for Al-Shabab membership. In Puntland alone, over two dozen children have been charged in military courts since 2016 ("Somalia: Military courts used to prosecute and punish Children," 2017).

The Juvenile Justice law drafted by Somaliland in 2007 clearly mentioned the need for different courts at different levels. They have talked about regional and district courts dealing with juveniles. A presiding judge and two public assessors will make up a Children's Court, and within 48 hours of the arrest, the child must be taken to a Children's Court. If the 48-hour period runs out on a non-court day, the child must be taken to court before the close of the first court day. At the preliminary hearing, judges must also clarify to the child his or her legal rights and remind the child of the existence of the charges against him or her, as prescribed by the Juvenile justice law ("Juvenile Justice Law," 2007).

According to juvenile courts and reformatories of 1970, A Juvenile Court has special authority to hear and decide cases involving children and young people who have committed crimes other than murder. When a child or adolescent is charged with a crime, the court may, at its discretion, demand the presence of his parent or guardian and issue any orders necessary for the purpose (Juvenile Courts and Reformatories, 2025). Regarding offenses committed by minors, there is no legal prohibition of the death penalty, life imprisonment, or corporal punishment as court punishments.

PRISON

Even if a child has committed a violent offense, they need protection. Detention can only be used as a last resort and for the shortest possible time, as it harms youngsters, according to Somalia's international legal obligations. They need communication with their family members as well as legal counsel. Separation from adults is therefore essential (Wabwire & Bader, 2018). Currently, only one jail in Somalia divides children from adults (Mandera Prison in Somaliland). The other children in Somalia's custody are being held with adults. (Unicef, 2016). There is only one prison for juveniles in Somalia, and the conditions are poor. Even if children and adults sleep in separate buildings, they interact with adults in a shared space during the day, including at mealtimes. Apart from playing in a huge open-air courtyard that the adults often use, they seemed to have no space for exercise. The children lacked access to schooling, though we recently learned that they might be beginning to have some (Bader & Wabwire, 2018).

STREET CHILDREN

It is one of the challenges faced by Somalia. The constitution mentions that a child is entitled to parental protection, which includes education and guidance. When family members cannot afford this service, others must do it. This right extends to children on the street and children of uncertain guardians, whose interests the State has a special responsibility to fulfill and defend (Constituteionnet, 2016). The government often fails to address these children's need for care and protection. Estimates in 2008 placed the overall number of street children at over 5,000. However, Somalia suffered the worst famine in over 60 years in 2011, decimating livestock and crops for many households. Many parents were left without a job or a way to afford their children as a result of this. As a result, more children took to the streets searching for income, and in 2015 the number dramatically increased to 11000 street children ("The Street Children of Mogadishu," 2015).

A Somali proposal to end recruiting child soldiers is supposed to exacerbate the problem; child soldiering is also an unfortunate way for disadvantaged youth to get off the streets. Other reasons behind street children are domestic issues such as divorce or neglect, and others are being drawn into cities from rural areas due to drought. These institutions for placing children, which the government runs, has a prison-like structure with bed, education, and food. But the drawback is that these centers can only accommodate a very limited number of children. The number of street children is comparatively higher than the number of accommodations in these centers (Vickery, 2017).

CHILD SOLDIERS

Children under 18 who are used for military purposes are known as child soldiers. In the Somali civil war, 1,915 children were recruited and used as of 2016. Because of a surge in al-Shabab abduction cases, the number of child soldiers in Somalia has nearly doubled since 2015. Al-Shabab was responsible for 87 percent of the 950 children kidnapped since 2015. Children have been used in warfare, as spies, and in support positions by all Somali warring parties, including government troops, clan militias, and Islamist insurgent factions ("It's Like We're Always in a Prison," 2018). Al-Shabaab, which forcibly enlisted children as young as eight years old into war, was blamed for the brunt of these atrocities. In the Galgadud and Middle Shabelle areas, the groups continued to force populations to "volunteer" children to join its ranks. Al-Shabaab enlisted the help of children or "taxed" families to provide male children for use as child soldiers. These kids planted bombs, served as human shields, carried out assassinations and suicide bombings, gathered intelligence, and supported domestic services. Young women were often compelled to perform sexual servitude (United States Department of State, n.d.).

There are many ways by which children join these militant groups. Firstly, children may willingly enter the army or are recruited by commanders because they have no other means of obtaining a living outside of armed groups, creating a temporary yet erroneous sense of material protection and group affinity. Somali children were born into a world of existential and material insecurity, where abuse was normalized and routined. As a result, their sense of morality was diminished or eliminated, leading them to see enlistment in military struggle as religiously justified and essential for existential survival (Regilme & Spoldi, 2021). Al-Shabaab profits from domestic factors, luring children into their ranks with promises of jobs, wages, or a bigger role in the so-called holy war. Al-Shabaab profits financially from child recruiting because the latter increases the number of warriors and performs other support functions during the war. Al-Shabaab largely ignores universal conventions on armed struggle and public international law surrounding children's rights. The party, led by a powerful religious-political philosophy, seeks to gain authority in Somalia and establish itself as the only legitimate government capable of providing social, religious, military, and economic necessities to the people without the help of outsiders (Regilme & Spoldi, 2021).

Al-Shabaab carried out raids on schools, madrassas, and mosques and harassed and coerced clan leaders to recruit youngsters. Al-Shabaab recruitment camps exposed them to arduous physical training, poor nutrition, firearms training, physical torture, and compulsory religious training in accordance with the group's philosophy. Children were also forced to punish and kill other children as part of the instruction (United States Department of State).

REVICTIMISATION OF CHILDREN BY THE GOVERNMENT

Somali federal and regional officials have unlawfully arrested children with suspected links to Al-Shabab and have tried children for terrorism-related crimes in military courts. The government has struggled to implement juvenile justice policies, especially for children convicted of Al-Shabab-related offenses (Human Rights Watch, 2020). Since 2015, authorities in Somalia have arrested hundreds of boys accused of being illegally affiliated with Al-Shabab, according to the UN. Under international law, Somalia is obliged to consider the unique condition of minors, identified as those under the age of 18, who have been recruited or used in armed conflict, including terrorism-related acts, and to assist them in their rehabilitation and reintegration.

Children who join armed groups will face criminal charges, but legal proceedings must adhere to juvenile justice guidelines, and non-judicial interventions must be weighed (Human Rights Watch, 2018). Mass searches are often carried out by security forces to barricade an area where a recent attack occurred. They then apprehend local young men or boys for further questioning. Any boys, including those with no ties to Al-Shabab, who are apprehended in mass sweeps on questionable evidence, never get a chance to tell their side of the truth. Boys detained for security violations will spend months in jail, locked in dark cells for harsh interrogations, and unable to sleep for days due to a lack of room to lie down (Wabwire & Bader, 2018).

Human Rights Watch discovered that factors such as socioeconomic status, clan history, and external pressure could affect the outcome of a boy's case, despite government officials admitting to detaining boys they identified as "high danger." Officials and guards have exposed children to coercive discipline and interrogations, including isolating them from their families and legal representation, intimidating them, and, on rare occasions, beating and torturing them, primarily to elicit confessions or as punishment for speaking out or causing the disturbance in the cells. Although criminal prosecution of children is uncommon in Somalia, the authorities use an outdated legal system to prosecute children in military trials, mainly as adults, for security offenses, even solely for involvement in Al-Shabab. (Human Rights Watch, 2018).

The State has established a National Coordination Working Group for Children Associated with Armed conflict to enact their rescue, rehabilitation, and reintegration strategies. The Ministry of Defense is in charge of rescue operations, while the Ministry of Women and Human Rights Development, in collaboration with UNICEF and child protection CSOs, is in charge of the recovery, resettlement, and reintegration of children rescued from armed groups (United Nations, 2024).

REFERENCES

Bader, L., & Wabwire, A. (2018). *Interview: How Security Forces in Somalia Fail to Protect Children*. Human Rights Watch. Retrieved May 15 2021, from https://www.hrw.org/news/2018/02/21/interview-how-security-forces-somalia-fail-protect-children

BENREY. L. (2016). *History of Child Soldier Policies - End Slavery Now*. Endslaverynow.org. Retrieved May 14 2021, from https://www.endslaverynow.org/blog/articles/history-of-child-soldier-policies

Briefing to the Security Council on the humanitarian situation in Somalia. Reliefweb.int. (2019). Retrieved May 15 2021, from https://reliefweb.int/sites/reliefweb.int/files/resources/ASG%20Statement%20to%20SC%20on%20Somalia%20-%20as%20delivered%20-%2022%20May%202019.pdf

Child Protection. UNSOM. Retrieved May 15 2021, from https://unsom.unmissions.org/child-protection

Constituteionnet (2016). *The Federal Republic of Somalia: Provisional Constitution, adopted August 1, 2012 as of Sep 19, 2012*. https://constitutionnet.org/vl/item/federal-republic-somalia-provisional-constitution-adopted-august-1-2012-sep-19-2012

Countries and their cultures (2009). *History, people, women, beliefs, food, customs, family, social, dress*. Everyculture.com. https://www.everyculture.com/Sa-Th/Somalia.html

Failing law leaves children unprotected in Somaliland. The New Humanitarian. (2011). Retrieved May 15 2021, from https://www.thenewhumanitarian.org/report/94054/somalia-failing-law-leaves-children-unprotected-somaliland

Harper, M. (2021). *Somali leaders back new constitution*. BBC News. Retrieved May 15 2021, from https://www.bbc.com/news/world-africa-19075685

Human Rights Watch. (2018). *Somalia: Detained Children Face Abuse*. Retrieved May 15 2021, from https://www.hrw.org/news/2018/02/21/somalia-detained-children-face-abuse

Human Rights Watch. (2020, January 7). World Report 2020: Rights Trends in Somalia. Human Rights Watch. https://www.hrw.org/world-report/2020/country-chapters/somalia

It's Like We're Always in a Prison. Hrw.org. (2018). Retrieved May 16 2021, from https://www.hrw.org/sites/default/files/report_pdf/somalia0218_web.pdf

Juvenile Courts and Reformatories. (2025). *Juvenile Courts and Reformatories Law no. 13 of 8 March 1970.* Uniroma3.It. http://hdl.handle.net/2307/26144

Juvenile Justice Law. Africanchildforum.org. (2007). Retrieved May 16 2021, from http://www.africanchildforum.org/clr/Legislation%20Per%20Country/somalia/somalia_juvenilejustice_2007_en.pdf

Juvenile Justice - Somalia. Sites.google.com. Retrieved May 15 2021, from https://sites.google.com/site/justiceinsomalia/juvenile-justice

Metz, H. (1992). *Somalia*. Countrystudies.us. Retrieved May 14 2021, from https://countrystudies.us/somalia/

Nations, U. (2021). *About Us | United Nations*. United Nations. Retrieved May 15 2021, from https://www.un.org/en/about-us/

Pandian, D. (2020). *As the fifth anniversary of Somalia's ratification of the convention on the Rights of the Child approaches, protection violations against children continue to rise*. Unicef.org. Retrieved May 15 2021, from https://www.unicef.org/somalia/press-releases/fifth-anniversary-somalias-ratification-convention-rights-child-approaches

Regilme, S., & Spoldi, E. (2021). Children in Armed Conflict: A Human Rights Crisis in Somalia. *Global Jurist*, *0*(0). Advance online publication. DOI: 10.1515/gj-2020-0083

Schauer, E., & Elbert, T. (2010). The Psychological Impact of Child Soldiering. *Trauma Rehabilitation After War And Conflict*, 311-360. https://doi.org/DOI: 10.1007/978-1-4419-5722-1_14

Singer, P. (2006). *The Enablers of War: Casual Factors behind the Child Soldier Phenomenon*. Files.ethz.ch. Retrieved May 14 2021, from https://www.files.ethz.ch/isn/28063/2006_6_Enablers_of_War.pdf

Somali leaders back new constitution. BBC News. (2012). Retrieved May 15 2021, from https://www.bbc.com/news/world-africa-19075685

Somalia. Cia.gov. (2021). Retrieved May 14 2021, from https://www.cia.gov/the-world-factbook/countries/somalia/

Somalia: Military courts used to prosecute and punish Children. Garowe Online. (2017).

Somalia: Penal Code. Refworld. (1962). Retrieved May 15 2021, from https://www.refworld.org/docid/4bc5906e2.html

The Street Children of Mogadishu. The Borgen Project. (2015). Retrieved May 16 2021, from https://borgenproject.org/street-children-mogadishu/#:~:text=In%202008%2C%20estimates%20placed%20the,of%20supporting%20for%20their%20children

UN lauds Somalia as country ratifies landmark children's rights treaty. UN News. (2015). Retrieved May 15 2021, from https://news.un.org/en/story/2015/01/488692-un-lauds-somalia-country-ratifies-landmark-childrens-rights-treaty

Unicef. (2016). *Situation Analysis of Children in Somalia 2016*. Retrieved May 15 2021, from https://www.unicef.org/somalia/reports/situation-analysis-children-somalia-2016-0

United Nations. (2024). OHCHR | Committee on the Rights of the Child. OHCHR. https://www.ohchr.org/en/treaty-bodies/crc

United States Department of State. (n.d.). *Somalia*. United States Department of State. https://www.state.gov/countries-areas/somalia/

Vickery, M. (2017). *Homeless children sniff glue to take 'away the pain' of surviving Somalia's streets*. Usatoday.com. Retrieved May 16 2021, from https://www.usatoday.com/story/news/world/2017/09/05/somalia-children-homeless-african-cities/613912001/

Wabwire, A., & Bader, L. (2018). *Interview: How Security Forces in Somalia Fail to Protect Children*. Human Rights Watch. Retrieved May 15 2021, from https://www.hrw.org/news/2018/02/21/interview-how-security-forces-somalia-fail-protect-children

Chapter 12

The Juvenile Justice System in the Arab Republic of Egypt

Sherie Sam
Prairie View A&M University, USA

ABSTRACT

Egyptian society is heavily rooted in ancient traditions and religious practices. Islam is the cornerstone of Egypt's social, intellectual, and political cohesion, offering the logical force that bonds communities into a broad nation. Since independence, the Egyptians have modeled the criminal justice system on the existing religious and colonial ideological influences. Despite being one of Africa's largest countries, only a few scholars have examined the Egyptian juvenile justice system. The chapter will explore various aspects of the juvenile justice system in Egypt, its history, organization, and contemporary issues in juvenile justice. The chapter highlights the age of majority and criminal responsibility, trends and statistics of youth crimes, and custodial and non-custodial treatment of young offenders. Through the comparison with western juvenile justice systems, the chapter intends to offer policy implications for the existing problems that youth face and suggest future research areas on youth crime and the juvenile justice system.

INTRODUCTION

Egyptian law prevents the use of the death penalty for young offenders. However, in January 2016, Karim Hemada, aged 17, was apprehended from his house on the charge of being in a terrorist group and was sentenced to death. According to a document sent to the Minister of Interior and the Public Prosecutor, he was reported

DOI: 10.4018/978-1-6684-9343-4.ch012

to be tortured with electric shocks, to extract a confession. Amnesty International then appealed for a retrial to ensure that punishment was fair and in adherence to the juvenile justice principle in Egypt (Amnesty International, 2019). The case demonstrates Egypt's unique history and ever-so-conflicted present. The country is a blend of natural and the supernatural, the old and the contemporary, the religious and the secular, and the indigenous and the foreign (Souryal, 1992). The Egyptian justice system is a complex, centuries-old amalgamation of Islamic law, Napoleonic law, and indigenous customs and practices. The system is based on civil law, where judges interpret and apply the rule rather than create it through precedent (Wahab, 2019). This chapter intends to shed light on the juvenile justice system in the Arab Republic of Egypt while comparing it with juvenile justice systems of the West. There are several differences between the juvenile justice systems of the West and Egypt, including the age of criminal responsibility, the treatment of juvenile offenders, and the availability of rehabilitation programs. The chapter includes sections on the treatment of children in both ancient and contemporary Egypt, youth crime by Egyptian youth, the juvenile justice system, the problem of street children, and the comparison with the Western juvenile justice system.

CHILDREN IN ANCIENT EGYPT

Children were highly treasured, and households frequently had numerous children to continue their lineage in Ancient Egypt. Several pharaohs had multiple spouses and offspring to secure the continuance of their families (Brewer & Teeter, 2017). The parents were responsible for the health and education of their children. They thought children were gifts from the gods and must be appropriately reared to ensure their future prosperity. Consequently, parents provided their children received sufficient diet, medical treatment, and education (Hornung et al., 2006). Education in Ancient Egypt was not reserved for the privileged. Children were strongly encouraged to attend school to learn to read and write. Although education was not required, it was viewed as a road to success, especially for males.

In contrast, females were frequently schooled at home and taught crafts like weaving and cooking. Boys attended school from ages 5 to 15 and were instructed in reading and writing by literate scribes. In addition, they were taught mathematics, history, and religion. Children from poor homes might attend school if they had the resources to do so (Johnson, 2011). In Ancient Egypt, children's social standing was defined by their family's wealth and rank. Children from affluent homes were more likely to have successful jobs because they had access to higher education and more resources.

However, children from impoverished households were more likely to work in agriculture as workers. Socioeconomic standing does not dictate a child's value or potential, and there are several examples of people who ascended to prominent positions despite lowly beginnings. For instance, Imhotep, who designed the Step Pyramid of Djoser, was a commoner who ascended to a high-ranking official at the pharaoh's court (Robins, 2008).

CHILDREN IN CONTEMPORARY EGYPT

Despite the pedigree and reverence youth got in ancient Egypt, children in contemporary Egypt are challenged with a wide range of obstacles linked to poverty, lack of education, poor health, and social inequity. According to a report by the United Nations Children's Fund (2019), Egypt has one of the worst child poverty rates in the Middle East and North Africa, with over a third of children living below the poverty line. It substantially influences children's access to school, health care, and basic amenities and can hinder their social and economic mobility. According to Human Rights Watch (2018), access to education is one of the most critical concerns affecting Egyptian youngsters. Despite the government's attempts to enhance access to education, particularly for females and children from underprivileged areas, Egypt continues to face substantial obstacles to providing a decent education. Children's health is another concern, particularly regarding hunger and access to medical treatment. According to a survey by the World Health Organization (2016), over one-third of children under five in Egypt have stunted growth. According to the research, inadequate nutrition may substantially influence children's physical and cognitive development, restricting their capacity to learn and grow.

Social inequality is also a significant concern, particularly those from marginalized populations such as street children, refugees, and children with disabilities. According to Save the Children (2018), street children encounter various obstacles like poverty, violence, and exploitation. The research states that many street children have limited access to schooling and medical care and are at significant risk of being involved in criminal activity.

Street Children in Egypt

Street children in Egypt are at high risk of ending up in juvenile institutions due to their lack of access to necessities such as food, shelter, and education. Amer & Hassanein (2018) found that most street children are boys between 10 and 14 years old, come from families with low education and income levels, and are at an increased likelihood of experiencing depression, anxiety, and substance abuse

(Elzalabany, 2020). To survive, many street children are forced to engage in illicit activities such as drug trafficking, prostitution, and theft, which increases their risk of being arrested and detained. Human Rights Watch (2019) reported minors arrested for these illicit activities are frequently detained in overcrowded and unsanitary pretrial detention for extended periods. They are frequently abused and neglected by guards and other detainees and lack access to competent medical care and legal counsel. The report also notes that children apprehended for minor offenses such as loitering or soliciting are frequently detained in juvenile institutions without trial or due process. These children are frequently subjected to physical maltreatment and forced labor and are not provided with adequate education or rehabilitation services. The Egyptian government enacted a new child protection law in 2017 to address some of these problems and provide protection for street children. However, the law's implementation has been sluggish, and many street children continue to confront significant challenges and risks (UNICEF, 2015; Osman & Saleh, 2015)

Juvenile justice is a crucial issue in Egypt, where a significant proportion of the population is under 18. The Egyptian government has developed a distinct system for dealing with juvenile criminals, controlled by Law No. 12 of 1996 on Children and its amendments. This system seeks to protect children's rights and facilitate their rehabilitation and reintegration into society. This law was intended to deal with juvenile criminals and protect children's rights, particularly their right to a fair trial (Egyptian Child Law, 1996).

YOUTH CRIME IN EGYPT

Juvenile delinquency is a complicated issue that several social, economic, and cultural variables may impact. Youth crime has been a worry in Egypt for several years, with reports of crimes perpetrated by youth on the rise in recent years. United Nations Office on Drugs and Crime (UNODC) (2019) reported that Egypt had experienced a considerable increase in juvenile offenders in correctional institutions over the previous decade. Poverty, unemployment, a lack of education, and social marginalization contribute to youth criminality. Theft, drug addiction, graffiti, and violent crimes, including assault and robbery, are the most common offenses youth commit (UNODC, 2019). According to the Egyptian Ministry of the Interior (2019), there were 76,000 documented occurrences of juvenile delinquency in Egypt in 2018, with stealing being the most prevalent violation perpetrated by youth. The COVID-19 epidemic has also affected youth crime in Egypt since lockdowns and economic disruptions have increased poverty and social instability, all of which can lead to higher crime rates (The National, 2020).

According to Souryal (1992), Egyptians believe that emotional and intellectual immaturity, which is generated by social imbalances in the immediate surroundings of the juvenile, is the root cause of juvenile criminality. Adverse conditions surrounding the child's rearing, such as affiliation with the wrong crowd in the neighborhood, school, or employment, can also contribute to developing deviant behavior. Before the institutionalization of juvenile delinquents, it was considered that the misbehavior of children and adolescents was a public problem that could be solved by adopting several social initiatives (Souryal, 1992).

JUVENILE JUSTICE IN EGYPT

The Egyptian government has taken several steps to combat adolescent crime, including the establishment of specialist police units and courts to handle juvenile offenders, the implementation of youth rehabilitation programs, and the provision of educational and job possibilities for youth. Yet, more comprehensive and successful methods are still required to reduce youth crime and address its core causes.

The law defines a child as someone under 18 (Egyptian Child Law, 1996). The Egyptian Child Law was enacted for the first time in 1996 and revised in 2008. The purpose of the law is to promote and protect children's rights, including their right to education, healthcare, and protection from violence, abuse, and neglect. The law also establishes a juvenile justice system dedicated to rehabilitating and reintegrating juvenile offenders. Children under 18 are considered minors under the law, and special provisions are in place to ensure that they are appropriately treated (Davis, 2015). The age of criminal responsibility in Egypt is 12 years old. Children between 12 and 18 who commit crimes are considered juvenile delinquents and are subject to a separate justice system (Eldefrawi, 2018).

There are specific essential provisions of the Egyptian Child Law. It includes protecting minors from maltreatment, exploitation, and violence; the right to a name, nationality, and family identity for offspring; the entitlement to education and healthcare for youth. The law intended to create a juvenile justice system emphasizing rehabilitation and reintegration over punishment and eliminating the death penalty and life sentences for juveniles. It stresses the establishment of specialized juvenile courts and institutions. The law requires that an attorney represent minors in legal proceedings; the condition that children be detained and tried separately from adult offenders; minors must be provided with education, vocational training, and other support during rehabilitation.

Child Law has been lauded for its emphasis on children's rights and best interests and its endeavors to establish a separate, specialized juvenile justice system (Egyptian Child Law, 1996). The legislation requires that juvenile criminals be handled differently than adult offenders. The purpose of the juvenile justice system is to rehabilitate and reintegrate young offenders into society (Egyptian Child Law, 1996). This is accomplished through various means, such as diversion programs, therapy, and alternatives to jail.

The purpose of diversion programs is to steer juvenile offenders away from the formal criminal system and into community-based initiatives (UNICEF, 2017). These programs try to address the underlying causes of juvenile delinquency and give assistance and counseling to help young people avoid future involvement in criminal activity. When incarceration is required, the law mandates that juvenile offenders be detained apart from adult criminals (Egyptian Child Law, 1996). Moreover, the law forbids the application of the death penalty or life without the chance of release for crimes committed by juveniles (Egyptian Child Law, 1996). In most instances, juvenile offenders are prosecuted in specialized juvenile courts presided over by judges with specific expertise in juvenile justice (UNICEF, 2017). These courts are intended to be less formal than adult courts and to offer juvenile offenders a more supportive atmosphere.

Structure of the Juvenile Justice System

The Egyptian juvenile justice system is supposed to be independent of the criminal justice system for adults. Child Law No. 12 of 1996 defines a child as any individual less than 18 years of age. Juvenile offenders are handled by specialist juvenile courts presided over by judges who have received specific training in juvenile justice. These courts are intended to be less formal than adult courts and to offer juvenile offenders a more supportive atmosphere.

Procedures in the Juvenile Justice System

The Egyptian juvenile justice system is designed to safeguard children's rights and facilitate their rehabilitation and reintegration into society. The statute offers unique processes for handling young offenders, such as diversion programs and alternatives to incarceration. Diversion programs aim to redirect juvenile offenders from the formal criminal system and towards community-based initiatives. These programs try to address the underlying causes of juvenile delinquency and give assistance and counseling to help young people avoid future involvement in criminal activity.

When incarceration is required, the law mandates that juvenile criminals be detained apart from adult offenders. In addition, the law forbids the use of the death penalty and life sentences without the chance of parole for crimes committed by juveniles. The purpose of detention in the juvenile justice system is to give young offenders education, training, and rehabilitation. There are four juvenile detention/correctional facilities. First, social investigation centers are organizations that attend to the social environment of adolescents. Caseworkers compile reports on children's living, social, and economic conditions, then present them in court. The second function of observation homes is to shelter juveniles detained by the courts during the pretrial phase and under investigation (Fouad, 2007). Thirdly, guest homes shelter minors in custody by the courts for committing offenses deemed vulnerable to danger (e.g., sleeping on the street or abandoning school). These guesthouses also house youth who have voluntarily sought refuge due to fleeing a violent home or for other reasons. Lastly, social observation centers are the typical juvenile detention facilities that hold youth sentenced to state custody. Some juveniles are confined in these facilities for less than three months, while others receive assistance with court appearances and make routine visits with probation officers (Ammar, 2009).

Outcomes of the Juvenile Justice System

Egypt's juvenile justice system has had mixed results. On the one hand, the system has effectively preserved children's rights and fostered their rehabilitation and reintegration into society. Using diversion programs and alternatives to imprisonment has helped lower the number of juveniles detained in the formal judicial system.

On the other hand, the Egyptian juvenile justice system still faces some substantial obstacles. There are insufficient resources and infrastructure to provide diversion programs and alternatives to incarceration (Eldefrawi, 2018). This indicates that many young people who may benefit from these programs are nonetheless detained in the formal justice system. Moreover, there are issues over the quality of Egyptian incarceration facilities. There are still allegations of overcrowding, poor cleanliness, and insufficient medical attention despite the Egyptian government's efforts to improve the circumstances in these institutions. Concerns exist in the overuse of physical punishment and other abuse at these facilities.

The juvenile justice system in Egypt has faced criticism from both domestic and international organizations for its lack of resources and inadequate rehabilitation programs for juvenile offenders. One of the major criticisms of the system is its lack of resources. A report by the United Nations Office on Drugs and Crime (UNODC) in 2014 noted that many juvenile detention facilities in Egypt suffer from poor conditions, including overcrowding, inadequate sanitation, and limited access to healthcare. The report also indicated that the government's budget for juvenile justice is insufficient, resulting in a lack of trained personnel and equipment. Another issue with the juvenile justice system in Egypt is the inadequate rehabilitation programs for juvenile offenders. According to Human Rights Watch (2020) report, many juveniles in Egypt are detained for prolonged periods without access to education or vocational training. The report also notes a lack of mental health services and counseling programs for juveniles who have experienced trauma or abuse. In addition to these criticisms, there have been reports of abuse and mistreatment of juvenile detainees by law enforcement officials. Human Rights Watch reported in 2020 that some juvenile detainees in Egypt had been subjected to physical abuse, including beatings, electric shocks, and the death penalty. According to Amnesty International (2021) report, Egypt has one of the highest rates of executions in the world, with minors being among those executed. The report states that at least four juveniles were executed in 2020. Human Rights Watch (2021) said that Egyptian authorities continue to sentence children to death, despite international law prohibiting the practice.

Moreover, children were often tried in adult courts and subjected to torture and other ill-treatment (ACHPR, 2020). These issues with the juvenile justice system in Egypt have led to calls for reform. In 2018, the Egyptian government passed a new law on juvenile justice that aimed to improve the treatment of juvenile offenders and provide better rehabilitation services. However, implementation of the law has been slow, and many of the issues with the system remain (El-Masry & Hegazy, 2018).

The political climate in Egypt has had a significant impact on juveniles, particularly in terms of their rights and freedoms. Under President el-Sisi's government, there have been widespread allegations of human rights abuses, including the detention of political dissidents, journalists, and activists. There have been claims that children have been jailed without trial, subjected to abuse and cruelty, and refused access to legal representation. The influence of Egypt's political atmosphere on the country's youth has also been felt in the country's educational system. According to a study by Amnesty International (2019), Egyptian authorities have enacted measures to repress dissent and limit academic freedom, including detention and dismissing instructors who express political opinions or oppose government policies. This has created an environment of fear and self-censorship among instructors and students, which can impede young people's capacity to express themselves and participate in the political conversation.

THE WEST AND EGYPT

The juvenile justice system in the West is essentially different from the realities of the youth system in Egypt. For instance, depending on the jurisdiction, the age of criminal culpability in the West varies between 10 and 18 years. However, in Egypt, the age of criminal responsibility is 12 (United Nations Office on Drugs and

Crime, 2021). Even 12-year-old minors can be prosecuted and punished for their crimes. Recognizing that children have distinct levels of maturity and responsibility, the juvenile justice system in the West is designed to deal with young offenders differently than adults. Typically, juvenile offenders are placed in specialized facilities or programs designed to rehabilitate them and address the root causes of their criminal behavior (Fagan & Tyler, 2005). In Egypt, however, juvenile offenders are frequently subjected to severe and punitive treatment. Children can be tried and sentenced in the same tribunals as adults and may face the same punishments, including imprisonment (Human Rights Watch, 2020). Various programs and interventions are available in the West to assist juvenile offenders in turning their lives around. These may include counseling, rehabilitation, training, vocational education, and community service (American Psychological Association, 2016). However, Egypt lacks the necessary infrastructure and resources to support rehabilitation programs for juvenile offenders. Most minors interacting with the justice system are punished and returned to their communities without support or follow-up (Human Rights Watch, 2020).

COMPARING THE JJS IN THE USA AND EGYPT

The juvenile justice systems of Egypt and the United States are designed to address young offenders' unique needs. Still, they differ significantly in their legal frameworks, historical development, and treatment of juvenile offenders. It should be noted that the two countries have different approaches to justice, with the U.S. focusing on punishment and Egypt emphasizing rehabilitation. Moreover, it is worth remembering that cultural factors play a significant role in shaping stakeholders' and peoples' attitudes toward juvenile justice (Fagan and Tyler, 2005). While both the U.S. and Egypt have made progress in protecting the rights of juveniles, there are still significant challenges in ensuring that these rights are fully respected (Abdelaal, 2017).

The legal frameworks of the juvenile justice systems in Egypt and the United States differ significantly. In the United States, juvenile justice is governed by state laws, which set out the rules for treating juvenile offenders. The main focus of the juvenile justice system in the United States is rehabilitation rather than punishment. It is based on the principles of parens patriae, which means that the state acts as a parent to the child (Mack, 2019). In contrast, the legal framework of the juvenile justice system in Egypt is governed by the Child Law of 1996, enacted to protect the rights of children, including those in conflict with the law (Al-Attar, 2021). However, the law lacks proper provisions for rehabilitating and reintegrating juvenile offenders, and children as young as 12 can be prosecuted as adults for criminal offenses.

The historical development of the juvenile justice systems in Egypt and the United States also differs significantly. In the United States, the first juvenile court was established in 1899 in Cook County, Illinois, and it marked the beginning of a new era in the treatment of juvenile offenders (Mack, 2019). The juvenile justice system was created to provide individualized treatment and rehabilitation for young offenders. It has since evolved to focus on keeping juveniles out of the criminal justice system. In contrast, the juvenile justice system in Egypt has a long history dating back to the Pharaonic era, when children were treated leniently in criminal cases (Al-Attar, 2021). However, Egypt's modern juvenile justice system has faced challenges providing proper rehabilitation and reintegration services for juvenile offenders. For instance, children, in Egypt commonly face barriers within the juvenile justice system, owing to a lack of age-appropriate resources and surroundings, extended legal processes, and lengthy delays in outcomes (Council of Europe, 2010). Juvenile offenders frequently find themselves in environments that are insensitive to their age, such as insufficient communication techniques and inadequate facilities (Council of Europe, 2010) where both young offender and their families are typically unaware of children's rights (national and international) and struggle to determine where and how to seek help in specific circumstances and are often overlooked (Davidson et al., 2019).

The treatment of juvenile offenders in Egypt and the United States also differs significantly. In the United States, the juvenile justice system strongly emphasizes rehabilitation and provides counseling, education, and other services to help juveniles reintegrate into society (Puzzanchera & Adams, 2017). Incarceration is seen as a last resort, and children are often held in separate facilities from adult offenders to prevent their exposure to more hardened criminals. In contrast, the treatment of juvenile offenders in Egypt is often punitive rather than rehabilitative. Young offenders can face harsh punishments, including imprisonment and flogging, and a lack of access to proper healthcare, education, and counseling services (Al-Attar, 2021). Juvenile offenders are often held in overcrowded facilities where they are exposed to adult criminals and can face physical and sexual abuse. The correctional institution is overcrowded with minors arrested for political reasons where they are abused physically and kept in unhygienic conditions. Despite the Egyptian Child Law being thorough, there is stark distinction between the reality and what is not the paper (Chang, 2015).

CONCLUSION

Ancient Egypt placed great importance on children and thought they must be adequately reared to ensure their future prosperity. In Ancient Egypt, parents were responsible for their children's well-being, which included their education, and education was highly prized. Although socioeconomic standing determined a child's possibilities, it did not define their value or potential (Johnson, 2011). Egypt's system for dealing with juvenile offenders is now controlled by Child Law No. 12 of 1996 and its amendments. This system seeks to rehabilitate and reintegrate young offenders into society using various methods, such as diversion programs and alternatives to imprisonment (Egyptian Child Law, 1996). Despite the Egyptian Child Law (2008) being highly progressive and essentially in line with international juvenile justice conventions, standards, and regulations, its application does not necessarily reflect the same image. According to human rights organizations and media reports, authorities did not always separate juveniles from adults and sometimes held pretrial detainees with convicted prisoners. Reports that guards abused prisoners, including youths in adult facilities, were usual (U.S. Mission Egypt, 2023). The Egyptian Organization of Human Rights has consistently reported minors being detained with adults by security authorities (Organisation Mondiale Contre la Torture, 2002).

Moreover, the juvenile justice systems in Egypt and the West differ significantly in their legal frameworks, historical development, and treatment of juvenile offenders. For instance, the United States strongly emphasizes rehabilitation and keeping juveniles out of the criminal justice system. The juvenile justice system in Egypt lacks proper rehabilitation services and often punishes juvenile offenders harshly. The different approaches to juvenile justice reflect broader legal and cultural framework differences between the two countries. However, it is pertinent to see the young offenders as children, rather than miniature adults, deserving punishments apt for an adult (Chang, 2015). According to Ahmad (2015), there are several ways in which changes in the treatment of children can be ensured. The Child Law (2008) can be revisited, and specific articles can be amended, especially those contradicting international treaties and guidelines. There can be sound preventive mechanisms to implement active community-based prevention programs. There can be initiatives to promote the development of a comprehensive social safety network that focuses on child and family welfare as a frontline to reduce child delinquency and responds to the increased number of children at risk. Furthermore, effective measures to address street children's challenges can be employed before they become children in conflict with the law or juvenile offenders. Future studies should assess programs implemented in the juvenile justice systems in Egypt and help improve the programs if they are found lacking. It is vital that stakeholders should pay attention to what is happening within the correctional institution – which is completely tainted with the political climate.

REFERENCES

Abdelaal, R. A. (2017). The rights of the child in the juvenile justice system: A comparative study between Egypt and the United States of America. *International Journal of Humanities and Social Science Invention*, *6*(8), 33–37.

Al-Attar, M. (2021). *Child law in Egypt*. Oxford Research Encyclopedia of Criminology and Criminal Justice.

Amer, M. M., & Hassanein, E. A. (2018). Street children in Egypt: Demographic and socioeconomic profile. *Child Abuse & Neglect*, *76*, 159–167.

American Psychological Association. (2016). Juvenile Justice: APA Advocacy Fact Sheet. https://www.apa.org/about/offices/ogc/amicus/juvenile-justice-facts

Ammar, N. H. (2009). The relationship between street children and the justice system in Egypt. *International Journal of Offender Therapy and Comparative Criminology*, *53*(5), 556–573. PMID: 18664552

Amnesty International. (2019). Egypt: Education under threat as authorities crackdown on academic freedom. Retrieved from https://www.amnesty.org/en/latest/news/2019/06/egypt-education-under-threat-as-authorities-crackdown-on-academic-freedom/

Amnesty International. (2021). Death Sentences and Executions 2020. https://www.amnesty.org/download/Documents/ACT5097452021ENGLISH.PDF

Brewer, D. J., & Teeter, E. (2017). *Egypt and the Egyptians*. Cambridge University Press.

Chang, C. (2015). *Inside Egypt's El-Marg juvenile detention centre*. Middle East Eye. https://middleeasteye.net/news/inside-egypts-el-marg-juvenile-detention-centre

Council of Europe. (2010). Council of Europe guidelines on child-friendly justice. https://www.coe.int/en/web/children/council-of-europe-guidelines-on-child-friendly-justice

Davidson, J., Martino, A., & Woodward, C. (2019). Child rights in the context of civil justice: Access to justice, procedural fairness and protection of the child's best interests (Study commissioned by the European Union Agency for Fundamental Rights). https://fra.europa.eu/en/publication/2019/child-rights-context-civil-justice-access-justice-procedural-fairness-and

Davis, E. (2015). Yale University. Egypt | Representing Children Worldwide. Retrieved April 17, 2023, from https://rcw.law.yale.edu/jurisdiction-research/egypt

Egyptian Child Law No. 12 of 1996, available at http://www.ilo.org/dyn/natlex/docs/ELECTRONIC/46681/80017/F-1605235635/EGY46681%20Eng.pdf

Egyptian Initiative for Personal Rights. (2021). Egypt's Juvenile Justice System: An Overview of Key Issues. https://eipr.org/sites/default/files/reports/pdf/EIPR%20Juvenile%20Justice%20Report%202021%20English.pdf

El-Masry, N., & Hegazy, I. (2018). Juvenile delinquency in Egypt: A social and legal perspective. *Child Abuse & Neglect*, *76*, 324–333.

Eldefrawi, M. H. (2018). Juvenile Delinquency in Egypt: An Overview. In Handbook of Juvenile Delinquency and Juvenile Justice (pp. 305-322). Springer.

Elzalabany, M. M. (2020). Psychological and social problems of street children in Egypt. *Journal of Child and Adolescent Behavior*, *8*(1), 1–5.

Fagan, J., & Tyler, T. R. (2005). Legal socialization of children and adolescents. *Social Justice Research*, *18*(3), 217–242.

Hornung, E., Krauss, R., & Warburton, D. A. (2006). Ancient Egyptian Chronology. Brill. https://eg.usembassy.gov/egypt-2021-human-rights-report/ https://www.amnesty.org/en/latest/press-release/2019/06/egypt-must-not-sentence-to-death-a-young-man-forcibly-disappeared-and-tortured-at-17/

Human Rights Watch. (2018). Egypt: Death Penalty for Children Approved. https://www.hrw.org/news/2018/02/15/egypt-death-penalty-children-approved

Human Rights Watch. (2020). Egypt: Children Among Thousands Disappeared and Tortured. Retrieved from https://www.hrw.org/news/2020/02/12/egypt-children-among-thousands-disappeared-and-tortured

Human Rights Watch. (2021). World Report 2021: Egypt. https://www.hrw.org/world-report/2021/country-chapters/egypt

Johnson, J. H. (2011). *Life in Ancient Egypt*. ABC-CLIO.

Mack, K. (2019). *Juvenile justice in the United States*. Oxford Research Encyclopedia of Criminology and Criminal Justice.

Osman, T. M., & Saleh, M. A. (2015). Street children in Egypt: From an invisible population to a priority for intervention. *International Journal of Social Science Studies*, *3*(1), 24–31.

Puzzanchera, C. & Adams, B. (2017). Juvenile arrests 2015. Juvenile Justice

Robins, G. (2008). *The Art of Ancient Egypt*. Harvard University Press.

Save the Children. (2018). Egypt Street Children Report. Retrieved from https://www.savethechildren.org/content/dam/usa/reports/advocacy/Egypt_Street_Children_Report.pdf

Souryal, S. S. (1992). Juvenile Delinquency in the Cross-Cultural Context: The Egyptian Experience. *International Journal of Comparative and Applied Criminal Justice*, *16*(1-2), 329–352.

The National. (2020). Egypt's youth crime rate rising as economic crisis hits home. Retrieved from https://www.thenationalnews.com/world/mena/egypt-s-youth-crime-rate-rising-as-economic-crisis-hits-home-1.1050631

UNICEF. (2017). Children in Egypt: A statistical digest. Available at https://www.unicef.org/egypt/media/1676/file/Children%20in%20Egypt%20A%20Statistical%20Digest%20Final%20-%20EN.pdf

UNICEF. (2019). Children in Egypt. Retrieved from https://www.unicef.org/egypt/children-egypt

United Nations Children's Fund (UNICEF). "Street Children in Egypt." 2015. https://www.unicef.org/egypt/street-children-egypt

United Nations Office on Drugs and Crime. (2014). Juvenile Delinquency in Egypt: A Situational Analysis. https://www.unodc.org/documents/egyptandarabstates//Juvenile_Delinquency_in_Egypt_2014.pdf

United Nations Office on Drugs and Crime. (2019). Global Study on Homicide 2019: Executive Summary. Retrieved from https://www.unodc.org/documents/data-and-analysis/gsh/2019/Executive_summary_GSH2019.pdf

United Nations Office on Drugs and Crime. (2021). Handbook on Children Recruited and Exploited by Terrorist and Violent Extremist Groups: The Role of the Justice System. https://www.unodc.org/documents/terrorism/Publications/Handbook_on_Children_recruited_and_exploited_by_terrorist_and_violent_extremist_groups.pdf

Wahab, M. (2019). Update: An overview of the Egyptian legal system and Legal Research. UPDATE: An Overview of the Egyptian Legal System and Legal Research - GlobaLex. Retrieved April 16, 2023, from https://www.nyulawglobal.org/globalex/Egypt1.html

World Health Organization. (2016). Malnutrition in Egypt. Retrieved from https://www.who.int/nutrition/topics/2_background/en/

Chapter 13
Reframing Juvenile Justice Through a Human Rights Lens:
Kenya and the U.S. Case Studies

Simeon P. Sungi
https://orcid.org/0000-0003-4172-6222
United States International University-Africa, Kenya

ABSTRACT

This chapter explores the reframing of juvenile justice through a human rights lens, using Kenya and the United States as comparative case studies. Both nations offer contrasting yet insightful approaches to juvenile justice, shaped by their legal frameworks and socio-political contexts. Kenya, as a signatory to key international treaties like the UN Convention on the Rights of the Child, emphasizes rehabilitation and diversion in its juvenile justice system. Conversely, the U.S., with its decentralized and punitive-focused approach, grapples with systemic issues such as racial disparities, the transfer of juveniles to adult courts, and over-incarceration. Through a comparative analysis, this chapter examines how each country's juvenile justice system aligns with or diverges from international human rights norms, highlighting implementation challenges, including resource constraints in Kenya and racial disparities in the U.S. The chapter underscores the need for reforms that prioritize the rights, dignity, and rehabilitation of young offenders globally.

DOI: 10.4018/978-1-6684-9343-4.ch013

1. INTRODUCTION

Juvenile justice systems around the world are faced with the difficult task of balancing public safety, the welfare of young offenders, and broader societal goals of justice and rehabilitation. Historically, many of these systems have leaned toward punitive measures, often treating juveniles in ways similar to adult offenders. However, in recent decades, there has been a growing recognition that children in conflict with the law are fundamentally different from adults in terms of their development, psychological maturity, and capacity for rehabilitation. This shift in thinking is encapsulated in the increasing emphasis on applying a human rights framework to juvenile justice, which centers on protecting children's rights, rehabilitation, and social reintegration over punishment.

This chapter, *Reframing Juvenile Justice through a Human Rights Lens: Kenya and the U.S. Case Studies*, delves into the evolving landscape of juvenile justice by focusing on two nations—Kenya and the United States. Despite their stark differences in history, culture, and legal systems, these countries provide rich comparative insights into how juvenile justice is approached, implemented, and aligned with international human rights standards. Both jurisdictions face unique challenges in the administration of juvenile justice. However, they aim to create systems prioritizing protecting and rehabilitating children while addressing crime and societal safety.

1.1 The Human Rights Framework for Juvenile Justice

The human rights framework for juvenile justice is grounded in the principles of child protection as outlined in critical international instruments such as the *United Nations Convention on the Rights of the Child* (UNCRC), the *Beijing Rules*, the *Havana Rules*, and the *African Charter on the Rights and Welfare of the Child* (ACRWC). These documents emphasize that children require special protection due to their vulnerability and developmental differences. Their involvement in criminal activities should be met with measures that promote their dignity, well-being, and social reintegration rather than punitive or harsh treatment (United Nations, 1989).

The UNCRC, in particular, is the cornerstone of international efforts to protect children's rights. It highlights vital principles such as the child's best interests, non-discrimination, and the right to be heard, all of which must be central considerations in any juvenile justice system. The convention calls for using detention only as a last resort and encourages states to develop systems that offer alternatives to incarceration, focusing on rehabilitation and reintegration into society. Despite these clear international standards, applying these principles varies widely between countries, shaped by legal traditions, resource availability, and social attitudes toward youth crime.

1.2 The Kenyan Context

Kenya's juvenile justice system has been heavily influenced by international human rights instruments, particularly the UNCRC, which the country ratified in 1990. Kenya's legal framework includes the *Children's Act of 2001*, which enshrines children's rights, including those conflicting with the law. The Act promotes a child-centered approach that focuses on the child's best interests and mandates that detention and other punitive measures should be used only as a last resort. In line with the UNCRC, Kenya's juvenile justice system aims to rehabilitate young offenders and reintegrate them into society through alternative measures, such as probation, counseling, and community service (Government of Kenya, 2001).

Despite these progressive legal provisions, Kenya faces significant challenges in implementing its juvenile justice system. Resource limitations, overcrowded detention facilities, and a lack of trained personnel often result in the substandard treatment of young offenders. Additionally, the socio-economic conditions in Kenya, including poverty and lack of access to education, play a critical role in pushing children into conflict with the law. These factors complicate the full realization of the human rights framework in the Kenyan context, but efforts are ongoing to reform the system and improve its alignment with international standards (Mujuzi, 2014).

1.3 The U.S. Context

The United States, with its decentralized criminal justice system, presents a stark contrast to Kenya. The U.S. juvenile justice system is shaped by a long history of treating juvenile offenders through a punitive lens, especially during the late 20th century when "tough on crime" policies led to harsher sentencing and the transfer of juveniles to adult courts. However, in recent years, there has been a gradual shift toward recognizing the developmental differences between juveniles and adults, and the U.S. Supreme Court has played a pivotal role in advancing this shift. Landmark cases such as *Roper v. Simmons* (2005), *Graham v. Florida* (2010), and *Miller v. Alabama* (2012) have established that juveniles cannot be subjected to the death penalty or life without parole for non-homicidal crimes, underscoring the importance of treating children in conflict with the law differently from adults (Roper v. Simmons, 543 U.S. 551, 2005).

Despite these legal advancements, the U.S. juvenile justice system continues to face critical issues, particularly racial and socio-economic disparities. Minority youth, especially African American and Latino children, are disproportionately represented in the juvenile justice system, often receiving harsher punishments compared to their white counterparts (The Sentencing Project, 2021). Furthermore, the punitive approach to juvenile justice in the U.S. still prevails in many states, and the use of incarceration remains high compared to international norms, raising questions about the country's compliance with human rights standards.

Kenya and the United States offer unique case studies examining how the human rights framework can be applied to juvenile justice systems. As a developing nation, Kenya grapples with the challenges of implementing a child-centered legal framework in the context of limited resources and a strained infrastructure. Despite these hurdles, its legal commitment to children's rights is clear, and ongoing reforms aim to bring the juvenile justice system more in line with international standards. The U.S., on the other hand, while economically more advanced, struggles with systemic issues such as racial disparities and the persistence of punitive measures in many states. Both nations offer essential lessons on the need for reform and the complexities of balancing justice, rehabilitation, and human rights in treating young offenders.

Reframing juvenile justice through a human rights lens is crucial in addressing the evolving needs of children in conflict with the law. This reframing emphasizes rehabilitation over punishment, supports social reintegration, and underscores the importance of treating juveniles in a manner that respects their rights and dignity. The international human rights framework provides a roadmap for these reforms, offering guidance on how states can design juvenile justice systems that align with global norms and respond to the unique needs of children. Kenya and the United States, despite their different contexts, both illustrate the need for ongoing efforts to reform juvenile justice systems to protect children's rights better and ensure their future well-being.

This research intends to contribute to comparative juvenile justice research since comparing Kenya, and the United States provides valuable insights into how juvenile justice systems can evolve to better align with international human rights standards. While both countries face distinct challenges, their efforts to reform juvenile justice systems show a growing recognition of the importance of a child-centered, rights-based approach. This chapter will further explore the legal frameworks, implementation challenges, and opportunities for reform in both jurisdictions, highlighting the critical role that a human rights lens can play in transforming the treatment of young offenders. Through this lens, we can better understand how to protect children's rights, promote rehabilitation, and create systems that foster positive societal reintegration for juvenile offenders.

1.4 Research Questions

This chapter addresses fundamental questions regarding the reframing of juvenile justice systems in Kenya and the United States through a human rights lens:

1. How do the criminal justice systems in Kenya and the United States treat juvenile offenders, and to what extent do they align with international human rights standards?
2. What are the key challenges and gaps in implementing human rights principles in the juvenile justice systems of both countries?
3. How can Kenya and the United States reform their juvenile justice systems to protect young offenders' rights better and promote rehabilitation and reintegration into society?

To this end, the chapter explores how juvenile justice can be reframed through a human rights perspective, focusing on Kenya and the United States case studies. Both countries present distinct but illustrative examples of juvenile justice systems shaped by their unique legal traditions, socio-economic conditions, and cultural contexts. However, each system faces challenges in fully realizing the human rights of juvenile offenders. The United States, with its decentralized and punitive approach, has been criticized for practices such as the incarceration of minors alongside adults and the imposition of life sentences without parole for juveniles. On the other hand, while incorporating international human rights frameworks such as the United Nations Convention on the Rights of the Child (UNCRC) into its legal system, Kenya struggles with institutional shortcomings and regional disparities in administering justice for juveniles. By examining these questions, the chapter aims to contribute to the ongoing global conversation about juvenile justice reform. Through a comparative analysis of Kenya and the United States, it seeks to highlight best practices, identify areas for improvement, and provide policy recommendations for developing juvenile justice systems grounded in human rights principles.

1.5 Methodology: The Selection of Kenya and the United States for Comparative Case Study

The selection of Kenya and the United States as case studies for examining juvenile justice through a human rights lens is grounded in several key justifications.

While Kenya and the United States have adopted the Common Law system, they represent two distinct legal traditions and socio-political environments, allowing for a rich comparative analysis. Kenya's legal system is a blend of common law, customary law, and international human rights law, making it an ideal case for exploring the integration of human rights frameworks into a developing country's justice system. On the other hand, with its federalist legal structure and significant influence on global legal trends, the United States provides a contrasting example of how a highly developed nation, despite its resources, often needs help to align with international human rights norms in juvenile justice fully.

The juxtaposition of these two countries helps illuminate the diverse ways different legal, economic, and cultural factors can shape juvenile justice. As a signatory to international instruments like the *United Nations Convention on the Rights of the Child (UNCRC)* and the *African Charter on the Rights and Welfare of the Child (ACRWC)*, Kenya offers insight into how international obligations are translated into national policy. In contrast, the U.S., which has yet to ratify the UNCRC, exemplifies how domestic legal frameworks can sometimes resist or diverge from global human rights standards, particularly concerning treating children in conflict with the law.

Furthermore, Kenya and the United States adopt fundamentally different approaches to juvenile justice, making them instructive for comparative analysis. Kenya's juvenile justice system, as outlined in the *Children's Act of 2001*, reflects a commitment to rehabilitation and reintegration, as enshrined in international human rights instruments. The focus is on protecting the rights of children, diverting them from the criminal justice system where possible, and ensuring that detention is used only as a last resort. The United States, by contrast, has historically emphasized a more punitive approach, with practices such as trying juveniles in adult courts and imposing harsh sentences, including life without parole for minors. Although recent U.S. Supreme Court decisions, such as *Roper v. Simmons* (2005) and *Miller v. Alabama* (2012), have signaled a shift towards recognizing the developmental differences between juveniles and adults, the U.S. system still faces criticism for its harsh treatment of young offenders. This divergence in approaches enables an exploration of the strengths and weaknesses of both rehabilitative and punitive models and the potential for reform.

Kenya and the United States face significant challenges in aligning their juvenile justice systems with human rights norms, but these challenges vary widely. In Kenya, challenges include limited resources, regional disparities, and the influence of customary law, sometimes conflicting with formal legal protections for children (Mujuzi, 2014; Nyamu, 2010). The Kenyan case highlights the difficulties many developing countries face in implementing human rights standards, particularly in strained judicial and social welfare systems.

In contrast, the United States grapples with systemic issues such as racial and socio-economic disparities, the criminalization of school-related behavior (the "school-to-prison pipeline"), and the over-incarceration of minority youth (Feld, 1999; Heitzeg, 2009). Despite its economic resources, the U.S. system has been criticized by international human rights bodies for practices such as solitary confinement for juveniles and the transfer of minors to adult courts. Including both countries provides a comprehensive view of the barriers to human rights compliance in juvenile justice, from resource constraints in developing countries to entrenched institutional biases in developed nations.

Kenya and the United States are strategically chosen because their juvenile justice systems represent broader global trends. Kenya's experience as a developing nation working to align its legal framework with international human rights obligations is relevant to many other countries in Africa and the Global South, where similar challenges regarding resources, legal pluralism, and regional disparities exist. Conversely, the U.S. experience is pertinent to other developed nations facing issues like mass incarceration, racial disparities, and resistance to international human rights frameworks.

This chapter compares these two systems to draw conclusions that can be generalized to both developing and developed nations. The insights gained from Kenya and the United States can help inform global discussions on juvenile justice reform, particularly the implementation of human rights standards in diverse legal and cultural contexts. Therefore, the comparative study of Kenya and the United States opens up opportunities for cross-learning. Despite its challenges, Kenya has made significant strides in incorporating international human rights standards into its juvenile justice system, mainly through establishing specialized children's courts and focusing on rehabilitation. The United States, with its advanced legal infrastructure, could potentially benefit from adopting similar approaches that emphasize rehabilitation and diversion.

Conversely, Kenya can learn from the recent judicial reforms in the U.S., particularly the Supreme Court's growing recognition of the developmental differences between juveniles and adults, which has led to landmark rulings restricting harsh sentences for minors (*Roper v. Simmons*, 2005; *Graham v. Florida*, 2010; *Miller v. Alabama*, 2012. This cross-learning is particularly valuable in the context of global juvenile justice reform, where countries can draw on each other's experiences to develop more effective, rights-based systems. The historical and cultural differences between Kenya and the United States also offer a rich context for understanding how juvenile justice systems evolve and societal values' role in shaping legal responses to juvenile crime. In Kenya, traditional justice mechanisms, often based on restorative principles, continue to influence the treatment of juveniles in some communities, even as the formal legal system strives to align with international standards (Rwezaura, 1998; Chokothe, 2013). In contrast, the United States legal system is deeply influenced by a culture of punitive justice, which has led to high rates of juvenile incarceration, particularly among marginalized populations (Mears, 2001; Bishop, 2005).

This chapter examines these historical and cultural factors to provide a nuanced understanding of how legal frameworks and societal attitudes toward youth, crime, and punishment shape juvenile justice systems.

2. HUMAN RIGHTS FRAMEWORK FOR JUVENILE JUSTICE

The human rights framework for juvenile justice is grounded in the understanding that children, including those who come into conflict with the law, are entitled to special protection due to their vulnerability and developmental differences from adults (Steinberg & Scott, 2003; Cipriani, 2009). Various international human rights instruments emphasize the need to treat children in conflict with the law with dignity, focusing on their reintegration into society and prioritizing rehabilitation over punishment. For instance, the *Convention on the Rights of the Child* (United Nations, 1989) underscores the right of children to be treated in a manner that promotes their dignity and self-worth. Similarly, the *Beijing Rules* emphasize that any response to juvenile offenders should prioritize their well-being and ensure proportionality to the circumstances (United Nations, 1985). Furthermore, the *Havana Rules* state that depriving juveniles of their liberty should be a last resort and only in exceptional cases (United Nations, 1990a). Additionally, the *Riyadh Guidelines* call for efforts to prevent juvenile delinquency, stressing the importance of the harmonious development of adolescents (United Nations, 1990b). This framework establishes global standards that States are encouraged to adopt and implement within their legal systems to protect children's rights in conflict with the law.

2.1 Key International Instruments

Several international instruments provide the foundation for the human rights framework that guides juvenile justice systems globally and regionally (continentally).

2.2 United Nations Convention on the Rights of the Child (UNCRC)

The *United Nations Convention on the Rights of the Child (UNCRC)*, adopted by the U.N. General Assembly in 1989, is the most comprehensive international treaty dedicated to protecting children's rights. It explicitly addresses juvenile justice in Article 37 and Article 40. Article 37 prohibits the imposition of capital punishment or life imprisonment without the possibility of parole for offenses committed by individuals under the age of 18. It also mandates that a child's arrest, detention, or imprisonment must be used only as a last resort and for the shortest appropriate period.

Article 40 of the UNCRC outlines several essential principles for treating children in conflict with the law. These include the right to be treated in a manner that promotes the child's sense of dignity and worth, the right to legal representation, and the right to a fair trial. This chapter focuses on promoting the child's reintegration into society and assuming a constructive role in the community (United Nations, 1989).

2.3 Beijing Rules

The *United Nations Standard Minimum Rules for the Administration of Juvenile Justice* (also known as the Beijing Rules), adopted in 1985, provide additional guidance on how juvenile justice systems should operate. The rules emphasize the need for a juvenile justice system that is distinct from adult criminal justice systems, focusing on the protection of children's rights and their rehabilitation. Rule 17 stipulates that any reaction to juvenile offenders must be proportionate to the offender's circumstances and the offense, highlighting the principle of proportionality (United Nations, 1985).

The Beijing Rules also promote diversionary measures, encouraging alternatives to formal judicial proceedings such as community service, counseling, and education. These measures aim to prevent the stigmatization of young offenders while addressing the root causes of their behavior.

2.4 Havana Rules

The *United Nations Rules for the Protection of Juveniles Deprived of their Liberty* (Havana Rules), adopted in 1990, provide guidelines for treating incarcerated or otherwise deprived of their liberty. These rules stress that juvenile detention should be used only as a last resort and for the shortest possible duration, in line with the principle articulated in the UNCRC. They also establish minimum standards for detention conditions, including access to education, healthcare, and opportunities for social reintegration (United Nations, 1990).

2.5 Riyadh Guidelines

The *United Nations Guidelines for the Prevention of Juvenile Delinquency* (Riyadh Guidelines), adopted in 1990, aims to prevent juvenile delinquency by addressing its underlying causes. The Riyadh Guidelines emphasize the importance of early intervention through social, economic, and educational measures, rather than punitive responses, to prevent youth from conflict with the law. They encourage governments to create policies that provide young people with positive opportunities, focusing on prevention through community involvement and family support (United Nations, 1990).

2.6 African Charter on the Rights and Welfare of the Child (ACRWC)

In the African context, the *African Charter on the Rights and Welfare of the Child* (ACRWC) complements the UNCRC by providing region-specific guidance on children's rights. The ACRWC, adopted by the Organization of African Unity (now the African Union) in 1990, echoes many of the protections found in the UNCRC and addresses specific cultural and social contexts within Africa. Article 17 of the ACRWC deals with juvenile justice, stating that children accused of or recognized as having violated the law should be treated with respect for their dignity and in a manner that takes into account their age and the desirability of promoting their reintegration (Organization of African Unity, 1990).

3. CORE PRINCIPLES OF THE HUMAN RIGHTS FRAMEWORK

The human rights framework for juvenile justice is built upon several core principles derived from international instruments. These principles emphasize the need to treat children in conflict with the law in a manner that reflects their age, developmental stage, and capacity for rehabilitation. The *Convention on the Rights of the Child* (United Nations, 1989) underscores that children are entitled to special protection and treatment that considers their developmental differences from adults. The *Beijing Rules* (United Nations, 1985) further stress that juvenile justice should prioritize the child's well-being and ensure proportionality in sentencing, while the *Havana Rules* (United Nations, 1990a) highlight the need for rehabilitation and reintegration over punitive measures. Additionally, the *Riyadh Guidelines* (United Nations, 1990b) promote preventive measures to prevent minors' criminalization and encourage positive development.

3.1 The Best Interests of the Child

One of the primary principles of the UNCRC is that the child's best interests must be a primary consideration in all decisions affecting them (Article 3, UNCRC). This principle is essential in juvenile justice, where decisions about the treatment of a child offender must prioritize their well-being and prospects. The aim is to avoid punitive measures that could harm the child's development and instead seek solutions that encourage their reintegration into society.

3.2 Non-Discrimination

Article 2 of the UNCRC enshrines the principle of non-discrimination, requiring states to protect the rights of all children without distinction of any kind. This principle is fundamental in juvenile justice systems, where marginalized or disadvantaged children—such as those from racial or ethnic minorities, low-income families, or children with disabilities—may be disproportionately affected by punitive policies. The human rights framework emphasizes equal treatment and eliminating discriminatory practices within juvenile justice systems (United Nations, 1989).

3.3 Detention as a Last Resort

A critical component of the human rights framework is the principle that detention should be used only as a last resort and for the shortest appropriate period (UNCRC, Article 37). This principle reflects the understanding that detaining children can negatively affect their development and reintegration prospects. Alternatives to detention, such as community-based rehabilitation programs, are encouraged to promote the child's social reintegration and prevent the negative impacts of institutionalization.

3.4 Right to Fair Treatment and Due Process

The right to fair treatment and due process is fundamental in any justice system, including juvenile justice. Article 40 of the UNCRC guarantees children the right to be presumed innocent until proven guilty, to be informed of the charges against them, to have access to legal assistance, and to have their cases heard by a competent, independent, and impartial authority. This aligns with broader international human rights principles, such as those articulated in the *Universal Declaration of Human Rights* (United Nations, 1948).

3.5 Rehabilitation and Reintegration

The overarching goal of the human rights framework for juvenile justice is the rehabilitation and reintegration of young offenders. International instruments stress the importance of addressing the underlying causes of delinquent behavior, providing education opportunities, and creating environments where young people can develop into responsible members of society. Punitive measures, particularly those that lead to long-term incarceration or the deprivation of liberty, are discouraged in favor of approaches that promote social reintegration (United Nations, 1989).

4. CHALLENGES IN IMPLEMENTING THE HUMAN RIGHTS FRAMEWORK

Despite the robust protections offered by international human rights instruments, implementing juvenile justice systems that fully respect children's rights remains a significant challenge globally. Several factors contribute to the gap between legal frameworks and their practical application. Below is a discussion of these factors:

4.1 Lack of Resources

Many countries, particularly in the Global South, face significant resource constraints that limit their ability to implement child-friendly juvenile justice systems. Inadequate funding for rehabilitation programs, social services, and specialized juvenile courts means that many children are subjected to prolonged detention or adult criminal justice procedures. For example, countries like Kenya have established legal frameworks that align with the UNCRC, but infrastructure and resource allocation challenges hinder full compliance (Netswera, 2020).

4.2 Cultural and Social Norms

Cultural and social norms also play a critical role in shaping the implementation of juvenile justice systems. In some countries, customary law and traditional justice mechanisms may conflict with the principles of the human rights framework. For instance, community-based justice systems that rely on customary law may only sometimes prioritize the child's best interests or respect their right to due process. Harmonizing formal legal frameworks with traditional practices is necessary to protect children's rights (Sloth-Nielsen, 2008).

4.3 Racial and Ethnic Disparities

In some jurisdictions, racial and ethnic disparities continue to affect the treatment of children in the justice system. In the United States, for example, minority youth—particularly African American and Hispanic children—are disproportionately represented in the juvenile justice system and are more likely to face harsher penalties than their white counterparts. This reality contradicts the principle of non-discrimination and highlights the need for reforms that address systemic biases (The Sentencing Project, 2021).

The human rights framework for juvenile justice provides a comprehensive set of principles to protect children's dignity, rights, and development in conflict with the law. Grounded in international instruments such as the *Convention on the Rights of the Child* (United Nations, 1989), the *Beijing Rules* (United Nations, 1985), and the *African Charter on the Rights and Welfare of the Child* (Organization of African Unity [OAU], 1990), this framework emphasizes the importance of rehabilitation, reintegration, and detention only as a last resort. However, the gap between legal standards and implementation remains significant in many jurisdictions, requiring sustained efforts to address resource constraints, cultural norms, and systemic disparities. Through continued advocacy, reform, and investment, the global community can work toward juvenile justice systems that respect the rights and well-being of all children.

5. INTERNATIONAL HUMAN RIGHTS INSTRUMENTS ON JUVENILE JUSTICE

International human rights law establishes a robust framework for protecting juveniles within the criminal justice system. The most important instrument is the *United Nations Convention on the Rights of the Child (UNCRC)*, ratified by every country except the United States. Article 40 of the UNCRC specifically addresses juvenile justice, mandating that states ensure that "no child shall be subjected to torture or other cruel, inhuman or degrading treatment or punishment," and that "every child accused of infringing the penal law shall be treated in a manner consistent with the promotion of the child's sense of dignity and worth."

The *Beijing Rules* (United Nations, 1985) and the *Riyadh Guidelines* (United Nations, 1990) further supplement the *Convention on the Rights of the Child* (CRC), emphasizing the importance of rehabilitation over punishment. These international instruments promote principles of proportionality, individualization, and non-discrimination in juvenile justice, urging states to develop separate legal frameworks for juveniles that focus on reintegration into society rather than incarceration.

5.1 Regional Human Rights Instruments

In Africa, the *African Charter on the Rights and Welfare of the Child* (ACRWC), adopted by the Organization of African Unity, provides additional protections specific to the African context. Article 17 of the ACRWC reinforces the rights of juveniles to special treatment, focusing on their reintegration and assuming that the child's best interests should be a primary consideration.

While the U.S. has not ratified the UNCRC, it is bound by other human rights treaties that affect the treatment of juveniles, including the *International Covenant on Civil and Political Rights* (ICCPR) and the *Convention against Torture and Other Cruel, Inhuman or Degrading Treatment or Punishment.*

6. KENYA'S JUVENILE JUSTICE SYSTEM THROUGH A HUMAN RIGHTS LENS

6.1 Legal Framework

Kenya's juvenile justice system is primarily governed by the *Children's Act of 2001*, which incorporated elements of the *United Nations Convention on the Rights of the Child* (UNCRC) and the *African Charter on the Rights and Welfare of the Child* (ACRWC) into domestic law. The Act defines a child as anyone under 18, which aligns with international standards and provides specific protections for juveniles in conflict with the law. It establishes a dedicated system of children's courts and includes provisions prioritizing the child's welfare, such as the requirement that detention be used as a last resort (Republic of Kenya, 2001). The *Children's Act* underscores Kenya's obligation to prevent juvenile delinquency by addressing the root causes of youth crime, such as poverty, lack of access to education, and family breakdown. However, despite this solid legal foundation, significant challenges must be addressed in implementing a human rights-centered approach to juvenile justice in Kenya.

6.2 Judicial Interpretation and Application

Kenya's judiciary has increasingly embraced human rights principles in interpreting juvenile justice laws. In *Francis Karioko Muruatetu v Republic* (2017), the Supreme Court of Kenya found mandatory death sentences unconstitutional, a decision that has implications for juveniles. However, the death penalty is not applied to minors under Kenyan law. This case reflects the broader judicial trend of recognizing the rights of individuals within the criminal justice system and could pave the way for greater juvenile protection. Under the *Children's Act of 2001*, capital punishment is prohibited for anyone under 18 (Republic of Kenya, 2001), in alignment with Kenya's obligations under international human rights frameworks, such as the *United Nations Convention on the Rights of the Child* (United Nations, 1989) and the *African Charter on the Rights and Welfare of the Child* (Organization of African Unity, 1990).

Nevertheless, the Kenyan system struggles with the tension between traditional punitive approaches and children's rights. Customary law, still influential in many communities, often contradicts formal legal protections (Kameri-Mbote, 2002). Additionally, juvenile detention facilities remain overcrowded, and alternative methods of rehabilitation, such as diversion programs, are underdeveloped (Kenya National Commission on Human Rights, 2015).

6.3 Challenges and Gaps

Kenya faces significant challenges in aligning its juvenile justice system with human rights obligations. According to a report by *The African Child Policy Forum* (ACPF), systemic issues such as corruption, inadequate legal representation for minors, and insufficient resources for the children's courts undermine the effectiveness of the juvenile justice system. The country also struggles with the social reintegration of juvenile offenders, as many rehabilitation centers lack the infrastructure and personnel to provide adequate support (Karanja, 2018). There are also regional disparities in how juvenile justice is administered in Kenya. Rural areas often lack access to the dedicated children's courts and rehabilitation services available in urban centers, leading to inconsistent application of the law and, in some cases, the violation of children's rights (Kenya National Commission on Human Rights, 2015).

6.4 The U.S. Juvenile Justice System: A Human Rights Evaluation

6.4.1 Legal Framework

The United States has a highly decentralized juvenile justice system, with individual states setting the rules and procedures governing juvenile offenders. However, federal law, such as the *Juvenile Justice and Delinquency Prevention Act (JJDPA)*, establishes specific minimum standards, including the requirement that juveniles be kept separate from adults in detention facilities and that efforts be made to reduce disproportionate minority contact with the juvenile justice system.

One key feature of the U.S. system is the discretionary transfer of juveniles to adult court for serious offenses, a practice that human rights advocates have widely criticized (Feld, 2017). Despite some reforms aimed at curbing this practice, the transfer of minors to adult courts remains prevalent in many states (Campaign for Youth Justice, 2020).

6.4.2 Judicial Interpretation and Challenges

In recent years, the U.S. Supreme Court has issued landmark decisions that reflect a growing recognition of the human rights of juveniles. In *Roper v. Simmons* (2005), the Court held that the death penalty for minors violated the Eighth Amendment's prohibition on cruel and unusual punishment. This decision was followed by *Graham v. Florida* (2010), which abolished life without parole for juveniles convicted of non-homicide offenses, and *Miller v. Alabama* (2012), which extended this ban to all juveniles.

These rulings indicate a shift in U.S. jurisprudence towards recognizing that children are constitutionally different from adults and thus require special protections (*Roper v. Simmons*, 2005; *Graham v. Florida*, 2010). Nevertheless, these decisions have not fully rectified the systemic challenges faced by juveniles in the American legal system. For example, racial disparities remain pervasive, with Black and Latino youth disproportionately represented in the juvenile justice system (Puzzanchera & Hockenberry, 2022; Rovner, 2021).

6.4.3 Human Rights Concerns

The U.S. juvenile justice system has been widely criticized for its failure to adhere to international human rights standards. The practice of solitary confinement, which is still legal for minors in some states, has been condemned by the United Nations Committee on the Rights of the Child as a form of torture (United Nations, 2016). Moreover, the U.S. has one of the highest rates of juvenile incarceration in the world, a trend that stands in stark contrast to the human rights principle of using detention as a last resort (Sawyer, 2019; Human Rights Watch, 2020).

In addition, the criminalization of school-related behavior, often referred to as the "school-to-prison pipeline," has drawn scrutiny from human rights organizations. Policies such as zero-tolerance discipline disproportionately affect marginalized communities, contributing to a cycle of incarceration that undermines the human rights of minors (American Civil Liberties Union, 2021; Advancement Project, 2018). These policies have been particularly harmful to Black and Latino students, exacerbating racial disparities in the juvenile justice system (NAACP Legal Defense Fund, 2017).

7. COMPARATIVE ANALYSIS: KENYA AND THE UNITED STATES

The juvenile justice systems of Kenya and the United States present two distinct yet insightful case studies for understanding how different legal frameworks address the treatment of children in conflict with the law. Although both countries aim to protect juveniles and uphold their rights, how their legal systems are structured and how laws are implemented varies significantly. This section delves into the legal frameworks of Kenya and the United States, examining how each country incorporates international human rights standards and the challenges and successes associated with the implementation of these frameworks.

7.1 Legal Frameworks for Juvenile Justice in Kenya

Kenya's juvenile justice system is primarily governed by the *Children's Act of 2001*, which was established to align the country's legal system with international human rights norms, particularly the *United Nations Convention on the Rights of the Child* (UNCRC). The Act recognizes children with inherent rights and offers specific protections for those conflicting with the law. It emphasizes using alternatives to incarceration, such as probation, counseling, and community-based rehabilitation programs (Government of Kenya, 2001).

7.2 Key Principles of Kenya's Legal Framework

Kenya's *Children's Act* is grounded in several core principles that are reflective of the UNCRC's guidelines:

1. **The Best Interests of the Child**: The Act prioritizes the child's best interests in all legal decisions, aligning with Article 3 of the UNCRC. This principle underpins all judicial decisions regarding children, ensuring their welfare is the primary consideration (United Nations, 1989).
2. **Non-discrimination**: The Act mandates equal treatment of all children, regardless of their background or circumstances, and prohibits discrimination on any grounds. This principle is essential in ensuring that the justice system does not disproportionately target children from marginalized communities (United Nations, 1989).
3. **Detention as a Last Resort**: Echoing the UNCRC's emphasis on rehabilitation, the Act states that detention should only be used as a last resort and for the shortest possible duration. Alternatives such as diversion, probation, and rehabilitation are encouraged to avoid the adverse effects of institutionalization on children's development (Government of Kenya, 2001).
4. **Rehabilitation and Reintegration**: The primary goal of Kenya's juvenile justice system is to rehabilitate young offenders and reintegrate them into society. This is consistent with the human rights framework, which prioritizes social reintegration over punitive measures (African Union, 1990).

7.3 Challenges in Implementation in Kenya

Despite Kenya's progressive legal framework, the government needs to work on implementing these principles effectively. Resource constraints are a significant issue, as Kenya lacks the necessary infrastructure and trained personnel to fully support juvenile offenders' rehabilitation and reintegration (Kenya National Commission on Human Rights, 2015; UNICEF, 2020). Without sufficient resources, efforts to prioritize rehabilitation over punishment and to reintegrate juveniles into society remain limited. Many children are held in overcrowded detention facilities where they do not receive adequate education, healthcare, or psychological support. Furthermore, there is often a gap between the legal standards in the *Children's Act* and the actual law enforcement practices, particularly in rural areas where traditional justice systems may need to align with formal legal protections (Mujuzi, 2014).

Moreover, poverty and social inequality continue to drive many children into conflict with the law, complicating efforts to address juvenile delinquency through a purely legal framework. Economic hardship, lack of access to education, and family breakdowns contribute to the high rates of juvenile crime in Kenya (Mutua, 2019; Kenya National Bureau of Statistics, 2020). These socio-economic factors often exacerbate juvenile delinquency, highlighting the need for holistic approaches that address underlying causes beyond the legal system. These socio-economic factors present a formidable challenge to successfully implementing the human rights-based approach to juvenile justice envisioned in the *Children's Act* (Netswera, 2020).

7.4 Legal Frameworks for Juvenile Justice in the United States

The United States has a highly decentralized juvenile justice system, with individual states having significant autonomy in handling juvenile offenders. There is no single national juvenile justice law; each state has its own set of laws and regulations governing the treatment of children in conflict with the law. However, the federal government provides guidelines through legislation such as the *Juvenile Justice and Delinquency Prevention Act* (JJDPA) of 1974, which emphasizes the separation of juveniles from adults in detention facilities, the deinstitutionalization of status offenders, and the need for a focus on prevention (U.S. Department of Justice, 2015).

7.5 Key Principles of the U.S. Legal Framework

i. **Diversion and Rehabilitation**: Like Kenya, the United States has made strides in moving away from a purely punitive approach to juvenile justice. Many states have implemented diversion programs to prevent first-time offenders from entering the formal justice system. Rather than punishment, rehabilitation is a critical focus in many state-level juvenile justice systems (Howell, 2003).
ii. **Developmental Differences**: U.S. Supreme Court rulings, such as *Roper v. Simmons* (2005) and *Miller v. Alabama* (2012), have emphasized the developmental differences between juveniles and adults, leading to the abolition of the death penalty for juveniles and limitations on life sentences without parole for

minors. These decisions reflect a growing recognition of international human rights standards prioritizing treating children as distinct from adults in the justice system (Roper v. Simmons, 543 U.S. 551, 2005).

iii. **Racial Disparities**: Despite these advances, racial disparities remain a significant issue in the U.S. juvenile justice system. African American and Latino youth are disproportionately represented at every stage of the justice process, from arrest to sentencing. Studies show that minority youth are more likely to receive harsher penalties and are overrepresented in juvenile detention centers (The Sentencing Project, 2021).

iv. **Transfer to Adult Courts**: One of the most controversial aspects of the U.S. juvenile justice system is transferring juveniles to adult courts for serious offenses. This practice varies by state, but it often leads to minors receiving adult-level sentences, including long-term incarceration. Critics argue that this practice contradicts the rehabilitation principles and violates international human rights norms, including those articulated in the UNCRC, which the U.S. has signed but not ratified (Feld, 2017).

7.6 Challenges in Implementation in the U.S.

The United States faces significant challenges in implementing a juvenile justice system that fully aligns with international human rights standards. While the federal government provides guidelines, the decentralized nature of the system means that practices vary widely across states. Some states have embraced reform, focusing on rehabilitation and reducing reliance on detention, while others maintain more punitive approaches, particularly for serious offenses (Feld, 2017).

Racial and socio-economic disparities continue to plague the U.S. system. Minority youth are disproportionately targeted by law enforcement, and economic inequality exacerbates these disparities. Poor communities often lack access to quality legal representation and support services, leading to higher rates of juvenile incarceration. These disparities raise concerns about the fairness and effectiveness of the U.S. juvenile justice system, particularly in light of international human rights standards that emphasize non-discrimination and equal treatment (The Sentencing Project, 2021).

7.7 Comparative Analysis of Implementation in Kenya and the U.S.

Despite their differences in wealth and legal structures, Kenya and the United States face significant challenges in implementing juvenile justice systems that fully respect children's rights. In Kenya, resource limitations and socio-economic conditions hinder the realization of the legal protections enshrined in the *Children's Act*. In the United States, racial and economic disparities undermine the fairness and effectiveness of the juvenile justice system, particularly for minority youth.

Kenya's legal framework, which is more centralized and directly influenced by international human rights norms, provides a more straightforward path toward protecting children's rights. However, the lack of resources and infrastructure creates a gap between the law and its implementation. In contrast, the U.S. system is decentralized and fragmented, leading to inconsistencies in how juvenile offenders are treated across different states. While the U.S. has made progress in recognizing the developmental differences of juveniles, its continued reliance on punitive measures, especially the transfer of juveniles to adult courts, highlights ongoing challenges in aligning with international human rights standards.

Kenya and the United States offer essential lessons in the ongoing effort to create juvenile justice systems that align with human rights norms. Kenya's centralized legal framework and commitment to international treaties provide a strong foundation, but it must address resource limitations to fully implement its progressive laws. The United States, while economically more advanced, faces significant challenges related to systemic inequality and the decentralization of its justice system. Both jurisdictions must continue to work toward systems that prioritize rehabilitation, protect children's rights, and reduce the reliance on punitive measures. Through reforms that address these challenges, both Kenya and the U.S. have the potential to build juvenile justice systems that genuinely serve the best interests of children.

7.8 Legal Frameworks and Implementation

Kenya and the United States have legal frameworks incorporating some aspects of international human rights standards in juvenile justice. However, the extent of implementation varies significantly. While Kenya has integrated international human rights instruments such as the UNCRC and ACRWC into its domestic law, the U.S. operates outside of the UNCRC framework, relying instead on constitutional protections and federal statutes like the JJDPA.

Both countries face challenges in aligning their juvenile justice systems with human rights obligations. In Kenya, legal protections for juveniles are undermined by institutional shortcomings and resource constraints. At the same time, in the U.S., systemic issues like racial disparities and punitive policies often contradict the rehabilitative goals of juvenile justice.

7.9 Cultural and Societal Influences

Cultural differences also play a significant role in shaping juvenile justice in both countries. In Kenya, customary practices often conflict with formal legal standards, particularly in rural areas (Kameri-Mbote, 2002). The influence of community-based justice mechanisms, which may not always prioritize children's rights, complicates efforts to establish a uniform approach to juvenile justice (Omboto, 2013). In contrast, the U.S. system is influenced by a deeply ingrained punitive culture, particularly regarding marginalized communities. The notion of "tough on crime" policies has historically led to the over-incarceration of juveniles, particularly those from minority backgrounds (Rovner, 2021; Feld, 2017).

8. CONCLUSION

This chapter has examined the juvenile justice systems of Kenya and the United States through the human rights lens, focusing on their legal frameworks and implementation. By comparing the two countries, it becomes evident that while both have made strides in aligning their juvenile justice systems with international human rights standards, significant challenges remain. The analysis reveals critical insights into how each country's approach to juvenile justice reflects its historical, socio-economic, and political context and the global standards set forth by the *United Nations Convention on the Rights of the Child* (UNCRC) and other relevant human rights frameworks.

The chapter focused on the following vital discussions. First, the Legal Frameworks and Human Rights Standards in Kenya and the United States have both incorporated, to some extent, international human rights treaties. However, their approaches to juvenile justice are markedly different due to divergent legal traditions and societal needs. Kenya's *Children's Act of 2001* draws heavily from the UNCRC, emphasizing protecting children's rights, rehabilitation, and using detention as a last resort. In contrast, the United States follows a decentralized system where juvenile justice laws vary from state to state, leading to inconsistencies in how juveniles are treated. Although the U.S. has taken steps to address juvenile rights in line with international standards, such as prohibiting life sentences without parole for juveniles in non-homicidal cases (*Graham v. Florida*, 2010), it still retains punitive practices like transferring juveniles to adult courts.

Second, the implementation challenges. Both countries face significant challenges in implementing their respective juvenile justice laws. In Kenya, resource constraints, overburdened facilities, and a lack of adequately trained personnel hinder the implementation of the *Children's Act*. These issues often lead to a gap between the legal framework and the actual treatment of juveniles. In the United States, the persistence of racial and socio-economic disparities complicates the realization of a just and equitable juvenile justice system. Minority youth are disproportionately represented in juvenile detention, and systemic inequalities continue to undermine efforts to reform the system.

Third is the international human rights framework governing juvenile justice law globally. The chapter highlighted the importance of aligning juvenile justice systems with international human rights norms. The UNCRC, *Beijing*, and *Havana Rules* provide clear guidelines for treating juveniles in conflict with the law, emphasizing non-discrimination, rehabilitation, and reintegration into society. Kenya and the United States have incorporated some of these principles into their legal frameworks, but gaps still need to be fully implemented.

Fourth is the debate between rehabilitation and punishment as it applies to juvenile delinquency. A key theme throughout this chapter has been the need to prioritize rehabilitation over punishment. The human rights framework calls for juvenile justice systems to focus on the well-being and future potential of the child rather than imposing punitive measures that may harm their development. Kenya's legal framework explicitly embraces this approach, although practical challenges impede its full realization. The United States has also begun to shift toward rehabilitative models, but the continued use of punitive measures, particularly for minority youth, indicates that further reform is needed.

The research, therefore, recommends the following based on the analysis of Kenya and the United States, several recommendations can be made to improve the effectiveness and fairness of juvenile justice systems in line with human rights standards:

1. Strengthening implementation mechanisms is essential when responding to juvenile delinquency. In Kenya, efforts should be made to bridge the gap between the progressive legal framework and its implementation. This includes investing in resources for the juvenile justice system, such as better facilities, personnel training, and increased access to rehabilitative services like education, counseling, and vocational training. A focus on building capacity at the local level, particularly in rural areas, is essential to ensure that juvenile justice standards are upheld throughout the country.
2. There is a need to address racial and socio-economic disparities when it comes to responding to juvenile delinquency in the United States. In the United States, racial and socio-economic disparities within the juvenile justice system must be addressed. Policy reforms should focus on reducing the overrepresentation of minority youth in detention and ensuring that all juveniles, regardless of race or economic background, have access to fair legal representation and support services. This could involve increased investment in community-based diver-

sion programs, greater oversight of law enforcement practices, and reforming sentencing laws that disproportionately affect minority populations.

3. The importance of moving towards a more centralized U.S. juvenile justice framework. The decentralized nature of the U.S. juvenile justice system needs to be more consistent in how juveniles are treated across different states. A move toward more excellent centralization or establishing more robust federal guidelines could help ensure that all juveniles, regardless of their state of residence, are treated following international human rights standards. This could involve expanding the scope and enforcement of the *Juvenile Justice and Delinquency Prevention Act* to ensure nationwide adherence to rehabilitative principles and the deinstitutionalization of juvenile offenders.
4. The need to promote restorative justice practices. Kenya and the United States should explore the wider adoption of restorative justice practices, which focus on repairing harm, engaging the community, and providing opportunities for offenders to make amends. Restorative justice is effective in reducing recidivism and promoting the reintegration of juveniles into society. This could be aligned with traditional justice mechanisms focusing on reconciliation in Kenya. In the United States, restorative justice programs could be expanded as alternatives to detention and incarceration, particularly for non-violent offenses.
5. There is a need to enhance international cooperation and support. International cooperation, particularly in sharing best practices and providing financial and technical support, is crucial for developing effective juvenile justice systems in countries like Kenya. International organizations, such as the United Nations and the African Union, can play a crucial role in facilitating cross-border cooperation, training, and capacity-building initiatives. The United States, as a global leader, should also ratify the UNCRC and take a more active role in promoting juvenile justice reforms that align with international human rights standards.

The comparative analysis of Kenya and the United States offers essential insights into the challenges and opportunities for reforming juvenile justice systems. However, several areas warrant further research:

1. While both countries emphasize rehabilitation, more empirical research is needed on the long-term effectiveness of rehabilitative programs for juvenile offenders. Studies that track recidivism rates, educational attainment, and social reintegration outcomes could provide valuable data to inform future policy decisions.
2. The interplay between formal legal systems and traditional justice mechanisms in Kenya deserves closer examination. Future research could explore how traditional systems of justice can be integrated into the formal juvenile justice

framework to promote reconciliation and rehabilitation. This research could also analyze the impact of socio-cultural factors on the effectiveness of juvenile justice systems in various regions.

3. Both Kenya and the United States experience high levels of juvenile crime linked to poverty, lack of education, and family instability. Further research could examine the socio-economic drivers of juvenile crime in both countries and identify interventions that address these root causes, such as poverty alleviation programs, community development initiatives, and access to education.
4. Comparative studies of juvenile justice reforms in other countries, particularly those that have successfully reduced reliance on incarceration, could provide valuable lessons for Kenya and the United States. Exploring models from countries like Norway, which has focused on rehabilitation and drastically reduced youth incarceration rates, could offer new perspectives on how to reform juvenile justice systems in a way that aligns with human rights norms.
5. The psychological well-being of children in conflict with the law is a critical aspect of their rehabilitation. Future research should focus on the mental health impacts of juvenile detention, as well as the availability and effectiveness of psychological and counseling services in both Kenya and the United States.

Reframing juvenile justice through a human rights lens is essential for creating systems that hold juveniles accountable for their actions, protect their rights, and promote their development. While Kenya and the United States have made progress in aligning their juvenile justice systems with international standards, much work remains to be done. By addressing the implementation challenges, promoting rehabilitative and restorative practices, and reducing disparities, both countries can move toward juvenile justice systems that genuinely serve the best interests of children and society.

REFERENCES

Advancement Project. (2018). *We Came to Learn: A Call to Action for Police-Free Schools*. https://advancementproject.org/wecametolearn/

African Charter on the Rights and Welfare of the Child. O.A.U. Doc. CAB/LEG/24.9/49 (1990).

African Child Policy Forum (ACPF). (2011). *Juvenile Justice in Africa: A Guide to Good Practice*. Addis Ababa: ACPF.

American Civil Liberties Union. (2021). *School-to-Prison Pipeline*. https://www.aclu.org/issues/juvenile-justice/school-prison-pipeline

Amnesty International. (2018). *Trapped in the Justice System: Children in Conflict with the Law in the U.S.A*. Amnesty International.

Bishop, D. M. (2005). The Role of Race and Ethnicity in Juvenile Justice Processing. *The Future of Children*, *18*(2), 67–92. DOI: 10.1353/foc.0.0019

Campaign for Youth Justice. (2020). *Key Facts: Youth in the Adult Criminal Justice System*. Retrieved from https://cfyj.org/reports/key-facts-youth-in-the-adult-criminal-justice-system/

Chokothe, T. K. (2013). Restorative Justice as an Alternative Model for Juvenile Justice in Kenya. *International Journal of Humanities and Social Science*, *3*(6), 235–241.

Cipriani, D. (2009). *Children's Rights and the Minimum Age of Criminal Responsibility: A Global Perspective*. Ashgate Publishing.

Feld, B. C. (1999). *Bad Kids: Race and the Transformation of the Juvenile Court*. Oxford University Press.

Feld, B. C. (2017). *The Evolution of the Juvenile Court: Race, Politics, and the Criminalizing of Juvenile Justice*. New York University Press.

Francis Karioko Muruatetu v Republic, Supreme Court of Kenya, Petition No. 15 of 2015 (2017).

Government of Kenya. (2001). *The Children's Act, No. 8 of 2001*. National Council for Law Reporting.

Graham v. Florida, 560 U.S. 48 (2010).

Heitzeg, N. A. (2009). Education or Incarceration: Zero Tolerance Policies and the School to Prison Pipeline. *Forum on Public Policy Online*, *2009*(2), 1–21.

Howell, J. C. (2003). *Preventing and Reducing Juvenile Delinquency: A Comprehensive Framework*. SAGE Publications.

Human Rights Watch. (2005). *The Rest of Their Lives: Life Without Parole for Child Offenders in the United States*. Human Rights Watch.

Human Rights Watch. (2020). *US: Scale Back Solitary Confinement in Prisons*. https://www.hrw.org/news/2020/09/02/us-scale-back-solitary-confinement-prisons

Juvenile Justice and Delinquency Prevention Act, Public Law No. 93-415, 42 U.S.C. § 5601 et seq. (1974).

Kameri-Mbote, P. (2002). The Impact of International Law on Children's Rights in Kenya. *African Human Rights Law Journal*, *2*(2), 131–153. DOI: 10.17159/1996-2096/2002/v2n2a6

Karanja, M. (2018). Assessing the Challenges Facing the Rehabilitation and Reintegration of Juvenile Offenders in Kenya. *Journal of Human Rights and Social Work*, *3*(2), 66–74. DOI: 10.1007/s41134-018-0086-2

Kenya National Bureau of Statistics. (2020). *Economic Survey 2020*. Nairobi: Government Printer. https://www.knbs.or.ke/?page_id=3142

Kenya National Commission on Human Rights. (2015). The Status of Juvenile Justice in Kenya: A Human Rights Perspective. Nairobi: KNCHR. Available at: https://www.knchr.org/Portals/0/Reports/Status_of_Juvenile_Justice_in_Kenya_A_Human_Rights_Perspective.pdf

Mears, D. P. (2001). "Get Tough" Juvenile Justice Reforms: The Impact of Punitive Policies on Juvenile Offenders and Juvenile Justice. *Criminal Justice Policy Review*, *12*(2), 125–146. DOI: 10.1177/0887403401012002002

Miller v. Alabama, 567 U.S. 460 (2012).

Mujuzi, J. D. (2014). The African Committee of Experts on the Rights and Welfare of the Child and the Right to Education. *Journal of African Law*, *58*(1), 144–161.

Mutua, J. (2019). Socioeconomic Factors Contributing to Juvenile Delinquency in Kenya. *Journal of African Law and Criminology*, *12*(1), 45–58. DOI: 10.1093/africlaw/jac004

NAACP Legal Defense and Educational Fund. (2017). *Locked Out of the Classroom: How Implicit Bias Contributes to Disparities in School Discipline*. https://www.naacpldf.org/wp-content/uploads/Locked-Out-of-the-Classroom-Implicit-Bias-Report.pdf

Netswera, F. (2020). The implementation of children's rights in Kenya. *Journal of African Law*, *64*(2), 249–264.

Nyamu, C. I. (2010). Children and the Law in Kenya: A Comparative Overview. *African Human Rights Law Journal*, *10*(2), 382–405.

Omboto, J. O. (2013). The Challenges Facing Rehabilitation of Prisoners in Kenya and the Mitigation Strategies. *International Journal of Research in Social Sciences*, *2*(2), 39–43.

Organization of African Unity. (1990). *African Charter on the Rights and Welfare of the Child*. Retrieved from https://au.int/en/treaties/african-charter-rights-and-welfare-child

Puzzanchera, C., & Hockenberry, S. (2022). *Juvenile Court Statistics 2019*. National Center for Juvenile Justice. https://www.ojjdp.gov/ojstatbb/njcda/pdf/jcs2019.pdf

Republic of Kenya. (2001). *The Children's Act, 2001*. Government Printer.

Roper v. Simmons, 543 U.S. 551 (2005).

Rovner, J. (2021). *Racial Disparities in Youth Incarceration Persist*. The Sentencing Project. https://www.sentencingproject.org/reports/racial-disparities-in-youth-incarceration-persist/

Rwezaura, B. (1998). The Politics of Law Reform, Customary Law and Children's Rights in Kenya. *International Journal of Law, Policy and the Family*, *12*(1), 56–69.

Sawyer, W. (2019). *Youth Confinement: The Whole Pie 2019*. Prison Policy Initiative. https://www.prisonpolicy.org/reports/youth2019.html

Sentencing Project. (2017). *Disproportionate Minority Contact in the Juvenile Justice System*. Sentencing Project.

Sloth-Nielsen, J. (2008). *Children's rights in Africa: A legal perspective*. Ashgate Publishing, Ltd.

Steinberg, L. (2013). The Influence of Neuroscience on U.S. Supreme Court Decisions about Adolescents' Criminal Culpability. *Nature Reviews. Neuroscience*, *14*(7), 513–518. PMID: 23756633

Steinberg, L., & Scott, E. S. (2003). Less Guilty by Reason of Adolescence: Developmental Immaturity, Diminished Responsibility, and the Juvenile Death Penalty. *The American Psychologist, 58*(12), 1009–1018. DOI: 10.1037/0003-066X.58.12.1009 PMID: 14664689

The Judiciary of Kenya. (2001). *Children's Act of 2001*. Government of Kenya.

The Sentencing Project. (2021). *Racial Disparities in Youth Incarceration Persist*. Retrieved from https://www.sentencingproject.org

UNICEF. (2020). *Juvenile Justice Systems in Kenya: Gaps and Challenges*. https://www.unicef.org/kenya/reports/juvenile-justice-systems-kenya

United Nations. (1948). *Universal Declaration of Human Rights*. Retrieved from https://www.un.org/en/about-us/universal-declaration-of-human-rights

United Nations. (1985). *United Nations Standard Minimum Rules for the Administration of Juvenile Justice* (The Beijing Rules). https://www.un.org/ruleoflaw/files/TH007.PDF

United Nations. (1989). *Convention on the Rights of the Child*. https://www.ohchr.org/en/instruments-mechanisms/instruments/convention-rights-child

United Nations. (1990a). *United Nations Rules for the Protection of Juveniles Deprived of their Liberty* (The Havana Rules). https://www.ohchr.org/en/instruments-mechanisms/instruments/united-nations-rules-protection-juveniles-deprived-their-liberty

United Nations. (1990b). *United Nations Guidelines for the Prevention of Juvenile Delinquency* (The Riyadh Guidelines). https://www.un.org/ruleoflaw/files/UN_Riyadh%20Guidelines.pdf

United Nations Committee on the Rights of the Child. (2016). *General Comment No. 10: Children's Rights in Juvenile Justice*. https://www.refworld.org/docid/42dd174b4.html

United Nations Convention on the Rights of the Child, adopted November 20, 1989, 1577 UNTS 3.

U.S. Department of Justice. (2015). *Juvenile Justice and Delinquency Prevention Act*. Office of Juvenile Justice and Delinquency Prevention.

Compilation of References

Aazami, A., Valek, R., Ponce, A. N., & Zare, H. (2023). A Systematic Assessment of Risk and Protective Factors and Interventions to Reduce Juvenile Delinquency. *Soc. Sci.*, *12*, 474.

Abdelaal, R. A. (2017). The rights of the child in the juvenile justice system: A comparative study between Egypt and the United States of America. *International Journal of Humanities and Social Science Invention*, *6*(8), 33–37.

ACOG. (2023). Obesity And Pregnancy. *The American College Of Obstetricians And Gynecologists*. Https://Www.Acog.Org/Womens-Health/Faqs/Obesity-And-Pregnancy

Adams, M. S., Robertson, C. T., Gray-Ray, P., & Ray, M. C. (2003). Labeling and delinquency. *Adolescence*, *38*(149), 171–186.

Advancement Project. (2018). *We Came to Learn: A Call to Action for Police-Free Schools*. https://advancementproject.org/wecametolearn/

African Charter on the Rights and Welfare of the Child. O.A.U. Doc. CAB/LEG/24.9/49 (1990).

African Child Policy Forum (ACPF). (2011). *Juvenile Justice in Africa: A Guide to Good Practice*. Addis Ababa: ACPF.

African Union. (1990). *African Charter on the Rights and Welfare of the Child (ACRWC)*. African Union. Retrieved from https://au.int/en/treaties/african-charter-rights-and-welfare-child

Ageton, S. S., & Elliott, D. S. (1974). The Effects of Legal Processing on Delinquent Orientations. *Social Problems*, *22*(1), 87–100.

Akande, L. (2007). Nigerians in the Diaspora list Tasks for Bankole. *Guardian Newspaper*, *7*(December), 3.

Akers, J. F., Jones, R. M., & Coyl, D. D. (1998). Adolescent friendship pairs: Similarities in identity status development, behaviors, attitudes, and intentions. *Journal of Adolescent Research*, *13*(2), 178–201.

Akers, R., & Sellers, C. (2009). *Criminological theories: Introduction, evaluation, and application* (5th ed.). Oxford University Press.

Al-Attar, M. (2021). *Child law in Egypt*. Oxford Research Encyclopedia of Criminology and Criminal Justice.

Alawiye-Adams, A. A., & Babatunde, A. (2013). Street Children Phenomenon in Nigeria: The Challenges and Way Forward *SSRN*: https://ssrn.com/abstract=2325114 or http://dx.doi.org/DOI: 10.2139/ssrn.2325114

Allard, T., Chrzanowski, A., & Stewart, A. (2015). The Effectiveness of Juvenile Diversion Programs in Australia. *Australian and New Zealand Journal of Criminology*, *48*(4), 543–559.

American Civil Liberties Union. (2021). *School-to-Prison Pipeline*. https://www.aclu.org/issues/juvenile-justice/school-prison-pipeline

American Psychological Association. (2016). Juvenile Justice: APA Advocacy Fact Sheet. https://www.apa.org/about/offices/ogc/amicus/juvenile-justice-facts

Amer, M. M., & Hassanein, E. A. (2018). Street children in Egypt: Demographic and socioeconomic profile. *Child Abuse & Neglect*, *76*, 159–167.

Ammar, N. H. (2009). The relationship between street children and the justice system in Egypt. *International Journal of Offender Therapy and Comparative Criminology*, *53*(5), 556–573. PMID: 18664552

Amnesty International. (2016). *Nigeria: Trapped in the Cycle of Violence: Nigeria's Justice System and the Detention of Children*. Amnesty International. Retrieved from https://www.amnesty.org/en/documents/afr44/4961/2016/en/

Amnesty International. (2018). *Trapped in the Justice System: Children in Conflict with the Law in the U.S.A.* Amnesty International.

Amnesty International. (2019). Egypt: Education under threat as authorities crackdown on academic freedom. Retrieved from https://www.amnesty.org/en/latest/news/2019/06/egypt-education-under-threat-as-authorities-crackdown-on-academic-freedom/

Amnesty International. (2021). Death Sentences and Executions 2020. https://www.amnesty.org/download/Documents/ACT5097452021ENGLISH.PDF

Ankomah, A. K., & Omoregie, P. (2019). Street children in Ghana: A neglected problem that requires urgent attention. *Journal of Social Science Studies*, *6*(1), 54–70. DOI: 10.5296/jsss.v6i1.14384

Annie E. Casey Foundation. (2013). *Juvenile Detention Alternatives Initiative: Lessons from the States*. Annie E. Casey Foundation. Retrieved from https://www.aecf.org/resources/juvenile-detention-alternatives-initiative/

Antwi Bosiakoh, T., & Obeng, B. A. (2021). Socio and ethno-cultural embeddedness of transnational Nigerian immigrant entrepreneurs in Ghana. *CMS*, *9*, 55. DOI: 10.1186/s40878-021-00271-z

Aparicio, E., Canals, J., Arija, V., De Henauw, S., & Michels, N. (2016). The Role Of Emotion Regulation In Childhood Obesity: Implications For Prevention And Treatment. *Nutrition Research Reviews*, *29*(1), 17–29. PMID: 27045966

Apel, R., & Sweeten, G. (2010). The Impact of Incarceration on Employment during the Transition to Adulthood. *Social Problems*, *57*(3), 448–479.

Aptekar, L. (1994). Street Children in the Developing World: A Review of Their Condition. *Cross-Cultural Research*, *28*(3), 195–224. DOI: 10.1177/106939719402800301

Aransiola, J. O. (2013). Providing Sustainable Supports for Street Children in Nigeria: Stakeholders Challenges and the Policy Options Available. *Advances in Applied Sociology*, *03*, 172–177. DOI: 10.4236/AASOCI.2013.33023

Aspers, P., & Corte, U. (2019). What is qualitative in qualitative research. *Qualitative Sociology*, *42*, 139–160.

Atilola, O., Abiri, G., & Ola, B. (2020). Psychiatric morbidity among adolescents and youth involved with the juvenile justice system in sub-Saharan Africa: Systematic scoping review of current studies and research gaps. *International Journal of Law and Psychiatry*, *73*, 101633.

Austin, A. E. (2009). Cognitive apprenticeship theory and its implications for doctoral education: A case example from a doctoral program in higher and adult education. *The International Journal for Academic Development*, *14*(3), 173–183.

Awati, R., & Fitzgibbons, L. (2024). *What is social learning theory?* WhatIs. https://www.techtarget.com/whatis/definition/social-learning-theory

Ayenew, M., Kabeta, T., & Woldemichael, K. (2020). Prevalence and factors associated with substance use among street children in Jimma town, Oromiya national regional state, Ethiopia: A community based cross-sectional study. *Substance Abuse Treatment, Prevention, and Policy*, *15*, 61. DOI: 10.1186/s13011-020-00304-3

Bader, L., & Wabwire, A. (2018). *Interview: How Security Forces in Somalia Fail to Protect Children*. Human Rights Watch. Retrieved May 15 2021, from https://www.hrw.org/news/2018/02/21/interview-how-security-forces-somalia-fail-protect-children

Bagley, B. M., & Rosen, J. D. (2017). *Drug trafficking, organized crime, and violence in the Americas today*. University Press of Florida.

Bailey, C., & Coore-Desai, C. (2009). Offender abuse history: Findings from Her Majesty's Prison, Barbados. Caribbean Journal of Criminology and Public Safety, 14(1–2), 49–80. https://sta.uwi.edu/conferences/09/salises/documents/C%20Bailey.pdf

Bakta, S. (2016). *A critical examination of the child justice system in mainland Tanzania*. South Africa: Doctorate thesis, University of Cape Town.

Barbados Government Information Services. (2015). *Reforming juvenile laws in Barbados*. Retrieved May 25, 2023 Reforming Juvenile Laws In Barbados | GIS (gisbarbados.gov.bb)

Barbados Today (2019). *Cabinet approves new Juvenile Justice Bill* Retrieved May 25, 2023 Cabinet approves new Juvenile Justice Bill - Barbados Today

Barretto, C., Miers, S., & Lambie, L. (2018). The views of the public on youth offenders and the New Zealand criminal justice system. *International Journal of Offender Therapy and Comparative Criminology*, *62*(1), 129–149.

Bazemore, G., & Umbreit, M. (1995). Balanced and Restorative Justice for Juveniles: A Framework for Juvenile Justice in the 21st Century. *Juvenile & Family Court Journal*, *46*(1), 1–26.

BBC. (2019). Nigeria profile - Timeline. BBC News. https://www.bbc.com/news/world-africa-13949550

Beauchemin, E. (1999). *The Exodus: The growing migration of children from Ghana's rural areas to the urban centers*. CAS & UNICEF.

Becker, H. S. (1963). *Outsiders: Studies in the sociology of deviance*. Free Press Glencoe.

Becker, H. S. (1963). *Outsiders: Studies in the Sociology of Deviance*. Free Press.

Bedoya, M., & Martinez, J. (1991). *From football supporter to gang member*. El Propio Bolsillo.

Bennett, R. R., & Lynch, J. P. (1996). Towards a Caribbean criminology: Prospects and problems. *Caribbean Journal of Criminology and Social Psychology*, *1*(1), 8–37.

BENREY. L. (2016). *History of Child Soldier Policies - End Slavery Now*. Endslaverynow.org. Retrieved May 14 2021, from https://www.endslaverynow.org/blog/articles/history-of-child-soldier-policies

Bergman, M., Seepersad, R., Safranoff, A., & Cafferata, F. (2020). *Regional comparative report: Survey of individuals deprived of liberty: Caribbean 2016-2019*. Inter American Development Bank., DOI: 10.18235/0002651

Bernburg, J. G., & Krohn, M. D. (2003). Labeling, Life Chances, and Adult Crime: The Direct and Indirect Effects of Official Intervention in Adolescence on Crime in Early Adulthood. *Criminology*, *41*(4), 1287–1318.

Birkbeck, C. (1999). By your theories you shall be known: Some reflections on Caribbean criminology. *Caribbean Journal of Criminology and Social Psychology*, *4*(1), 1–31.

Bishop, D. M. (2005). The Role of Race and Ethnicity in Juvenile Justice Processing. *The Future of Children*, *18*(2), 67–92. DOI: 10.1353/foc.0.0019

Blum, R. W. (2007). Youth in Sub-Saharan Africa. *The Journal of Adolescent Health*, *41*(3), 230–238. DOI: 10.1016/j.jadohealth.2007.04

Boakye-Boaten, A. (2006). An examination of the phenomenon of street children in selected communities in Accra (Ghana) [Doctoral dissertation, Ohio University*]*. *OhioLINK Electronic Theses and Dissertations Center*. https://rave.ohiolink.edu/etdc/view?acc_num=ohiou1162599630

Boakye-Boaten, A. (2008). Street children: Experiences from the streets of Accra. *Academia.edu*. https://www.academia.edu/65589458/Street_Children_Experiences_from_the_Streets_of_Accra

Boateng, A., & Dako-Gyeke, M. (2022). Child Labor in Ghana: Current Policy, Research, and Practice Efforts. In Ssewamala, F. M., Sensoy Bahar, O., & McKay, M. M. (Eds.), *Child Behavioral Health in Sub-Saharan Africa*. Springer., DOI: 10.1007/978-3-030-83707-5_13

Branch, N. T. (2012). *Reconsidering Labeling Theory: A Case Study of Juvenile Delinquency in Barbados*. Howard University.

Brewer, D. J., & Teeter, E. (2017). *Egypt and the Egyptians*. Cambridge University Press.

Briefing to the Security Council on the humanitarian situation in Somalia. Reliefweb.int. (2019). Retrieved May 15 2021, from https://reliefweb.int/sites/reliefweb.int/files/resources/ASG%20Statement%20to%20SC%20on%20Somalia%20-%20as%20delivered%20-%2022%20May%202019.pdf

Briggs, A., Mayhew, H., & Bradley, J. L. (1966). Review of Selections from "London Labour and the London Poor,". *Scientific American*, *215*(1), 123–126. https://www.jstor.org/stable/24930998

Buckner, J. C., & Bassuk, E. L. (2016). Mental disorders, substance abuse, and their comorbidity among homeless youth. In *Handbook of Homelessness in the United States* (pp. 263–277). Springer.

Bynum, J. E., & Thompson, W. E. (1996). *Juvenile delinquency: A sociological approach* (3rd ed.). Allyn & Bacon.

Cameron, E. (2020). The crisis of criminal justice in South Africa. *South African Law Journal*, *137*(1), 32–71.

Campaign for Youth Justice. (2020). *Key Facts: Youth in the Adult Criminal Justice System*. Retrieved from https://cfyj.org/reports/key-facts-youth-in-the-adult-criminal-justice-system/

Case, S., & Haines, K. (2021). Abolishing youth justice systems: Children first, offenders nowhere. *Youth Justice*, *21*(1), 3–17.

Casey, S. (2019). *Diversion of Children in Conflict with the Law: International Models and Best Practices*. UNICEF ESARO.

Cassidy, C. (1991). The Good Body: When Big Is Better. *Medical Anthropology*, *13*(3), 181–213. PMID: 1961102

Cavadino, M., & Dignan, J. (2007). *The Penal System: An Introduction* (4th ed.). Sage Publications.

CDC. (2023). Health Effects Of Overwright And Obseity. *Centers For Disease Control And Prevention* Https://Www.Cdc.Gov/Healthyweight/Effects/Index.Html

Chang, C. (2015). *Inside Egypt's El-Marg juvenile detention centre*. Middle East Eye. https://middleeasteye.net/news/inside-egypts-el-marg-juvenile-detention-centre

Chanila, D. S., Mohamed, F., & Pittman, S. (2024). Re implementation of the diversion program in juvenile justice administration in Dar es salaam, Tanzania: Benefits and challenges. *Institute of Social Work Journal*, *3*(1), 1–32.

Chesney-Lind, M., & Okamoto, S. K. (2001). Gender Matters: Patterns in Girls' Delinquency and Gender Responsive Programming. *Journal of Forensic Psychology Practice, 1*(3), 1–28.

Chesney-Lind, M., & Sheldon, R. G. (1998). *Girls, Delinquency and Juvenile Justice.* Wadsworth Publishing Co.

Child Protection. UNSOM. Retrieved May 15 2021, from https://unsom.unmissions.org/child-protection

Children Act, 2022

Chitsamatanga, B. B., & Rembe, N. (2019). Exploring the Challenges of Juvenile Diversion Programmes in Africa: A Case Study of Zimbabwe. *African Journal of Criminology and Justice Studies, 12*(1), 71–85.

Choi, J. J., Green, D. L., & Gilbert, M. J. (2011). Victim-Offender Mediation: A Meta-Analysis of Program Effectiveness. *Justice Quarterly, 28*(4), 745–772.

Chokothe, T. K. (2013). Restorative Justice as an Alternative Model for Juvenile Justice in Kenya. *International Journal of Humanities and Social Science, 3*(6), 235–241.

Cipriani, D. (2009). *Children's Rights and the Minimum Age of Criminal Responsibility: A Global Perspective.* Ashgate Publishing.

Clifford, W. (2024). Zambia. In *African Penal Systems* (pp. 237–258). Routledge.

Collins, C. S., & Stockton, C. M. (2018). The Central Role of Theory in Qualitative Research. *International Journal of Qualitative Methods, 17*(1). Advance online publication. DOI: 10.1177/1609406918797475

Constituteionnet (2016). *The Federal Republic of Somalia: Provisional Constitution, adopted August 1, 2012 as of Sep 19, 2012.* https://constitutionnet.org/vl/item/federal-republic-somalia-provisional-constitution-adopted-august-1-2012-sep-19-2012

Coppin, J. (2022). *Examine root causes of violence among youth.* The Nation News. Retrieved May 27, 2023 https://www.nationnews.com/2022/09/26/examine-root-causes-violence-among-youth/

Corrado, D., Wichter, T., Link, M. S., Hauer, R., Marchlinski, F., Anastasakis, A., & Calkins, H. (2015). Treatment of arrhythmogenic right ventricular cardiomyopathy/dysplasia: An international task force consensus statement. *European Heart Journal, 36*(46), 3227–3237.

Council of Europe. (2010). Council of Europe guidelines on child-friendly justice. https://www.coe.int/en/web/children/council-of-europe-guidelines-on-child-friendly-justice

Council on Foreign Relations. (2021). Boko Haram in Nigeria. Council on Foreign Relations. https://www.cfr.org/backgrounder/boko-haram-nigeria

Countries and their cultures (2009). *History, people, women, beliefs, food, customs, family, social, dress.* Everyculture.com. https://www.everyculture.com/Sa-Th/Somalia.html

Creswell, J. W., & Báez, J. C. (2020). *30 essential skills for the qualitative researcher*. Sage Publications.

Crime, U. N. O. O. D. A., & Unicef. (2007). *Manual for the Measurement of Juvenile Justice Indicators*. United Nations Publications.

Criminal Procedure Code (Cap. 75)

Cunneen, C., Goldson, B., & Russell, S. (2018). Human rights and youth justice reform in England and Wales: A systemic analysis. *Criminology & Criminal Justice, 18*(4), 405–430.

Dadwal, L. (2018). Juvenility: From criminality to responsibility. *International Journal of Reviews and Research in Social Sciences, 6*(4), 381–395. DOI: 10.5958/2454-2687.2018.00031.x

Dag, H. Y. A.; Altikrdesler, Ö. K. & Törün, S. H. (2021). A Child Abuse: Marriage At Childhood Age. *Turkish Archives Of Pediatrics*(6). Https://Doi.Org/Doi: DOI: 10.5152/Turkarchpediatr.2021.21093

Dahlberg, L. L., & Potter, L. B. (2001). Youth violence: Developmental pathways and prevention challenges. *American Journal of Preventive Medicine, 20*(1), 3–14.

Dankyi E, Huang KY. (2021). Street Children in Ghana's Golden Triangle Cities: Mental Health Needs and Associated Risks. *Child Psychiatry Hum Dev*. 53(4):840-851. DOI: . Epub. PMID: 34350504.DOI: 10.1007/s10578-021-01223-5

Davidson, J., Martino, A., & Woodward, C. (2019). Child rights in the context of civil justice: Access to justice, procedural fairness and protection of the child's best interests (Study commissioned by the European Union Agency for Fundamental Rights). https://fra.europa.eu/en/publication/2019/child-rights-context-civil-justice-access-justice-procedural-fairness-and

Davis, E. (2015). Yale University. Egypt | Representing Children Worldwide. Retrieved April 17, 2023, from https://rcw.law.yale.edu/jurisdiction-research/egypt

Dean, J. (2018). *The use of diversion in juvenile justice settings in Australia with particular focus on the state of Victoria.* Retrieved August 2024, from Institute for Criminal Justice Reform: http://icjr. or. id/wp-content/uploads/2018/05/The-Use-of-Diversion-in-Juvenile-Justice-Diala, A. C., & Kangwa, B. (2019). Rethinking the interface between customary law and constitutionalism in sub-Saharan Africa. *De Jure Law Journal*, 52(1), 189-206.

Deosaran, R. (2010). *Caribbean Encyclopedia of Crime and Punishment.* Sage Publication.

Dewees, A., & Klees, S. J. (1995). Social Movements and the Transformation of National Policy: Street and Working Children in Brazil. *Comparative Education Review*, *39*(1), 18.

Dillman, D. A. (2007). *Mail and internet surveys: The Tailored Design Method 2007 update with new internet, visual, and mixed-mode guide*. John Wiley & Sons, Inc.

Dosumu, M., Olumide, A. O., & Omotade, O. O. (2016). Predictors of psychoactive substance use among street children in Ibadan Municipality, Nigeria. *International Journal of Child and Adolescent Health, Suppl.Special Issue: Developmental Issues in Children and Adolescents: Promotion of Positive Youth Development*, 9(2), 195-202. https://login.pvamu.idm.oclc.org/login?url=https://www.proquest.com/scholarly -journals/predictors-psychoactive-substance-use-among/docview/2410492384/se-2

Egyptian Child Law No. 12 of 1996, available at http://www.ilo.org/dyn/natlex/docs/ELECTRONIC/46681/80017/F-1605235635/EGY46681%20Eng.pdf

Egyptian Initiative for Personal Rights. (2021). Egypt's Juvenile Justice System: An Overview of Key Issues. https://eipr.org/sites/default/files/reports/pdf/EIPR%20 Juvenile%20Justice%20Report%202021%20English.pdf

Eldefrawi, M. H. (2018). Juvenile Delinquency in Egypt: An Overview. In Handbook of Juvenile Delinquency and Juvenile Justice (pp. 305-322). Springer.

Elliot, D. S., & Menard, S. (1996). Delinquent friends and delinquent behaviour: temporal and developmental patterns. In Hawkins, J. D. (Ed.), *Delinquency and crime: current theories* (pp. 28–67). Cambridge University Press.

El-Masry, N., & Hegazy, I. (2018). Juvenile delinquency in Egypt: A social and legal perspective. *Child Abuse & Neglect*, *76*, 324–333.

Elzalabany, M. M. (2020). Psychological and social problems of street children in Egypt. *Journal of Child and Adolescent Behavior*, *8*(1), 1–5.

Emotional Abuse. (2022). Psychology Today. Https://Www.Psychologytoday.Com/Us/Basics/Emotional-Abuse

Espinosa, E., & Sorensen, J. (2015). The influence of gender and traumatic experiences on length of time served in juvenile justice settings. *Criminal Justice and Behavior*.

Esposito, A. (2021). Force-Feeding And Drug Abuse: The Steep Price Of Beauty In Mauritania. *Harvard International Review*. Https://Doi.Org/Https://Hir.Harvard.Edu/Force-Feeding-And-Drug-Abuse-The-Steep-Price-Of-Beauty-In-Mauritania/

Fagan, J., & Tyler, T. R. (2005). Legal socialization of children and adolescents. *Social Justice Research*, *18*(3), 217–242.

Failing law leaves children unprotected in Somaliland. The New Humanitarian. (2011). Retrieved May 15 2021, from https://www.thenewhumanitarian.org/report/94054/somalia-failing-law-leaves-children-unprotected-somaliland

Farrington, D. P. (1998). Predictors, Causes, and Correlates of Male Youth Violence. In Tonry, M., & Moore, M. H. (Eds.), *Youth Violence* (pp. 421–475). University of Chicago Press.

Farrington, D. P., Ohlin, L. E., & Wilson, J. Q. (1986). *Understanding and Controlling Crime*. Springer-Verlag.

Federal collaboration. Federal Collaboration | Youth.gov. (n.d.). https://youth.gov/feature-article/federal-collaboration

Feld, B. C. (1993). *Justice for Children: The Right to Counsel and the Juvenile Courts*. Harvard University Press.

Feld, B. C. (1999). *Bad Kids: Race and the Transformation of the Juvenile Court*. Oxford University Press.

Feld, B. C. (2017). *The Evolution of the Juvenile Court: Race, Politics, and the Criminalizing of Juvenile Justice*. New York University Press.

Feld, B. C. (2019). *The evolution of the juvenile court: Race, politics, and the criminalizing of juvenile justice* (Vol. 4). NYU Press.

Ferguson, K. M., Dortzbach, K., Dyrness, G. R., Dabir, N., & Spruijt-Metz, D. (2008). Faith-based programs and outcomes for street-living youth in Los Angeles, Mumbai, and Nairobi. *International Social Work*, *51*(2), 159–177. DOI: 10.1177/0020872807085856

Francis Karioko Muruatetu v Republic, Supreme Court of Kenya, Petition No. 15 of 2015 (2017).

Freemon, K., Nuño, L., & Katz, C. (2020). The status of youth incarceration in the Caribbean. *Caribbean Journal of Criminology*, *2*(1), 48–74.

Gallinetti, J. (2009). *Getting to Know the Child Justice Act*. Child Justice Alliance. Retrieved from https://www.childjustice.org.za/

Gallinetti, J. (2009). *The Impact of the Child Justice Act on Juvenile Offenders in South Africa*. University of Cape Town.

Garg, R. (2021). *Juvenile delinquency : a social problem* - iPleaders. https://blog.ipleaders.in/juvenile-delinquency-social-problem

Gentle-Genitty, C., Kim, J., Yi, E.-H., Slater, D., Reynolds, B., & Bragg, N. (2017). Comprehensive assessment of youth violence in five Caribbean countries: Gender and age differences. *Journal of Human Behavior in the Social Environment*. Advance online publication. DOI: 10.1080/10911359.2016.1273811

Gibbons, D. C., & Blake, G. F. (1976). Evaluatin the Impact of Juvenile Diversion Programs. *Crime and Delinquency*, *22*(4), 411–420.

Gilliss, S. (2023). *Children's Rights Awareness, Rights-Informed Practices and Child-Friendly Justice in a Secure Custody Facility in Canada* (Doctoral dissertation, Université d'Ottawa/University of Ottawa).

Goldson, B. (2015). Child criminalisation and the mistake of early intervention. *Criminal Justice Matters*, *102*(1), 27–28.

Gonnerman, J. (2015). Kalief Browder, 1993–2015. *The New Yorker, 7*.

Government of Kenya. (2001). *The Children's Act, No. 8 of 2001*. National Council for Law Reporting.

Goyal, A. (2022). Juvenile Justice system in india. *ResearchGate*. https://www.researchgate.net/publication/360540963_Juvenile_Justice_system_in_india

Graham v. Florida, 560 U.S. 48 (2010).

Griffin, P. (2003). *Trying and sentencing juveniles as adults: An analysis of state transfer and blended sentencing laws. Pitts-burgh*. National Center for Juvenile Justice.

Grilo, C. M., Masheb, R. M., Brody, M., Toth, C., Burke-Matindale, C. H., & Rothschild, B. S. (2005). Childhood Maltreatment In Extremely Obese Male And Female Bariatric Surgery Candidates. *Obesity Research*, *13*(1), 123–130. PMID: 15761171

Grusec, J. E. (1992). Social learning theory and developmental psychology: The legacies of Robert Sears and Albert Bandura. *Developmental Psychology*, *28*(5), 776–786.

Gustafson, T. B., Gibbons, L. M., & Sarwer, D. B. (2006). History Of Sexual Abuse Among Bariatric Surgery Candidates. *Surgery for Obesity and Related Diseases, 2*(3), 369–374. PMID: 16925354

Haines, K., & Case, S. (2015). *Positive Youth Justice: Children First, Offenders Second*. Policy Press.

Hansen, W. W., Jima, K., Abbas, N., & Abia, B. (2016). Poverty and Economic Deprivation Theory: Street Children, Quranic Schools/Almajirai and the Dispossessed as a Source of Recruitment for Boko Haram and other Religious, Political and Criminal Groups in Northern Nigeria. *Perspectives on Terrorism, 10*(5), 83–95. https://www.jstor.org/stable/26297656

Harper, M. (2021). *Somali leaders back new constitution*. BBC News. Retrieved May 15 2021, from https://www.bbc.com/news/world-africa-19075685

Hart, D. (2014). *Pre-court arrangements for children who offend*. National Association for Youth Justice.

Hasan, L. (2008). Mauritania Tries To Reverse Obesity Tradition: Women In This West African Country Are Still Force-Fed To Stay Fat. *ABC News*. Https://Abcnews.Go.Com/GMA/Story?Id=4322187&Page=1

Haworth, A. (2021). Forced To Be Fat. Https://Doi.Org/Http://Www .Marieclaire.Com/World-Reports/News/Forcefeeding- In-Mauritania.

Heitzeg, N. A. (2009). Education or Incarceration: Zero Tolerance Policies and the School to Prison Pipeline. *Forum on Public Policy Online, 2009*(2), 1–21.

Henggeler, S. W., Schoenwald, S. K., & Borduin, C. M. (2009). *Multisystemic therapy for antisocial behavior in children and adolescents, 2nd ed.* https://psycnet.apa.org/record/2009-06165-000

Henry, B. (1996). 'Temperamental and Familial predictors of violent and nonviolent criminal convictions: Age 3 to age 18'. *Developmental Psychology, 32*, 614–623.

Herz, D. C. (2017). Juvenile Mental Health Diversion: A Collaborative Court Approach. *Children and Youth Services Review, 83*, 91–100.

Herz, D. C., & Ryan, J. P. (2010). Exploring the Effectiveness of Juvenile Mental Health Courts. *Youth Violence and Juvenile Justice, 8*(2), 136–152.

Hill, S. M. & Morris, P. K. (2017). Drug Trafficking and Gang Violence in the Caribbean. *Crime, Violence and Public Safety in the Caribbean*, 52-75. https://doi.org/DOI: 10.4324/9781315525778-3

Hine, J. (2007). Youth-A Waste of space? *CCJ Newsletter*, (17), 4.

Hine, J. (2020). The Role of Peer Courts in the UK Juvenile Justice System. *Journal of Youth Studies, 13*(5), 587–604.

Hipwell, A., Loeber, R., Stouthamer-Loeber, M., Keenan, K., White, H. R., & Kroneman, L. (2002). Characteristics of girls with early onset disruptive and antisocial behaviour. *Criminal Behaviour and Mental Health, 12*, 99–118.

Holman, B., & Ziedenberg, J. (2006). *The Dangers of Detention: The Impact of Incarcerating Youth in Detention and Other Secure Facilities.* Justice Policy Institute.

Hornung, E., Krauss, R., & Warburton, D. A. (2006). Ancient Egyptian Chronology. Brill. https://eg.usembassy.gov/egypt-2021-human-rights-report/ https://www.amnesty.org/en/latest/press-release/2019/06/egypt-must-not-sentence-to-death-a-young-man-forcibly-disappeared-and-tortured-at-17/

Howell, J. (2009). *Preventing and reducing Juvenile Delinquency: A Comprehensive framework.* https://doi.org/DOI: 10.4135/9781452274980

Howell, J. C. (2003). *Preventing and Reducing Juvenile Delinquency: A Comprehensive Framework.* SAGE Publications.

Howell, J. C., Lipsey, M. W., & Wilson, D. B. (2013). A Handbook of Evidence-Based Juvenile Diversion Programs. *Crime and Delinquency, 62*(5), 823–841.

Human Rights Watch. (2005). *The Rest of Their Lives: Life Without Parole for Child Offenders in the United States.* Human Rights Watch.

Human Rights Watch. (2018). Egypt: Death Penalty for Children Approved. https://www.hrw.org/news/2018/02/15/egypt-death-penalty-children-approved

Human Rights Watch. (2018). *Somalia: Detained Children Face Abuse.* Retrieved May 15 2021, from https://www.hrw.org/news/2018/02/21/somalia-detained-children-face-abuse

Human Rights Watch. (2020). Egypt: Children Among Thousands Disappeared and Tortured. Retrieved from https://www.hrw.org/news/2020/02/12/egypt-children-among-thousands-disappeared-and-tortured

Human Rights Watch. (2020). *US: Scale Back Solitary Confinement in Prisons.* https://www.hrw.org/news/2020/09/02/us-scale-back-solitary-confinement-prisons

Human Rights Watch. (2020, January 7). World Report 2020: Rights Trends in Somalia. Human Rights Watch. https://www.hrw.org/world-report/2020/country-chapters/somalia

Human Rights Watch. (2021). World Report 2021: Egypt. https://www.hrw.org/world-report/2021/country-chapters/egypt

ILO supports Nigeria's response to Child Labor Emergency. (2021). *Supports Nigeria's Response to Child Labour Emergency.* https://www.ilo.org/africa/about-us/offices/abuja/WCMS_803364/lang--en/index.htm

India's juvenile Justice dilemma: balancing punishment and potential. (2024). *Bharat Law AI.* https://www.bharatlaw.ai/post/balancing-justice-and-rehabilitation-transforming-juvenile-offenders-in-india-for-a-safer-society

It's Like We're Always in a Prison. Hrw.org. (2018). Retrieved May 16 2021, from https://www.hrw.org/sites/default/files/report_pdf/somalia0218_web.pdf

Jensen, G. F. (2015). Delinquency, Sociology of. In *Elsevier eBooks* (pp. 68–74). https://doi.org/DOI: 10.1016/b978-0-08-097086-8.45021-x

Johnson, J. H. (2011). *Life in Ancient Egypt.* ABC-CLIO.

Johnson, J. L., Adkins, D., & Chauvin, S. (2020). A review of the quality indicators of rigor in qualitative research. *American Journal of Pharmaceutical Education, 84*(1), 7120.

Juvenile Courts and Reformatories. (2025*). Juvenile Courts and Reformatories Law no. 13 of 8 March 1970.* Uniroma3.It. http://hdl.handle.net/2307/26144

Juvenile Justice - Somalia. Sites.google.com. Retrieved May 15 2021, from https://sites.google.com/site/justiceinsomalia/juvenile-justice

Juvenile Justice and Delinquency Prevention Act, Public Law No. 93-415, 42 U.S.C. § 5601 et seq. (1974).

Juvenile Justice Law. Africanchildforum.org. (2007). Retrieved May 16 2021, from http://www.africanchildforum.org/clr/Legislation%20Per%20Country/somalia/somalia_juvenilejustice_2007_en.pdf

Kadilu, M. (2017). *Protecting the rights of detained juvenile delinquents: Tanzania's compliance with international standards.* India: Phd Thesis, Acharya Nagarjuna University.

Kameri-Mbote, P. (2002). The Impact of International Law on Children's Rights in Kenya. *African Human Rights Law Journal, 2*(2), 131–153. DOI: 10.17159/1996-2096/2002/v2n2a6

Karanja, M. (2018). Assessing the Challenges Facing the Rehabilitation and Reintegration of Juvenile Offenders in Kenya. *Journal of Human Rights and Social Work*, *3*(2), 66–74. DOI: 10.1007/s41134-018-0086-2

Kaur, A. (2023). *Juvenile delinquency in India*. iPleaders. https://blog.ipleaders.in/juvenile-delinquency-related-legislations-india/

Kelly, B. T., Loeber, R., Keenan, K., & DeLamatre, M. (1997). "Developmental Pathways in Boys' Disruptive and Delinquent Behavior". *Juvenile Justice Bulletin*. Retrieved December 11, 2010 (https://www.ncjrs.gov/pdffiles/165692.pdf)

Kenya Law. (2022). *National Authority for the Campaign Against Alcohol and Drug Abuse Act*. Kenyalaw.org. https://new.kenyalaw.org/akn/ke/act/2012/14/eng@2022-12-31

Kenya National Bureau of Statistics. (2020). *Economic Survey 2020*. Nairobi: Government Printer. https://www.knbs.or.ke/?page_id=3142

Kenya National Bureau of Statistics. (2021). *Economic Survey Report*. Government Printers.

Kenya National Commission on Human Rights. (2015). The Status of Juvenile Justice in Kenya: A Human Rights Perspective. Nairobi: KNCHR. Available at: https://www.knchr.org/Portals/0/Reports/Status_of_Juvenile_Justice_in_Kenya_A_Human_Rights_Perspective.pdf

KHRC KBS. (2018). The Economic Survey. KNBS Sitienei. Life Experiences of children living on the streets in Kenya. Journal of Child and Adolescent trauma]. *E (Norwalk, Conn.)*, •••, 92020.

Kierkus, C. A., & Baer, D. (2003). Does the Relationship Between Family Structure and Delinquency Vary According to Circumstance? An Investigation of Interaction Effects. *Canadian Journal of Criminology and Criminal Justice*, *45*(4), 405–429.

Kilkelly, U. (2008). Youth justice and children's rights: Measuring compliance with international standards. *Youth Justice*, *8*(3), 187–192.

Kiniti, J. W. (2013). *The Criminal Justice Process: the Enforcement of Rights of the Children in Kenya* (Doctoral dissertation, University of Nairobi).

Knox, M. (2021). FAT SHAME: 'I Was Force-Fed Five Times A Day To Fatten Me Up For Marriage Aged 12 – If I Refused Or Threw Up I'd Be Beaten'. *The Sun*. Https://Www.Thesun.Co.Uk/News/13727356/Force-Fed-5-Times-Day-Beaten

Kruttschnitt, C. (2016). The politics and place of gender in research on crime. *Criminology*, *42*(2), 307–336.

Kury, H., Obergfell-Fuchs, J., & Ferdinand, T. (2002). The Background of Illegal Drug Abuse: a German View. In Brochu, S., Da Agra, C., & Cousineau, M. (Eds.), *Drugs and Crime Deviant Pathways* (pp. 197–218). Ashgate Publishing.

Lacombe, É. F. (2017). Prioritizing children's best interests in canadian youth justice: Article 3 of the un convention on the rights of the child and child-friendly alternatives. *Windsor Yearbook of Access to Justice*, *34*(2), 209–233.

Larkin, H., Aykanian, A., & Streeter, C. L. (2019). Homelessness Prevention and Intervention in Social Work. doi:DOI: 10.1007/978-3-030-03727-7

Legal Aid Act, 2016

Leiter, S. (2020). *Force-Feeding In West Africa: 5 Facts About Leblouh In Mauritania.* Https://Borgenproject.Org/Leblouh-In-Mauritania/

Lemert, E. M. (1951). *Social Pathology*. McGraw-Hill.

Lewin, K. (1943). 'Defining the "Field at a Given Time". *Psychological Review*, *50*, 292–310.

Lipsey, M. W. (2009). The Primary Factors that Characterize Effective Interventions with Juvenile Offenders: A Meta-Analytic Overview. *Victims & Offenders*, *4*(2), 124–147.

Lipsey, M. W., Howell, J. C., Kelly, M. R., Chapman, G., & Carver, D. (2010). Improving the Effectiveness of Juvenile Justice Programs: A New Perspective on Evidence-Based Practice. *Juvenile Justice Research and Policy*, *11*(1), 27–45.

Loeb, R. C., Waung, M., & Sheeran, M. (2015). Individual and familial variables for predicting successful completion of a juvenile justice diversion program. *Journal of Offender Rehabilitation*, *54*(3), 212–237.

Lofland, J. (1969). *Deviance and identity*. Prentice-Hall.

Lundman, R. J. (1993). *Prevention and control of juvenile delinquency*. Oxford University Press.

Lundman, R. J. (1994). Demeanor or crime? The Midwest city police-citizen encounters study. *Criminology*, *32*(4), 631–656.

MacDonald, J., & Chesney-Lind, M. (2001). Gender bias and juvenile justice revisited: A multiyear analysis. *Crime and Delinquency*, *47*, 173–195.

Mack, K. (2019). *Juvenile justice in the United States*. Oxford Research Encyclopedia of Criminology and Criminal Justice.

Makoae, M. G. (2015). *Experiences of caregivers implementing HIV and AIDS services within community-based organizations (CBOS) in rural Maseru: Lesotho* (Doctoral dissertation, University of the Free State).

Males, M (1994) 'Bashing Youth: Media Myths about Teenagers', *Fair News bulletin,* March.

Malimath, V. S. Government of India, Ministry of Home Affairs, Varadachary, S., Gupta, A., Menon, N. R. M., Rao, D. V. S., Gupta, D., Basavarya, C. M., Girither, K., Menon, B., Reddy, S. M., Raja, V., & Uthaiah, M. K. (2003). Report. In *Committee on Reforms of Criminal Justice System.* Government of India, Ministry of Home Affairs. https://www.mha.gov.in/sites/default/files/criminal_justice_system_2.pdf

Marshall, A. (2018). Restorative Justice for Indigenous Youth in Canada: Addressing Historical Injustices. *Canadian Journal of Criminology and Criminal Justice, 60*(3), 289–306.

Marwah, A. (2020). RESTORATIVE JUSTICE AND REFORMATION OF OFFENDERS. In *ILI. Law Review, 2020*(Winter Issue), 157–159. https://ili.ac.in/pdf/amar.pdf

Matsueda, R. L. (1992). Reflected appraisals, parental labeling, and delinquency: Specifying a symbolic interactionist theory. *American Journal of Sociology, 97*(6), 1577–1611. DOI: 10.1086/229940

McAlpine, K., Henley, R., & Mueller, M.. (2010). A Survey of Street Children in Northern Tanzania: How Abuse or Support Factors May Influence Migration to the Street. *Community Mental Health Journal, 46*, 26–32. DOI: 10.1007/s10597-009-9196-5

McAra, L., & McVie, S. (2018). Transformations in youth crime and justice. In Goldson, B. (Ed.), *Juvenile Justice in Europe: Past, Present and Future. Abingdon* (pp. 74–103). Routledge.

McCord, J. (1979). Some child rearing antecedents of criminal behaviour in adult men. *Journal of Personality and Social Psychology, 37*, 1477–1486.

Meade, A. C. (1974). The labeling approach to delinquency: State of the theory as a function of method. *Social Forces, 53*(1), 83–91.

Mears, D. P. (2001). "Get Tough" Juvenile Justice Reforms: The Impact of Punitive Policies on Juvenile Offenders and Juvenile Justice. *Criminal Justice Policy Review, 12*(2), 125–146. DOI: 10.1177/0887403401012002002

Mears, D. P., Hay, C., Gertz, M. G., & Mancini, C. (2007). Public opinion and the foundation of the juvenile court. *Criminology*, *45*(1), 223–257. DOI: 10.1111/j.1745-9125.2007.00077.x

Mears, D. P., Kuch, J. J., Lindsey, A. M., Siennick, S. E., Pesta, G. B., Greenwald, M. A., & Blomberg, T. G. (2016). Juvenile court and contemporary diversion. *Criminology & Public Policy*, *15*(3), 953–981.

Mears, D. P., Shollenberger, T. L., & Willison, J. B. (2014). Juvenile Diversion Programs: A Meta-Analysis of Program Effects. *Youth Violence and Juvenile Justice*, *12*(4), 325–348.

Melograno, V. (2022). Childhood Interruped: Child Marraige In Mauritania. *The Borgen Project*. Https://Borgenproject.Org/Child-Marriage-In-Mauritania/

Mendel, R. A. (2011). *No Place for Kids: The Case for Reducing Juvenile Incarceration*. Annie E. Casey Foundation. Retrieved from https://www.aecf.org/resources/no-place-for-kids/

Mensa-Bonsu, M. A. (n.d.). The Trouble with Judicial Amendments: Lessons from Ghana.

Metz, H. (1992). *Somalia*. Countrystudies.us. Retrieved May 14 2021, from https://countrystudies.us/somalia/

Miller v. Alabama, 567 U.S. 460 (2012).

Miller, D.. (2016). Vocational Skills Programs for At-Risk Youth: An Evaluation. *Journal of Youth Development*, *11*(2), 45–61.

Miller, G. E., & Prinz, R. J. (1990). Enhancement of social learning family interventions for childhood conduct disorder. *Psychological Bulletin*, *108*(2), 291.

Milner, A. (2024). *African penal systems*. Taylor & Francis.

Ministry of Gender. (2015). *Children and Social Protection*. Child and Family Welfare Policy.

Mishra, A. (2019). Juvenile Justice and the role of Police: Indian Scenario - Academike. *Academike*.https://www.lawctopus.com/academike/juvenile-justice-role-police-indian-scenario/

Mishra, H. (2024). Delhi teen stabbed to death for refusing to throw party over new phone. *India Today*. https://www.indiatoday.in/cities/delhi/story/delhi-boy-stabbed-dies-party-new-phone-purchase-shakarpur-2605626-2024-09-24

Mittal, Y., & Law, L. (2024). Supreme Court: Juvenile accused cannot be tried as adult without preliminary assessment by JJB. *Live Law*. https://www.livelaw.in/supreme-court/jj-act-juvenile-accused-cant-be-tried-as-adult-in-absence-of-preliminary-assessment-report-by-jjb-supreme-court-253459

Moore, R. S. (2018). The touchy topic of juvenile delinquency. The Barbados Advocate. Retrieved April 15, 2023 The touchy topic of juvenile delinquency | Barbados Advocate

Morangi, R. (2013). Effectiveness of street children intervention in Eldoret. *International Journal of Smart Technologies*, *6*, 14.

Mudeizi, H. M. (2022). *Determinants of Children's Rights Violations in Prosecution: A Case of Nairobi City County, Kenya* (doctoral dissertation, kenyatta university).

Muema, F. M., Nyangwencha, S. K., & Njoroge, M. (2023). *Perceptions of Justice Involved Children on the Child Justice System in Nairobi County*. The University Journal.

Mugambi, M. K. (2013). *Effects of e-government strategy on service delivery in the government ministries in Kenya* (Doctoral dissertation, University of Nairobi).

Mujuzi, J. D. (2014). The African Committee of Experts on the Rights and Welfare of the Child and the Right to Education. *Journal of African Law*, *58*(1), 144–161.

Muncie, J. (2008). *Youth and Crime* (3rd ed.). SAGE.

Muntingh, L. (2011). *Diversion Programmes for Juvenile Offenders in Africa: Challenges and Opportunities*. University of the Western Cape.

Murhula, P. B., & Singh, S. B. (2019). A critical evaluation of the literature on the rehabilitation technique for offenders in South Africa. *African Journal of Criminology and Justice Studies*, *12*(1), 12.

Musiega, R. (2021). *Enhancing Child Justice in Kenya: an Appraisal of the Implementation of the Rights of Child Offenders* (Doctoral dissertation, University of Nairobi).

Mutua, J. (2019). Socioeconomic Factors Contributing to Juvenile Delinquency in Kenya. *Journal of African Law and Criminology*, *12*(1), 45–58. DOI: 10.1093/africlaw/jac004

Myburgh, C., Moolla, A., & Poggenpoel, M. (2015). The lived experiences of children living on the streets of Hillbrow. *Curationis*, *38*(1), 1274. DOI: 10.4102/curationis.v38i1.1274

NAACP Legal Defense and Educational Fund. (2017). *Locked Out of the Classroom: How Implicit Bias Contributes to Disparities in School Discipline*. https://www.naacpldf.org/wp-content/uploads/Locked-Out-of-the-Classroom-Implicit-Bias-Report.pdf

National Census Street Families Report (2018). Street families rehabilitation fund. Ministry of Labor and Social Protection

National Crime Research Centre. (2023). *Efficacy and adequacy of criminal Justice agencies in Kenya: the case of children in conflict with the law*. NCRC.

National Juvenile Justice Network. (2023). *Raising the Minimum Age for Prosecuting Children*. Retrieved May 16, 2023 Raising the Minimum Age for Prosecuting Children (njjn.org)

National Strategy on Justice for Children 2023-2028

Nations, U. (2021). *About Us | United Nations*. United Nations. Retrieved May 15 2021, from https://www.un.org/en/about-us/

NeMoyer, A., Gale-Bentz, E., Goldstein, N. E., & Pema Harvey, L. (2020). Factors associated with successful completion of a community-based, postarrest juvenile diversion program and subsequent rearrest. *Crime and Delinquency*, *66*(5), 603–626.

Netswera, F. (2020). The implementation of children's rights in Kenya. *Journal of African Law*, *64*(2), 249–264.

Nhapi, T. G., & Agere, L. (2019). Street Children Revisited: Critical Perspectives on Street-Connected Children in a Fragile Zimbabwean Socioeconomic Climate. *Social Development Issues*, *41*(1), 64–82. https://login.pvamu.idm.oclc.org/login?url=https://www.proquest.com/scholarly-journals/street-children-revisited-critical-perspectives/docview/2295417072/se-2

Nickerson, C. (2023). *Merton's Strain Theory of Deviance and Anomie in Sociology*. Simply Psychology. https://www.simplypsychology.org/mertons-strain-theory-deviance.html

Nigeria agrees to end military detention of children. *Human Rights Watch*. (2023). https://www.hrw.org/news/2022/10/03/nigeria-agrees-end-military-detention-children

Nkirote, K. J. (2016). *An Analysis of The Adequacy of The Legal Framework in Protecting The Rights Of Child Offenders in Kenya* (Doctoral dissertation, University Of Nairobi).

Nnama-Okechukwu, C. U., Ebimgbo, S. O., Agha, A. A., & Onalu, C. E. (2023). Vulnerable children aiding visually challenged beggars in Nigeria: Need for social work intervention. *Children & Society*, *37*, 616–633. DOI: 10.1111/chso.12618

Nolterieke, L. (2020). Delinquency in the Caribbean: Stakeholder perceptions of root causes. Honors Theses, University of New Heaven. https://digitalcommons.newhaven.edu/honorstheses/31

Number of children without critical social protection increasing globally. *UNICEF.* (n.d.). https://www.unicef.org/press-releases/number-children-without-critical-social-protection-increasing-globally

Nyamu, C. I. (2010). Children and the Law in Kenya: A Comparative Overview. *African Human Rights Law Journal*, *10*(2), 382–405.

Obondo, A., & Pthieno, J. (2020). Patterns of Substance abuse among Kenyan Street Children. *AJOL. VOl*, *12*, 2.

Odongo, G. (2012). Juvenile Justice in Kenya: A Human Rights Perspective. *African Human Rights Law Journal*, *12*(2), 274–293.

Oduor, A. J., & Nyaata, V. M. (2022). A survey of children's rights in the juvenile justice system in Kenya. [JLJ]. *Journal of Law and Jurisprudence*, *1*(1), 1–7.

Office of the Director of Public Prosecutions (2020) 'A Prosecutor's Guide to Children in the Criminal Justice System'

Okorie, M. A. (2020). *Juvenile Justice Systems in Nigeria: Challenges and Opportunities. Nigerian Journal of Legal Studies, Hartjen, C. A. (2008). Youth, crime, and justice: A global inquiry*. Rutgers University Press.

Olowa, O. W. (2020). Street children in Nigeria: Challenges and prospects. *Journal of Social and Political Sciences*, *3*(4), 968–974. DOI: 10.31014/aior.1993.03.04.155

Olowu, D. (2008). The Impact of Colonization on African Juvenile Justice Systems. *African Legal Review*, *42*(1), 103–117.

Omale, D. J. O. (2009) Restorative justice as an alternative dispute resolution model: opinions of victims of crime and criminal justice professionals in Nigeria, PhD Thesis submitted to De Montfort University, Leicester. Available at: https://dora.dmu.ac.uk/items/879404ae-0e77-454c-b56d-4768cdee1d10

Omale, D. J. O. (2005). *Understanding restorative justice: A Handbook for criminal justice stakeholders*. Trinity Biz.

Omale, D. J. O. (2006). Justice in History: An Examination of the African Restorative Traditions and the Emerging Restorative Justice Paradigm. *African Journal of Criminology and Criminal Justice*, *2*(2), 30–60. http://www.umes.edu/WorkArea/showcontent.aspx?id=7012

Omale, D. J. O. (2012). *Restorative Justice and Victimology: Euro-Africa Perspectives.* Wolf Legal Publishing.

Omboto, J. O. (2013). The Challenges Facing Rehabilitation of Prisoners in Kenya and the Mitigation Strategies. *International Journal of Research in Social Sciences*, *2*(2), 39–43.

OPEC. (2021). Nigeria. OPEC. https://www.opec.org/opec_web/en/about_us/169.htm

Oputa, C. A. (1975). Crime and the Nigerian Society. In Elias, T. O., Nwagbara, S. N., & Akpamgbo, C. O. (Eds.), *African Indigenous Laws*. Government Printer.

Organization of African Unity. (1990). *African Charter on the Rights and Welfare of the Child.* Retrieved from https://au.int/en/treaties/african-charter-rights-and-welfare-child

Orr, J. (2020). Public Perceptions of Police Interactions with Juveniles. Undergraduate Review, 15, 256-275. https://vc.bridgew.edu/undergrad_rev/vol15/iss1/22

Oshiomole, A. (2008). Osunbor Needs Time to pack out of Government House. *Thisday Newspaper*, (March), 1.

Osman, T. M., & Saleh, M. A. (2015). Street children in Egypt: From an invisible population to a priority for intervention. *International Journal of Social Science Studies*, *3*(1), 24–31.

Ouldzeidoune, N. K. J., Bertrand, J., & Rice, J. (2013). A Description Of Female Genital Mutilation And Force-Feeding Practices In Mauritania: Implications For The Protection Of Child Rights And Health. *PLoS One*, *8*(4). Https://Doi.Org/Doi: 10.1371/Journal.Pone.0060594 PMID: 23593257

Overview. *World Bank*. (2021). https://www.worldbank.org/en/region/afr/overview

Owoaje, E. T., Adebiyi, A. O., & Asuzu, M. C. (2009). Socio-demographic characteristics of street children in rural communities undergoing urbanization. *Annals of Ibadan Postgraduate Medicine*, *7*(1), 10–15. DOI: 10.4314/aipm.v7i1.64055

Ozturk, B., Bell, A., McLeod, D., & Gentzler, R. (2022). Criminal justice diversion and the importance of program retention. *Journal of Forensic Social Work*, *6*(1), 43–56.

Panag, S., Ganguli, T., & Chopra, L. (2024). The Practitioner's Guide to Global Investigations. *Global Investigation Review*. https://globalinvestigationsreview.com/guide/the-practitioners-guide-global-investigations/2024/article/india

Pandian, D. (2020). *As the fifth anniversary of Somalia's ratification of the convention on the Rights of the Child approaches, protection violations against children continue to rise*. Unicef.org. Retrieved May 15 2021, from https://www.unicef.org/somalia/press-releases/fifth-anniversary-somalias-ratification-convention-rights-child-approaches

Pappas, L. N., & Dent, A. L. (2023). The 40-year debate: A meta-review on what works for juvenile offenders. *Journal of Experimental Criminology*, *19*(1), 1–30.

Paternoster, R., & Iovanni, L. (1989). The labeling perspective and delinquency: An elaboration of the theory and assessment of the evidence. *Justice Quarterly*, *6*(3), 359–394.

Penal Code (Cap. 63) Laws of Kenya

Penal Reform International. (2013). *UK Aid The Minimum Age of Criminal Responsibility (Justice for Children Briefing No. 4)*. Penal Reform International.

Physical Abuse. (2023). American Psychological Association. Https://Dictionary.Apa.Org/Physical-Abuse

Poe-Yamagata, E., & Jones, M. (2000). And justice for some: Building blocks for youth. *Retrieved July, 12*, 2009.

Prinsloo, J. (2008). In the best interest of the child: The protection of child victims and witnesses in the South African Criminal Justice System. *Child Abuse Research in South Africa*, *9*(2), 49–64.

Pti. (2017). Ryan school murder case: Class 11 student confessed he killed Pradyuman Thakur, says CBI. https://www.livemint.com/Politics/acQQwygFhJcUqOdo2VkrbM/Ryan-School-murder-Accused-Class-XI-student-admits-killing.html

Puzzanchera, C. & Adams, B. (2017). Juvenile arrests 2015. Juvenile Justice

Puzzanchera, C., & Hockenberry, S. (2022). *Juvenile Court Statistics 2019*. National Center for Juvenile Justice. https://www.ojjdp.gov/ojstatbb/njcda/pdf/jcs2019.pdf

Regilme, S., & Spoldi, E. (2021). Children in Armed Conflict: A Human Rights Crisis in Somalia. *Global Jurist*, *0*(0). Advance online publication. DOI: 10.1515/gj-2020-0083

Reiner, R. (2007). *Law and Order: An Honest Citizen's Guide to Crime and Control*. Polity Press.

Republic of Kenya. (2001). *The Children's Act, 2001*. Government Printer.

Republic v BC [2022] KEHC 17153 (KLR)

Robin-D'Cruz, C. (2019). *Mapping youth diversion in England and Wales*. Retrieved August 2024, from https://justiceinnovation.org/portfolio/mapping-youth-diversion

Robins, G. (2008). *The Art of Ancient Egypt*. Harvard University Press.

Robinson, W. S. (2009). Ecological correlations and the behavior of individuals. *International Journal of Epidemiology, 38*(2), 337–341.

Roper v. Simmons, 543 U.S. 551 (2005).

Rovner, J. (2021). *Racial Disparities in Youth Incarceration Persist*. The Sentencing Project. https://www.sentencingproject.org/reports/racial-disparities-in-youth-incarceration-persist/

Rovner, J. (2016). *Racial Disparities in Youth Incarceration Persist*. The Sentencing Project.

Rwezaura, B. (1998). The Politics of Law Reform, Customary Law and Children's Rights in Kenya. *International Journal of Law, Policy and the Family, 12*(1), 56–69.

Sanjuan, A. M. (1998). Youth and Violence in Caracas: the paradoxes of a loss of citizenship. In Pinheiro, P. S. (Ed.), *Sao Paul without fear: a diagnosis of urban violence* (pp. 155–171). Garamond.

Sarwanto, A. (2023). The Phenomenon of Juvenile Delinquency that Occurs in the Era of Globalization. *The Easta Journal Law and Human Rights, 1*(02), 45–50.

Sarwer, D. B. P., H. M. (2018). The Psychological Burden Of Obesity. *Endocrinology and Metabolism Clinics of North America, 45*(3), 677–688. PMID: 27519139

Save the Children. (2018). Egypt Street Children Report. Retrieved from https://www.savethechildren.org/content/dam/usa/reports/advocacy/Egypt_Street_Children_Report.pdf

Sawyer, W. (2019). *Youth Confinement: The Whole Pie 2019*. Prison Policy Initiative. https://www.prisonpolicy.org/reports/youth2019.html

Schauer, E., & Elbert, T. (2010). The Psychological Impact of Child Soldiering. *Trauma Rehabilitation After War And Conflict*, 311-360. https://doi.org/DOI: 10.1007/978-1-4419-5722-1_14

Scheff, T. J. (1966), 1984 2nd ed., 1999 3rd ed. Being mentally ill: A sociological theory. Aldine, Chicago

Schur, E. M. (1971). *Labeling Deviant Behavior: Its Sociological Implications*. Harper & Row.

Schwalbe, C. S. (2008). A Meta-Analysis of Juvenile Risk Assessment Instruments: Predictive Validity by Gender. *Criminal Justice and Behavior, 35*(11), 1367–1381.

Schwartz, S. H. (2009). Basic human values. *sociologie, 42*, 249-288.

Scott, E. S., Reppucci, N. D., Antonishak, J., & DeGennaro, J. T. (2006). Public attitudes about the culpability and punishment of young offenders. *Behavioral Sciences & the Law, 24*(6), 815–832. DOI: 10.1002/bsl.727

Sentencing Project. (2017). *Disproportionate Minority Contact in the Juvenile Justice System*. Sentencing Project.

Sexual Exploitation of Children. (2015). Office of Juvenile Justice and Delinquency Prevention. *Office of Juvenile Justice and Delinquency Prevention*. https://ojjdp.ojp.gov/programs/sexual-exploitation-children

Shah, C. (2024). India's juvenile Justice dilemma: balancing punishment and potential. *Bharat Law AI*. https://www.bharatlaw.ai/post/balancing-justice-and-rehabilitation-transforming-juvenile-offenders-in-india-for-a-safer-society

Sharma, K., & Gupta, K. (2023). An analysis of social learning theory to the changing nature of juvenile crimes and legal responses to…ResearchGate. https://www.researchgate.net/publication/378976490_AN_ANALYSIS_OF_SOCIAL_LEARNING_THEORY_TO_THE_CHANGING_NATURE_OF_JUVENILE_CRIMES_AND_LEGAL_RESPONSES_TO_NAVIGATE_THE_CHANGE

Shaw, M (2005) *Youth and Gun Violence: The Outstanding Case for Prevention*, International Centre for the Prevention of Crime (ICPC)

Shaxon, N. (2007). *Poisoned Wells: The Dirty politics of African Oils*. Macmillian.

Shelden, R. G. (1999). *Delinquency and Juvenile Justice in American Society*. Waveland Press.

Sherman, L. W., Strang, H., & Woods, D. J. (2015). Recidivism Outcomes for Restorative Justice Diversion Programs. *Journal of Youth Studies, 18*(6), 725–742.

Shoemaker, D. J. (2000). *Theories of delinquency: An examination of explanations of delinquent behaviour* (4th ed.). Oxford University Press.

Sickmund, M., & Puzzanchera, C. (2014). *Juvenile Offenders and Victims: 2014 National Report*. U.S. Department of Justice.

Sigonda, G. G. G. (2000). *The Impact of Infrastructural Projects on the Environment in Tanzania: The Case of Mindu Dam*. The University of Manchester.

Singer, P. (2006). *The Enablers of War: Casual Factors behind the Child Soldier Phenomenon*. Files.ethz.ch. Retrieved May 14 2021, from https://www.files.ethz.ch/isn/28063/2006_6_Enablers_of_War.pdf

Skelton, A., & Tshehla, B. (2008). *Child Justice in South Africa*. Google Books. https://books.google.co.in/books/about/Child_Justice_in_South_Africa.html?id=WWYxAQAAIAAJ&redir_esc=y

Skelton, A. (2015). Juvenile Justice in Africa: Reflections on Restorative Justice and Children's Rights. *International Journal of Children's Rights*, *23*(2), 335–351.

Skelton, A., & Batley, M. (2006). *Restorative Justice in South Africa: From Traditional Practice to Formal Adoption*. South African Legal Reform Institute.

Skelton, A., & Tshehla, B. (2008). Child Justice in South Africa. *Institute for Security Studies Monographs*, *2008*(150), 72.

Sloth-Nielsen, J. (2008). *Children's rights in Africa: A legal perspective*. Ashgate Publishing, Ltd.

Smith, A. (2007) 'Parental time a key factor in gang violence', *Leicester Mercury*, 29 August, p.15

Smith, A. (2009). Girls Being Force-Fed For Marriage As Fattening Farms Revived. *The Observer*.

Smith, M. (2018). For the Love of 'Bad, Foreign Habits': Anglo-Saxon and Scandinavian Cultural Development and Identity Differentiation from 750 to 950 CE.

Smith, C. A., & Stern, S. B. (1997). Delinquency and Antisocial Behavior: A Review of Family Processes and Intervention Research. *The Social Service Review*, *71*, 382–420. DOI: 10.1086/604263

Smith, J. D. F., E. & Kobayahi, M. A. (2020). Prevention And Management Of Childhood Obesity And Its Psychological And Health Comorbidities. *Annual Review of Clinical Psychology*, •••, 351–380. PMID: 32097572

Somali leaders back new constitution. BBC News. (2012). Retrieved May 15 2021, from https://www.bbc.com/news/world-africa-19075685

Somalia. Cia.gov. (2021). Retrieved May 14 2021, from https://www.cia.gov/the-world-factbook/countries/somalia/

Somalia: Military courts used to prosecute and punish Children. Garowe Online. (2017).

Somalia: Penal Code. Refworld. (1962). Retrieved May 15 2021, from https://www.refworld.org/docid/4bc5906e2.html

Souryal, S. S. (1992). Juvenile Delinquency in the Cross-Cultural Context: The Egyptian Experience. *International Journal of Comparative and Applied Criminal Justice*, *16*(1-2), 329–352.

Steinberg, L. (2013). The Influence of Neuroscience on U.S. Supreme Court Decisions about Adolescents' Criminal Culpability. *Nature Reviews. Neuroscience*, *14*(7), 513–518. PMID: 23756633

Steinberg, L., & Scott, E. S. (2003). Less Guilty by Reason of Adolescence: Developmental Immaturity, Diminished Responsibility, and the Juvenile Death Penalty. *The American Psychologist*, *58*(12), 1009–1018. DOI: 10.1037/0003-066X.58.12.1009 PMID: 14664689

Straw, J. (2007) 'What Next for Our Democracy', *Leicester Mercury*, 11 December, p.5

Street children worldwide - abuse, violence, impunity, poverty, addiction & HIV. *Compass Children's Charity*. (2021). https://www.compasschildrenscharity.org.uk/about-us/street-children-worldwide/

StudyCorgi. (2023). *How Social Learning Theories Impact Juvenile Delinquency and Crime*. https://studycorgi.com/how-social-learning-theories-impact-juvenile-delinquency-and-crime/

Surgeon-General Report, U. S. (2001). *Youth Violence: A Report of the Surgeon-General*. US Department of Health and Human Services.

Sutton, H., & Ruprah, I. J. (2017). *Restoring paradise in the Caribbean: Combatting violence with numbers*. Inter-American Development Bank.

Swick, K. J., & Williams, R. D. (2006). An analysis of Bronfenbrenner's bio-ecological perspective for early childhood educators: Implications for working with families experiencing stress. *Early Childhood Education Journal*, *33*(5), 371–378.

Tannenbaum, F. (1938). *Crime and the community*. Ginn and Company.

Tatia, P., & Patel, D. N. (2011). Training of child welfare officers on special juvenile police unit on the juvenile justice. In Report Regarding Compliance of Direction of Hon'ble Supreme Court of India in Sampurna Behrua V Union of India. https://jhalsa.org/pdfs/JJB_Report.pdf

The Editors of Encyclopaedia Britannica. (2024). *Strain theory | Social Control, Anomie & Deviance*. Encyclopedia Britannica. https://www.britannica.com/topic/strain-theory-sociology

The Judiciary of Kenya. (2001). *Children's Act of 2001*. Government of Kenya.

The Judiciary. (2024) 'CRJ Mokaya underscores need for increased budgetary allocation for Child Justice Sector' available at https://judiciary.go.ke/crj-mokaya-underscores-need-for-increased-budgetary-allocation-for-child-justice-sector/

The juvenile justice system in India and children who commit serious offences – reflections on the way forward. (2013). *Observatorio Internacional De Justicia Juvenil*. https://www.oijj.org/sites/default/files/documentos/the_juvenile_justice_system_in_india_and_children_who_commit_serious_offences.pdf

The McKinney-Vento homeless assistance act. Institute for Children Poverty Homelessness. (n.d.). https://www.icphusa.org/mkv/

The Nation Newspaper. (2008). *Gone to pot*. Retrieved September 30, 2009 (http://archive.nationnews.com/archive_detail.php?archiveFile=2008/January/28/LocalNews/52442.xml&start=0&numPer=20&keyword=Gone+to+Pot&sectionSearch=&begindate=1%2F1%2F2008&enddate=4%2F28%2F2010&authorSearch=&IncludeStories=1&pubsection=&page=&IncludePages=1&IncludeImages=1&mode=phrase&archive_pubname=Daily+Nation%0A%09%09%09)

The National. (2020). Egypt's youth crime rate rising as economic crisis hits home. Retrieved from https://www.thenationalnews.com/world/mena/egypt-s-youth-crime-rate-rising-as-economic-crisis-hits-home-1.1050631

The Sentencing Project. (2021). *Racial Disparities in Youth Incarceration Persist*. Retrieved from https://www.sentencingproject.org

The Street Children of Mogadishu. The Borgen Project. (2015). Retrieved May 16 2021, from https://borgenproject.org/street-children-mogadishu/#:~:text=In%202008%2C%20estimates%20placed%20the,of%20supporting%20for%20their%20children

Theories of delinquency. (2018). https://sandratrappen.com/2018/12/30/theories-of-delinquency/

Thompson, C. (2014). Body Image In Mauritania: Bigger Is Better. *Utah Historical Review*, 1-7.

Thorpe, D. H., Smith, D., Green, C. J., & Paley, J. H. (2024). *Out of care: The community support of juvenile offenders*. Taylor & Francis.

Tönnies, F. 1887. "Community and Society." Pp. 16-22 in *The Urban Sociology Reader*. Jan Lin and Christopher Mele (Eds.). London: Routledge.

Torbet, P., Griffin, P., Hurst, H., & MacKenzie, L. (2000). *Juveniles facing criminal sanctions: Three states that changed the rules*. US Department of Justice, Office of Justice Programs, Office of Juvenile Justice and Delinquency Prevention.

U.S. Department of Justice. (2015). *Juvenile Justice and Delinquency Prevention Act*. Office of Juvenile Justice and Delinquency Prevention.

Umbreit, M. S. (1994). Crime victims confront their offenders: The impact of a Minneapolis mediation program. *Research on Social Work Practice*, *4*(4), 436–447.

Umbreit, M. S., & Armour, M. P. (2010). *Restorative Justice Dialogue: An Essential Guide for Research and Practice*. Springer Publishing Company.

UN lauds Somalia as country ratifies landmark children's rights treaty. UN News. (2015). Retrieved May 15 2021, from https://news.un.org/en/story/2015/01/488692-un-lauds-somalia-country-ratifies-landmark-childrens-rights-treaty

UN-HABITAT. (2004) Strategy Paper on Urban Youth in Africa: A focus on the most vulnerable groups, Policy Dialogue Series No.2, Nairobi, Kenya: UN-HABITAT Safer Cities Project.

UNICEF Nigeria, & Nigeria. (2012). *Situation analysis of children and women in Nigeria*. Related UNICEF Websites. https://www.unicef.org/nigeria/reports/situation-analysis-children-and-women-nigeria

UNICEF. (2012). Children living in the streets. Retrieved from https://www.unicef.org/media/54896/file/UNICE

Unicef. (2016). *Situation Analysis of Children in Somalia 2016*. Retrieved May 15 2021, from https://www.unicef.org/somalia/reports/situation-analysis-children-somalia-2016-0

UNICEF. (2017). *A Familiar Face: Violence in the Lives of Children and Adolescents*. United Nations. Retrieved from https://data.unicef.org/resources/a-familiar-face/

UNICEF. (2017). Children in Egypt: A statistical digest. Available at https://www.unicef.org/egypt/media/1676/file/Children%20in%20Egypt%20A%20Statistical%20Digest%20Final%20-%20EN.pdf

UNICEF. (2019). Children in Egypt. Retrieved from https://www.unicef.org/egypt/children-egypt

UNICEF. (2020). *Juvenile Justice Systems in Kenya: Gaps and Challenges.* https://www.unicef.org/kenya/reports/juvenile-justice-systems-kenya

UNICEF. (2023). *Diversion of Children in Conflict with the Law in Eastern and Southern Africa Diversion programmes in the Eastern and Southern Africa Region: Best practices, opportunities and challenges.* UNICEF.

UNICEF. n.d. Legal minimum ages and the realization of adolescents' rights. Retrieved May 16, 2023 PDF Minimum age for criminal responsibility.pdf (unicef.org)

United Nations (2020) Single Convention on Narcotic Drugs The Kenyan Constitution (2010) Kinyanjui. M 92021) City Hall to spend 40 million to rehabilitate street children. *The Star. April 2021* Children's Act No. 8 of 2000

United Nations Children's Fund (UNICEF). "Street Children in Egypt." 2015. https://www.unicef.org/egypt/street-children-egypt

United Nations Committee on the Rights of the Child. (2016). *General Comment No. 10: Children's Rights in Juvenile Justice.* https://www.refworld.org/docid/42dd174b4.html

United Nations Convention on the Rights of the Child, adopted November 20, 1989, 1577 UNTS 3.

United Nations Office on Drugs and Crime. (2014). Juvenile Delinquency in Egypt: A Situational Analysis. https://www.unodc.org/documents/egyptandarabstates//Juvenile_Delinquency_in_Egypt_2014.pdf

United Nations Office on Drugs and Crime. (2018). *Introductory handbook on the prevention of recidivism and the social reintegration of offenders.* Retrieved July 2024, from. https://www.unodc.org/documents/justice-and-prison-reform/18-02303_ebook.pdf

United Nations Office on Drugs and Crime. (2019). Global Study on Homicide 2019: Executive Summary. Retrieved from https://www.unodc.org/documents/data-and-analysis/gsh/2019/Executive_summary_GSH2019.pdf

United Nations Office on Drugs and Crime. (2021). Handbook on Children Recruited and Exploited by Terrorist and Violent Extremist Groups: The Role of the Justice System. https://www.unodc.org/documents/terrorism/Publications/Handbook_on _Children_recruited_and_exploited_by_terrorist_and_violent_extremist_groups.pdf

United Nations. (1948). *Universal Declaration of Human Rights.* Retrieved from https://www.un.org/en/about-us/universal-declaration-of-human-rights

United Nations. (1985). *United Nations Standard Minimum Rules for the Administration of Juvenile Justice* (The Beijing Rules). https://www.un.org/ruleoflaw/files/TH007.PDF

United Nations. (1989). *Convention on the Rights of the Child (CRC).* United Nations. Retrieved from https://www.ohchr.org/en/instruments-mechanisms/instruments/convention-rights-child

United Nations. (1989). *Convention on the Rights of the Child.* https://www.ohchr .org/en/instruments-mechanisms/instruments/convention-rights-child

United Nations. (1990a). *United Nations Rules for the Protection of Juveniles Deprived of their Liberty* (The Havana Rules). https://www.ohchr.org/en/instruments -mechanisms/instruments/united-nations-rules-protection-juveniles-deprived-their -liberty

United Nations. (1990b). *United Nations Guidelines for the Prevention of Juvenile Delinquency* (The Riyadh Guidelines). https://www.un.org/ruleoflaw/files/UN _Riyadh%20Guidelines.pdf

United Nations. (2019). Convention on the Rights of the Child. Retrieved May 17, 2023 from General comment No. 24 (2019) on children's rights in the child justice system | OHCHR

United Nations. (2024). OHCHR | Committee on the Rights of the Child. OHCHR. https://www.ohchr.org/en/treaty-bodies/crc

United States Department of State. (n.d.). *Somalia.* United States Department of State. https://www.state.gov/countries-areas/somalia/

UNODC. (2005) *Strategies and Best Practices in Crime Prevention, in relation to Urban Areas and Youth at Risk,* Background Paper, in Workshop No.3 at the 11th UN Congress on Crime Prevention and Criminal Justice, Bangkok, Thailand: 18-25 April. Also available as File: A/CONF.203/11 at www.unodc.org

Unruh, D., Povenmire-Kirk, T., & Yamamoto, S. (2009). Perceived Barriers and Protective Factors of Juvenile Offenders on their Developmental Pathway to Adulthood. *Journal of Correctional Education*, *60*(3), 201–224.

US Department of Justice. (2021). *Juvenile Injustice: Police Abuse and Detention of Street children in Kenya. USDJ KNCHR (2018).* Human Rights and Drug Abuse.

Van Blerk, L. (2015). *Growing up on the streets: Building networks of knowledge exchange for delivering impact*. University of Dundee., https://gtr.ukri.org/projects?ref=ES/M006107/1

Van Ness, D. W., & Strong, K. (2014). *Restoring Justice: An Introduction to Restorative Justice* (5th ed.). ResearchGate., https://www.researchgate.net/publication/287587203_Restoring_Justice_An_Introduction_to_Restorative_Justice_Fifth_Edition

Vashishth, A., Dudeja, S., & Teena, N. (2024). System of Restorative Justice and Juvenile Justice in India: A Brief Comparative Study with Latin American System. *Mexican Law Review*, •••, 131–143. DOI: 10.22201/iij.24485306e.2024.2.18895

Vickery, M. (2017). *Homeless children sniff glue to take 'away the pain' of surviving Somalia's streets*. Usatoday.com. Retrieved May 16 2021, from https://www.usatoday.com/story/news/world/2017/09/05/somalia-children-homeless-african-cities/613912001/

Vidya. (2021). Shakti Mills gang rape case: Bombay HC asks Maha govt to "shun unscientific two-finger test" *India Today*. https://www.indiatoday.in/india/story/shakti-mills-gang-rape-case-bombay-high-court-two-finger-test-maharashtra-1881118-2021-11-26

Vincent, G. M., Guy, L. S., & Grisso, T. (2012). *Risk Assessment in Juvenile Justice: A Guidebook for Implementation*. Models for Change Initiative.

Viola, M. W. (2009). The protection of rights of juveniles in the criminal justice system in Kenya.

Wabwire, A., & Bader, L. (2018). *Interview: How Security Forces in Somalia Fail to Protect Children*. Human Rights Watch. Retrieved May 15 2021, from https://www.hrw.org/news/2018/02/21/interview-how-security-forces-somalia-fail-protect-children

Wachaya, D., Fandel, G., Byrne, J., Watts, J., Bellinger, F., & Phillips, S. (2022). *Understanding the Nigerian child soldier crisis - Thred Website*. Thred Website. https://thred.com/change/understanding-the-nigerian-child-soldier-crisis/

Wadsworth, M. E. J. (1978). 'Delinquency Prediction and its uses: The experience of a 21-year follow-up study. *International Journal of Mental Health*, *7*, 43–62.

Wahab, M. (2019). Update: An overview of the Egyptian legal system and Legal Research. UPDATE: An Overview of the Egyptian Legal System and Legal Research - GlobaLex. Retrieved April 16, 2023, from https://www.nyulawglobal.org/globalex/Egypt1.html

Walker, J. T., & Maddan, S. (2019). *Statistics in criminology and criminal justice*. Jones & Bartlett Learning.

Wanjiru, F. W. (2015). *The effect of dividend pay out ratio on the financial performance of companies listed on the Nairobi Securities Exchange* (Doctoral dissertation, University of Nairobi).

WBI working papers - World Bank. (n.d.). https://documents1.worldbank.org/curated/en/344301468763803523/pdf/263880WBI0Street0children.pdf

Weijers, I. (2004). The Moral Dialogue: Juvenile Justice, Criminal Law, and Restorative Justice. *Journal of Social Philosophy*, *35*(3), 466–480.

WHO. (2023). Obesity. *World Health Organization*. Https://Www.Who.Int/Health-Topics/Obesity#Tab=Tab_1

Williams, C. (1993). Who are "street children?" A hierarchy of street use and appropriate responses. *Child Abuse & Neglect*, *17*(6), 831–841. DOI: 10.1016/s0145-2134(08)80013-0

Wilson, H. A., & Hoge, R. D. (2012). The effect of youth diversion programs on recidivism. *Criminal Justice and Behavior*, *40*(5), 497–518. DOI: 10.1177/0093854812451089

Wirth, L. 1930. "Urbanism as a Way of Life." Pp. 32-41 in *The Urban Sociology Reader*. Jan Lin and Christopher Mele (Eds.). London: Routledge.

Wong, J. S., Bouchard, J., Gravel, J., Bouchard, M., & Morselli, C. (2016). Can at-risk youth be diverted from crime? A meta-analysis of restorative diversion programs. *Criminal Justice and Behavior*, *43*(10), 1310–1329. DOI: 10.1177/0093854816640835

Wood, J., & Kemshall, H. (2010) 'Effective multi-agency public protection: learning from research', in K.Harisson (ed) *Managing high risk and sex offenders in the community: Risk management, treatment and social responsibility*, Collompton: Willan, pp 39-60

World Atlas. (2021). Ethnic Groups Of Nigeria. *WorldAtlas*. https://www.worldatlas.com/articles/ethnic-groups-of-nigeria.html

World Bank. (2021). Nigeria. *World Bank*. https://data.worldbank.org/country/nigeria

World Health Organization. (2016). Malnutrition in Egypt. Retrieved from https://www.who.int/nutrition/topics/2_background/en/

Young, H., & Giller, C. (2021). Juvenile Delinquency in the United States of America. *Journal of Sociology, Psychology &. Religious Studies*, *3*(4), 1–7.

Young, S., Greer, B., & Church, R. (2017). Juvenile delinquency, welfare, justice and therapeutic interventions: A global perspective. *BJPsych Bulletin*, *41*(1), 21–29. DOI: 10.1192/pb.bp.115.052274

Zai, A. F., & Zani, G. (2020). Juvenile Delinquency: A global challenge in modern society. *ResearchGate*, *10*, 2020. DOI: 10.61841/V24I10/400370

Zehr, H. (1990). *Changing lenses: A new focus for crime and justice*. Herald Press.

Zehr, H. (2002). *The Little Book of Restorative Justice*. Good Books.

Zehr, H., & Mika, H. (1998). Fundamental concepts of restorative justice. *Contemporary Justice Review*, *1*, 47–55.

About the Contributors

Simeon P. Sungi holds an LL.B (Hons), LL.M in International Human Rights Law, M.A. in Criminology and Criminal Justice and a Ph.D. in Criminal Justice. Dr. Sungi is an Associate Professor of Criminal Justice at the United States International University in Nairobi, Kenya. He is a lawyer by profession and is licensed to practice law in Tanzania and Kenya. He is also a former United Nations International Criminal Tribunal for Rwanda staff member. His research focuses on law and justice and policy reform issues in the global south. Dr. Sungi is a passionate advocate on human rights and crime prevention policies that are scientifically driven. He has published in numerous scholarly journals and edited books.

***

Nicole Branch-Ellis hails from Barbados. She earned her Ph.D. from Howard University and seeks to bridge research with advocacy. Her research has focused on juvenile delinquency, justice reform and alternates to incarceration, which includes providing recommendations for juvenile justice reform to the government of Barbados. Her current research focuses on racial injustice, police impunity and restorative justice. As an Assistant Professor at Bowie State University, she teaches courses in juvenile and criminal justice, incorporating comparative international justice systems. Throughout her career, Dr. Branch-Ellis has held a variety of research and youth advocacy positions with government agencies and non-profit organizations, the National Institute of Justice, DC Alliance of Youth Advocates, Child Trends Incorporated and the National Crime Prevention Council. Passionate about the healthy well-being of children, she has volunteered with the Coalition for Juvenile Justice (CJJ) and Court Appointed Special Advocates (CASA) in Washington, DC.

Don John O. Omale is a Professor of Criminology & Security Studies, UNODC Expert on Restorative Justice; and a British Chevening Scholar of Criminology. He was two times Head of Department at the Federal University Wukari Taraba State, Nigeria from 2018-2022, and presently teaches Criminology at University of Derby, UK. He holds BSc Psychology (University of Nigeria, Nsukka), MSc Criminology (University of Leicester, UK) and PhD Criminology with specialism in Restorative Justice & Victimology at the Centre for Community and Criminal Justice, De-Montfort University Leicester, England, UK. He is an alumnus of the Rotary Foundation International "Group Study Exchange Programme" to California, District 5230 USA (2002); an Economic and Social Council (ECOSOC) Delegate to the Model United Nations Congress in New York, USA (2003) funded by the UK Foreign and Commonwealth Office, London. He voluntarily disengaged from the Nigerian Prisons Service as Assistant Controller of Prisons (ACP), and has directed Research and Training at the Police College Oji-River, Prisons Staff College Kaduna, and the Nigerian Defence Academy Kaduna respectively. He is internationally published.

Poorvi Ravikumar is an undergraduate psychology student at PES University, RR campus, Bengaluru. Her research interests include topics related to human behaviour, mental health, and psychological abnormalities.

Michael Sang holds a Master of Laws (LLM) in International Law from the University of Cape Town, South Africa and a Bachelor of Laws (LLB) from Moi University, Eldoret. The author is also an Advocate of the High Court with a Post Graduate Diploma in Law and employed in public service as a Prosecutor currently holding the position of Acting Deputy Director of Public Prosecutions (Ag. DDPP). The author is in charge of the Department of Regional, County Affairs and Regulatory Prosecutions and also the Head of the Counter - Terrorism and Transnational Organized Crimes Division at the Office of the Director of Public Prosecutions and is based in Nairobi. The author can be contacted through emails sang7michael@gmail.com or michael.sang@odpp.go.ke

Danielle E. Wetuski, M. A., is a doctoral student at Prairie View A&M University studying Juvenile Justice with a background in Psychology. Her research centers on religion and attitudes about sexual assault, sexual assault victimization and perpetration, fear of crime, and human rights.

Index

A

B

C

D

G

H

I

J

P

Q

R

S

U

W

Y

www.ingramcontent.com/pod-product-compliance
Ingram Content Group UK Ltd.
Pitfield, Milton Keynes, MK11 3LW, UK
UKHW052003041026
15590UKWH00008B/2115

9 781668 49347